D0845293

The United States and Cuba

The
United States
& Cuba

Hegemony and Dependent Development, 1880—1934

JULES ROBERT BENJAMIN

University of Pittsburgh Press

Published by the University of Pittsburgh Press, Pittsburgh, Pa. 15260
Feffer and Simons, Inc., London
Manufactured in the United States of America

Library of Congress Cataloging in Publication Data

Benjamin, Jules R
  The United States and Cuba.

  (Pitt Latin American series)
  Bibliography: p. 243
  Includes index.
  1. United States—Relations (general) with Cuba.
2. Cuba—Relations (general) with the United States.
3. Cuba—History—Revolution, 1933—Causes.   I.   Title.
E183.C9B42   301.29'7291'073   77-74550
ISBN 0-8229-3347-0

Some of the material in chapter 4 appeared in the *Hispanic American Historical Review*, 55, no. 1 (February 1975). Copyright © 1975, Duke University Press. Some of the material in chapter 7 originally appeared in *The Business History Review*, 51, no. 1 (Spring 1977). Copyright by the President and Fellows of Harvard College, 1977.

To my parents,
Harry W. Benjamin
and
Ada Gold Benjamin

Contents

Preface

THE TWENTIETH CENTURY has been characterized as the age of egalitarianism. Nevertheless, the problems of the age have arisen in great measure from disparities of wealth and power, both within and between states. Moreover, these disparities—most clearly observed in the division between industrialized and nonindustrialized areas—show no signs of abating. The present work is an attempt to understand the chronic nature of this division by studying the relationship between two states of greatly unequal wealth and power.

For purposes of this study, unequal relations between two states are taken to be those wherein one party has the ability to define the issues which arise between them in its own terms (ideological hegemony), to effect its will in regard to these issues (political hegemony), and to be the principal beneficiary of their resolution (material hegemony). While the stronger state's dominance is rarely absolute, it is often the major factor in determining the course and outcome of events within the weaker state. Furthermore, such strength can affect the social and economic structure of the weaker state so as to render it less resistant to subsequent influence. That is, under certain circumstances, there is a tendency for hegemonic relationships to be self-perpetuating. Once inequality becomes imbedded in the structure of a relationship, only epochal events can significantly alter its terms.

This work is an attempt to illustrate the structure and course of the hegemonic element in the relations between the United States and Cuba in the years leading up to the Cuban revolution of 1933. It involves a study of both U.S. foreign policy and Cuban social movements. Its thesis is that the political upheaval of 1933 sprang from tensions in Cuban society which derived in great measure from the structure of its relationship with the United States, and that the Cuban response to these tensions was greatly circumscribed by that relationship.

This project had its origins in a graduate seminar at the University of Pennsylvania led by Gabriel Kolko. Under the supervision of Fredrick Pike, an earlier version was presented as a doctoral dissertation in history to that institution. Material support came from a dissertation-year fellowship from the University of Pennsylvania and grants from the Rabinowitz Foundation and the American Philosophical Society. Assistance also took the form of two teaching fellowships from the History Department of the University of Pennsylvania and the moral support of two of its members—Alfred Rieber and John Shover. My work was further facilitated by the cooperation of the staffs of the Library of Congress, the National Archives, the Franklin Delano Roosevelt Library, the Houghton Library of Harvard University, the Sterling Library of Yale University, and the Van Pelt Library of the University of Pennsylvania. My wife Elaine was the principal typist and proofreader and the source of emotional support which was inestimable.

My greatest debt is to the moral and political ferment of the 1960s, in which I had the good fortune to participate. During that decade, in the course of working out an understanding of the origins and effects of power, I came to possess the insights and analytical tools which form the bases for this study. It is my hope that this work may in some way help to sustain the temper of those times.

The United States and Cuba

The Origins of Hegemony, 1880–1902

The Cuban Economy in the Nineteenth Century

THE BASIS for U.S. dominance in Cuban affairs was established even before the Spanish-Cuban-American War of 1898. It was a natural consequence of the integration of the Cuban economy into the international trading structure, a process which began in the eighteenth century. This integration process brought about the slow dissolution of the vast royal land-grant estates which had been typical of Cuban landholdings since the sixteenth century, and to their replacement by tracts devoted to commercial agriculture. Land usage began to pass from cattle-grazing to sugar production. Nevertheless, even the new commercialized agriculture remained extension-oriented, and production was still based upon slavery in most cases, so that the social impact of the changes in land use was slow to appear. When land or workers wore out, they were replaced, and little modern technology was employed.[1]

Technological change was added to international commercial influence in the nineteenth century. The productive capacity of the cane mills was increased, leading to an increased demand for cane land. With the introduction of the railroad in the 1830s, the basis for the modern sugar *central* and its latifundium had been created. The Ten Years' War (1868–1878) destroyed much of the remaining base of the old agricultural class and began the transfer of the sugar industry from Cuban hands to those of Spaniards and North Americans.[2]

The subsequent pace of expansion in sugar responded to European and U.S. demand, and to the fate of other sugar-growing regions.[3] Despite cyclical declines, the Cuban sugar industry grew throughout the nineteenth century and up until the 1920s. However, the Napoleonic period in Europe brought about the growth of the beet sugar industry under government support. It, too, had a generally sustained growth, eventually coming to supply much of the European market, thus limiting long-range growth of the international cane market. Beet sugar culture arose in the United States later in the nineteenth century with similar competitive effects on cane culture.

3

However, in this case there were direct political effects on Cuba: to gain access to the U.S. market, Cuba now had to run the gauntlet of congressmen from states where the sugar beet industry was influential.[4]

Technological innovation and concentration in the Cuban sugar industry gained momentum in the last decade of the nineteenth century. Increased competition and changing market standards lowered sugar prices, leaving competitive only those Cuban mills which could achieve large-scale production and financing.[5] A division of labor set in whereby milling and growing operations were separated, the former being increasingly accomplished by large mills which were supplied with the raw product by a developing planter class which contracted for the sale of their cane.[6]

International economic pressure caused the breakdown of Spanish control of Cuban trade in the course of the nineteenth century. Despite tariff preferences favoring Spain, by 1860 the United States was taking 62 percent of Cuba's exports and Spain only 3 percent. The Cuban sugar industry was beginning its long career as the supplier for the U.S. market.[7]

Changes also occurred in the marketing and financing of sugar. Large commercial and banking houses became middlemen in sugar sales. Market crises tended to force small Cuban firms out of this line of business, and it came to be dominated by U.S. and Spanish capital. A further effect of these crises was to transform some of the brokerage firms into mill owners through foreclosure.[8]

The oligopolization and rationalization of the sugar industry undermined the economic base of the most powerful Cuban class—the sugar estate owners. These men, though barred from political power by Spanish rule, were the wealthy owners of mills, sugar lands, and cattle ranches, and many were small merchant-bankers as well. After the 1860s this group slowly began to lose control of the financing and milling of sugar, though many held onto their cane and cattle lands into the twentieth century.[9]

With the passing of this autonomously based upper class, Cuba would no longer possess a wealthy class independent of U.S. capital. The decline of this landed aristocracy meant that until the rise of the proletariat in the 1920s there was no large and powerful Cuban class whose interest was to articulate and organize opposition to foreign ownership of land. Indeed, as we shall see, those of the Cuban upper class who remained wealthy usually did so by directly attaching their fortunes and enterprises to U.S. firms. Moreover, they sent their children to live and study in the United States, often owned homes there, and generally became "Americanized." They were, in effect, bringing their life-style into conformity with their economic interests. As the twentieth century progressed, sectors of the professional middle class were to follow their example. Many took out U.S. citizenship as well, erasing legal distinctions along with cultural ones.[10]

The U.S. Presence in the Cuban Economy, 1880–1898

Even before U.S. military power was used to eliminate Spanish control over Cuba, the U.S. economic presence in the island was imposing. By 1881 the value of U.S.-Cuban trade was over six times that of Cuban commerce with Spain. Nevertheless, the island's tariffs still favored Spanish shipping and goods and were resented in the United States, occasionally provoking retaliatory duties. In the 1880s the United States offered the carrot of reciprocity rather than the stick of discrimination. From 1891 to 1894 a U.S.-Spanish reciprocity treaty regulated the Cuban trade, resulting in the doubling of U.S. exports to the island.[11]

The changing nature of the sugar industry also led to an increased U.S. presence. As the sale of refined sugar grew rapidly in the late nineteenth century, U.S. refiners sought to increase their capacity and thus reduce their operating expenses. By 1880, Henry O. Havemeyer had combined nineteen refineries in the United States into the American Sugar Refining Corporation, which until World War I furnished from 70 to 80 percent of all refined sugar consumed in the United States. This rationalization of refining lowered the price of raw sugar as well, once more forcing marginal Cuban mills out of business and leaving their owners to operate as planters for the large, mechanized *central* or to sell their lands to large sugar companies.[12]

The profit squeeze due to the lower prices created by the refiners' trust forced small Cuban millers who managed to stay in business to go more deeply into debt. This eventually led to further foreclosures by U.S. sugar merchants with each price downturn. Edwin Atkins of Boston, whose E. Atkins and Company had financed the Cuban sugar trade since 1838, was the first U.S. merchant to come into ownership of large Cuban sugar estates in this manner. Others, like Havemeyer, seeking reliable sources of supply for their refineries, also began investing in Cuban mills as early as 1892.[13]

Other preindependence investments in Cuba included the Havana waterworks and lighting system, a Standard Oil refinery, and iron mines in Oriente owned by Bethlehem Iron Mines. However, when war came in 1898, U.S. investments were valued at only $30 to $50 million, and other than mining, U.S. capital did not dominate any internal sector of the Cuban economy. Nevertheless, U.S. dominance in the market for Cuban sugar implied an economic power that could be used to gain access to the economy as a whole.[14]

Psychological and Social Effects of Tutelary Independence

In 1898, the United States directly exerted its power in Cuba and forced the removal of Spanish authority. It then formally established its dominance by grafting onto the island's legal structure recognition of special U.S. rights concerning military intervention, naval bases, and financial supervision. This recognition was the price exacted from the island's independence movement for removing U.S. troops.[15] Thus, the "independence" generation in Cuba came to power under U.S. tutelage. Their tutelary position was to keep the leaders of this generation from achieving true popularity among their people. The Cuban Republic was to have few heroes. Because of the uncharismatic quality of the leadership, and the opportunist character of the political parties, nonparty forces were able to gain a hearing for ideological arguments, with the majority of Cubans eventually coming to accept some form of militant nationalism, and with a large minority influenced by Marxism.

The U.S. presence created a resentment among many elements of the postindependence generation of Cubans which was to give popular opinion a strong anti-U.S. bias. Since each Cuban president had to make his peace with the United States, none of them was able to avoid for very long the accusation of having betrayed the nation. Hence Cuban governments never achieved true legitimacy, and the more they depended upon the United States for the indispensable tools of stability (such as recognition, loans, and sugar quotas), the less legitimate they became.

As damaging as were the political results of U.S. influence, the economic presence cut an even deeper wound. Cuba's independence war came at a later stage of industrial development in the major western economies than had those of the other Latin American states. It was not to be the intermittent and partial economic influence of the British or Yankee trader that was felt, but the full force of an industrial and capital-exporting economy which needed not merely the rights of trade but access and protection in the subsoil, land, and internal markets of Cuba. To make matters worse for Cuba, the U.S. farmer still had enough political power to force a compromise upon the industrial and capital exporter's plans for an economic protectorate. The struggle between these two forces caught the Cuban economy in a crossfire which on the one hand tended to make of it a sugar plantation to feed U.S. East Coast refineries, while on the other placed the benefits to be gained from such a role in the hands of U.S. congressmen hostile to the rational functioning of such an arrangement.[16]

The alienation of Cuban land by large U.S. sugar companies, and the diminishing returns of plantation status at the hands of farm-state congressmen, made it impossible for Cuban leaders either to deny the loss of economic sovereignty or to show that such loss was leading to significant and secure economic gain for most Cubans. As a result, Cuban opinion tended to polarize around programs for either total economic integration with the U.S. market or the closing of Cuba to U.S. capital while diversifying production and trade.[17]

The Occupation

The U.S. Military Government of Cuba from 1898 to 1902 vainly sought to establish morality and stability in Cuba. Its task was hopeless, however, because the basis for morality and stability was steadily underminded by the power and growing economic presence of the United States, for which the occupation government was a major agent. People like Governor Leonard Wood and War Secretary Elihu Root were to explain their difficulties by means of a racist disdain for Cuban capacities (especially on the part of the Cuban masses), concluding that if the United States was to have any success at all it must place power in the hands of the white, conservative Cuban upper class and the wealthy Spanish community. To achieve this, Wood established a restricted franchise (limited by literacy and property requirements, among others) to undercut the power of the masses, whom he felt to be both ignorant and foolishly nationalistic (that is, anti-American).[18]

Cuban nationalism was a constant problem for the occupation authorities, and in the final analysis only the combination of Root's appeasing "interpretation" of the Platt Amendment and the threat to continue the occupation (and hints about good treatment for Cuban sugar) brought about Cuban acceptance of protectorate status.[19] Despite the franchise restriction, the municipal elections of 1900 were won overwhelmingly by nationalists, as were the elections for delegates to the Constitutional Convention. This was lamented by Wood, who considered the victorious candidates a "revolutionary element." The facts of U.S. power were explained to the elected Cuban leaders, who thereafter tried to walk the tightrope of balancing a nationalist image with the electorate while making compromises with U.S. wishes.[20]

Another potential source of anti-U.S. nationalism (and even insurrection) was the Cuban Liberation Army, which the occupation government was able to disband by agreeing to set up a $3 million demobilization fund. In its place the United States created the Rural Guard, led by the most cooperative officers of the independence forces, whose task was to assure the security of agricultural properties.[21]

While Cuban nationalism was an irritant, it was not a true threat to U.S. interests. With a few notable exceptions, most of the Cuban leadership, while uneasy about U.S. tutelage, accepted a close economic relationship with the United States.[22]

U.S. influence was most pervasive among upper-class Cuban families. As noted earlier, many of these families had already begun a process of integration with Yankee culture that paralleled the integration of their economic interests. U.S. occupation authorities furthered this integration of the "*nortecubanos*" by appointing them to offices under the Military Government.

Many of these men became the leading politicians of the republican period, and their integrated position regarding the United States simplified U.S. diplomacy.[23]

The conservative upper classes often favored not only close ties to the United States but actual annexation. Moreover, this annexationist desire, going back to the early nineteenth century, was shared by many members of the U.S. occupation government, especially Governor Leonard Wood. General James H. Wilson (departmental commander for Matanzas and Santa Clara), a milder annexationist than Wood, favored protectorate status for Cuba and a customs union which would eventually lead to political union.[24]

The growing economic presence of the United States lent substance to such expectations. In 1900 the Cuba Company, capitalized at $80 million, was formed to build a railroad the length of the island.[25] The United Fruit Company had begun to expand its original landholdings of 1898. In 1901, changing their focus from bananas to sugar, they acquired 200,000 acres on Nipe Bay and built a huge sugar mill ("Boston") at Banes. Another early sugar company (later to become the Cuban-American Sugar Company) was formed by U.S. Representative R. B. Hawley, a Texas Republican. The firm was promoted in Cuba by an early collaborator with U.S. capital, Mario G. Menocal, later president of Cuba (1912–1920). In 1901 the Hawley interests built *central* Chaparra, which became the largest sugar estate in the world. The Hawley interests also bought two other mills at this time and the only refinery remaining from the preindependence period.[26] Though these pioneer elements already foresaw the vast prospects of Cuban sugar, it was not until such promise was certified by the Platt Amendment and the Cuban-American Trade Treaty (with its preference to Cuban sugar) that the major investment took place.

In these years, however, it was tobacco and not sugar that drew the most U.S. capital. At the end of the occupation in 1902 there was $25 million of U.S. capital in sugar and $45 million in tobacco. Before 1899, with the exception of the English firm of Henry Clay and Block and a few German interests, the tobacco industry was in the hands of Cubans and Spaniards. However, in that year, the Havana Commercial Company, owned by the American H. B. Hollins and the Cuban-American Rafael Govin, brought in U.S. capital to purchase cigar and cigarette factories and tobacco plantations.[27]

With Cuba's independence coming at the time of the building of large U.S. trusts, investments in Cuba often followed the pattern of monopoly being established in the United States.[28] This was especially true of tobacco. The American Tobacco Company had in 1901 combined twenty U.S. factories into the American Cigar Company, which in turn had a worldwide marketing arrangement with British tobacco interests. In 1902 American Cigar entered Cuba and purchased Clay and Block and Havana Commercial, thereby gaining control over 90 percent of Cuba's cigar exports and nearly 50 percent of all Cuban production. American Cigar also formed the Cuban Land and Leaf Tobacco Company to run its tobacco plantations.[29] Tobacco capital from the United States thus did not pioneer a market but rather absorbed one, and at a single stroke.

Before 1898, Cuban banking and finance had been dominated by two large Spanish banks: the Banco de Comercio and the Banco Español de la Isla de Cuba. The banking scene also included several of the major merchant houses which dealt in remittances (Zaldo and Company, H. Upmann and Company, N. Gelats and Company). In 1899 the Banco de Comercio was bought by the Merchants Bank of Halifax, which became in 1902 (with the aid of Chicago capital) the Royal Bank of Canada. The bank of Nova Scotia also opened a small branch at this time. In 1899, two New York promoters founded the North American Trust Company and obtained the contract as fiscal agents for the occupation government. North American Trust was reorganized in 1901 as the Banco Nacional de Cuba with the addition of capital from J. P. Morgan interests, and some Cuban-American capital as well.[30] Because of the seasonal nature of Cuba's basic export, sugar, the year-round economy ran largely on credit, so banks were very powerful institutions. The refusal to lend was often tantamount to foreclosure. Thus, the growing foreign influence in banking would be of immense significance.

At the end of the occupation in 1902, U.S. investment in Cuba was more than double what it had been before the Independence War. This increase took place despite the fact that congressional opposition to annexation, as manifested in the Teller Amendment, threatened to hobble the U.S. government's ability to control the course of events in Cuba directly. A still greater impediment to this control took the form of the Foraker Amendment, which forbade the granting of business concessions by the occupation authorities.[31] Senator Foraker apparently felt that if the War Department became involved in such affairs it would never extricate itself from Cuba, and that pressures for annexation would become stronger. Few senators were willing to defend the granting of franchises or concessions, and the resolution passed easily.[32] Nevertheless, throngs of Yankee entrepreneurs made trips to Havana to survey the territory and, in the ensuing months, the Foraker law, like the Teller resolution before it, was found to be less constricting than had originally been thought.

The Military Government under General Leonard Wood fostered the development of the island by U.S. capital and promoted tariff reciprocity to enhance Cuba's trade with the United States. General Wood, like most U.S. policy makers after him, saw stability in Cuba arising from her ability and willingness to obtain U.S. capital. He especially championed railroad development, strongly supporting the Cuba Company in its effort to build a central railroad. Through connections in Washington with Secretary Root and Senator John C. Spooner, the Cuba Company was able to circumvent the Foraker law. While the company was busily acquiring right-of-way properties, Platt and Root used the device of revokable permits rather than the forbidden "concessions" to allow the railroad to cross the public domain, and they authorized Governor Wood to condemn other lands for the railroad by right of eminent domain. Wood also established freight rates for Cuban railroads at levels which he hoped would make the island more attractive to U.S. capital.[33] In another breach of the Foraker law, mining rights were ruled exempt by Wood. He granted 218 concessions in this area, mostly to U.S. companies, and further induced such investment by exempting it from the property tax.[34]

The Foraker law was no barrier to outright purchases. Governor Wood was able to pave the way for the massive purchase of Cuban lands by U.S. corporations. In support of the economic forces already at work to break down the structure of the old royal land grants, the U.S. Military Government promulgated decrees facilitating their dissolution. On the other hand, Wood refused to extend credit to small Cuban farmers to rebuild war-devastated properties.[35]

The occupation government also carried out the first in a long series of infrastructural studies which U.S. experts were to continue periodically over the years. These studies generated the statistical data upon which U.S. policy makers and businessmen based many of their decisions, and were often more accurate and complete than those in the hands of the Cuban government itself.

As early as 1898, Robert B. Porter, a friend of the president's, was sent by McKinley to make a survey of economic conditions on the island. Not long after this, General Wood commissioned a report on Cuba's geological resources which was carried out by a team of three prominent U.S. geologists. The occupation government also conducted a census of the island in 1899.[36]

Tariff reciprocity was an essential part of the economic program of the occupation. The Military Government had reduced the taxes on U.S. imports to Cuba and eliminated Spanish preferences. It thus ended the last vestiges of Spanish mercantile policy in Cuba and set the stage for the almost complete domination of the island's trade by the United States.[37] General Wilson suggested a long-range program of tariff preferences, including a special rate for Cuban sugar, which was supported by Root and by the Cuban sugar industry. The latter had undergone great material destruction in the war and now faced a low world market price for sugar. Only preferential U.S. treatment could make Cuban sugar profitable for the Cuban and U.S. investors. Governor Wood agreed, moreover, because he saw reciprocity as a step toward the annexation he preferred.[38]

Again the question of congressional approval rose as an obstacle. Lower tariffs for Cuba meant more competition for U.S. agriculture, and agriculture controlled votes in the Congress. The division between those who saw Cuba as a competitor and those who saw her as a market was continual and kept the United States from fully exploiting its dominant position. It also kept Cuba from reaping whatever rewards would flow from free trade.

As president, Theodore Roosevelt generally favored agricultural protection, but because of his attachment to Cuban "independence" he was convinced that Cuba was a special case. He urged Congress to adopt reciprocity with Cuba. Governor Wood assigned General Tasker Bliss to draft a reciprocity agreement. The move for reciprocity was, of course, joined by U.S. investors in Cuban sugar and by East Coast refining interests who formed the Associated American Interests in Cuba, of which E. F. Atkins was chairman.[39]

Opposition to reciprocity came from the U.S. beet sugar industry. This was a young industry which had experienced significant growth only since 1897, when the U.S. Department of Agriculture began assisting its development by distributing seed and cultivation information. By 1900 many counties in the upper Midwest, the Rocky Mountain region, and the Pacific Coast were sugar beet areas.[40]

The hearings of the House Ways and Means Committee on the reciprocity bill developed as a battle between these two forces, each with its own allies. The reciprocity forces, somewhat on the defensive, stressed the "obligation" of the United States to assure Cuban prosperity and stability; and they held out a thriving Cuba as a great market for U.S. goods. They denied that Cuban sugar would destroy beet farming, which could in any event supply only a small portion of the domestic demand for sugar.[41]

The beet interests claimed that they would be harmed and demanded protection from the same government that had originally encouraged them to take up beet culture. They saw low-priced Cuban sugar as spelling the end of beet expansion and perhaps the extinction of a crop that was sustaining a growing number of farmers. "Responsibility" toward Cuba, they felt, should not be shouldered exclusively by them, but rather should be borne equally by all citizens. In their most effective argument they charged that the "refining trust" wished to utilize reciprocity as a source of cheap raw materials and huge profits, which would be of no help to the Cuban cane planter extolled by the defenders of reciprocity.[42]

A reciprocity bill, watered down to a 20 percent mutual preference, passed the House in April 1902, but with an amendment by antitrust and beet sugar congressmen reducing the tariff on refined sugar to the level of that on raw sugar, thus opening U.S. refiners to the same kind of competition facing beet farmers. In this form the bill was unpalatable to almost everyone and had little prospect in the Senate. The Committee on Cuban Relations of that body diluted the bill even more, limiting its duration to five years, and stipulating presidential power to terminate it if it was determined

that U.S. refiners and not Cuban planters were deriving the principal benefit. The low tariff on refined sugar was retained, and the bill was killed in
committee.[43]

During 1902, U.S. negotiators with the now independent Cuban government obtained agreement to Cuban preferences ranging up to 40 percent for
U.S. goods, thus sweetening the package even more for U.S. exporters. The
Congress took up this new treaty in 1903. By that time, another change had
taken place in the situation. The beet sugar industry in Europe was declining, and there was the prospect that Cuban cane sales to Europe would
increase. This could have led to decreased Cuban dependence on the U.S.
market, rendering the island less willing to give tariff concessions on U.S.
goods. Greater Cuban economic independence would have undercut the
rationale of reciprocity and, indeed, the whole basis of the Cuban protectorate.[44]

However, before the Cubans had time to reconsider, the main opposition
to the treaty in the United States strangely disappeared. The American Beet
Sugar Association, leader of the fight against Cuban reciprocity, suddenly
dropped its objections to the treaty. The reason was simple. The American
Sugar Refining Company had spent the year of 1902 buying stock in the
major beet sugar companies. By 1903, the two competing interests (U.S.
beet millers and cane refiners) were one, with the massive sugar trust calling
the tune.[45] The prospect of cheap and secure cane supplies was just too
attractive to the Havemeyer interests. In effect, they literally bought out the
beet industry, using the capital leverage which their refining monopoly gave
them to compensate for their "underrepresentation" in the popular-based
legislature.

With the beet sugar states now in line, and with eastern Republicans
facing the prospect of a Cuban market moving out of the U.S. orbit, the
treaty passed both houses by large majorities. By tying the basis of the
Cuban economy to the U.S. market, the treaty rendered true Cuban independence "irrational" in that only by faithfully fulfilling her dependent position as a raw-material supplier could she hope to benefit completely from
reciprocity.

The reciprocity treaty and its political counterpart, the Platt Amendment,
established the framework of U.S. domination. These two documents also
became the focus of a sixty-year contest between the United States and those
Cubans who continued to be inspired by the romantic sense of justice and
sovereignty which infused the life and writings of José Martí. This utopian
strain revived episodically, threatening to rend the fabric of the protectorate.
The intense awareness of an independence denied was the psychological
component of the structural antagonism between the needs of U.S. capital
and the desire of the popular forces which had supported the struggle against
Spain to enter the mainstream of national life.

CHAPTER TWO

The U.S. Economic and
Political Presence, 1902–1924

THE ECONOMIC PRESENCE of hegemonic states within dependent states takes many forms. These forms are usually the result of the particular stage of economic development of the hegemonic power and the opportunities for enhancing or succeeding that stage of development which exist within the economic base of the dependent state.[1]

The most important expressions of foreign economic presence within dependent states have traditionally been found in the following areas: (1) trade, in which the goods and commerce of the foreign state dominate the import structure of the dependent state; (2) raw materials, in which the production of foreign-owned or foreign-controlled subsoil deposits dominate the export structure of the dependent state; (3) agriculture, in which the land base and food and fiber production of large-scale agricultural units are owned or controlled by foreign firms; and (4) infrastructure and industry, in which the networks of communication and sources of energy and the mass production of consumer and capital goods are owned by or heavily indebted to foreign capital.

The U.S. economic presence in Cuba became dominant in *all* of these areas. This was almost unique, for elsewhere in Latin America (especially outside the Caribbean area), the U.S. economic presence faced some European and even native competition in one or more areas of the economy. Native competition was often strongest in the plantation sector. In Cuba, however, the U.S. plantation investment (almost wholly in sugar) dominated that sector of the economy. In fact, it was the largest of such investments by the United States anywhere in the world.[2]

Domination of the plantation sector, in addition to all the others, meant that the foreign economic presence in Cuba stunted the growth not only of an independent industrial bourgeoisie (as was the case in most nonwhite colonial and dependent areas), but of the agrarian capitalist class as well. Moreover, the massive sugar investment built a huge industrial plant in addition to its vast acquisition of land. This was so because sugar, unlike other tropical raw material and food extractions, required large on-site instal-

13

lations to ready the raw product for refining. Furthermore, the returns to scale in the milling process increased up to very large units.

All of these factors led to the creation of an agro-industrial-commercial complex: that is, vast cane fields encompassing entire metropolitan centers. These centers contained milling structures, stores, worker housing, transportation, and other ancillary services, all owned or regulated by the sugar company. In this manner large areas of Cuba came under the effective sovereignty of private U.S. firms.

Economic Presence
Sugar and Banking

The structural bases of hegemony led to concrete economic and political arrangements which facilitated the growth of the U.S. economic presence in Cuba. Under the psychological and political protection of the Platt Amendment and the 20 to 40 percent tariff preferences provided U.S. goods under the 1903 trade treaty, U.S. capital and goods began to move into Cuba during the early years of the republic.[3]

The most massive influx of capital was into the sugar industry. From 1902 to 1924 investment in this area went from around $50 million to $600 million.[4] In 1906, the Hawley interests were consolidated as the Cuban-American Sugar Company, while the Rionda group (international sugar brokers based in New York) continued to acquire properties and in 1910 formed the Washington Sugar Company. In 1913, the West Indies Sugar Finance Corporation was formed to manage and finance Caribbean sugar properties, some of them in Cuba. By the outbreak of World War I, investment in sugar was almost four times what it had been before independence.[5]

The Great War brought a boom in sugar prices which caused a further intensification in investment, mill construction, and consolidation. The Atkins group organized the Punta Alegre Company in 1916, consolidating its expanded holdings. Warner Sugar Refining Company built a large *central* in Oriente, and the West Indies Finance Corporation took over three more properties.[6] The largest investment of this period was made by the Rionda interests (backed by J. and W. Seligman Company, bankers), which created the Cuba Cane Sugar Corporation in 1915 and bought up fourteen mills in the following year.[7]

Most of the large new mills built or bought by the U.S. sugar companies were in eastern Cuba (Camaguey and Oriente provinces), where large tracts of virgin land were available. Hundreds of thousands of acres of forested land were cleared, and thousands of additional cane and mill workers were brought in from Haiti and Jamaica.[8]

The original entrepreneurial initiative for the sugar expansion of the war period was taken by Cuban sugar men, but most of their new mills were quickly bought up by U.S. sugar companies.[9] Though the entry of U.S. firms into Cuba has often been explained as the result of the failure of Cuban entrepreneurs to raise sufficient capital or run risks, this appears not to have been the case with the Cuban sugar industry. U.S. sugar capital was attracted not only by the lure of possible future profits, but by the very real present profits being made by Cuban mills.[10] Indeed, the largest U.S. sugar company, the Cuba Cane Sugar Corporation, was created for the very purpose of buying out profitable Cuban operations.

Another group of U.S. sugar investors was made up of companies which used large quantities of sugar in their manufacturing businesses. The Hershey Chocolate Company bought Cuban cane land and mills at this time, as did the Charles E. Hires Company, the United Drug Company, Loft Candy Company, and the Coca-Cola Company.[11]

Throughout the war, most of the U.S. companies made handsome profits and reinvested heavily. But 1920 brought an end to the sugar boom, and the price of the commodity dropped from twenty-two cents per pound in May to three cents per pound in December. No portion of the industry was organized to function at such price levels, and massive bankruptcies and reorganizations occurred in 1921, especially among the financially weaker Cuban firms. The end of the Dance of Millions (as the 1919–1920 period of high sugar prices was known) brought a new element of U.S. capital to prominence—U.S. banking houses.

The first U.S. bank had entered Cuba as the fiscal agent of the U.S. Military Government (1898–1902). In 1901 this agent, the North American Trust Company, was reorganized as the Banco Nacional de Cuba, with New York capital. In a rare turn, the Cuban millionaire José López Rodríguez (known as Pote) bought control of this bank in 1912 and installed a president who began to train Cubans as administrators. By 1920, Banco Nacional was the leading bank in Cuba and had 121 branches. However, the bank was heavily involved in Pote's speculative ventures and was to disappear from the scene in the bank crash of 1921.

In 1905 another U.S. bank, the Trust Company of Cuba, was organized. After 1912 this bank represented the Morgan interests, which had been bought out of the Banco Nacional by Pote. Also in 1905, the National City Bank of New York took control of the Banco de la Habana, whose president, Carlos de Zaldo, acted as agent for American Sugar Refining Company interests in Cuba. The Upmann Bank became associated with Speyer and Company, and the National City Bank began opening its own branches in 1914.

The First World War greatly increased the demand for sugar, thereby producing the need for additional capital to raise and move an ever larger crop. This need drew more U.S. banks into Cuba. The Mercantile Bank of the Americas founded a Cuban subsidiary related to the Cuba Cane Sugar Corporation. The Chase National subsidiary—American Foreign Banking

Corporation—set up shop in Havana, as did the Guaranty Trust Company and the Canadian Bank of Commerce. At the same time, the National City Bank began to spread its branches across the island, and a Cuban bank, the Banco Internacional de Cuba, was organized.[12]

The sugar crash of 1920–1921 brought U.S. banks directly into the sugar business. The postwar recovery of production in Europe, and the expansion of beet sugar in the continental United States and of cane in its island possessions, led to a surplus sugar situation, especially in the markets in which Cuba sold its crop. Prices dropped over 80 percent, and sugar companies with short-term notes based on sugar collateral had to default to their bankers, who soon were left holding millions in worthless paper and were thus unable to cover their demand deposits with local capital. By October 1920, there was a run on the banks and many suspended payment. On October 10, the Cuban government declared a bank moratorium.

Enoch Crowder, the special representative of the U.S. president in Cuba (and soon to become the first U.S. ambassador), steered a bill through the Cuban Congress which ended the moratorium under conditions which most of the Cuban banks (unable to call on reserves outside the country) could not meet. Only four small native banks were able to reorganize under the terms of the legislation, known as the Torriente Laws. The remainder, including the two largest banks on the island, folded, leaving the field to the U.S. banks and the Royal Bank of Canada. Whereas in 1920 Cuban banks dispensed 70 percent of all loan money and had 80 percent of all deposits, after the banking crisis of 1921 these same percentages were 18 and 31, respectively.[13]

The bank closings also brought down many of the large Cuban sugar merchants, leading to the suicide of Pote and the flight of José I. Lezama, the two largest. The bank failures also carried away the savings of much of the Cuban middle class and created great resentment against the increased sugar dependency which the crisis revealed.[14]

Pote's Banco Nacional, the largest in Cuba, had closed in April and the Banco Internacional, the other major Cuban bank, in May. By the end of June 1921, eighteen other banks had folded, mostly Cuban and Spanish. The only major banks to survive the crisis relatively unscathed were the National City Bank and the Royal Bank of Canada. The Spanish and Cuban banks simply disappeared.[15]

Through foreclosure, the surviving banks became heirs to many sugar mills. National City alone came into possession of sixty mills as a result of the crisis, which properties it organized under the General Sugar Company. Other banks also set up corporations to pool and manage their properties. After 1920, Cuban sugar and U.S. banks were inextricably intertwined. In the 1920s, foreign banks controlled about 80 percent of sugar production, with financing directed toward favored customers.[16]

The crisis of 1920–1921 not only shook the Cuban and Spanish banks out of the industry, but further concentrated sugar production in foreign hands. The Cuban and Spanish mills which were not tied to the large U.S. sugar corporations or banks for financing could not survive the collapse of their creditors (the Cuban banks). In the next five years, thirty-three *centrales* closed down, while others put themselves in the hands of U.S. banks. Whereas before the war, U.S.-controlled mills had ground 35 percent of the crop, by 1927, this figure stood at 62 percent.[17]

Most of the U.S. sugar companies had earned large profits and paid good dividends before 1921, especially during World War I, and some had greatly reduced their bonded indebtedness. However, in the expectation of continuing high prices they had continued reinvesting in the 1919–1921 period and now faced small prospect of significant return on this investment. By 1921, most of the U.S. companies were heavily in the red. Cuba Cane, for example, had an operating loss of $21 million and bank debts of $29 million. Even some of these large U.S. companies fell under the aegis of the consolidation corporations being set up by the banks.[18] Despite their commanding position, the U.S. sugar companies were ailing giants. The rationalization of their debt structure was often as important to them as the production of sugar.

The remaining companies, as well as those under bank management, tried to meet their heavy overhead charges by lowering unit costs through further mechanization and increased production. Without the financial backing for a similar expansion, the "independent" Cuban and Spanish mills were rendered even more marginal. Their position became more precarious still, as expanded production by U.S. mills further depressed the declining sugar market.[19]

Other Industries

Whereas sugar and banking were the major areas of investment for U.S. capital in the early republic, the economic protectorate embraced other sectors of the economy as well. Subsidiaries of large U.S. companies came to dominate the public utilities industry. In 1907, U.S. interests organized by Frank Steinhart, the former U.S. consul general in Cuba, gained control of the Havana Electric Railway.[20] By the second decade of the twentieth century, utilities investments in Cuba were the province of the massive economic units spawned by the oligopolization of that industry in the United States. The Electric Bond and Share Company (the large utility holding company organized by General Electric), through its subsidiary, American and Foreign Power Company, began acquiring public utility franchises throughout Cuba in 1921. In the mid-twenties, Electric Bond and Share consolidated its Cuban holdings under the Cía Cubana de Electricidad.[21] After 1926, this company had, in effect, a monopoly of the Cuban market.

The Cuban telephone industry experienced a similar development. In

1909 the Cuban government granted the right to establish islandwide service to the Cuban Telephone Company, a Delaware corporation and, after 1920, a subsidiary of International Telephone and Telegraph. Though not given monopoly rights, Cuban Telephone eventually acquired most of the existing services and soon was serving every Cuban town. By the mid-twenties Cuban Telephone also controlled the Havana Subway Company and the Radio Corporation of Cuba. The latter firm had received a government concession covering wireless service throughout Cuba.[22]

The major port facilities in Cuba also came under U.S. ownership. Sosthenes Behn (president of International Telephone and Telegraph and chairman of the Cuban Telephone Company) was president of the Port of Havana Docks Corporation, which owned the principal docks in Havana harbor. Other important docks belonged to the Ward Line, Munson Line, Grace Line, Atlantic Fruit and Steamship, and the Cuban and Pan American Express Company.[23]

Cuban railroads also underwent a period of U.S. investment and consolidation during the early republic. Cuba was unusual in that about two-thirds of all rail mileage was owned by sugar companies. These private railroads brought cane to the *centrales* and carried the milled product to company-owned ports. This integrated system reflected the massive economic presence of the sugar companies.

The "public service" railroads were consolidated in the 1920s under British and U.S. capital. The western provinces were served by the United Railways of Havana, in which extensive U.S. capital was invested but which was under British management. The eastern provinces were served by the Cuba Railroad (owned by the U.S.-based Cuba Company) and the Cuban-owned Cuba Northern Railway. In the mid-twenties, the Cuba Northern was merged with the Cuba Railroad to form the U.S.-dominated Consolidated Railways of Cuba.[24]

The mining industry in Cuba began to attract U.S. capital even before independence. It was spurred on by the concessions granted during the first occupation. By the 1920s, Cuban ore deposits of commercial value were almost wholly in U.S. hands, mostly under the control of Bethlehem Steel Corporation and the United States Steel Corporation.[25]

U.S. manufacturing firms also began to set up shop in Cuba. Aided by their size and proximity and by the favorable tariff structure, the products of U.S. manufacturers had come to dominate the Cuban market. By the 1920s some of these firms had established branch plants in the island, a move which lowered their costs vis-à-vis their competitors (Cuban and U.S.) and furthered their penetration of that market. Companies such as Armour, Coca Cola, Pabst, Ford, Fleischmans, Procter and Gamble, and Colgate-Palmolive began producing in Cuba during this period.[26]

Nonsugar agricultural holdings were also extensive. Thirteen thousand

U.S. farmers owned tracts of land, mostly on the Isle of Pines. Lykes Brothers had large cattle ranches, and International Harvester had several thousand acres of sisal. Extensive banana lands were owned by United Fruit Company, Atlantic Fruit Company, and De Georgio Fruit Company.

U.S. oil companies were present as well, though no large deposits had been discovered. Petroleum products were marketed in Cuba by subsidiaries of Sinclair, Standard, Texas Corporation, and Tidewater Oil.[27]

A major U.S. investment in an area of great influence was the holdings of the Cuban-American Govin family of New York. The Govin brothers owned four major Havana dailies—*El Mundo, La Prensa*, the *Havana Post*, and the *Evening Telegram.*[28]

Total U.S. investment in Cuba by the 1920s was over $1 billion, about half in sugar. This represented over 25 percent of all U.S. direct investments in Latin America. The Cuban sugar investment represented over half of all U.S. agricultural investments in Latin America.[29]

To summarize, by the 1920s large tracts of Cuban land, some 20 to 30 percent of all Cuban territory, were owned or leased by U.S. companies. The economic infrastructure (railroads, utilities, shipping, mining, banking, industry) was in foreign—and in most cases U.S.—hands.[30] Moreover, because those sectors of finance, commerce, and merchandising which remained in Cuban hands were closely tied to the sugar economy, they were dependent on U.S. capital as well, in that supply and demand in the sugar market were determined by the large U.S. mills, and by tariff and consumption levels in the United States.

Political Presence

Interference

The political presence of the United States in Cuba during the early republic was as great as that of U.S. capital. This presence included not only official U.S. foreign policy but the many connections between those responsible for that policy and those who directed the economic presence in Cuba. While diplomacy necessitated considerations sometimes at variance with one or more specific economic interests, the basic aims of Cuban policy— stability and the opportunity for U.S. economic development—did not differ fundamentally from those of U.S. business interests.[31]

The general goals of U.S. foreign policy, like its goals in Cuba, focused upon peace, stability, and economic expansion. For nonindustrialized countries this implied support for stable governments and dominant classes, as long as they espoused "open" economies, and it further implied opposition to expansionist, nationalist, or revolutionary movements, especially when they espoused "closed" economies.[32] In Latin America, as the century progressed, nationalism became the greatest obstacle in the path of these goals.

Although nationalism at times served the cause of stability by tying emerging masses to dominant upper or aspiring middle classes, it often threatened to take as the price for such stability a reduced accessibility to Latin economies.[33]

Accessibility was of prime importance because the U.S. economy structurally, and the Open Door philosophy intellectually, based U.S. welfare on economic opportunities abroad. The long-range problem for the United States in the hemisphere was to make enough of an accommodation to nationalism to enable nonradical forces to govern, preferably through legal majorities, while negotiating with the leaders of such forces to modify the economic repercussions of such nationalism. Accommodation was a more difficult and dangerous process where socialists threatened to attract the nationalist masses, or where the emerging nonradical elements were still locked in combat with remnants of feudal forces. Moreover, the racism, conservatism, and chauvinism of many U.S. policy makers made it especially difficult for them to accommodate to nationalism in Latin America. By and large, however, U.S. policy since the twenties has managed a tolerable adjustment, although it is unlikely that it can do so indefinitely.

Nevertheless, in the early Cuban Republic, the United States could still afford the luxury of a protectorate policy which ignored the masses and resisted nationalism. During this period, the United States attempted and indeed expected to restructure Cuban society so that both stability and access would be built into Cuban institutions. In doing so the United States also hoped to avoid the complications attendant upon military occupation. It preferred what was known as a "preventive policy," that is, seeing to it that order was maintained by the Cuban government itself so that the United States would not have to intervene. In the effort to assure that the Cuban government would be willing and able to do so, however, the United States had to interfere in the Cuban political process. Political differences within the island had to be muted and made compatible with the goal of stability. In effect, the Cubans were not to have politics, only elections.

Cuban stability, however, broke down almost from the start. The reelection in 1905 of the first president, Tomás Estrada Palma,[34] brought forth a revolt. At the urging of William Howard Taft, whom he had sent to conduct an investigation on the island, President Theodore Roosevelt reluctantly ordered a second U.S. occupation, which ruled Cuba from 1906 to 1909. Charles Magoon, the U.S. governor, believing that "the stability of all governments comes from the business element and property owners," felt that in order to solve Cuba's political problems it was necessary "to induce the property owning and commercial classes to engage in active politics."[35]

The failure of the "better classes" to take political leadership, and their willingness to depend upon the Platt Amendment to protect their interests, was the result of their alienation from Cuban society. Many had opposed independence or were still Spanish citizens, which made them ineligible for political office. Contests for such positions were in practice restricted to officers of the Independence Army and the political leaders of the independence movement. This group of men, even when they were sons of the old upper class, were not truly conservative. On the other hand, their need to accommodate to U.S. interests kept them from fulfilling the nationalism espoused by José Martí. Their aspirations came to be confined to the search for wealth and power, and they developed no serious programs for social order or progress.

It was with such totally political men that the United States had to work in its attempt to create Cuban stability and economic accessibility. The second occupation government attempted to instill this stability by reforming the electoral and governmental process. Magoon set up an Advisory Law Commission to bring order to the Cuban political arena. Its head, Colonel Enoch Crowder,[36] created an electoral code which for the next twenty years would bear witness to the disparity between ideal and reality in Cuban politics and which would serve as the basis upon which aggrieved political groups, alleging its violation, would make constant appeal to the United States.[37]

Despite Crowder's attempt to elaborate an Anglo-Saxon system of electoral guarantees, Magoon sought political stability in the short run by increasing the government bureaucracy to absorb the opposition to Estrada into the government. This bloated the administration, emptied the treasury, and established sanction for a spoils and graft system which later Cuban politicians elevated to the level of an art. This decision by Magoon also became a theme of Cuban nationalism: that Magoon had introduced corruption into Cuban government.[38]

Though U.S. policy makers were slowly disabusing themselves of the hope of significantly altering Cuban character or even procedure, they remained firmly convinced that dollars were ultimately redemptive. Magoon granted many contracts to U.S. firms and was closely advised by the former U.S. consul general to Cuba, by then a prominent Havana businessman, Frank Steinhart.[39]

Another purported reform, and one which seemed to hold out the most direct possibility of producing stability, was the expansion of the Cuban armed forces. The Rural Guard was augmented, and U.S. officers set up schools to train a Cuban officer corps for that body. Provision was also made for the expansion of the army. Because the revolt against Estrada had fielded more men than the Cuban Army itself, the expansion of that army was a direct expression of the U.S. desire that there be no revolutionary changes of power in Cuba.[40]

With the end of the second occupation in 1909, the Taft administration raised prevention to the level of official policy.[41] In 1912 a revolt by veterans of the Independence War (directed against Spaniards who remained in the civil service after the war) and another by blacks led Taft's secretary of state to call upon the Cuban government to maintain law and order and "to prevent a threatened situation which would compel the government of the United States, much against its desire, to consider what measures it must take in pursuance of the obligation of its relation to Cuba."[42]

Cuban blacks had founded the Independent Party of Color in 1907. The grievances voiced by this party rested upon the conviction that although blacks had composed 85 percent of all troops who fought for Cuban independence, the republic had brought them no reward. President José Miguel Gómez (1909–1912) had made extensive promises to the blacks when elected, but in 1910 the black party was banned by Congress. In 1912 blacks responded with strikes and angry demonstrations which were especially strong in Oriente, where in many places nonwhites formed a majority. The whites reacted to this, and to their own deep-seated fears of black revolution, with a fearsome repression in which three to five thousand blacks were killed.[43]

The U.S. response to the unrest caused by the veterans' and blacks' revolts was to protect U.S. citizens and property by sending gunboats which landed a force of marines at Guantanamo. Secretary of State Philander C. Knox told the Cuban government that he hoped the presence of U.S. forces would help it suppress the revolt.[44]

Such "antirevolutionism" became standard policy under Wilson, and it reflected the continuity of aims of Cuban policy between Taft's "Dollar Diplomacy" and Wilson's "Constitutionalism." When Mario Menocal manipulated his reelection in 1916, the Liberals again threatened revolt. The United States felt especially inconvenienced by unrest in Cuba at the time because the massive wartime demand for sugar made the island's stability more important than usual. In February 1917, Alfredo Zayas, Gerardo Machado, Carlos Mendieta, and other Liberal leaders took to the field, while they appealed to Wilson to intervene and ensure an honest election. Wilson declared U.S. support for constitutional government and warned the revolutionaries to desist.[45] The United States sent arms to Menocal and landed marines in Oriente once again to protect U.S. property.

When the United States entered World War I in April 1917, it was necessary for Cuba to do so also, because its neutrality might threaten the Allies' vital sugar supplies and U.S. use of naval bases in Cuba. With Menocal willing to follow the U.S. lead, Wilson had even less desire to see him replaced. By May, Menocal had defeated the insurrection and, after a further round of rigged elections, was declared officially reelected. Supposedly as a war measure, Menocal had asked the U.S. troops in Oriente to stay. Approximately 2,600 men stationed in Oriente and Camaguey remained in Cuba on "training missions"—until 1923! Their real mission was to protect U.S. sugar properties, mines, and railroads in eastern Cuba from labor unrest and Liberal sabotage, and to inhibit renewed opposition to Menocal.[46]

Other examples of interference in Cuban affairs were less obviously related to the question of stability. The U.S. desire for expansion of its economic position in Cuba implied opposition to foreign (that is, non-U.S.) capital on the island. U.S. interference in Cuba on several occasions was for the purpose of opposing the entrance or expansion of foreign, usually British, capital.[47] The State Department vigorously opposed the granting of a concession to British capitalists for construction of a railroad in north-central Cuba. When the real backers of the project were found to be the Cuban magnate José Miguel Tarafa and a group of New York investors, objections were dropped. In a related matter, Special Representative Enoch Crowder suggested that the U.S. Federal Reserve System establish a presence in Cuba to back U.S. banks in the face of expanding influence by British and Canadian banking houses.[48]

Military intervention, support for U.S. capital, prevention of instability, and support for constitutionality did not exhaust the expressions of the U.S. political presence in the early republic. Two additional themes were the politics of loans and tariffs.

Loan Policy and the Sugar Tariff

State Department thinking, in the days before the U.S. government learned to lend tax revenues abroad to support policy, was slowly coming to accept the necessity of close monitoring of private foreign lending.[49] Though conservatives both inside and outside of government opposed this trend, the Platt Amendment, with its article 2 setting out the conditions under which the Cubans could borrow externally, gave to those who favored loan supervision (so as to render capital lending consistent with policy) a precedent from which to expand.

Even the earliest Cuban loan, that of 1904, was cleared through the U.S. State Department by the bankers. The second loan, of 1909, was directly authorized by Magoon during the second occupation. A further loan in 1913 was not closely supervised, "since it was designed to cover an outstanding obligation to American contractors."[50]

Menocal's appeal for a U.S. loan in 1917 was answered by the State Department with the condition that he settle claims of two U.S. firms, the Ports Company and the Cuba Railroad. After Menocal agreed to make settlement with these companies, the U.S. loan was granted.[51]

A loan in 1922, under President Zayas, was the occasion of demands by J. P. Morgan and Company and the State Department that Cuban internal revenues be increased and that a commission acceptable to the United States administer the loan and the revenues pledged to its repayment. A banker–State Department delegation pressed these conditions upon Zayas and also considered a customs receivership and a tax revision program. By the time Zayas' assent had been obtained, however, Cuban finances had reached a perilous stage, and the bankers feared default on their earlier loans. They now supported a no-strings emergency loan to which the State Department reluctantly agreed. In 1923, when the situation had stabilized, a large loan of $50 million, with requirements for budget and tax reforms, was successfully negotiated.[52]

The politicization of the loan process retreated temporarily in the late twenties owing to the failure of the "moralization program" and to the buoyant economic conditions and expectations within the United States.[53] Moreover, once rule in Cuba by opportunist political leadership was accepted, it became contradictory to the goal of stability to demand that these men refrain from concern for power and enrichment. If cooperation on accessibility was to be maintained, a certain freedom in the use of public monies was necessary. There was, of course, a dilemma in such an approach. Too much fiscal freedom would allow Cuban leaders to ensure the welfare and position of their supporters and block access by the opposition to the seats of power. This, quite obviously, would have destabilizing effects.

When Zayas obtained the $50 million loan in 1923, he became less cooperative. Subsequent loans (prior to 1933) did not carry with them the same level of State Department intervention as before, but the more discreet method of consulting with the bankers prior to such loans was continued, and some control over Cuban finances was retained in this manner.[54]

Cuban-U.S. trade was of great importance to the United States and, as it became the very basis of the Cuban economy, vital to that state. The value of this trade grew steadily between 1902 and 1920 and remained at a high level until the mid-twenties. At its height the United States supplied 73 percent of Cuban imports and took 84 percent of her exports. In good years the small island of Cuba provided one of the largest markets in the world for U.S. goods.[55]

An essential element in the trade between the United States and Cuba was, of course, sugar. Cuban producers were hostage to the political forces which determined the level of the tariff on that product in the United States. While the refiners of the "sugar trust" had overcome the objections of the beet industry in the 1903 tariff fight, the tariff battles of the twenties were a more even contest. The war-born demand for sugar had brought expansion not only to Cuban cane but to U.S. beet production as well. When the sugar market declined after 1920, the beet industry asked for more protection against Cuban cane, with its far lower cost of production. The beet industry succeeded in obtaining an emergency increase in the tariff in 1921.[56]

U.S. exporters, refiners, and sugar companies with Cuban properties argued that a high sugar tariff would destroy the extensive Cuban trade, damage the huge investment in the island, and lead to depression and even revolution in Cuba. Despite such opposition, the expansion of beet agriculture had created a formidable beet "bloc" in the Congress,[57] to which were added other representatives from rural areas who saw low-tariff sugar as a bonanza for the East Coast refiners led by the American Sugar Refining Company.[58]

With growing strength, the beet forces also began to demand a limitation on Cuban production. At this point the banks which had become heirs to sugar mills stepped in, and so did the Cuban government. This combination was able to defeat the demand for limitation, but despite certain obeisances to freer trade, the Fordney-McCumber Act of 1922 retained the high duty on sugar.[59]

Banker-industrialist support of Cuban sugar was generally unsuccessful in the twenties because these interests were not merely fighting for a general lowering of tariffs in order to expand capital and goods exports; they were further demanding the freer entry of a specific competing agricultural product. The farm bloc, whose constituents were in almost continual recession during this period, saw beet-growing as a protected haven from crops which were in domestic oversupply, and they wanted nothing to destroy its growth potential.

Moralization

Another expression of U.S. hegemony over Cuba was the policy of "moralization": that is, reforming the Cuban political process so as to have it conform to U.S. political preferences and to enable it to serve U.S. interests in the island better. Even more than the larger policy of stabilization, "moralization" touched upon the choice of Cuban political leaders. This was an arena in which the United States had no proprietary or treaty rights as a basis for interference. As a result, Cubans were especially resentful of meddling in this area, and the U.S. effort was generally unsuccessful.

In 1919, in an attempt to rationalize the electoral process (which was deemed to be the central roadblock to political stability), Enoch Crowder was sent to Cuba as presidential representative to revise the electoral code. This initial attempt was only superficially successful; despite the new code, the election of 1920 which brought Alfredo Zayas to power led to charges of fraud and to a request by the opposition that the United States supervise new elections. The U.S. response was a broad-based attempt to reform Cuban politics known as the "moralization program."[60]

Crowder was sent to Cuba once again in 1921 to obtain guarantees that future elections would be honest.[61] The core of the moralization program was embodied in fifteen secret memoranda which Crowder delivered to the new Cuban president. These memoranda carried interference further than ever before. They called for a series of economic and political reforms and claimed a U.S. right to investigate even the departments of the Cuban government and to obtain from them reports and statistics which would form the bases of later requests. Numerous U.S. experts arrived and, among other activities, conducted investigations of the tax system (John Herd), public works (the U.S. military attaché), and banking (W. P. G. Harding of the Federal Reserve).[62]

The central demand of the reform program was the request that Zayas name an "honest cabinet," the members of which would be approved by Crowder.[63] When finally appointed, the cabinet generally contained men who were sympathetic to U.S. interests.[64] Nevertheless, Zayas' administration was one of the most corrupt to date, and in late 1922 there was talk of his impeachment. Crowder generally favored such an act, but feared that the substitute chosen by the Cuban Congress would prove no more amenable to U.S. advice than was Zayas.[65]

By 1923 Zayas had obtained his loan from the U.S. bankers and had weathered the domestic political storm. He now began openly to liberate himself from Crowder's "advice." When he dismissed the "honest cabinet," the State Department accepted the failure of moralization and refused to back Crowder in his desire to threaten intervention.[66] U.S. policy makers during this period were beginning to conclude that interference, rather than reducing the need for intervention, often made it more likely. In Cuba intervention, or the threat of it, was felt now to lead to less "responsible" leadership and increased instability. After Crowder became U.S. ambassador to Cuba in 1923[67] he was told not to threaten intervention for fear that the threat would have to be carried out. The United States was willing to give up the possibility of honesty and democracy in Cuba as long as its basic aims of economic security and stability were reasonably attended to. The economic boom of the twenties seemed to make this likely.[68]

Ironically, it was about this time that reform forces within Cuba— incensed by Zayas' corruption and U.S. intervention—began to gain strength. Despite its own constant calls for reform, the United States was frightened by the nationalism and radicalism of much of the reform movement. Thus, it chose to support Zayas, whom it viewed as the representative of stability.

The ending of the moralization program presented a dilemma for the budding reform movement. Much of the intellectual leadership of this movement had supported Crowder in his struggle with Zayas. They did so because the declining standard of Cuban political life was leading them toward the conclusion that the island might be unready for self-government. Indeed, the dominant theme of the political and aesthetic literature of the early republican era—to which these men made significant contributions— was that of *decadencia*. This school of thought traced the failure of true Cuban independence, not to U.S. interference, but rather to weaknesses in Cuban society deriving from the long period of Spanish colonial rule. The pessimistic conclusion of much of this literature was that these weaknesses had become inherent in Cuban society. The failure of moralization undercut the influence of this school within the broader reform movement and gradually brought to the fore a group of intellectuals with an antihegemonic outlook.[69]

The antihegemonists were beginning to define Cuba's instability in terms of its failure to resist the rapid changes in the social and political order deriving from the U.S. presence in the island. Such thinkers perceived the malaise of Cuban society as the result of the culture-destroying accommodations made by Cuban politicians, businessmen, and landowners to that presence.[70]

Even this budding anti-U.S. nationalism remained ambivalent as long as the U.S. presence which bore the economic penetration they decried also seemed to espouse the political reforms they demanded. However, as Washington abandoned moralization and began to define the antigovernment reformers as a source of instability, this school began to shed its schizophrenic character. After 1925, when the United States clearly sacrificed reform for stability and lined up behind the oppressive Machado administration, these two enemies fused into one clear target. As the decade progressed, this wing of Cuban nationalism became increasingly anti-Yankee, with one element turning toward socialism—a fact not without subsequent significance.

CHAPTER THREE

Hegemony and Depression: The U.S. Economic Presence, 1925–1932

The Latifundium at Its Height

BY THE MIDDLE of the 1920s, when the last of the major U.S. sugar investments had been made, the economic presence of the latifundium towered over the Cuban economy. Consolidation had reduced the number of active mills from 1,100 in 1894 to 176 in 1926. Of the latter number, about 100 were partly foreign-owned, and 75 of these were wholly owned by U.S. sugar companies or banks. Since the U.S.-owned mills were in almost all cases the largest, these mills ground over 60 percent of all cane. The U.S. sugar investment was over $600 million and had a mill capacity of 3 to 4 million tons. In addition, the U.S. sugar companies controlled some 4 or 5 million acres in the island. Moreover, the bulk of the mill capacity and acreage under U.S. control was itself concentrated among roughly a dozen U.S. firms.[1]

These powerful companies, drawn by the enormous sugar profits created by World War I, had supplanted much of the native mill-owning class. They had also begun to drive a large portion of the planting class either off their land or into dependent status. They had proletarianized large segments of the rural agricultural class and had imported tens of thousands of West Indian laborers to complement their work force.[2] All of this took place amidst the Dance of Millions, the most intense sugar boom in modern Cuban history.

Though the social changes and tensions created by this powerful foreign presence were masked by the years of prosperity, the sugar decline and bank crash of 1920–1921 had foreshadowed the stark form that economic hegemony would take in times of depression. When a long period of economic decline set in after 1925, the workings of hegemony proved to be an unbearable burden upon Cuban society. In this period economic privation and foreign control combined to form the dual basis for a rising nationalism and radicalism which would culminate in the revolutionary upheaval of 1933.

The Sugar Depression of the Twenties

The overwhelming reality of the Cuban economy in the late twenties and early thirties was depression. Cuban exports declined over 80 percent by value between 1919–1921 and 1932. Sugar production, the heart of the economy, fell 50 percent from 1922 to 1932, while sugar prices dropped over 60 percent. Wages fell from 50 to 75 percent over the same period. In the early thirties, agricultural workers, by far the largest segment of the work force, were paid around fifty cents per day, and mill workers about eighty cents per day, for the two to four months of the sugar harvest. Most were unemployed for the remainder of the year.[3]

This unprecedented decline had come swiftly. The prosperity of the war years had ended in the sugar crash of 1920–1921, when average sugar prices fell 66 percent. By 1923–1924 prices had climbed up to their prewar levels, but they declined again in 1925 and continued to do so until 1934. The downward spiral in prices was reinforced after 1929 by decreasing sugar sales, which fell 50 percent between that date and 1932.[4] This simultaneous decline in price and sales signaled not only deep depression for Cuba but the end of seller dominance in sugar. The period marked the beginning of a secular decline in sugar profits which thereafter colored the workings even of the latifundium.[5] The pressure of the latifundium on the Cuban economy would henceforth be paralleled by the pressure of world industrial depression on the latifundium itself.

Sugar Controls

The post-1925 sugar depression ended the rising prosperity which Cuba had experienced since 1900. The island was never again to experience a similar period of sustained growth,[6] and the social and economic relations forged in the first two decades of the republic were now to be called into question.

The end of easy profits in sugar meant that an industry born in prosperity would now have to adjust itself to operating in depression. The principal question was whether economic laws would be allowed to operate, eliminating all but the wealthiest and most efficient producing units, or whether political forces would intervene in an effort to have the various segments of the industry bear a legislatively determined share of the burden.

Under depression conditions, differing interests within the Cuban sugar economy came to light. Despite the sharp price decline in 1925, the massive mills that the large U.S. companies had built were still profitable. However, these mills needed peak-output production to reach their minimum costs, and their initial response to the price decline was to increase production.[7]

The response of the Cuban mill owners, who generally owned the older and smaller mills, and whose cost of production was above the prevailing price levels even at full capacity, was to press for production control as a way of raising market prices. This last remaining element of an agrarian owning class (who now produced only one-third of the sugar crop) hoped to save themselves from total eclipse by state intervention. In particular, those Cuban owners close to the newly elected Machado administration (Machado and many of his cabinet were mill owners) hoped that a system of mill quotas would be initiated and would be arranged to their advantage. Because the return to scale in these mills was small, they had much less to lose by being held below capacity. [8]

Another segment of the industry was the U.S. sugar refiners who controlled sugar companies operating in Cuba. In regard to the desire for high-level production, their immediate interests coincided with those of the other U.S. companies which owned mills. As mill owners, they too wished to produce at the lowest unit cost. But they differed with U.S. mill interests concerning the latter's long-range goal (shared by both U.S. and Cuban millers) of raising prices. The refiners were not squeezed by a low world market price because they sold their cane, not in that market, but rather to themselves. Since for them cane was a raw material, cheap raw sugar lowered the cost of their final product. Their profits derived for the most part from the spread between the prices of raw and refined sugar and not, as in the case of cane operations which sold on the open market, on that between the cost of milling and the raw price. [9]

A final segment of the industry was composed of the U.S. banks in Cuba. Those banks which had large mill interests, like Chase National and National City, generally favored the high-production solution advocated by the big sugar companies. Nevertheless, their attitude toward production controls was influenced by the magnitude of their lending operations in the sugar economy as a whole. They and those banks acting exclusively as lenders rather than millers provided over 80 percent of the credit with which planters, millers, and brokers operated. If any one sector came under too much pressure, debts would go into default and the banks would wind up with more unwanted sugar, land, or mills. [10] As a result, the banks tended to take a larger view of the problems posed by the sugar depression.

Historically, the first controls over the Cuban sugar industry during the republic had come at the time of the First World War, when a fixed price for the entire crop was negotiated between the Cuban government and the U.S. Sugar Equalization Board, which purchased it for the Allied war effort. At the end of the war, regulation of prices and exports was ended, but the vicious price fluctuations of 1921 caused the Cuban government to return to controls. The Zayas administration (1921–1924) set up the Sugar Finance Commission to prevent the collapse of the credit structure of the industry.

The commission was dominated by representatives of U.S. banks and sugar companies. These interests wished to restore the confidence and liquidity of the sugar market which had been damaged by the violent movement of quotations. The U.S. refiner interests, however, suspected the commission of desiring only to raise prices and so opposed it.[11] Because of this division the commission ceased functioning in 1922, and the stronger prices of 1923 and 1924 put off the question of controls for the time being.[12]

These rising prices of 1923 and 1924 were taken to signify a return to "normal" pre-1920 profitability, and the massive U.S. mills, especially those owned by banks wishing to recover the debt losses sustained in acquiring them, produced at capacity and pushed 1925 production over 5 million tons—for the first time in Cuban history. The expanded output of other world sugar producers in these years soon led to a sharp drop in prices and to renewed demands for production controls.[13]

Even though the high-technology, high-volume U.S. mills had lower unit costs than the older, smaller Cuban and Spanish mills, the former's heavy indebtedness made necessary an especially high rate of return. A long period of low prices, even though it might eliminate inefficient competitors, would make such a rate of return impossible and might also undermine the confidence of these companies' bondholders, thus making it difficult to raise capital at a later date. Even more sobering to the high-production propensities of the big U.S. mills was the intimation, proceeding from the rising anti-Yankeeism of the period, that Cuban nationalism might not accept, and a pro–U.S. government in Cuba might not survive, the destruction of the one-third of sugar production still in Cuban hands.[14]

The first serious attempt to control the production of Cuban sugar was made in 1926 under pressure from Cuban mill owners. Known as the Verdeja Act, it provided for a shortened period of cane-grinding and set maximum quotas for each mill to reduce the total crop by 10 percent each year for three years. It was hoped that by that time world surplus sugar stocks would have been absorbed.[15]

While the long price decline was working a slow change in the attitude of the U.S. sugar companies, they were not about to accept a production limitation program in which they made the greatest sacrifice. They were able, by virtue of their economic strength, to change the principal effect of the Verdeja Act from one which would have reduced output to one which reduced surplus sugar stocks; that is, the delay of the grinding season left more time to sell off the surplus left from the last crop. Thus, despite its origins, the major thrust of the sugar program under the Verdeja Act was to change the form of the sugar surplus from unsold raw sugar in the hands of millers and brokers (predominantly U.S.) to uncut cane in the hands of *colonos* (predominantly Cuban). The shortened cane-cutting season also reduced the yearly income of the largest segment of the Cuban working class. Thus, the financial burden imposed by overproduction was borne by the native segment of the industry.[16]

The Verdeja control program led to the formation of the Sugar Export Corporation, whose function was to handle all sales of cane outside the U.S. market. Sales to the United States (which represented 70 to 80 percent of the total) were not controlled, because most large U.S. mills had important structural ties to that market. Moreover, the U.S. sugar companies retained a majority on the board of directors of the Sugar Export Corporation.[17]

By 1928 the control program had reduced Cuban production by about 2 million tons. Even though Cuba produced about 20 percent of the world's sugar, Cuban retrenchment could not effect a rise in the world market price. Other sugar-growing states expanded production during this period, and world sugar surpluses were actually higher in 1928 than they had been in 1926.[18]

While the hope of higher prices had induced the high-volume U.S. mills to accept production controls, they had no incentive to bear their heavy overhead and unused capacity in the light of continued price declines. The U.S. sugar companies and the banks involved with Cuban sugar now called for an end to controls.[19]

In the face of such opposition, production controls were removed in 1928, causing the 1929 crop to be the largest on record. Protectionism in the other sugar-producing states, however, kept low-cost Cuban sugar from eliminating marginal producers. Thus, the expanded Cuban production merely added to the growing sugar surpluses around the world. Prices now dropped even more sharply, and most segments of the industry began to accept the need for some form of international production control as the only way out.

Attempts at international agreement had failed in the late twenties owing to the resistance of refiners and low-cost growing areas like Java. Nevertheless, the situation had deteriorated so badly by 1930 that some form of international cooperation had become imperative. By that year, the average price of sugar dropped below two cents per pound for the first time since before World War I, and surplus stocks were higher than ever.[20] Even the most efficient producers were pressed at these prices, and political considerations (in the form of subsidies and tariffs) tended to keep many high-cost producers in the world market despite the price.

The call for a return to an uncontrolled market made by U.S. sugar producers in Cuba in 1928–1929 came at a time when marketplace laws would have necessitated the elimination of hundreds of thousands of beet and cane growers and millions of beet pickers and cane cutters around the world. While the structural development of cane sugar production since the turn of the century had been in the direction of oligopoly, the movement had taken place over a period of thirty years. That the nonrationalized segments of that industry (which were still significant) would be allowed to disappear almost overnight, while the respective state governments stood by, was not likely. Moreover, such a situation would have been particularly disruptive of the Cuban economy, with consequences that were incalculable. Any entity with a significant economic stake in Cuba would run great risks in such an eventuality, regardless of the long-run benefits predicted by classical economic theory.[21]

As noted earlier, many U.S. banks had other interests in addition to their large Cuban mill holdings. They dominated the entire credit structure of the island (especially crop-financing) and had underwritten most of the state debt as well. Moreover, they were uneasy in their role as sugar producers and hoped eventually to sell off their mill properties. As another tariff battle in the U.S. Congress loomed in 1928, there arose the possibility that even sales in the U.S. market might soon be below cost. It was about this time also that the large U.S. sugar companies first began to run large deficits.[22] What is more, as the sugar price decline spread deep economic depression across the island, U.S. interests began to fear that rising Cuban nationalism would call for radical solutions.[23] All of these factors made U.S. sugar interests desirous of a reorganization of the Cuban industry.

In 1929, U.S. interests, fearing another rise in the U.S. tariff, had sought to allay the fears of beet growers by accepting sales controls for Cuban sugar moving to the U.S. market. Once again, as with the Sugar Export Corporation, however, this new single-seller—now called the Cooperative Sugar Sales Agency—was dominated by U.S. interests. The arrangements made for crop-financing under this new control body greatly favored U.S. producers, and this led to a hostile response from the Cuban segment of the industry, causing President Machado to dissolve the agency in 1930. The free marketing of the 1930 crop that ensued drove prices down even further and set the scene for a major effort at both Cuban and international controls.[24]

The Chadbourne Plan

By 1930, non-Cuban sugar interests in the United States had achieved another increase in the sugar tariff—to the highest levels since 1890. Moreover, broadening industrial depression in the United States was reducing U.S. sugar consumption. The unsold surpluses of Cuban sugar built up since the record cane crop of 1928 were accumulating in unprecedented amounts in the hands of U.S. banks and sugar brokers (whose loans the bankers held). Just as the banks were recovering their losses from the crash of 1920–1921 by refinancing the mills they had acquired, they faced the disturbing possibility of coming into possession of vast quantities of unsold and perhaps unsalable sugar stocks. The banks' most pressing concern, therefore, was to salvage their commodity loans, the collateral for which resided in warehouses across Cuba. A comprehensive program of production controls could render these surpluses salable.[25]

As a result of these factors, a committee representing U.S. banks and sugar companies with Cuban interests was formed in New York City. The chairman of the committee was Thomas L. Chadbourne, a New York corporation lawyer with a direct interest in two Cuban *centrales*. In August 1930 this committee called a meeting of sugar representatives from all the areas supplying sugar to the U.S. market. To avoid the possibility of antitrust proceedings, the program issuing from this meeting was formulated as a "gentlemen's agreement." The "agreement" set limits on the marketing of each sugar-producing group in the U.S. market, limiting producers in Cuba to 2.8 million tons and those in Hawaii, the Philippines, Puerto Rico, and the U.S. mainland to their present shares of the U.S. market.[26]

Despite the fact that no binding commitments had been made, the Cuban government was prevailed upon to implement the agreement by means of legislation. This led to the Cuban Sugar Stabilization Law of 1930, which requested that each mill set aside a portion of its production to be turned over to the Sugar Export Corporation in return for government bonds. The Export Corporation was pledged by the "gentlemen's agreement" to market its sugar outside the United States and over a five-year period.[27] Since the bonds were backed in part by a tax on all Cuban sugar produced, the burden of sugar surpluses, mostly in the hands of the U.S. banks and brokers, was shifted from them to the Cuban sugar industry as a whole. As with all previous "Cuban" regulatory bodies, most members of the Export Corporation were Americans, with Chadbourne himself as president.[28]

With Cuban controls established, the next step was an international production and marketing agreement to complement them. In May 1931 an international convention was negotiated in Brussels by a Cuban delegation headed by Chadbourne. This agreement, generally known as the Chadbourne Plan, was concerned ultimately with price recovery but was immediately interested in holding new production off the market until accumulated sugar stocks could be sold. This priority was necessary because the capital-lending institutions had to be allowed to recover their assets from previous crops before they would finance future ones. However, because the plan was inspired by bank interests and worked in the first instance to their specific benefit, the program was opposed by U.S. refinery interests. These interests were free of banker influence because they were strong enough to finance their cane operations from refining profits. They feared that a growers' cartel (which the Chadbourne Plan approximated) could withhold enough raw sugar to raise their cost of production.[29]

The Chadbourne Plan called for the nine participating nations to limit production and to export only the quota amounts of sugar provided for by the agreement. The heaviest production decline was suffered by Cuba, whose quota was 25 percent below her current (already reduced) output. Surplus stocks (70 percent of which were Cuban sugars) were to be released over a period of four years, but in a manner that, including new production, would not exceed a state's quota. That is, surplus exports reduced the amount of the quota remaining for new production. The banks and brokers were thus to precede the millers and growers in the long climb upward.[30]

For a number of reasons the Chadbourne Plan was a failure. In addition to refiner opposition, the agreement nations accounted for only 60 percent of world sugar exports. States whose production was sold in preferential or duty-free areas were not included. While the agreement countries reduced output over 6 million tons, nonagreement states expanded their production. This particularly hurt Cuba, because the nonduty suppliers of the U.S. market, ignoring the "gentlemen's agreement," took advantage of Cuban restriction and a higher tariff to supplant Cuba even further in the U.S. market. Cuban sugar, which had dominated that market (57 percent in 1922) and had one-quarter of the world's output just after World War I, had been reduced to only 28 percent of the U.S. market and less than 10 percent of world production by 1932.[31]

The Chadbourne Plan countries had assumed that world sugar consumption would rise and that tariff-protected sugar would decline. These hopes were dashed by the world depression and the increased autarky it fostered. While the native segments of the Cuban sugar industry might have suffered as much had the Chadbourne Plan not been in existence, the fact is that the plan entailed exceptional sacrifice from Cuban producers. This sacrifice, most heavily felt by the Cuban *colono* and cane worker, led to the gravest economic conditions experienced by Cuba in the century. As it became clear that the U.S. banks were the only beneficiaries of the Cuban sugar debacle, the nationalist movement churned up by the economic crisis began to take on an anti-Yankee and even anticapitalist complexion.[32] The workings of hegemony, previously hidden within the complex arrangements of an economy in ascent, now stood out more starkly as depression reduced economic affairs to their most basic components.

The Tariff Struggle of 1930

Cuba suffered two levels of economic hegemony. One was the presence within the island of U.S. firms, especially sugar companies. The other was the continental U.S. economy. While this economy provided the capital and market base for the U.S. presence in Cuba, it also—at least in the case of sugar—competed with that presence. The tariff relations between the

United States and Cuba provide an example of the competitor function of the domestic U.S. sugar industry.

Cuba needed a low tariff for her sugar. But to obtain such a tariff, Cuba (and those U.S. sugar interests in the island) had to influence a congressional coalition large enough to overcome U.S. protectionism, especially beet sugar protection. She had only one major resource to attract such a coalition: her ability and willingness to buy U.S. exports and to provide profitable opportunities for U.S. capital. In prosperous times, supporters of U.S. economic hegemony could point to the "advantages" of such an arrangement, but in depression the situation was much more difficult. First of all, the ability of Cuba to consume generally high-priced U.S. exports was one of the first casualties of the declining Cuban economy. More important, however, was the fact that with a rising tariff barrier in the United States, the profits of U.S. sugar enterprises in Cuba, if they were to be maintained, would have to come out of the now frail body of the native segment of the economy. Thus, Cuba was caught in a particularly vicious cycle. To stem the severe economic deprivation which was tearing their society apart, Cuban leaders had to fight the tendency of the sugar companies to reduce their losses by further depressing the Cuban standard of living. Yet at the same time, these very companies were held by such leaders to be the essential allies of Cuba in the attempt to arrest the decline of the world sugar market and secure a more profitable entry for Cuban cane into the United States. [33]

Because of its belief that the only way out of depression was in concert with U.S. economic interests, the Cuban government developed no serious alternative to the program carried out by those interests. When the efforts of the U.S. companies failed to stem the decline of sugar prices, and when these same companies continued to charge prices and pay wages which the domestic economy could not accept, the strategy of alliance with U.S. interests was discredited, as was the Cuban government which espoused that alliance.

In addition to efforts at production control, U.S. interests in this period sought to defeat another increase in their country's sugar tariff. Despite the total dependence of the Cuban government on the success of the tariff struggle, however, its impotence to promote or even articulate its interests can be seen by the entirely secondary role which it played in the formulation of the Smoot-Hawley tariff of 1930. Except for a few wealthy Cuban sugar mill owners (José Miguel Tarafa and Viriato Gutiérrez), [34] the entire cast of the production was made up of the contending U.S. economic interests. Though the depression of the late twenties and early thirties was to wipe out twenty-five years of economic advance in Cuba and to bring on political revolution, Cuba stood as a spectator to most of the major events of the period.

Like their opponents in cane agriculture, the beet farmers of the United

States spent the 1920s trying to arrest the declining price of sugar. The solution they adopted was the protective tariff. Beet sugar was generally more expensive to produce than cane sugar, and only barriers to cane imports could make beet sugar salable in the United States. The major threat to beet interests appeared to come from Cuban sugar, which had the lowest costs of all the cane-supplying areas and, despite the already existing tariff, had captured about half of the U.S. market by the early twenties.[35] These interests hoped that further tariff increases would both lower the amount of Cuban cane coming into the United States and drive the price of sugar upward.

The big *centrales* in Cuba attempted to compensate for the rising sugar tariff with a reduction in their cost by increasing and intensifying production, by lowering wages and cane payments, and by generally using their dominant position in the Cuban economy to pass on a portion of their costs to the native economy and government. But the lower Cuban costs fell, the more insistently beet interests demanded higher tariffs. And so the cycle went: overproduction and depression drove sugar prices down faster than the tariff could raise them, and to a point lower than that which the most excruciating economies of the *centrales* in Cuba could reach. The result was a return of feudal conditions and semistarvation in the Cuban cane fields and undisguised exploitation of beet workers in the United States.[36] The ultimate outcome would be New Deal regulation for the beet industry—and revolution in Cuba.

The first round of the tariff fight had begun late in 1928. The main Cuban interests were represented by the American Chamber of Commerce of Cuba (nonsugar interests) and the United States Sugar Association (sugar companies with Cuban interests). While calling for a lower duty, these opponents of the sugar tariff privately conceded the difficulty of winning on that issue and put their main effort into a covert arrangement with the continental sugar producers. Under this agreement, continental producers would get a production subsidy, and both groups would cooperate on limiting the access of insular sugars to the U.S. market. Some of the domestic producers responded with their own proposal to accept a "sliding-scale" tariff (one inversely related to the price of sugar) if Cuba would limit her sugar exports to the United States.[37]

As noted earlier, the Cuban sugar interests were willing to accept import controls. The beet interests, for their part, were unsure of obtaining adequate protection through a higher tariff and thus were attracted by the possibility of a subsidy and limits on insular sugar. But the beet bloc in the House of Representatives was powerful enough to vote through a higher tariff, and the beet interests opted for one last try at protection via the tariff rather than the untried arrangement offered by the Cuban cane interests. In May 1929, the House passed a higher rate for sugar.[38]

As the tariff bill moved to the Senate in 1929, the State Department stepped in with a defense of the Cuban position. The department, sensitive to rising anti-Americanism in Latin America, stated to President Hoover that a higher sugar tariff would give fuel to such propaganda and that this would be of advantage to the United States' "commercial competitors."[39]

The Cuban cane interests, rebuffed in their efforts at an alliance with beet forces, now tried to reduce the rate passed by the House. When they appeared to be having some effect, there came to light, in hearings by the Senate Judiciary Committee, the existence of a $95,000 "sugar defense fund" created by the Cuban cane and banking interests to support their lobbying effort. Antimonopoly senators were able to use the specter of plutocratic interests to defeat rate reduction. The level for Cuban sugar finally arrived at in the Smoot-Hawley Tariff Act of 1930 was the highest rate in forty years.[40]

The outcome of this last tariff struggle prior to the New Deal convinced most of the Cuban interests (with the exception of a group of refiners) that the only way to end the chaos and decline of the sugar market was to move toward controls both within the United States and in international markets. These forces also concluded from their experience with the Congress that the Democratic party would be more receptive to such an arrangement than the Republicans.[41]

Cuban Tariff of 1927

Many Latin American states experienced internal demands for protected, import-substituting production during the late twenties and thirties. Native capitalists operating principally in the depression-rocked domestic market pressured governments to protect their access to that market. In Cuba, a small group of native businessmen had grown up along the fringes of the booming sugar economy and acted to protect themselves similarly once that economy floundered. These forces found an outlet for their needs in the Liberal party, which under Machado's leadership became something of a political expression of this commercial and manufacturing group. His election in 1925 had, in fact, signaled a shift in power away from the landlord-based Conservative party that was dominant during the Menocal years.[42]

Despite the domestic business interests of many members of Machado's administration, however, his regime by no means represented a regnant national bourgeoisie. The depth of U.S. hegemony required the principal job of the Cuban president to be that of maintaining conditions in the island conducive to the interests of U.S. capital. Therefore, nationalist legislation in Cuba expressed the contradiction between the native capitalist's need for legislation which worked against the prevailing market forces set in motion by the U.S. economic presence and the U.S. capitalist's need for a free working of these forces.

The native bourgeoisie, weak owing to the extent of the U.S. presence and appealing to an administration dependent upon Washington's benevolence, would have had no success at all had not the depression and rising nationalism created an atmosphere in which some action had to be taken. Nevertheless, their links to the United States (few were independently financed or without the need for U.S. inputs) and their unwillingness to form domestic mass-based alliances led the administration which reflected their interests to produce tariff and tax reforms and agricultural diversification schemes of a very moderate nature. In the final analysis, these reforms represented not a challenge to hegemony, but rather the Havana government's very immediate need for legitimacy and, as a means thereto, revenues.[43]

The government under the republic was a major employer of the professional class in Cuba. This resulted from the fact that the non-Cuban segment of the economy generally used its own managerial and technical personnel, so that the Cuban civil service was the only area of the economy able to absorb large numbers of degree-holding natives. Government revenues also supported the army (whose allegiance was crucial to the incumbent president) and the payment of foreign loans and political supporters. Upon the ability of the Cuban government to meet its payroll, its foreign debts, and its unofficial obligations to supporters depended its very existence. By the late twenties, as trade decline followed sugar depression, the revenues of the government (over 50 percent of which derived from customs receipts) plummeted.[44]

To maintain government revenues, and in some measure to respond to the nationalist call for greater autonomy, the Machado government in 1927 established a new tariff schedule. The changes of rate and classification were not large, the most significant being a slight increase in the duty on manufactured goods except machinery and equipment. Though certain domestic industries expanded under this protection, it did not lead to significant competition for this type of U.S. import.[45]

The depressed economic conditions, however, did favor the tariff-protected expansion of domestic food production, because of both the high price of U.S. food imports and the large amount of acreage no longer needed for cane. The resulting decline in food imports from the United States, though it did not give rise to a strong Cuban agricultural industry, did disturb U.S. growers, and this was reflected in later attempts by this group to use the sugar tariff as a weapon to break down the Cuban tariffs on food products.[46]

One significant effect of the higher industrial duties was to enhance the tendency for U.S. firms to set up branch-plant operations. In many cases they were able to buy out competing Cuban firms, thus actually reducing the native segment of the domestic-oriented economy. U.S. plants in Cuba, even more than Cuban firms, imported most of their raw materials and equipment from the United States, thus tending to perpetuate the island's import dependence despite the increase in domestic production.[47]

In practice, the major function of tariff reform tended away from protection and toward the immediate economic and revenue problems of the Cuban government. The need for revenues, moreover, led to the establishment of a series of taxes—including consular invoice fees and customs surcharges, port improvements taxes, and a gasoline tax—all of which were levied on imports. It was these taxes, even more than the higher duties, which disturbed U.S. exporters to Cuba. Duty increases still preserved the U.S. preferential, but these import charges were based on value and weight, and thus not only raised the price of U.S. goods but lessened the preferential advantage of these goods against full-duty imports.[48]

The 1927 tariff never really threatened to close off the Cuban economy to the bulk of U.S. trade, and the decline of U.S. exports was due mostly to the depression and not to Cuban protectionism. Nevertheless, U.S. export interests worked to break down the duty and import tax structure erected by the Machado administration. The desires of these forces became one of the elements behind the major readjustment of U.S.-Cuban economic relations which culminated in the Reciprocal Trade Treaty of 1934.[49]

Because Cuban protectionism was not erected as a determined program of import substitution, and because it was elaborated as a response to immediate fiscal and political pressures, it led to no serious assault upon sugar dependency or the larger U.S. hegemony.[50] Nevertheless, because the new import controls hit hardest against that nation which supplied the majority of foreign goods (the United States), it alienated U.S. exporters and caused them to demand even greater privilege in the 1934 treaty than they had obtained in 1903.

Loans and Debt

The inability of the Machado government to reflect in a meaningful way the growing Cuban nationalism of the twenties was also due to the massive debt it contracted with U.S. banks. From the outset, Machado was saddled with the 1923 Morgan loan of $50 million granted to the Zayas government, the largest single loan Cuba had ever received. Since very little of the loan was used for expansion (it was employed in the main to liquidate previous indebtedness), no economic momentum flowed from it.[51]

Machado had pledged in his 1924 presidential campaign not to increase Cuba's foreign debt. However, he also promised a broad program of public works. As the post-1925 sugar depression reduced government revenues, the president cast about for some means of financing the public works program. U.S. bankers, then in the midst of a cycle of almost frantic foreign lending, competed eagerly for the opportunity to lend Cuba money. The bankers considered the right of U.S. intervention, the large U.S. investment in the island, and the probusiness attitude of Machado as guarantees of their loans.[52]

In 1927 Machado acquired from J. P. Morgan and Company a $9 million loan, once again for the purpose of retiring previous indebtedness. By this time, however, the Chase National Bank had established the closest ties to the Machado administration. Chase Securities worked through Henry Catlin, president of Electric Bond and Share Company, who reputedly had financed much of Machado's election campaign. Through Catlin, Machado's son-in-law was made notarial attorney for the Chase National Bank in Havana, and in 1927 the Chase Bank made a $10 million banking credit to the Machado government. This credit was the first part of some $100 million which would be lent to finance Machado's public works program—the greatest single public program expenditure to that date in Cuban history.[53]

The Chase Bank credit was used by the Cuban government to issue "public works certificates," that is, payment pledges of the Cuban government granted to contractors for work completed. These certificates were to be bought from the contractors by the Chase Bank so that the contractors could finance their continuing operations. The Chase Bank was to hold them until special new taxes imposed to finance the payment of the public works debt had brought in enough funds to retire the certificates. This somewhat tortuous procedure resulted from the fact that Cuban customs revenues were beginning to decline as a result of the sugar depression and were themselves already mortgaged in great degree to the repayment of previous loans. New taxes had to be levied to pay for the public works program, but the revenue from these taxes would not accrue swiftly enough to keep present contractors on the job. Moreover, the certificates and the Chase Bank credit did not technically come under the purview of article 2 of the Platt Amendment. Thus, the arrangement kept the eager bankers beyond the surveillance of a more cautious State Department.[54]

Once begun, the public works program—especially the seven-hundred-mile central highway and the new capitol building—ran to great sums. To finance the continuation of work, a syndicate headed by the Chase Bank extended a further credit of $50 million in 1928. Because the bankers were becoming somewhat wary, the entire credit of $60 million was to be repaid within five years. This large short-term debt soon doubled Cuba's yearly cost of repayment.[55]

By 1930, the $60 million had been spent, while corruption and mismanagement left major parts of the works program still unfinished. The fall in government revenues was accelerating, and the returns from the taxes pledged for repayment were not keeping pace with the six-month maturity dates of the certificates. The bankers were now in a bind. They had to protect their $60 million investment by a further credit and easier repayment schedule or Cuba would be forced into default. Moreover, the bankers and the State Department felt that a further loan was necessary to keep Machado in power. His government had so far proven to be the most effective of all Cuban governments in protecting U.S. interests and promoting stability. Though the sugar depression was undermining his ability to perform these functions, the bankers did not want to increase his burden by withholding funds.[56]

In February 1930 another syndicate headed by the Chase Bank lent Cuba a further credit of $20 million, again on short terms. In addition, the syndicate sold the Cuban government $38 million worth of the public works certificates they held, and accepted for marketing $40 million of new public works bonds with later maturity dates. This refinancing cost Cuba over $3 million.[57] These complex financial arrangements in effect lent Machado the money with which to pay past indebtedness now coming due. In short, the banks were advancing to Cuba just enough money to prevent default and the possible demise of the Machado government. The dependence of the Cuban government on U.S. banks now became almost total. Public works bonds and credit repayments were coming due every six months or less, and with ever declining revenues this meant a regular bailing out by the bankers. As political opposition against Machado's increasingly dictatorial regime became more intense in the early thirties, his growing dependence on U.S. bankers added to the momentum of Cuban nationalism.

In a very direct way, Machado's dependence on the banking segment of the U.S. economic presence was felt by the Cuban people. As foreign debt service began to pile up after 1930, Machado began to dip into the regular budget. As a U.S. State Department summary of the Cuban debt situation in 1933 stated:

> In order to meet its external debt payments Cuba has rolled up an enormous floating [internal] debt in the neighborhood of $42–50,000,000. The Government has anticipated taxes, retained salaries, looted special funds intrusted with it for safekeeping, piled up unpaid bills, all to enable it to meet its foreign debt payments.[58]

The banks and the State Department indirectly encouraged this procedure by insisting that Machado produce a balanced budget. However, balancing the budget (which had dropped over 50 percent between 1925 and 1931) meant failing to pay large segments of the civil service, which was the main source of employment for the lower-middle class. Moreover, as it became clear that government salaries and services were being withheld so that Machado could continue to pay the Chase Bank debt, another link in the association between the Machado regime and the U.S. economic presence was forged in the minds of most Cubans.

Machado for his part felt that he had no choice. His dependence on the banks was so great that he was sure default would remove U.S. political and economic support and lead to the destruction of his regime.[59] He therefore continued to extract from the severely depressed native economy the monies necessary to meet the large foreign debt, thus helping to assure that the threat to his regime would not be an economic one from the bankers, but rather a political and social one from the Cuban people.

With debt service mounting and revenues falling, Machado was ultimately forced to increase internal as well as customs taxes. By 1932 there were taxes on the domestic consumption of gasoline, chocolate, soap, clothing, butter, cheese, razor blades, and ham. Taxes were also levied on certain luxuries, on sales and gross incomes, insurance premiums, radio sets, installment purchases, sugar, and many other items.[60] In effect, Machado was taxing the very industries which the tariff of 1927 was presumed to foster. When added to the taxes on imports, these internal taxes kept price levels from deflating as fast as disposable income, forcing a great portion of Cubans out of the market for these goods. In addition, there was widespread evasion of taxes. Despite all of these tax measures, revenues declined steadily after 1925 and precipitously after 1930. By 1932 the Cuban government was, by any reasonable economic standard, bankrupt.[61]

By this time, the bankers feared a Cuban default despite all of their own efforts, as well as those of Machado. As bad as the economic situation had become, it was now the political unrest that most worried the bankers and the U.S. State Department. A revolution against the Machado government had broken out in August 1931. Though it had been put down, the opposition was still demanding Machado's resignation. The institutions of higher education were closed, and students and professional men were organizing antigovernment terrorism in the cities. Strikes were proliferating and Marxist ideas spreading. The bankers began to fear that if Machado fell to this growing nationalist and antidictatorial movement, there might be nothing left to save.[62]

The banks began to consider the possibility of allowing a partial moratorium covering the long-term public works debt in order to avoid complete debt default. They hoped in this way to give Machado something with which to bargain in making concessions to the more conservative elements of the opposition. To meet the December 1931 debt service, the bankers extended the 1930 credit of $20 million (due at the end of 1931) for six months. The same procedure was followed in June and December 1932, with the banks extending the high-interest credit to enable Machado to pay both that interest and the service due on the older debt.[63]

As the bankers tightened their rein, Machado became more restive. With government salaries two to three months in arrears, and with $15 million owed to suppliers, the president was coming to conclude that he might have more to fear from the wrath of the Cuban people than from the bankers. He proposed to float a $10 million internal loan to repurchase the loyalty of the civil service and appease the government's native creditors. U.S. Ambassador Harry F. Guggenheim bluntly told the president that such a loan would threaten Cuba's credit and discourage further advances from the Chase Bank. He threatened, as he had not done in regard to the Chase Bank credits, to invoke article 2 of the Platt Amendment if Machado tried to go through with the internal borrowing. Machado dropped the proposal.[64]

Nevertheless, by the end of 1932 the political situation was so desperate that Machado was forced to incur the bankers' displeasure by opposing their suggestion that the sugar production tax be pledged against a renewal of the credit. However, he gave in eventually and agreed to pledge the production tax as well as a new sugar consumption tax in return for a new credit from the Chase Bank and a prepayment of taxes by the U.S. oil companies operating in Cuba.[65]

But the additional Chase Bank advance and the tax prepayment by the oil companies could not save the day. To meet the December 1932 debt payment, tax collections up through 1934 were being pledged. Ambassador Guggenheim now differed with the bankers and opposed this procedure of putting off default by mortgaging more and more of Cuban revenues. He felt that the growing demand for a debt moratorium by the Cuban people had to be satisfied in some way and that a partial default might ease domestic political pressures. However, the State Department saw the alternative to continued debt payments as a general default and thus accepted the bankers' program.[66] Bit by bit, the dwindling proceeds of the entire Cuban economy, as well as the fate of the Cuban president, were becoming tied to the debt service.

Tariffs and Trade

Protectionism and internal borrowing were responses to the sugar depression that were influenced by the mainstream of Cuban nationalism. They were attempts, however timid, to lessen the economic hegemony of the United States. There were other forces in Cuba, however, which saw the way out of depression through even closer economic ties to the United States. The main efforts of these forces were directed toward a renegotiation of the 1903 trade treaty.[67]

The preferential treatment of Cuban sugar afforded in the 1903 treaty had allowed the island's product to underbid the rest of the duty-paying segment of U.S. sugar imports. Indeed, by 1910 it had practically eliminated them from the U.S. market. By that time, moreover, Cuban sugar had established itself as the lowest-cost of all sugars entering the United States and no longer needed the preference to compete with duty-paying sugar. The Cubans at that point claimed that the benefits they derived from the trade treaty had ceased and that the treaty should be renegotiated.[68]

The real competition faced by Cuban cane for a share of the U.S. market came from the non-duty-paying cane sugar grown in the United States' island possessions (Hawaii, Puerto Rico, and the Philippines) and the beet sugar grown in the continental United States. Against these duty-free sugars, the Cuban "preference" (20 percent less than the full sugar tariff) was no advantage. Moreover, as the beet sugar interests in Congress successively raised the tariff after 1921, Cuba's disadvantage increased, and its efforts to compete by lowering the cost of production only spurred beet forces to raise the tariff even higher. Cuba had tied its prosperity to its ability to compete in a market where the price of its product was controlled by its competitors. This arrangement was a central feature of the hegemonic position of the U.S. economy vis-à-vis Cuba.[69]

In an effort to escape this dilemma, and as a way of countering the autarkic sentiments of a rising Cuban nationalism, the Machado administration was forced to open once again the question of renegotiating the trade treaty. In April 1926, Machado's secretary of state officially informed Ambassador Crowder of his belief that the trade treaty was no longer benefiting Cuba and that the island needed a lower tariff or a higher preference for its sugar. Crowder passed on an official Cuban memorandum to this effect to the State Department. A study of the treaty was then ordered by the U.S. Tariff Commission, but no formal action was taken.[70]

Early in 1927 the new Cuban ambassador to the United States, Orestes Ferrara (a strong advocate of close economic ties between Cuba and the United States), again presented Cuba's request for the negotiation of a new treaty. The State Department showed no serious interest in the proposal, and nothing further occurred until a third Cuban request was made in December. This note reflected once again the necessity for prior Cuban concessions if negotiations were even to begin. It suggested that Cuba would increase the 20 to 40 percent preferences on U.S. goods to 30 to 50 percent in return for a larger preference for its sugar.[71] The note also raised the question of having the United States allow a set tonnage of Cuban sugar to enter duty-free in return for free entry of certain U.S. goods into Cuba. Secretary of State Frank B. Kellogg, responding to Ferrara's note, stated that Cuba had a favorable balance of trade with the United States and was still benefiting from the treaty. He also added that the Congress was unlikely to pass any proposal which called for easier access for Cuban sugar.[72]

Nevertheless, early in 1928 the State and Commerce departments set up an interdepartmental committee to study the question of renegotiation.

After investigation, however, Kellogg and Herbert Hoover (then secretary of commerce) agreed that the proposals were disadvantageous to the United States. In June Kellogg informed Ferrara of these findings, adding that opening up the question might cause Congress to make an arrangement less favorable to Cuba.[73]

This rebuff threatened to weaken the influence of those of Machado's advisors who were trying to stem the growth of autarkic proposals in Cuba. Ferrara, whose pro-U.S. sympathies could almost be called annexationist, tried another approach. He sought to gain support for renegotiation from the U.S. export community. In an address to the National Foreign Trade Council, the Cuban ambassador offered every concession to U.S. capital if only the United States would not force autarky upon the island through an unfair treatment of Cuban sugar. "Our country is willing . . . to effect all transactions, to accept every possible arrangement, in a word, to reach most satisfactorily the desideratum of the commerce of the United States," he told his audience. Unless viable trade arrangements were possible, Cuba, he warned, might have "to shut herself up, within her frontiers, imitating the protectionist policy of other nations." Nevertheless, he had "hope that we may be spared from taking such drastic action."[74]

The response of the U.S. export community was sympathetic, but by late 1928 the attention of all groups interested in Cuban trade was caught up in the eventually losing struggle to prevent an increase in the sugar tariff. Ferrara made further requests for renegotiation in 1929 and 1930, but the State Department failed to take any action on the matter.[75]

The frustration of the pro-U.S. forces in Cuba seemed to be leading them toward a dead end where the ideas of the nationalist, autonomist, and anti-U.S. forces would undoubtedly have become dominant. Despite the impotence of the integrationists, however, much of their position was salvaged by the fact that the Cuban sugar depression came to be seen as an integral part of the growing worldwide industrial depression in the resolution of which all segments of the U.S. sugar and export industries had a stake.[76]

As the destabilizing effects of the sugar depression mounted in 1931 and 1932, the State Department began more serious consideration of proposals for altering the trade treaty. Moreover, the great decline in U.S. exports to Cuba became more apparent and spurred interest in solving Cuba's economic problems.[77]

Though dismayed by the strength of the opposition to Cuban sugar shown in the tariff battle of 1928–1930, the State Department slowly moved toward the position of accepting some sort of program to save the Cuban economy. In December 1931 Ferrara moved again for renegotiation, citing now the seriously declining figures of the U.S.-Cuban trade.[78] The Office of the Economic Advisor of the State Department in response even moved to consider the most far-reaching proposal of the Cuban integrationists—a customs union. The economic advisor, Herbert Feis, who generally opposed protectionism, thought that "a prosperous Cuba would buy from the United States more per capita than any other country of the world." Feis went so far as to suggest that the noncompetitive segment of the tariff-supported domestic beet sugar industry be allowed to fail, and that some form of North American customs union including Cuba and Canada might be established to protect the United States from the effect of the emerging trade blocs, especially that of the British Empire. Feis acknowledged to Assistant Secretary Francis White, however, that his thoughts represented "only a technical survey."[79]

The mainstream of the State Department's discussion avoided the question of a customs union and tried to find some solution that would grant a stability-producing advantage to Cuba while at the same time being acceptable to non-Cuban sugar interests. Proposals to grant a sliding-scale subsidy (in place of the tariff) on beet production or a gradual duty against Philippine sugar imports were discussed.[80] Nevertheless, it was not until larger interests began to be involved that serious new proposals arose.

In March 1932, in an interview with Secretary of State Henry Stimson, Samuel Bertron, a New York financier active in foreign trade matters, formulated a proposal which moved the question away from the politically vulnerable issue of tariffs. Bertron suggested the formation of a nonprofit stabilization corporation made up of U.S. sugar producers (as provided for in the Agricultural Marketing Act of 1929) whose purpose would be to purchase a set amount of sugar from each growing region which sold sugar on the U.S. market.[81] This approach broadened the question from one of aiding Cuba to the larger concern of secular overproduction in sugar and world economic depression. It thus became more likely that the beet bloc in Congress would consider it in their interest to cooperate. Indeed, even before his meeting with the secretary of state, Bertron had discussed his proposals with Senators Reed Smoot, Key Pittman, and Cordell Hull, and had obtained a memorandum from the prestigious law firm of Sullivan and Cromwell to show that the proposal did not violate the Sherman Antitrust Act. Bertron had also contacted the refining interests, who agreed to be silent partners if a one-half-cent differential between the duties on raw and refined sugar was included in the proposal. Because of their unpopularity with the Congress, the "sugar trust" and the Cuban producers were not to take an active part in the lobbying effort.[82]

By the time the U.S. sugar industry as a whole was beginning to think of large-scale control schemes, Franklin D. Roosevelt was on the way to being elected president of the United States. Roosevelt's campaign had made reference to a lowering of tariffs—the sugar tariff among them—and all interested parties eagerly awaited the inauguration of the new president to see how he would respond to the various proposals percolating through Cuba, the State Department, and the U.S. sugar industry.

By the early twenties the U.S. economic presence in Cuba held the central position within the Cuban economy. This presence determined the response to, and allocated the costs of, the post-1925 sugar depression. It is true that the major element of this presence—the U.S. sugar investment—was itself beset by forces in the Congress and the world sugar market which were beyond its control; it is also true that most of the big U.S. mills incurred heavy losses in this period. Still, within the context of the Cuban economy, their immense power enabled them to thrust a good part of the economic burden of the depression onto the native segment of that economy, and most of these firms were strong enough to survive even the social upheaval which that heavy burden helped to bring forth.

The U.S. banking houses in Cuba were even less shaken by events, and despite the vast diminution of the economic substance upon which their loans rested, they were able to extract significant amounts of capital from Cuba, even as the ship went down.

In times of material growth, the sign of economic dominance is the ability to aggregate the lion's share of capital surplus; in times of decline, dominance is characterized by the ability to pass on the lion's share of capital loss. The U.S. economic presence in Cuba was able to do both, and it came out of the long Cuban depression (1925–1941) as strong in relation to the island's economy as it had gone in.

CHAPTER FOUR

Hegemony and Nationalism, 1925–1932

Noninterference and the Early Machadato, 1925–1928

BY THE MID-1920s, the goals of U.S. Cuban policy—stability and economic accessibility—entered a period of redefinition that was completed by the end of the decade. Stability was redefined to mean not honesty and efficiency in Cuban government, but merely the absence of armed opposition to the incumbent regime. The meaning of economic access focused no longer on the treatment received by a particular U.S. investment, but on the health of the Cuban economy as a whole. Direct supervision of internal Cuban political and economic affairs, exemplified by the moralization program of General Enoch Crowder, was ended about 1923, and a general trend toward less direct interference began. From then on, threats of intervention were less common and the tutelary role of U.S. diplomatic representatives was carried out by means of informal advice.

The altered manner in which U.S. hegemony was to operate in the decade after 1923 was the result of several forces. The great diminution of European economic and political influence in Latin America (especially in the Caribbean area) occasioned by World War I allowed the United States to respond less nervously to purely New World threats to its hegemony. Latin American states were now less likely to be able to call in the Old World to redress the imbalance of the New. The wartime destruction of European economic competition gave U.S. businessmen a confidence which allowed them to show greater circumspection in the defense of their interests. Indeed, by 1925, a postwar cooperation between business and government in the United States had brought about U.S. domination of the key economic sectors of communications, subsoil deposits (especially oil), and banking throughout much of Latin America—and a virtual monopoly within the Caribbean area.[1]

While the unchallenged nature of the U.S. presence in the Caribbean made it unnecessary to intervene to forestall or eliminate European rivals, nevertheless, the rise of Latin American nationalism following the Mexican Revolution of 1910 now posed an *internal* threat to U.S. hegemony. The

49

initial U.S. response to events in Mexico had actually helped to forge the identity between nationalism and Yankeephobia. Opposition to radicalism by both Wilson and the Republican presidents who followed him caused them initially to intervene, both diplomatically and militarily, to protect U.S. presence and influence in Mexico and also in Nicaragua. By the late twenties these interventions were perceived in Washington as not having produced stability and as having increased hostility toward the United States. Thereafter, an accommodation with Latin American nationalism was initiated by means of a more selective and subtle application of U.S. power and the nurturing of native (even nationalist) allies.[2]

Within Cuba, both the cessation of external competition with the U.S. presence and the diminution of interference as the typical response to nationalism had already occurred by the middle of the decade. Noninterference had been easier to initiate in Cuba because 1924 saw the election of a strong, popular leader—Gerardo Machado—who campaigned as a nationalist yet was committed to the enhancement of U.S. interests. Machado represented the epitome of the businessman-president. Like many other prominent Cuban politicians, he had been brought into Cuban politics under the U.S. military occupation, being named mayor of Santa Clara in 1899. He had served as secretary of the interior (1909–1911), gaining a reputation as an enemy of organized labor and a friend of public utilities. Though he became a sugar mill owner during the Danza, his basic business interests were in the light and power industry. Political favors to utility interests had brought him the vice-presidency and a half-ownership in the Santa Clara Light Company. He wed these utility interests to the larger fortunes of the Cuban Electric Company—subsidiary of the Electric Bond and Share Company—when the latter began its monopolization of the Cuban electric industry in the early twenties. Machado became a close friend of Henry Catlin, the president of the Cuban Electric Company, who in turn helped finance his presidential campaign.[3]

Even before taking office, the president-elect traveled to the United States and attended a banquet given in his honor by the president of the National City Bank, Charles E. Mitchell. At the banquet Machado told his audience that "in my administration there will be absolute guarantees for all business, and there is no reason to fear the outbreak of disorders, because I have sufficient force to suppress them." Machado also met with President Calvin Coolidge, whom he praised highly, and with the State Department, where Assistant Secretary Francis White felt that he made a "favorable impression."[4]

Machado's election in 1924 represented the coming to power of the Liberal party, which he led, and its conversion to a centrist position. This party during the early republic was the institutional expression of what remained of the nationalist fervor exemplified by such fallen heroes of independence as José Martí and Antonio Maceo. Its role was that of a generally reformist opposition to the more conservative political parties, especially in its call (however muted) for the repeal of the Platt Amendment. Its rhetoric had been generally nationalist, and it was given to mass appeals, especially among blacks and the urban middle and lower classes. Though Liberals had no political philosophy as such, their nationalist and populist appeals made U.S. business interests suspicious. Under Machado, however, the Liberals worked out a relationship between Cuban nationalism and the U.S. economic presence that was surprisingly amicable—it became known as "business nationalism"—and which led to almost unanimous support for his administration by business interests. By ending the contradiction between the only nationalist political party and the U.S. economic presence, Machado set the stage for the rise of a more ideological nationalism based outside the electoral political arena and for the eventual identification of both the Liberal party and the U.S. presence as prime targets of the critique formulated by that new nationalism.[5]

The business press in the United States supported Machado strongly at this time, praising his businesslike attitude and his action against labor "agitators."[6] Machado felt that business was a "neutral element" of society which needed tranquility in which to operate. The Cuban president was proud of his support of business, declaring in 1928 that "during all my political existence I have heard the producing classes complain because their petitions were not heard; that cannot be said today, because at times I have but been their direct mandatory, fulfilling all that has been requested of me."[7]

In 1927, Machado made another trip to the United States and was again feted by U.S. business interests. As Robert Smith describes it:

> Luncheons were given in honor of the Cuban President by the Chase National Bank, the Importers and Exporters Association, the Electric Bond and Share Company, J. P. Morgan and Company, the New York Chamber of Commerce, Sosthenes Behn [president of ITT], the National City Bank, Mayor Jimmy Walker, and others. The speeches given at some of these gatherings reflected the bond between these groups and Machado. William H. Woodin—later to be the first New Deal Secretary of the Treasury—stressed the point that it was a fine thing for any country to have a businessman for president since such a situation "is greatly to our advantage." At one of the banker's luncheons Machado assured the group that American capital in Cuba would be protected "at all hazards." Thomas Lamont then rose and expressed the hope that the Cuban people would find some way to keep Machado in office "indefinitely."[8]

Machado himself was thinking along the same lines. By 1926, the Cuban president had moved to bring all Cuban political parties under his power. By the spring of 1928, Machado had almost total control over Congress, which dutifully passed resolutions extending the president's term of office. These resolutions were adopted as constitutional amendments by a Machado-controlled constitutional convention, which also called upon Machado to accept a new term of office. All of the political parties then endorsed Machado's candidacy, and he was elected to a new and extended (six-year) term to run until 1935.[9]

This pseudoconstitutional (his opponents called it illegal) act of *continuismo* was condoned by the State Department and president of the United States. This acceptance was facilitated not only by Machado's protection of U.S. interests, but by his domestic popularity and his relationship with Ambassador Crowder, who at that time considered him cooperative. Crowder told the U.S. secretary of state that the United States should give "informal assurance" that it was not opposed to Machado's continuation in office.[10] During his 1927 visit to the United States, Machado had met with Coolidge and had discussed the then pending constitutional amendments. Coolidge told Machado—in a clear example of the new policy of noninterference—that "the United States felt that this was a question for the Cuban people and their government to decide."[11]

By accepting the constitutional "reforms" of 1928, U.S. policy identified itself with Machado's de facto second presidential term. Business support for Machado likewise identified the U.S. economic presence with the Cuban president, more so than with any previous regime. As the sugar depression forced Machado to take sides on the question of allocating economic hardship, he came down on the side of the "producing classes" and turned to repressive measures to make his policies stick. Within just a few years he was to become the most hated man in Cuba and the only president in Cuban history until Fulgencio Batista to be overthrown by popular revolt. The U.S. policy and economic presence which supported him almost shared his fate.

The Machadato and Cuban Nationalism, 1928–1932

While dependence on the United States had brought well-being to those Cuban merchants, professionals, and politicians allied to the U.S. economic presence, it had created structural deformities in the Cuban economy, leaving large segments of the population without a sense of efficacy or a satisfactory standard of living.[12] Those groups harmed either economically or psychologically by this dependency were the proletariat, the students and intellectuals, and certain elements of the middle and even upper classes. When the sugar depression increased the burdens upon these groups and mocked the expectations of the upwardly mobile among them, they began to attack the symbols of dependency with the weapon of Cuban nationalism. Because of its position as the locus of foreign hegemony and domestic repression, the center of this attack was the regime of Gerardo Machado.

The Cuban Labor Movement in the Early Republic

The modern Cuban labor movement arose during the last decades of Spanish colonial rule, with the introduction of radical labor doctrines by Spanish immigrants. In this period, anarchism and anarchosyndicalism vied with doctrines of labor peace based upon cooperatives. The combination of Spanish resistance to all forms of labor organizing and the depressed economic conditions of the late nineteenth century led to the victory of the anarchosyndicalist position by the 1890s. The Cuban labor movement was to be dominated by this philosophy for some thirty-five years.[13]

Organized labor in Cuba supported the independence struggle but failed to extract a political price for its efforts. The 1901 constitution contained no reference to the rights of labor, and the harsh restrictive legislation of the Spanish penal code remained in force.[14] Despite such legislation, and despite, moreover, a division within labor between native and immigrant (Spanish) workers, the first decade of the republic saw several militant strikes, especially among port workers. In addition to recognition and wage issues, an early concern of the labor movement was to prevent the importation of low-wage field labor from Haiti and Jamaica by the large *centrales*. Labor also struggled against a high cost of living occasioned by the impact of U.S. capital and goods upon the Cuban economy.[15]

The Cuban export economy, with its high prices, recurring inflation, and sharp cycles due to changes in sugar income, created within labor a complex combination of job insecurity and organizational militancy that tended to drive unions in the direction either of bureaucratic collaboration with government or of violent syndicalist struggles increasingly political in character. By the second decade of the century, the liberal, reformist unions had in the main become collaborationist, and the central ideological struggle within the labor movement was between anarchosyndicalists and socialists. By the early twenties, the socialists, too, had made their peace with government—with the exception of a small group of socialist intellectuals and labor leaders who helped to found the Cuban Communist party in 1925.[16] The cutting edge of the labor movement thus came under the control of anarchosyndicalists and their militant strike tactics.

Those unions which cooperated with the state were rewarded with protective legislation, and by the 1920s Cuban labor codes were more progressive than those in most states in Latin America. Thus, by the time of the severe depression of the late twenties, one part of labor had gained some protective legislation that enabled it, in part, to shift the burden of economic decline away from itself, while remaining segments of labor had a militant ideology and practice on which to base the defense of their interests. This combination of factors was to give Cuban labor organizations a prominent position in the social upheaval of the early thirties.[17]

Under President Alfredo Zayas (1920–1924), there were violent strikes by port workers, railway workers, and, for the first time, sugar mill workers. Severe repression by Zayas, and later by Machado, was aimed mainly at the direct-action leadership of the anarchosyndicalist unions which dominated most of the strike efforts. Assassination and deportation weakened the syndicalists vis-à-vis the reformist and the state-supporting socialist unions. More important, governmental destruction of the anarchosyndicalist leadership created an opening in the left wing of the labor movement which the newly founded Cuban Communist party would fill after 1928.[18]

Despite ideological and national divisions, and despite severe governmental repression, labor organizing was achieved in the 1920s on regional and even national levels. The most powerful labor organization from 1925 to 1935 was the Confederación Nacional Obrera de Cuba (CNOC), founded and until 1928 dominated by anarchist leadership. By the end of the decade, however, CNOC had come under the leadership of the young Partido Comunista de Cuba (PCC). The rival union federation, the Unión Federativa Obrera Nacional (UFON) and its allied Cuban Federation of Labor had been adopted by Machado as the "legal" labor movement. The leaders of these federations—much of whose membership was on paper only—were staunch supporters of the Machado regime and even accepted its brutal treatment of labor. Machado came down heavily against the noncollaborating unions, raiding their offices and jailing, deporting, and even murdering their leaders. Even the conservative American Federation of Labor (AFL) felt constrained to declare its opposition to Machado's tactics, though it remained affiliated through the Pan American Federation of Labor (PAFL) with the unions which supported the Cuban government.[19]

During the depression the Cuban proletariat responded to the organizing drives of the militant unions. By the early thirties, all the major trades, except sugar workers, were highly organized, with by far the largest number of workers belonging to unions strongly opposed to the Machado government. These latter unions—all of which Machado called "communist" though most were not—reacted to Machado's repression with strikes that included both economic and political demands. When Machado declared the most radical of these unions illegal in 1930, they called a general strike. The shutdown was only partially successful, but it was followed almost continually by a long series of militant work stoppages by one union or another. By this time, the legal structure of labor-management relations had all but disappeared, and the police state that was soon to descend on other opposition political elements had already begun to function in regard to labor. From this point on, there was a gradual coalescence of labor movement aims (though there was neither tactical nor philosophical unity) with those of the middle-class political opposition in regard to the expanding Machado dictatorship.[20]

At this time also, communist labor leaders were beginning to succeed in organizing on a mass scale the largest proletarian group on the island—the sugar mill and cane field workers. Faced with almost feudal conditions, sugar workers struck during the 1931–1932 harvest, and in late 1932 the first national sugar workers union (Sindicato Nacional de Obreros de la Industria Azucarera) was formed. By 1933, Cuban labor was more highly organized and more radically led than almost any proletariat in Latin America.[21] This fact, coupled with a dictatorial and antilabor government and severe economic hardship, made for an explosive situation.

The relationship between Machado and "Yankee imperialism"—which radical labor leaders were propounding as the key to the situation—now began to command public attention. Fear and hatred of the United States, basic components of Cuban nationalism from the very first days of the republic, were now to become the cement binding the labor rebellion to those posing more immediate threats to Machado's power—the university students and intellectuals and the disaffected middle class.

The Student Movement and the Machadato

During the U.S. occupation (1899–1902), the secretary of public instruction, Enrique José Varona, carried out a reform of the University of Havana, the only institution of higher learning in Cuba. Despite a somewhat more technically oriented curriculum, however, most students continued to study in the faculties of law and medicine. The inability of a dependent Cuban economy to absorb all these aspiring professionals, the influx of radical ideas from the Mexican and Russian revolutions and the Córdoba reform movement, and the conservative attitudes of most of the faculty all combined to turn the student generation of the twenties toward questions of university reform and social change.[22] These concerns, arising within the context of a hemisphere-wide climate of anti-Yankeeism among intellectuals, eventually led the more radical students to attacks upon U.S. influence.

Although student activism had included a demonstration against the granting of an honorary degree to Enoch Crowder, early protests centered on academic reforms. In 1923, the Federación de Estudiantes de la Universidad de la Habana (FEU) was formed to press for university autonomy, the dismissal of incompetent faculty, and student representation in university governance. The secretary of the FEU, Julio Antonio Mella, more radical than his fellow students, also raised the question of governmental corruption by President Zayas, thereby tending to enlarge the impact of student demands. Nevertheless, the mainstream of student protests remained focused on intramural matters. Sporadic student strikes achieved the removal of some professors and the occasional appointment of progressive rectors and deans. While President Zayas resisted the central demand for university autonomy, he nevertheless made enough concessions to weather the storm.[23]

By the time of the inauguration of Machado, the activist minority of the FEU led by Mella had come under the influence of Aprista or Marxist philosophy and were directing their energies away from the university, which had been generally quieted by the partial reforms gained under Zayas. Machado thus inherited an isolated radical fringe of students and a calm campus, one that even accepted the expulsion of Mella and the reinstatement of many professors removed by the progressive reforms of a few years before. Though Mella, who was now in jail and soon to be exiled, called Machado a "tropical Mussolini," the president did not run into trouble with the majority of student opinion until 1927–1928, when he engineered the irregular extension of his mandate. In response to this political maneuver, which even the Cuban Supreme Court found of doubtful legality, students carried out a series of anti-Machado demonstrations, to which the president responded (unlike Zayas) by dissolving the FEU, abolishing the reform commission to which Zayas had acceded, and even temporarily closing the university.[24]

Militants among the student body at the university created a new student organization, the Directorio Estudiantil Universitario (DEU), which issued a manifesto attacking the regime. The group was later expelled from the university, but it continued to meet nonetheless and to maintain contacts within the student body. In 1929, Mella was assassinated in Mexico City, where he was in exile. The students held Machado responsible, and support for the militant student position increased. In 1930 the Directorio was reestablished with a larger following, and it carried out a massive anti-Machado demonstration that ended in a confrontation with the police and the death of one of the student leaders. Machado, by now besieged on other fronts as well, suspended constitutional guarantees, declared the university a seat of communism, and closed the entire institution. Student opposition had by now spread beyond the university, and Machado was forced to close most of the high schools as well.[25]

The situation by this time had acquired a momentum of its own. Support for the students arose among the middle-class opponents of the regime, and the newly published program of the Directorio became a focal expression of militant anti-Machado Cuban nationalism. This program called for political change as a precondition to university reform and pledged the signatories to fight for "deep social transformation." Students now joined with middle-class professionals to carry out urban guerrilla warfare against the police apparatus of the regime, and murders and bombings by both sides became commonplace. In January 1931, most of the leaders of the Directorio were arrested, and indictments for conspiracy were issued against almost the entire university faculty because they had openly supported the Directorio program.[26]

An ideological split developed among the Directorio leaders while they were in prison in 1931, and a group of them with Marxist tendencies founded the Ala Izquierda Estudiantil. This group focused its attack, not on the Machado dictatorship, but on Yankee imperialism, and moved toward the position of the Cuban Communist party. The Ala Izquierda looked to the peasantry and proletariat rather than the university community and middle class as the force for overthrowing Machado. The majority of the Directorio, on the other hand, thought in terms of a multiclass uprising, similar to that of the struggle against the Spanish, and saw the symbol of imperialism less as Wall Street than as the Platt Amendment. Throughout 1931 and 1932 these moderate students joined forces with the middle- and upper-class nationalist movements, which were the main focus of the struggle against the Machadato.[27]

Middle- and Upper-Class Reform Movements and the Machadato

The abnormal development of the Cuban bourgeoisie due to U.S. economic predominance in the island placed this class in a difficult position when depression and dictatorship coincided to set the mainstream of Cuban nationalism against both the incumbent regime and U.S. hegemony. In the twenties, this class was still absorbing the effects on its life-style brought about by the immense onrush of investments in Cuba by oligopolized industries in the United States during the previous decade. Though most of the members of the Cuban bourgeoisie benefited enormously from the increasing U.S. presence, they were uneasy about their growing dependence and about the cultural shocks administered to Cuban society by the intensity and all-pervasiveness of the flow of foreign capital, goods, and ideas. When the sugar boom ended in the bank crash of 1921, the small but growing entrepreneurial segment of this class was decimated, and its remaining professional and commercial elements then stood out, more clearly than before, as mere adjuncts of U.S. dominance.

Cuban nationalism and the myths surrounding Cuba's long struggle for independence made it politically unwise, if not psychologically impossible, for even these beneficiaries of U.S. capital to accept the annexationist implications of such a situation. They attempted, through a moderate economic nationalism (which Machado in his first term tried vainly to reflect), to gain some control over the pace and direction of U.S. investment, though this did not imply or include opposition to U.S. capital.[28]

When Machado proved unable to use state intervention to stabilize the effects of U.S. economic penetration, and when economic depression forced him to accept the priority of protecting that penetration—in short, when moderate economic nationalism failed—the Cuban bourgeoisie was deprived of its major ideological weapon in the struggle against a rising anti-Yankee nationalism. Furthermore, when Machado responded to the social and economic tensions of depression by imposing constraints upon the political arena (party-government amalgamation, *continuismo,* suspension of constitutional guarantees, censorship, and so on), large numbers of the middle and even upper classes began to identify him as the prime cause of these tensions, and—without adopting the radical nationalism of the other opposition elements—joined the movement against the Machadato. This failure of the "business nationalism" of the twenties would cause the destruction of the regime which espoused it, and lead to a period of radical nationalism which broke with liberal economic theory and experimented with corporate and socialist alternatives. [29]

Artists and Intellectuals

Cuban intellectuals shared in the themes of Latinism, Indianism, and anti-Yankee nationalism that were attracting widening support in Latin America during the period surrounding the First World War. In addition, these intellectuals were still possessed by the idealism of the very recent independence period and were sensitive to the failure of the hopes (both economic and cultural) engendered during that struggle. [30]

The first significant action taken by intellectuals was their response to the corruption of Cuban life exemplified by the actions of the Zayas administration. Growing out of a group of young revisionist writers and poets, and coinciding with the early protests by the university students, this action was known as the *protesta de los trece.* It was triggered by the presence of Zayas' minister of justice at a meeting of the Academy of Science on March 18, 1923. To protest governmental corruption, thirteen of these writers, led by the poet Rubén Martínez Villena, walked out of the academy and the next day published their *protesta*, in which they promised to carry out similar acts whenever "unpatriotic" politicians appeared in public. [31]

Developing out of the *protesta* was the Grupo Minorista, a vanguardist literary movement with political implications in that its members criticized the apolitical escapism of the arts. The works of this group came to reflect social and political themes within Cuba as well as hemisphere-wide racial and cultural motifs. In a 1927 statement the group referred to its task of "ideological renovation," reiterated its stand against U.S. policy in Mexico and Nicaragua, and renewed its support of Cuban student protests. [32]

The populism and nationalism embraced by the early Machadato (1925–1928), and its lack of corruption compared to the Zayas years, temporarily deflected the rising political concerns of Cuban intellectuals away from their own government. But the growing political repression and economic depression after 1928 brought most of the Minorista intellectuals into the forefront of the struggle against the later Machadato (1929–1933). The struggle sent this generation of young Cuban intellectuals in many ideological directions. A few were attracted to fascism, some to Aprismo, and a few actually chose to stay on as advisors to Machado even after the extension of his mandate and the eclipse of his nationalist image. The majority, however, became supporters of either the moderate political opposition or one of the Marxist organizations, especially the Partido Communista de Cuba.[33]

The Moderate Political Opposition

Political reform movements had also arisen early in the twenties. Fernando Ortiz, the well-known Cuban anthropologist, formed the National and Civic Renovation Committee in 1923. Its manifesto reflected *decadencia* doctrine, which attributed the weaknesses in Cuban government to a lack of honesty, morality, and efficiency. These weaknesses, as noted previously, were seen as the result of four hundred years of Spanish colonial rule. In August of the same year the Veterans and Patriots Association (the organization of the veterans of the Independence War) began a campaign for governmental reforms, some of them similar to those of the defunct Crowder moralization plan. In April 1924, this organization actually fomented an armed uprising against Zayas. After its pleas for intervention against Zayas were ignored by the United States, the movement was easily suppressed by the government.[34]

Despite the veterans' movement, political reform up to this point was generally contained within the established political parties and dealt with in the electoral realm. However, in 1925, when Machado's pliant Congress prohibited the creation of new parties and fixed party control in members of Congress, reform politicians were frozen out of the legitimate political process. All of the official parties supported Machado's pseudo-legal act of *continuismo* in 1927, thus forcing anti-Machado elements to break with their parties and to form groupings outside the traditional party structure. This closing of the political arena rendered even moderate antigovernment organizations all but illegal and tended to blur the distinction between them and the radical and revolutionary groups that were gathering strength during this same period. This led in time to intermittent alliances between elements of the radical and moderate opposition, and for a time it fostered the impression of a unified movement against the dictator.[35]

Segments of the old parties led by Mario G. Menocal (insurgent Conservatives), and by Miguel Mariano Gómez and Carlos Mendieta (dissident Liberals), moved into formal opposition after 1928. These men were not really reformers as much as political rivals of Machado who refused to join his all-party coalition. (Only one of the groups created by these men—the Unión Nacionalista of Mendieta—had something of a moderate reformist base.) The efforts of these groups from 1928 to 1931 were directed toward convincing the United States to intervene against Machado and, failing that, toward directing enough U.S. pressure on Machado to force him to open up the legal political arena once again. These groups periodically undertook negotiations with the Cuban president to determine the conditions for their reentry into the political arena while also raising legal challenges to the regime before the Supreme Court. Despite minor concessions by Machado, the negotiations and the legal challenges failed. [36]

Machado, for his part, tried to frighten the moderate opposition away from alliance with radicals by references to the possibility of communist revolution should he be overthrown. He denied that he was a dictator and stated that restrictive laws were necessary to thwart the aims of "an implacable communist aggression directed by powerful, hidden, foreign powers." Economic depression was not, in Machado's opinion, the cause of the unrest, but merely a pretext utilized by subversive forces. [37]

By 1931, the Unión Nacionalista, the largest of the groups of the moderate political opposition, had become convinced that the U.S. policy of passive support for Machado would not be altered unless a serious internal challenge to the dictator arose. The more radical student and middle-class opposition did not favor a traditional armed uprising in the interior, especially at this time, for fear that it would provoke U.S. military intervention. Nevertheless, the Unión Nacionalista was able to arouse sufficient support to organize a guerrilla uprising, including a filibustering expedition from the United States. The revolt, which took place in August 1931, was an uncoordinated affair, and when an expected army uprising did not materialize, it was quickly overcome by Machado's forces.

With the failure of the revolt, Machado became more confident of his strength, while the moderate political opposition, despairing of a change in U.S. policy toward the dictator, resolved to win whatever protection they could through a new round of negotiations with him. Their removal from active opposition—and the discrediting of their tactics—brought more radical groups to the center of the struggle against the Machadato. [38]

The most intransigent and perhaps the only truly class-conscious middle-class opposition came from the secret terrorist organization known as the ABC. Its members were a mixture of the petty bourgeoisie, professionals, and students, and its pronouncements were couched in a broad range of classless nationalist and populist appeals. The original ABC ideology was generational, elitist, developmental, reformist, and corporatist. Some of its early statements also stressed anti-imperialism and Cubanization of the island's economy. Its program manifesto, issued in 1932, marked the end of middle-class acceptance of political and economic liberalism. The document, holding that Cuba's trouble derived from its dependent economic status, called for state intervention to control the latifundium, protect the native farming class, aid cooperatives, regulate major corporations, nationalize public services, establish a native banking system and progressive taxation, protect the small merchant and industrialist, and inaugurate protective labor legislation. Its political program called for a corporately based upper house and a narrowing of the franchise to literates, but it also included programs of civil liberties and demilitarization. The manifesto attempted to supplant liberalism and solve the problem of dependency without accepting the mass or class doctrines usually considered the only nonreactionary alternatives.[39]

The ABC was known not so much for its ideology, however, as for its tactics—urban terrorism. Its bomb attacks against well-known figures of the regime and its police apparatus (mainly carried out by student members) made ABC a popular symbol of the revolt against Machado. Moreover, the retributive torture and assassination against these sons and daughters of the Cuban middle class by the agents of the Machadato destroyed the cohesion of the bourgeoisie, splitting the portion of it desiring the overthrow of the regime from that which—for fear of the consequences—still supported the president. By the end of 1932, as both economic and political tensions approached crisis proportions, the ABC began to show signs of concern over its lack of a mass base and the possibility of radical revolution. Like so many in the reformist opposition before them, they began an effort to convince the United States (which alone had the power both to remove Machado and to suppress radical revolution) that theirs was a "realistic" nationalism which did not threaten the U.S. economic presence.[40]

The exile organizations were a final segment of moderate political opposition. Between the expulsion of the communist Julio Antonio Mella in 1926 and the emigration of much of the moderate political opposition early in 1933, many hundreds of anti-Machado Cubans left the island for Mexico City, Madrid, Paris, Miami, Washington, D.C., or New York City. Exile organizations were established in all these cities, with the largest and most influential—known as the New York Junta—based in New York City. The junta disseminated anti-Machado propaganda, raised money to support clandestine activities, debated internal political differences, and most important of all worked to obtain support for its cause from the U.S. government.[41]

Due to their strategic location, the U.S.-based exile organizations were able to keep the image of a bloody dictatorship before the Congress and the reform organizations of the United States. Their propaganda, combined with increasing repression within the island, slowly dissolved the existing general support for Machado, especially in business and government circles. Eventually, moreover, they were able to make contact with advisors to the newly elected Franklin D. Roosevelt.[42]

The Cuban Communist Party

The Cuban Communist party sprang from many sources: the Bolshevik Revolution and its attempt to create an international movement of communist parties under its direction, the Cuban student reform movement of the early twenties, the development of Cuban socialism and anarchosyndicalism, and the effects of U.S. hegemony on Cuban society. In an immediate sense, however, the party's founding was the work of a small number of Cuban intellectuals and an agent of the Comintern.

Prior to World War I, several abortive socialist parties had been established, most notably as a result of the efforts of Carlos Baliño (a founder of the Partido Revolucionario Cubano, which initiated the final anticolonial struggle against Spain), who had become a socialist around the time of independence. By the early twenties, when socialist and anarchist movements in Europe and the Western Hemisphere began to divide along Bolshevik and anti-Bolshevik lines, Baliño led a small group out of the Agrupación Socialista de Habana to found the Agrupación Comunista. Between 1923 and 1925 other communist *agrupaciones* sprang up, including one among Jewish immigrants from Poland.[43]

The student movement against the corruption of the Zayas regime brought the first new recruits to these *agrupaciones*. One of the leaders of the FEU, Julio Antonio Mella, was among the first of this generation of students to raise the question of class struggle within the university. When Mella met Baliño in 1923, he had already come under the influence of the Mexican Revolution and the thought of Víctor Raúl Haya de la Torre. The following year Mella and several fellow students joined Baliño's Agrupación Comunista. Mella had a very forceful personality and was the best known of the student leaders. He was a tireless worker and vibrant orator, and his conversion to socialism brought a prestige to left-nationalist sentiments that far outstripped their previous influence in Cuba even among intellectuals.[44]

In 1925 the Comintern took an interest in the Cuban situation and sent Enrique Flores Magón, then a member of the Mexican Communist party, to Havana to help form a Cuban Communist party. In August of that year, at a series of meetings in Havana, six of the *agrupaciones*, under the urging of Flores Magón, formed the Partido Comunista de Cuba. The party established a journal, formed a youth group, and applied for membership in the Comintern.[45]

The young Communist party attracted a small group of intellectuals, professionals, students, and workers. Almost immediately Machado's police moved against them, and the party itself was declared illegal in 1927. Under the unofficial leadership of the poet Rubén Martínez Villena, the party slowly rebuilt in 1928 and 1929. Its major success during this period came in the struggle against the anarchosyndicalist leadership of the Confederación Nacional Obrero de Cuba (CNOC). While the party's ideas and supporters gained influence in that labor federation's hierarchy, its membership worked to create "revolutionary fractions" within the railway and tobacco workers' organizations—the areas of strongest union activity up to that time. They also began the first tentative efforts at organizing the agricultural proletariat. By 1929, however, the party still had only a few hundred members, and its organ, the underground *El Comunista*, had a circulation of less than one thousand. The majority of its members were in Havana, and most of its working-class adherents were in light rather than basic industry.[46]

By 1930, though strained by policy disputes within the leadership,[47] the party had reorganized the CNOC under its control and had won leadership positions in most of its constituent unions. The CNOC was by then the largest union federation and had some sixteen thousand members. Party propaganda during this period was both anti-Machado and anti-imperialist. In addition, party spokesmen attacked the moderate opposition, especially the Unión Nacionalista, accusing it (correctly) of desiring U.S. intervention. While thus attempting to discredit the bourgeois political opposition, the party nevertheless took cognizance of the fact that the depression was impoverishing the petty bourgeoisie. Accordingly, it supported the petty-bourgeois boycotts then taking place to protest the high rates charged by the "imperialist" telephone and electric companies.[48]

A major test of the strength of the movement occurred in March 1930, when Machado suspended the legal rights of certain of the communist-led unions. The CNOC call for a general strike to demand their reinstatement resulted, for the first time, in a tie-up of the transportation network and many services in Havana. The general strike, however, failed to gain the support of the more moderate unions and did not bring about the withdrawal of sanctions. Indeed, as a result of the strike, Machado arrested the CNOC leaders and suspended the labor federation.

The more moderate unions, most of which were by now engaged in vigorous strike activities of their own, also suffered suspension or police harassment during this period. Machado's public position was that all unions, with the exception of the few which actually supported his regime, were "communist."

Despite its illegal status, the CNOC led a series of strikes in 1931 and 1932. Many of the moderate unions struck as well, occasionally in support of efforts by CNOC unions. By the end of 1932, the militant response of the Cuban proletariat to the depression and the dictatorship had become one of the major threats to the regime. Moreover, the CNOC, for the first time in Cuban history, had organized a large union of sugar workers. Given the central position of the sugar industry in the entire economy, an effective and communist-led harvest strike by large numbers of these workers had the potential of bringing down the government and possibly creating a revolutionary situation.[49]

Machado took this threat seriously and furnished the U.S. embassy with the files of his secret police to convince the State Department that his regime was under attack by a revolutionary labor movement that was directly tied to the Communist International. However, by the time it became apparent that the Red scare which Machado had falsely used to divide his opponents for the last five years was finally coming to have some substance, the threat to his regime from other opponents (students, noncommunist labor, middle-class opposition) was even more immediate. While the State Department took seriously the threat of communism in Cuba, it was forced to focus its attention on the more immediate possibility of middle-class revolt.[50]

The ideology of the Partido Comunista de Cuba (PCC) during this period generally conformed to the aggressive posture taken toward both the bourgeoisie and reformist movements within the "Third Period" of the Communist International. The party attacked the moderate nationalist opposition to Machado, although seeking to organize among the petty-bourgeois followers of these groups. Because the party was the strongest force among significant segments of organized labor, its unwillingness to join with the middle-class opposition meant that these two broad streams of protest would remain generally unsupportive of one another in the struggle prior to the overthrow of Machado. Indeed, they came into opposition in the attempt to construct a successor regime.[51]

Despite schisms, by late 1932 the party leadership had coalesced around a mass revolutionary line based on the proletariat. It analyzed the situation in Cuba as follows:

> The Cuban revolution is in its initial bourgeois-democratic stage and therefore takes the form of anti-feudalism and anti-imperialism. The victory of the [subsequent] agrarian and anti-imperialist revolution will be achieved by means of an alliance of the working class and the peasantry, carrying along with it the poorer stratum of the urban petit bourgeoisie, under the hegemony of the proletariat and the direction of the Communist Party, [and will] overthrow the power of imperialism, and the feudal (latifundist) elements and the native bourgeoisie tied to them, and [will] establish the revolutionary democratic dictatorship of the workers and peasants based upon soviets.[52]

By the beginning of 1933, although the "revolutionary proletarian" line of the central committee of the party was not yet fully effective in terms of party discipline, the mass line had established a powerful base for the party among labor, especially workers in sugar, urban transport, and tobacco. The party could claim membership of three thousand and organizations in all the major towns. It had a cell structure in many factories and plantations and a youth league of several thousand. In addition it had established Cuban branches of the Anti-Imperialist League and International Labor Defense. Among students, the Ala Izquierda Estudiantil represented Marxist ideology and boasted a university membership of some three hundred. The central committee of the Ala Izquierda, however, was not wholly Marxist, and among those who were, many rejected the "revolutionary proletarian" line.[53]

Thus the party, while isolated from the nationalist spearhead of the revolt against Machado, had a firm base among the proletariat. Its goal was to use this base (with timely additions from the peasantry, students, poor petty bourgeoisie, army ranks, and blacks) to expedite the overthrow of Machado and then to build upon that success to heighten the contradictions of the subsequent bourgeois nationalist regime and force the "growing over" of the bourgeois revolution into a socialist revolution.

The Cuban Army Under the Machadato

By the late 1920s, the Cuban Army played two important roles in Cuban society. The first was assigned to the military at the time of its organization by U.S. occupation authorities—as underwriters of a political and economic order compatible with U.S. interests. The second, which grew out of the extralegal character of domestic politics, was that of the armed expression of the political power of the incumbent president.

Machado perfected the latter role of the Cuban armed forces and wielded them against those groups protesting the closing of the political and economic order. Indeed, as the civil political situation deteriorated after 1928, the military began to function as the direct representative of the Machadato, taking over many of the executive and judicial functions of constituted authority on the provincial and local levels. In this way, the mercenary character of the Cuban army—a function of their role as defenders of the foreign economic presence—was duplicated on the domestic scene.

The rising nationalist opposition began to direct its attack against the military as the direct agent of its oppression. In the course of their war with the Cuban Army, nationalist reformers came to equate political and military dictatorship and adopted a strong antimilitarism as part of their program. As the military became more closely identified with Machado, it became clear to them that, barring some dramatic break with the dictator, they must share his fate. This set the scene for nationalist forces to attempt to pry loose from Machado not only sections of the officer corps who opposed the dictatorship, but also those who had come to conclude that such action had become the better part of valor. Thus, military conspiracies against the president were a concomitant of the nationalist movement beginning in the early 1930s. [54]

U.S. Policy and the Late Machadato, 1928–1932

The impact of U.S. intervention in Cuban affairs was so firmly established between 1898 and 1925 that the relative noninterference of 1925–1933 was itself a disturbing experience which Cuban politicians began to understand only as the policy was about to end. In the late twenties and early thirties, both Machado and his burgeoning opposition attempted to elicit the decisive support of the United States. Many in the U.S. State Department, however, were attempting to reduce U.S. responsibility for the outcome of events in Cuba. They feared that U.S. involvement with the rising Latin American nationalism of the period would only increase the likelihood of intervention and would heighten anti-Yankee feeling. The State Department thus attempted, especially after 1929, to avoid taking a strong public position regarding the growing crisis in Cuba, though its continuation of recognition and normal relations with Machado implied a tacit acceptance of the status quo.

The U.S. business community, for its part, was loud in its praise of Machado, almost to the very end. Articles in *American Industries* (the journal of the National Association of Manufacturers) and *Commerce and Finance* lauded economic conditions under the early Machadato. Business was also generally favorable to the 1928 extension of Machado's term of office. Even the prestigious *American Bar Association Journal* carried an article which cited the constitutional "amendments" as a stabilizing element. By 1930, however, economic and political conditions had badly deteriorated. An article in *Barron's* concluded that whatever hopeful economic signs existed were due to Machado's policies. Business periodicals at this time generally avoided commentary on Machado's dictatorial methods, while another *Barron's* article praised Machado as the Caribbean Mussolini. By late 1931, pieces in *Barron's* and *Commerce and Finance* began to reflect upon the possibility that the Machadato was partly responsible for the social unrest which was exacerbating already depressed economic conditions. These articles, however, still reflected a preference for Machado and a hope that he would weather the political storm. As late as December 1932, a *Barron's* article praised Machado for his "punctual fulfillment of debt obligations."[55]

The problems of the late Machadato were only a small part of the foreign policy problems of the State Department. For President Hoover and Secretary of State Stimson, the major concerns during this period were the growing threats to the international economic and political arrangements established in the decade after World War I, arrangements generally favorable to the United States. Armaments races in Europe and Japanese expansion in Asia in particular took up the greatest amount of time and led to extensive U.S. proposals on disarmament and peace-keeping, and to statements of opposition to military aggression. These initiatives were limited in some instances because public and congressional unconcern with balance-of-power politics inhibited any more forceful statements by the government and all but precluded a major commitment of U.S. power to achieve these ends.

Latin American policy under Hoover and Stimson was characterized by a more laissez-faire attitude which was reflected in the return to a de facto recognition policy, the publication of the Clark memorandum (narrowing the legitimation of U.S. intervention in Latin America), and the termination of the military interventions previously carried out in the circum-Caribbean area. The major problems facing the United States at the time were the mounting social tensions in Latin American societies due in part to the massive U.S. loans and investments of the twenties, the political instability caused by the economic hardship of the Great Depression, rising anti-Yankee nationalism, and the entry of the developing proletariat and middle class into the balance of power of Latin American societies. These tensions were arising just when many in the State Department were concluding that overt intervention in Latin America in favor of U.S. investors or against uncooperative governments would only make matters worse.[56]

Secretary of State Stimson felt that the forms of government favored by U.S. foreign policy circles could not be imposed upon Latin societies and that the effort to do so would only increase resentment in Latin America and provide a justification for the actions of non-American states (especially Japan) which were attempting to build their own spheres of influence. The secretary concluded that previous U.S. interventions in Latin America had "been used by the enemies and critics of the United States as proof positive that we are an imperialistic people.... And these accusations, however unjustifiable, have damaged our good name, our credit and our trade far beyond the apprehension of our own people."[57]

The injunction against military or aggressive political intervention did not imply opposition to support for an increased U.S. economic presence in Latin America. Herbert Hoover, as secretary of commerce, had been very much interested in expanding U.S. trade and investments in Latin America, and Stimson during his stewardship of the Nicaraguan intervention had concluded that capital imports were the only means by which that nation could solve its problems:

> The intelligent leaders in Nicaragua . . . realize that Nicaragua today lacks one of the principal foundations for a democratic government in that she has no well-developed middle class: . . . Such a middle class cannot come into existence until the industries of the country are developed. These industries cannot be developed without capital, and capital can be obtained only by foreign loans.[58]

The desire for a retreat from overt forms of intervention in Latin America expressed itself in terms of Cuban policy by a return to the Root interpretation of the Platt Amendment. Under this interpretation, U.S. intervention was to be a last resort to head off anarchy and not a way of assuring "good government" in Cuba. At first, this narrow interpretation was used to assure Cuban nationalists that the Platt Amendment was not an enemy of Cuban independence. Its later importance, however, was in parrying demands from the Cuban opposition and U.S. reform forces that the United States live up to its legal responsibilities and take action against the Machado dictatorship.[59]

Absolute noninterference was of course next to impossible for a nation so deeply imbedded in the affairs of another as was the United States with Cuba. The focal point of most of the inevitable pressures and temptations for intervention was the U.S. ambassador to Cuba. Though the Havana embassy had reported the opposition to Machado as early as 1928, Ambassador Noble B. Judah, who headed the embassy from November 1927 to October 1929, reported that Machado was in control. As tensions in Cuba increased, however, the new ambassador, Harry F. Guggenheim, found he could not ignore the pivotal role of the U.S. embassy, nor did he wish to do so.[60]

Ambassador Guggenheim, as the scion of an immensely wealthy family, was able to bring with him to Cuba a personal staff which included, in addition to existing embassy personnel, a personal legal advisor (Phillip Jessup), an economic advisor (Grosvenor Jones), and a private secretary (Burnham Carter). This personal staff carried out important studies of the Cuban debt structure and the effects of prior applications of the Platt Amendment. The ambassador also arranged for an extensive study of the Cuban system of taxation, and was often able to gain access to Cuban archives for U.S. researchers. Guggenheim felt that "a continuous and thorough study of Cuban economic and political conditions should be made, so that the mission could be in a position at all times to give, when desired and without obligation, unofficial advice and assistance to the Cuban government, in order to help Cuba's progress." In this way, a nonobjectionable form of interference—"unofficial advice"—would replace public moralization programs as the central vehicle for conveying U.S. influence.[61]

Guggenheim used his knowledge of the Cuban economy to attempt to find a way out of the economic impasse which was causing social unrest in the island. He also sought to conciliate the growing political rift between the Cuban president and the moderate political opposition. In 1930, Guggenheim began a series of discussions with the leaders of the Unión Nacionalista and other members of the moderate opposition. His aim was to persuade them to withdraw their demand that Machado resign and to accept a series of guarantees from the Cuban president that the laws barring them from future electoral contests would be removed. The ambassador also held talks with Machado in order to convince him to give such guarantees. However, as long as the United States continued (at least tacitly) to support his regime, and as long as his army remained loyal, Machado saw no need to conciliate the opposition. The opposition understood this and used their meetings with Guggenheim to press for U.S. intervention to remove the dictator or for at least the withdrawal of recognition of his regime. This latter position was the more public one in that the militant nationalism of the other elements of the opposition forced the moderate political opposition to deny their desire to have the United States invoke the hated Platt Amendment.[62]

Ambassador Guggenheim tried to convince the moderate opposition that the United States would not intervene in Cuba even to the extent of withdrawing recognition and that their only recourse was to bargain with Machado for political reforms. At the same time, recognizing his inability to force Machado to agree to such reforms as long as U.S. support for his regime was certain, Guggenheim attempted to obtain permission from Secretary of State Stimson to threaten Machado, at least indirectly, with the removal of such support. However, Stimson's strict adherence to the nonintervention policy, which in effect sustained Machado, left the U.S. ambassador with less leverage than the holder of that office normally possessed in shaping internal Cuban affairs. While Guggenheim accepted noninterference (and indeed was one of a growing group of State Department people who felt that the Platt Amendment made Cuban affairs less tractable by directing the appeals of Cuban political contestants toward Washington), he chafed under the pressure placed upon him by virtue of being the representative of a government which had the power and the treaty right to influence the outcome of Cuban political disputes, but which refused either to exercise that right or formally to revoke it.[63]

Nevertheless, as opposition grew during 1931, Machado agreed to discuss a compromise solution with moderate opposition leaders such as Mario Menocal and Carlos Mendieta. The negotiations, supported by Guggenheim, dealt with the possibilities of shortening Machado's term, guarantees of honesty for the November 1932 elections, and a coalition cabinet.[64]

While these negotiations were in progress, Guggenheim returned to Washington for conferences with Stimson and Assistant Secretary Francis White. Guggenheim explained the growing opposition to Machado, but generally misinterpreted it by discounting student and labor unrest. The ambassador concluded that economic stability and a willingness to compromise on Machado's part were essential elements of a solution, but that the president's resignation (which was the central demand of the opposition) would only lead to a breakdown of all order. Stimson, who hoped to avoid both intervention and revolution, sympathized with Guggenheim's desire to pressure Machado to make the compromises necessary to reenlist the support of the moderates. He therefore relented somewhat and allowed Guggenheim to express to Machado the desire of the U.S. government for certain constitutional reforms in Cuba, with the understanding that no overt interference was to be allowed.[65]

By August 1931, however, Machado's negotiations with the moderate opposition had broken down, and the latter launched an armed revolt. Faulty planning combined with U.S. neutrality (which meant the United States prohibited arms shipments for the rebels) doomed the uprising. The defeat of the moderates removed them (and the generation and political philosophy they represented) from the front ranks of the opposition and enabled Machado to claim that the only alternative to his regime was radical nationalism or even social revolution. Guggenheim had opposed the revolt and was now thoroughly disenchanted with the moderates, whom he characterized as political opportunists. Nevertheless, the worsening economic situation caused him to urge that Machado regain public support for established political processes by a guarantee of honest congressional elections in 1932. He further urged Machado to agree to step down in advance of the elections to prove his impartiality. (The incumbent invariably controlled the electoral machinery.) The U.S. ambassador even went so far as to draft a speech for the Cuban president which would announce these moves. Machado responded that he would be willing to step down, but that if he announced it in advance, his control over Congress and the army would disappear. [66]

By the beginning of 1932 Machado had concluded that the United States would not force him to step down and, while releasing the members of the moderate political opposition captured in the August 1931 revolt, he publicly stated his intention to serve until the end of his term in 1935. Guggenheim felt that economic programs necessary to the restoration of "moral peace" in Cuba were now imperative and that some conciliation of the middle and upper classes by the president was vital. Once again the ambassador sought some statement from the secretary of state that might indicate enough disapproval of Machado's policies to force him to change them lest he lose U.S. support. Once again, however, Stimson refused to intervene. [67]

As the year wore on, economic decline accelerated and the struggle between Machado and the militant student and labor organizations began to approach the level of civil war. Resolutions were introduced in the U.S. Congress asking for removal of support from Machado, and certain intellectuals and liberal organizations pressed petitions upon the State Department, as did the Cuban exile groups in the United States. The *Nation* and the *New Republic*, which had for over a year been calling for U.S. action against Machado, were now joined by the *Christian Century* and *World Tomorrow*. Even prestigious journals such as *Foreign Affairs*, *Current History*, and *Foreign Policy Reports* (an organ of the Foreign Policy Association) carried articles critical of the Machadato. [68]

As 1932 came to an end, there seemed no way out of the deepening social and economic crisis in Cuba. Sugar prices continued to fall, draining the life-blood of the Cuban economy. Economic hardship had propelled the proletariat into labor agitation which, infused with syndicalist and communist doctrine, bordered on civil conflict. Status deprivation and romantic libertarianism and egalitarianism were inflaming the entire postindependence generation of Cuban students. The middle and upper classes were in revolt against a regime that, partly owing to forces beyond its control, had frozen them out of the political and civic dialogue in which they had always been accustomed to participate. Forming the backdrop to this entire scene was the specter of Yankee hegemony, a force which now made even its beneficiaries uncomfortable and whose mixed blessings were turning to unmitigated burdens as the economic depression deepened.

In this context, the unwillingness of the United States to remove any of the essential U.S. buttresses of Machado's power intensified the anti-Plattist basis of Cuban nationalism in such a way as to threaten the structure of U.S. domination. To maintain its position, the United States would somehow have to disengage itself from the very office to which it had assigned the role of protector and stabilizer. More fundamentally, it would have to create a new foundation for its dominance, one that rested upon newly emerging forces in the island. The State Department under Stimson, with its sense that intervention would only worsen matters and that the storm could be ridden out, was not intellectually prepared for such a change. It remained to be seen whether his Democratic successors would measure up to the task.

CHAPTER FIVE

The New Deal Prepares for Power

The Latin American Policy Debate of the 1920s

TWO TRADITIONS of Democratic party policy in the 1920s seemed to equip the Democrats better than the Republicans for dealing with the Cuban crisis. First, they were less dogmatic concerning the issue of tariff protection, and second, the heritage of Wilsonian moralism disposed them to a deeper involvement in the affairs of Latin American states. While both the Hoover and Roosevelt administrations agreed on the need to eliminate overt interference in the internal affairs of Latin American states, the distinction between Hoover's policy and what became the Good Neighbor Policy was that the latter accepted the necessity of creating and aggressively utilizing powers of the U.S. federal government to establish effective yet less offensive means of maintaining U.S. influence in Latin America. While the Hoover administration initiated the process of changing the scope and nature of U.S. interventionism, it was the Good Neighbor Policy which established the specific institutions and procedures needed to meet the growing demands of economic depression, anti-Yankee nationalism, and the ideological challenges of New World fascism and socialism.

Despite the acceptance by both Republican and Democratic administrations of the basic assumptions of U.S. Latin American policy—economic expansion and political dominance—the twenties were marked by a debate between foreign policy spokesmen for both parties over which was responsible for the growing troubles of the United States in Latin America. The debate generally involved charges of "moral imperialism" by the Republicans against "Wilson" Democrats and accusations of "dollar diplomacy" by Democrats against "Wall Street" Republicans. Two of the "Wilson" Democrats of this period who were to be influential in determining U.S. policy toward Cuba in the thirties were the ex-assistant secretary of the navy and 1920 vice-presidential candidate, Franklin Delano Roosevelt, and the former chief of the Latin American Division of the State Department, Summer Welles.

72

The Early Career of Sumner Welles

Sumner Welles had known Roosevelt in his teens and had been a page at Roosevelt's wedding. Their families moved in the same social circles, and when FDR became assistant secretary of the navy in the Wilson administration, he recommended Welles for a position in the Foreign Service, to which the twenty-three-year-old Welles was appointed in 1915. Welles's career in diplomacy was highly successful, and by 1920, with the support of Under Secretary of State Norman Davis, he was named assistant and then chief of the Latin American Division of the State Department.[1]

It was upon Welles's recommendation that Enoch Crowder was sent to Cuba in January 1921 to deal with the disputed election of 1920. Welles favored a policy whereby the contesting candidates would withdraw in favor of a neutral candidate. As the "neutral" candidate, Welles preferred Carlos Manuel de Céspedes, primarily because of "his thorough acquaintance with the desires of this Government." Since none of the candidates withdrew, supervision of new elections was settled upon as the appropriate policy. Nevertheless, Welles's preference for Céspedes would play a role in the latter's appointment as provisional president upon the overthrow of Machado in August 1933.[2]

Welles also became involved in the granting of the 1923 Morgan and Company loan to Zayas. His role was as an "honest broker" between J. P. Morgan and Company and Cuban officials. Welles opposed the bankers' plan for a customs receivership, fearing that it would lead to military intervention and increased hostility to the United States in Latin America. Thus, he early displayed a sensitivity on the question of intervention, an attitude that would become basic to Latin American policy in the late twenties.[3]

Welles's connection with the banking community became rather close at this point, and he was seriously considering a job on Wall Street. Intending, as he wrote to Norman Davis, to "go into business," Welles resigned as chief of the Latin American Division in 1922. Before he found a suitable position, however, Secretary of State Charles Evans Hughes, just six weeks after the resignation, asked Welles to take the position of U.S. commissioner to the Dominican Republic, then under U.S. occupation. Believing that his assigned task of preparing a program for the withdrawal of the occupation would take only a few months, Welles accepted the post.[4] But the military evacuation was to take two years, and only after Hughes promised him a promotion within the department did Welles agree to stay on. Eventually Welles was prevailed upon to stay even beyond the military evacuation and to negotiate the political and financial conventions which succeeded it. In his position as U.S. commissioner, however, Welles incurred the wrath of the influential Senator Charles Curtis of Kansas by opposing the appointment of a friend of the senator's as the receiver general of Dominican Customs.

When Curtis blocked Welles's appointment as a judge of the Central American Court of Arbitration in 1925, Welles resigned his position as Dominican commissioner.[5]

In 1925, Welles again took up the possibility of a banking career and had discussions with officers of the Guarantee Trust Company of New York. He also attempted to get Dwight Morrow to put forward his name to President Coolidge for the position of assistant secretary of state for Latin American affairs. However, the banking position was not satisfactory, and the State Department post was not offered, so Welles settled down to write a book about the Dominican Republic.[6]

A study of Welles's State Department work in the Latin American field between 1920 and 1925 reflects the mind of a benevolent interventionist of the Wilson school. While he showed an interest in consultation with other Latin American states which was somewhat ahead of its time, his methods of dealing with hemisphere representatives was paternalistic and, when necessary, included the threat to use the power of the United States. His attitude toward military intervention was typical of the period, for he believed that it was acceptable, as a last resort, to protect U.S. citizens and their property or to prevent civil conflict. Of course, he preferred "friendly mediation" to restore "orderly constitutional government" when that was sufficient. In line with the more progressive elements of the State Department, Welles made a distinction between government support of "legitimate" business interests and of those which practiced "exploitation." At the same time he believed that "it is almost axiomatic that the development of commercial relations between countries brings about a better understanding and a clearer perception of their mutual advantages and common needs." By the time of his 1925 retirement, Welles had served both Democratic and Republican administrations, and his views were not considered controversial by any of the four secretaries of state under whom he served. Indeed, Frank Kellogg and especially Charles Evans Hughes thought very highly of him.[7]

By 1928, when Welles's massive two-volume study of the Dominican Republic appeared in print, his views on Latin American policy had mellowed somewhat. *Naboth's Vineyard*, as the work was entitled, praised the "preventive intervention" policy which he ascribed to Secretaries Elihu Root and Charles E. Hughes, and criticized the "meddling" manner and "remedial" policy which he ascribed to Secretaries Philander Knox and William Jennings Bryan. Welles made much of this distinction between a policy which used U.S. influence to prevent unrest in Latin American states and a policy which reacted only after the fact, and then too harshly. He favored the use of U.S. commerce, educational exchange, developmental lending, and technical aid as the normal forms of influence. Intervention, when necessary, was to be carried out with the "cooperation" of other Latin American nations. The military intervention in the Dominican Republic was judged harshly because its measures "conformed solely to the customs, habits and prejudices of the intervening power" and thus were not lasting, as were the indigenous reforms encouraged by lesser forms of intervention. The benefits of the occupation of the Dominican Republic were "of infinitesimal importance when compared to the suspicions, fears and hatred to which the Occupation gave rise throughout the American continent."[8]

These sentiments mark Welles as an early exponent of much of the tone and tactics of the Good Neighbor Policy. Yet, inconsistent with the traditional interpretation of that policy, they also mark him as an opponent of the policy of noninterference being introduced at that time by the new secretary of state, Henry Stimson. Preventive policy—intervening on the diplomatic level to avoid having to intervene on the military level—was itself judged by Stimson to lead to more military interventions. For Stimson, the way to break the cycle was to abjure intervention at all costs. These two contradictory positions on the ways to eliminate military interventions formed the basis of much of the Latin American policy debate between the Republicans and Democrats in the late twenties and early thirties. It is important to note that what became the Good Neighbor Policy position after 1933 was actually less in the spirit of nonintervention than was that of the Hoover administration.

The Early Career of FDR

The career of FDR in the twenties less directly reveals the evolution of his thinking on Latin American affairs, but he too established an attitude and philosophy which were to bear upon his role in the Cuban Revolution of 1933. As assistant secretary of the navy under Wilson, he expressed a strong interest in foreign affairs. He accepted an imperial role for the United States in the Caribbean and maintained a paternalistic attitude toward the peoples of that area. He vigorously defended the military intervention in Haiti, considering the natives as "little more than savages" before the occupation.[9]

In 1917, the assistant secretary made an inspection tour of U.S. operations in Haiti and the Dominican Republic. He stopped first, however, in Cuba, where he commented positively on the effects of U.S. tutelage in the island. He visited with President Menocal, whom he found to be a "business man—orderly progress type." Roosevelt concluded in his diary that Cuba "needs a continuation of orderly progress and not of radicalism for some time to come." Roosevelt's reputation as an astute political observer must have been damaged somewhat by the fact that less than a week after concluding of Menocal that "no opponent has questioned his honesty," a full-scale rebellion against the Cuban president broke out as a result of his having rigged his reelection in 1916.[10]

In Haiti, Roosevelt praised the bloody suppression of the Caco revolt by the U.S. Marines. Not all of the navy assistant secretary's thoughts, however, were on military matters. Like Welles, who tried to keep one foot in the banking industry, Roosevelt was alert to business opportunities during his stint in government. While on the north coast of Haiti, Roosevelt considered the possibility of building a resort in the area. Anticipating the U.S.-sponsored constitution of 1918 then under discussion (which would make generous provisions for foreign land ownership), FDR also investigated possible sites for plantations, including development plans for the Ile de la Gonâve. After his retirement from the Navy Department position in the early twenties, Roosevelt and John A. McIlhenny, the U.S. financial advisor to Haiti, planned to found a trading company in Haiti. However, nothing concrete came of their plans. [11]

After an unsuccessful campaign in 1920 as the Democratic vice-presidential candidate, Roosevelt engaged (despite his contracting polio in 1921) in a series of business ventures. He also kept his hand in New York state and Democratic national politics. [12] Roosevelt's interest in foreign affairs caused him to keep up a correspondence with Sumner Welles through this period. Even after Roosevelt's election as governor of New York in 1928, he frequently consulted with Welles on Latin American affairs. [13]

Roosevelt, Welles, and the Latin American Policy Debate of the Hoover Years

Welles's letters to Roosevelt during this period offer a further opportunity to study the development of his ideas on Latin American policy. A letter to Roosevelt in January 1928 spelled out in some detail Welles's attitude on intervention. It stated that if the United States had to intervene in the Caribbean or Central America in defense of its own interests, it should first *consult* with other Latin American states. If the purpose of intervention, however, was to deal with threats to the peace arising from disputes between Latin American states, such intervention should be undertaken with, if possible, the *cooperation* of other Latin American states. Welles felt that *cooperation* would apply to "remedial" intervention.

In the case of "preventive" interference, however, the United States would in most cases have to act on its own. [14] The unilateral nature of "preventive" actions can be seen in Welles's previous activities in initiating and supervising the work of the Washington Conference of Central American states in 1923 and in his mission the following year to mediate the civil war in Honduras. [15]

By consultation or cooperation Welles did not seem to contemplate any form of mutual policy formation. His main interest in multilateralism arose from the conviction that cooperation might transfer to other Latin American states some of the opprobrium attached to interventions. Thus, the United

States might escape in part the anti-Yankeeism attendant upon its unilateral acts. This appears to have been Welles's motive for including the other Central American states in the Pact of Amapala, which ratified the creation of a provisional government for Honduras during his mission there in 1924. Welles informed Secretary of State Hughes on that occasion:

> In view of the urgency of the situation here, it has appeared best to hasten the suspension of hostilities by proposing the selection of the Provisional President and the signing of a preliminary pact on an American warship in Amapala with the sole mediation of the United States. I have, however, favored the additional mediation of the Central American republics in the negotiation of the final agreement since in my opinion Central American participation . . . [will allay] criticism that the coming government was placed in power by the United States. . . . For this reason in particular I believe it desirable that our responsibility in effecting a satisfactory and equitable settlement of the present difficulties in this Republic be shared by all the countries represented in the last Central American conference.[16]

Not only was Welles's policy of "cooperation" more unilateral than it seemed, but his definition of the conditions under which it was proper for the United States to intervene on its own were sufficiently loose that they did not actually proscribe acts like the Caribbean military occupations of the past. Such interventions were then being repudiated by Stimson's nonintervention policy. Indeed, the old rationalizations of intervention—the Monroe Doctrine and the Roosevelt Corollary—were being divested of their legitimating status, as indicated by the Reuben Clark memorandum of December 17, 1928.[17] Welles's position thus represented a return to *greater* freedom of intervention.

Welles was not only more tolerant of intervention, but also more willing to accept interference by the United States in the internal affairs of Latin American states, if only to avoid the need for later intervention. Welles's quarrel with what he considered to be the remedial policy followed by Secretaries of State Kellogg and Stimson was that by dropping Secretary Hughes's preventive policy they were allowing conditions in Latin America to deteriorate to a point where either military intervention or total nonintervention would be the only alternatives left to the United States.[18]

Welles's letters to Roosevelt also influenced the latter's views on foreign policy. In July 1928, desirous of keeping his name before the public as a national Democratic spokesman, Roosevelt prepared, with Welles's aid, an article entitled "Our Foreign Policy: A Democratic View," which appeared in the influential journal *Foreign Affairs*. The article upheld the supposed distinction between Dollar Diplomacy, which "placed money leadership ahead of moral leadership," and Wilsonianism, which brought the "restoration of high moral purpose to our international relations." Roosevelt even managed to defend Wilson's Latin American policy and the Caribbean occupations undertaken during his administration. He implied that intervention was practically forced upon the United States by anarchy in the islands and that "we accomplished an excellent piece of constructive work" during our occupations of Haiti and the Dominican Republic. He then went on to condemn intervention in general while still defending the policies of Wilson in the Caribbean. He did so by concluding that while the motives and material works of the occupation were laudable, the Latin Americans had not appreciated or approved of U.S. actions. Therefore, he concluded:

> It is possible that in the days to come one of our sister nations may fall upon evil days; disorder and bad government may require that a helping hand be given her citizens as a matter of temporary necessity to bring back order and stability. In that event it is not the right or the duty of the United States to intervene alone. It is rather the duty of the United States to associate with itself other American Republics.... Single-handed intervention by us in the internal affairs of other nations must end; with the cooperation of others we shall have more order in this hemisphere and less dislike. [19]

Roosevelt's espousal of multilateral intervention was, however, the only new position taken in the *Foreign Affairs* article. The theme of Wilson's moralism versus Taft's Mammonism was an old one, and Roosevelt did not develop Welles's distinction between preventive and reactive policy.

Roosevelt and Welles were also involved in another attack on Republican policy in Latin America, this time in 1931. In that year, in a speech to the New York Council on Foreign Relations, Secretary of State Stimson issued a criticism of Wilson's Latin American policy, especially in regard to diplomatic recognition, and stated that the Hoover administration would employ a de facto recognition policy. Welles felt that a Democratic reply was necessary and wrote Roosevelt that he would be willing to help in preparing one if the latter wished to write it. Welles also mentioned Norman Davis as a possible author. Roosevelt answered that Davis was acceptable as an author but that Welles himself should consider writing it. Eventually it was agreed that Welles would prepare the article but that it would appear under Davis's better-known name. [20]

The Democratic answer to Stimson's speech appeared in July 1931, also in *Foreign Affairs*. The Welles-Davis article attacked Stimson's de facto recognition policy as leading to U.S. support for Latin American dictators, which would only increase anti-Yankeeism. A preventive policy was held out as encouraging orderly political and economic progress and reducing the likelihood of usurpation of power. This Wilsonian formula for stability was seen as the way to reduce the need for U.S. interference in Latin American affairs and thus the answer to hostility toward the United States.

One of the sharpest points of the article was its criticism of Republican tariff policy. Welles and Davis made a plea for the lowering of tariffs on Latin American goods and called for a tariff-making procedure which would incorporate the suggestions of the State Department as to the needs of foreign policy. This effort to increase executive influence in tariff-making was to take the form of reciprocal trade agreements (not treaties) under the New Deal. In a specific reference to Cuba, the sugar tariff was singled out as having destroyed Cuba's position as the largest importer of U.S. goods in Latin America.

While Republican protectionism, epitomized by the Smoot-Hawley tariff of 1931, was a poorly defended flank of Hoover's Latin American policy, on the question of nonintervention the Stimson position was more "neighborly" than that taken in the Welles-Roosevelt *Foreign Affairs* article of July 1928. In this latest piece, the Democratic authors tried to close the gap. In the light of the newly published Clark memorandum divorcing the Roosevelt Corollary from the Monroe Doctrine, Welles and Davis tried to go one better by calling for the multilateralization of that doctrine—though only by having other Latin American states proclaim it as *their* policy as well.

On the crucial question of intervention, the article reflected a slight move in the direction of self-abnegation (employing it only to protect "national safety," based on the right of "self protection"), and even "undue interference" was condemned. However, aside from failing to define the parameters of "undue" interference, the retention of a preference for "preventive" actions left the Democratic position the more "meddlesome" one.

The article ended with Welles's provision for cooperative or consultative interventions. However, in terms by now familiar, he still claimed the right to act unilaterally if cooperation were not forthcoming.[21]

Sumner Welles's proto–Good Neighborism displayed that sensitivity to Latin American criticism which was characteristic of the later policy. He also believed that military occupations, which were the source of much of the criticism, never produced the stability which was at the heart of U.S. interests in Latin America. Hence the thrust of Welles's thinking was on ways of avoiding the conditions which had led to past military interventions. Because Welles concluded that the breakdown of stability which prompted such intervention could be prevented by timely use of U.S. diplomatic "influence," his thinking contained an inherent tendency toward *increasing* political interference in Latin American affairs. "Advice," "consultation" and "cooperation" were to develop as ways of implementing such interference while at the same time neutralizing the Latin American resentment which that interference would otherwise engender.

The progress of Welles's thinking on Latin American policy between 1920 and 1931, and its influence upon the outlook of FDR, were to be reflected in U.S. Cuban policy in 1933.

The Imperatives of Trade Policy

The intervention debate of the twenties coincided with a debate on the tariff. This debate was of course concerned with broader questions than Latin American trade, but commerce with that area was an important consideration.

The social structure of Latin American states forced their governments to raise needed revenues through trade duties rather than internal taxation. As a result, U.S. trade with Latin America was faced with the problem of surmounting tariff barriers. At a time when U.S. exports to Latin America were uncompetitive with those of Europe, tariff reciprocity was a favored instrument of export interests within the United States. Reciprocity, however, was resisted by the United States' European competitors and was disapproved by domestic protectionist forces. Moreover, as reciprocity had to be cemented by treaty, that is, by approval of two-thirds of the Senate, it was a cumbersome and often politically infeasible method. Most reciprocity treaties failed of ratification for one reason or another. Tariff bargaining was also complicated by the fact that many Latin imports to the United States were deficit food products or necessary raw materials which entered free of duty. In such cases the United States could offer little in the way of incentives to Latin American trade. Sugar, however, was protected by a high tariff because, unlike most other agricultural products, it was both produced domestically on a significant scale and also heavily imported.[22]

Despite these dilemmas, industrial expansion in the United States, by the early years of the twentieth century, had made U.S. exports to Latin America competitive with those of Europe, and the demands for favored treatment characteristic of the 1880s and 1890s gave way to a call for the Open Door. The preferential tariff rates of the Cuban treaty of 1903 went against the trend of this period, but were accepted as the result of the special political relationship between the two states.[23]

U.S. competitiveness abroad resulted in great measure from the attainment of mass production, which had led to domestic surpluses of certain goods. Having outrun home markets, export interests argued that overseas expansion of trade was necessary to avoid the economic recession that would attend less than full production by domestic industry. Much of the intellectual climate of the period supported this expand-or-die philosophy.[24]

The growing strength of the position of U.S. goods in Latin America made this area a natural target for these expansionist forces. In the period surrounding World War I, even governmental promotion of Latin American trade was achieved. The Commerce, State, and Treasury departments worked with such organizations as the U.S. Chamber of Commerce and the National Foreign Trade Council to assist U.S. exporters. [25]

When U.S. free-trade doctrine had originated around the turn of the century, its main purpose was to gain access for U.S. goods to the colonial possessions and tariff-controlled areas of the European powers. It was less needed for Latin America, where few such European arrangements existed. Indeed, the Open Door, most forcefully espoused in the case of China, was anachronistic in what was fast becoming the United States' own sphere of influence. By 1918, U.S. goods so dominated the Latin American market that the problem for the United States was reduced to one of merely keeping out the postwar return of European goods.

Thus, there arose in the interwar period the contradictory effort by the United States to open the door to markets dominated by European goods while sealing off the markets of Latin America as its own preserve. The Europeans, for their part, had always defended their right to special tariff arrangements with areas under their political control. As the United States achieved hegemony in the Western Hemisphere, the Europeans could cite in their defense similar arrangements by the United States with Cuba, the Philippines, Puerto Rico, Hawaii, and Alaska. [26]

These preferential trade relationships by the United States were opposed by the small group of pure free-traders in the country, in part because they gave strength to European arguments against the Open Door. Even this group, however, accepted Cuban reciprocity as a special situation on geographical, political, or moral grounds. Some also believed that the Cuban treaty, even though it included special as opposed to general reductions in rates (and was therefore discriminatory), was a weapon against outright protectionism in that reciprocity at least embodied the goal of lower tariffs. [27] The more pragmatic Open Doorsmen (whose sole interest was in expanding opportunities for U.S. trade and who had no basic faith in the benefits of the free working of the "laws" of comparative advantage) also defended Cuban reciprocity, but solely because they saw it as a means of increasing the U.S. share of the Cuban market.

In addition to the problem of opening new markets for U.S. goods while protecting their position in Latin America, export interests faced the problem of domestic protection. The compromise solution of the twenties, which it was hoped would appease the demand for a high U.S. tariff while still exerting pressure for a lowering of foreign rates, was the "flexible" or "bargaining" tariff, to be implemented by an "impartial" tariff commission. A bargaining tariff, whose rates could be raised or lowered as reward or punishment for changes in tariffs of other states on U.S. goods, had its appeal for protectionist forces because it could be used to pressure other states into giving better treatment for U.S. goods without necessarily lowering any U.S.

rates. For their part, export forces hoped that, by placing tariff-making criteria in the hands of a tariff commission pledged to a national trade policy based upon "objective" economic criteria and responsible only to the president, they could undercut the strength of protectionist forces in the Congress and produce a "rational" tariff system.[28]

Both protectionist and export forces were temporarily satisfied to use a flexible tariff to attack colonial preference systems, especially the British imperial tariff system. There was, however, a subtle undermining of the protectionist position by virtue of their willingness to acknowledge the advantages to be gained from breaking down foreign barriers to U.S. trade. An attack on foreign tariffs could not, logically, be prevented from leading into an attack on protection, including U.S. protection.[29]

Nevertheless, Republican presidents in the twenties declined to use their power to lower tariffs while consistently threatening to raise them. Moreover, they generally refused to follow the advice of the new U.S. Tariff Commission when that advice would get them in trouble with Congress. Without a willingness to offer the carrot of lowered rates, and brandishing only the stick of threatened higher rates, the tariff bargainers made little headway against the growing economic nationalism of the late 1920s and early 1930s. As a result, the desire to aid overseas investment and exports, especially strong while Herbert Hoover was secretary of commerce, was generally frustrated in regard to the trade regions under European influence. As such regions grew in scope after the onset of the world industrial depression, and as Japan closed off larger areas of China (the Soviet Union had long since been cut off from significant U.S. trade), the Latin American market emerged as the only major outlet for expanded U.S. trade and capital lending.[30]

Thus, as the decade of the thirties began, the problems of expanding U.S. hemispheric trade took center stage. With trade expansion problems in this area now compounded by economic depression, renewed European competition, and anti-Yankee nationalism, the new administration elected in 1932 needed new trade policies. Observing the failure of the bargaining tariff either to overcome congressional and European protectionism or to support trade expansion, the New Deal would revert to the older theme of reciprocity. Because U.S. hegemony could help to ensure a "friendly" reception for reciprocal trade in Latin America, the New Deal would look first in that direction. Finally, because Cuba had been the exemplary case of the "benefits" of reciprocity, and because the trade of the United States with that island had been decimated by depression, protectionism, and European competition, that island was the best and most necessary place in which to illustrate the New Deal solution to the critical problem of trade expansion.

By the time the New Deal took office, Cuba was almost in the midst of revolution, but this did not deter the newly arrived Good Neighbor diplomats. They believed they could produce not only trade expansion for the United States but political stability for Cuba as well.

Preparation of a Cuban Policy, 1932–1933

The presidential campaign of 1932, because of the deepening depression, focused primarily on domestic matters. The only major issue of the campaign touching upon foreign affairs was the tariff. The Republicans defended high tariffs, compromising only to the extent of being willing to set them no higher than was necessary to equalize foreign and domestic costs of production. The Roosevelt campaign attacked the high levels of the Smoot-Hawley bill but, fearful of alienating the farm vote, elaborated no program for lowering duties other than a vague scheme of tariff bargaining.[31]

After the November election, foreign policy discussions among the Brain Trust and Roosevelt's other financial and political backers and advisors became more rigorous. The main division arising in these discussions was between those like Raymond Moley and Rexford Tugwell, who favored a period of economic nationalism to insulate the depressed U.S. economy from outside forces while domestic recovery programs got off the ground, and those like Norman Davis and Felix Frankfurter, who urged increased economic and diplomatic cooperation in the international arena.[32] The internationalist forces generally came off second best in their efforts to influence the president-elect, but FDR's own interest in foreign affairs and his desire not to ostracize the low-tariff wing of the party enabled them to win some minor concessions.

The acknowledged leader of the low-tariff Democrats was Tennessee senator and perennial free-trader Cordell Hull. Ever since 1911, Hull had been one of the most outspoken opponents of the protective tariff in Congress. His original belief that protection led to unfair profits and high prices had been complemented in later years by the conviction that trade barriers led to heightened international tensions and war. As a farm state congressman, he also saw freer trade as a way to foster the export of agricultural surpluses.[33]

Hull was not directly represented in the tariff discussions of Roosevelt's advisors during the interregnum. His position in most cases was filled by Charles William Taussig, a peripheral member of the Brain Trust. Taussig was president of the American Molasses Company and a close friend of Adolf Berle, who was counsel to American Molasses. Early in 1932 Taussig had imparted to Berle his ideas concerning reform of the stock and commodity exchanges and had gone to Washington to raise support among certain members of the Senate. In May, finding himself by accident on the same train as FDR, who was returning to New York from Warm Springs, Georgia, Taussig managed to gain an interview. The discussion ranged from exchange regulations to FDR's great-grandfather's molasses business, to tariffs and international trade. Roosevelt, apparently impressed, invited Taussig to get in touch with the newly formed Brain Trust.[34]

A man without a college degree, Taussig was never accepted into the inner councils of Roosevelt's advisors, and Raymond Moley only tolerated his presence because he expected a campaign contribution. Roosevelt, however, considered Taussig a representative of the Democratic party's low-tariff wing, and shortly after the party convention he asked Moley to send Taussig to see Hull and come back with ideas as to how the tariff issue should be presented in the election campaign. From then on, in tariff discussions among Roosevelt's advisors, Taussig represented Hull's low-tariff position. He was not able to obtain a commitment for lower duties from the candidate, whose speeches never went beyond advocating some general idea of "tariff by negotiation."[35]

While ineffective regarding the tariff, Taussig, whose experience with the sugar industry of the Caribbean had made him much concerned with its problems, was able to bring before the president-elect the problem of Cuba. Though the immensity of domestic economic problems caused the newly elected Roosevelt to spend the four months before his inauguration preparing to meet that crisis, it is instructive of the importance of U.S.-Cuban relations that even during this period, when the U.S. economy was plunging to the trough of its worst depression, several of FDR's advisors, and on occasion the president-elect himself, were engaged in a serious investigation of the Cuban crisis.

Roosevelt had maintained his interest in Latin American affairs during his governorship of New York (1928–1932) and on into the presidential election campaign. The correspondence with Sumner Welles, dating back to the early twenties, was continued after 1928. Early in 1932, when Roosevelt was preparing his fight for the Democratic party nomination, Welles had offered his service as an advisor, and FDR made plans to use the Latin American expert in that capacity. In the interregnum, Welles, in a series of discussions and letters, set before the president-elect the continuing development of his thinking on Latin American affairs. Welles's major concerns were with hemispheric questions of peace-keeping, trade, recognition, and intervention. He proposed confining the Monroe Doctrine to the principle of hemispheric self-defense and suggested its multilateralization through periodic conferences and consultation. He saw trade as a vehicle of interstate amity and proposed lowering barriers to Latin American products as a way of expanding U.S. markets in Latin America. Welles opposed armed intervention by the United States but felt that it could be acceptable if temporary, sanctioned by Congress, and necessary for the protection of the lives of U.S. citizens. He now favored a modified de jure recognition policy whereby the United States would recognize a regime which came to power illegally or by force if it subsequently was upheld by election. This modification of pure Wilsonian doctrine, Welles hoped, would not cause nonrecognition to be seen as a desire by the United States to weaken a de facto government, but rather would cause emphasis to be placed upon the unwillingness of such a regime to risk its fate with the electorate. In this manner, a de jure recognition policy might be made more compatible with Latin American nationalism. However, he realized it might also encourage rigged elections merely to placate the United States.[36]

In that Welles's overriding concern, like Wilson's, was for the fostering of constitutional and democratic processes in Latin America, phony elections might be as discrediting of bourgeois legality as no elections at all. In the final analysis, Welles's concern not merely with the prevention of anarchy but with the nature and direction of Latin American society implied a willingness to use U.S. power to influence that direction. He hoped, therefore, to employ a "preventive" policy which he defined as "an effective diplomacy that suggests rather than commands," and which could "prevent the growth of conditions which lead to the breakdown of orderly constitutional government in the small Republics."[37]

One of Welles's concerns during the interregnum was the Cuban crisis, especially the proposals being advanced by various banking houses for protecting their Cuban holdings.[38] The subject of Cuba was apparently also on Roosevelt's mind during this period, because it came up in the course of a foreign policy briefing the president-elect had with the outgoing secretary of state, Henry Stimson, in January 1933.

Ever since the November elections, Stimson, whose main concern in 1932 was Japanese expansion in Asia, had been trying to arrange a conference with the president-elect to obtain a commitment to his anti-Japanese policy. Hoover, for his part, was especially interested in approval of his policy on the question of payment of European debts. Roosevelt refused to be drawn into a statement on the debt issue, but in December agreed to meet with Stimson to discuss foreign policy.[39]

The meeting took place on January 9 at Roosevelt's home in Hyde Park. The broad-ranging discussion included the topics of war debts, the coming World Economic Conference, disarmament, and the Far East. Despite the pressing nature and gravity of these issues, Roosevelt's interest in Latin American affairs is indicated by the fact that he initiated discussions of recognition policy and of the current situations in Haiti and Cuba. Indeed, Cuba was the first subject broached by FDR. Roosevelt asked Stimson about conditions in Cuba and indicated that he thought a revolution against Machado was likely and that this might lead to U.S. intervention. Stimson, who had been following a policy of neutrality toward the Cuban conflict, thought that the major problem in Latin America was the Chaco War and told Roosevelt that conditions in Cuba were not threatening because

"Machado had had unusual success in controlling his position" and retaining the loyalty of the army.[40]

Roosevelt's interest in Cuba is further indicated by the fact that the very next day he sent Taussig, who began to function at this time as Roosevelt's advisor on Cuban affairs, to see Stimson for a further discussion of Cuban policy. The discussion left the secretary of state with the impression that Taussig was contemplating a policy of intervening in Cuba. Stimson told Taussig that intervention was not necessary because Machado was "able to hold the country safe and suppress revolution." When Taussig suggested U.S. supervision of a special Cuban election to replace Machado, Stimson argued that this would be feasible only with a large body of U.S. troops on the island, which would, in effect, amount to an occupation. A small force could not ensure an honest election and would result in the United States being blamed for endorsing an electoral fraud. The secretary felt he had convinced Taussig that neither of these outcomes was acceptable.[41]

Nevertheless, Taussig was becoming convinced that some active policy by the United States was necessary to head off serious trouble in Cuba. He approved of Ambassador Guggenheim's efforts to compromise the differences between Machado and the opposition and was critical of Stimson's refusal to give his Cuban ambassador more leeway and support in that effort. Taussig even suggested the possibility of Guggenheim's being retained for a while by the new administration.[42]

In mid-January, in the company of Adolf Berle, Taussig made an inspection trip to Cuba. He met with Guggenheim and certain influential Cubans. Though Stimson had called Guggenheim to warn him against Taussig's ideas and not to disclose confidential information to him, the ambassador and Taussig agreed upon Guggenheim's desire for a stronger hand in mediating Cuban difficulties. Taussig promised to try and arrange an interview for the ambassador with Roosevelt. Taussig also broached the subject of a new reciprocal trade agreement with some of the Cubans. His hope was that such a prospect might prevent the complete deterioration of the political situation in Cuba and provide the new administration with time to implement its Cuban policy.[43]

Taussig relayed the outline of this new policy to Roosevelt, then at Warm Springs, when he returned from his Cuban trip. Taussig's report contained several elements that would help to direct the policy of the Roosevelt administration in Cuba away from the hands-off attitude of the later Hoover years. Taussig was unequivocal in calling Machado a dictator and in stating that the vast majority of the island's people opposed him and that only the support of the Cuban Army kept him in power. (This was a position that no high-level State Department officer had ever taken.) Moreover, he laid the responsibility for the economic plight of Cuba upon the U.S. banks and sugar companies, more or less reflecting the position of moderate Cuban nationalism.

Taussig concluded that while military intervention would be unwise, a "strong" ambassador should be named whose task would be to "induce" Machado to resign and to have the leaders of the political opposition name a neutral provisional president.[44]

Taussig had also been in touch with members of the Cuban exile community in the United States. The opposition to Machado, in its frustration at being unable to overthrow the dictator, was still attempting to force U.S. intervention. On occasion they threatened to attack U.S. property or nationals in order to produce such an effect. Taussig, through J. J. Barrett of the New York brokerage firm of Barrett and Company, passed the word to the exiles that they should desist in their attacks until the new administration was inaugurated so as not to force its hand. Encouraged by the possibility of a less neutral U.S. policy toward Machado, the various moderate exile organizations formed a unified Junta Central in Miami on March 27. Taussig met with one of the leaders of this junta, Miguel Mariano Gómez, and discussed various proposals for easing the Cuban president out of office. During the next few months, the junta anxiously awaited word of the new U.S. policy and their place within it. They further expressed their willingness to have a new U.S. ambassador select a provisional president who would oversee elections.[45]

After the March inauguration of the Roosevelt administration, Cuban policy ceased to be confined to this holding operation and was taken over by the policy-making apparatus of the State Department and White House. On April 6, Sumner Welles was appointed assistant secretary of state and, as a sign of the importance of Cuban affairs, was then "promoted" to the post of Cuban ambassador on April 24.

The stage was now set for a new and vigorous Cuban policy. The attitudes and preinaugural activities of men like Taussig, Berle, and Welles indicated that the new administration was likely to bring forth policy makers less enthralled by strict rights-of-property concepts, men who, under the pressure of an incipient social revolution in Cuba and an industrial crisis in the United States, would be willing to experiment with market control mechanisms and unorthodox political alliances. Moreover, the eagerness of certain elements of the Cuban opposition to accept a U.S. program for terminating the Machadato—itself a sign of U.S. predominance—afforded the opportunity to divert the critical thrust of Cuban dissent and turn it onto paths compatible with the hegemonic relationship.

CHAPTER SIX

The New Deal and the Search for Cuban Stability—Part 1

ONE OF THE DISTINCTIVE FEATURES of New Deal policy toward Cuba was that it combined an economic policy and a political program. More than a narrow attempt either to protect U.S. investments or to establish a friendly regime, it was a broad-based effort to enhance the U.S. economic position in Cuba while so influencing internal Cuban political processes that the stability and progress upon which that economic position depended would be achieved. Because the economic program was slower to be implemented, it ran behind the political aspects of the policy. Thus, despite the unity of the policy, for reasons of convenience the political aspects will be taken up first. However, it would be best to keep in mind the fact that those implementing policy in this period were juggling both aspects at once. Political stability was felt to rest ultimately upon the revival of U.S.-Cuban commerce, while such revival depended upon the existence of a stable and accommodating Cuban regime with which new economic arrangements could be negotiated. Thus, the two components of Cuban policy had to move forward roughly in tandem.

There were two major stumbling blocks to the goals of Cuban stability and the enhancement of U.S. (and thereby, so it was maintained, Cuban) economic interests. One was the profound social and economic crisis in Cuba, and the other was the power of competing economic influences within the United States. Nevertheless, New Deal Cuban policy, even as the banks were closing at home, bravely sallied forth to "save" Cuba and, as the most far-sighted planners thought, the U.S. economy itself.

By early 1933 there was a growing chorus among the U.S. Congress, Cuban exiles, and liberal reform groups for action to end the chaotic conditions in Cuba. Even the banks were now wavering in their support of Machado and were contemplating ways of protecting their Cuban investment that might include cooperation with the incoming Roosevelt administration. Nevertheless, Secretary of State Stimson held tenaciously to his policy of nonintervention.[1]

Roosevelt's advisors, on the other hand, were in touch with both banking circles and exile groups, and three men in particular—Charles W. Taussig, Adolf A. Berle, Jr., and Sumner Welles—were working out a new Cuban policy. As early as January, Welles began gathering materials on the situation in Cuba, and in that same month, Taussig and Berle went to Cuba to assess the stability of the Machado regime. Another feature of the Taussig-Berle trip was the attempt to lay the groundwork for an economic solution to Cuban problems. The two emissaries discussed with Cuban leaders the idea of a reciprocal trade agreement. Such agreements were to be part of a general program for export expansion which the Brain Trust, at the urging of Cordell Hull, had decided upon during the interregnum.[2]

Many of Roosevelt's advisors had economic interests in Cuba, and they found it easy to perceive a relationship between Cuban stability and the export needs of the U.S. economy. Taussig was president of the American Molasses Company, whose subsidiary, Sucrest Corporation, used Cuban sugar. Berle was counsel to American Molasses, and Rexford Tugwell was to become a vice-president of the company for several years during the thirties. William Woodin, Roosevelt's secretary of the treasury, was a director of the Cuba Company and of the Consolidated Railways of Cuba, and a member of the "Cuban Chamber of Commerce in the United States." Daniel C. Roper, secretary of commerce, had been an attorney for U.S. sugar companies in Cuba and had represented them before the U.S. Tariff Commission. Norman Davis, a Roosevelt advisor on international economic and disarmament affairs, had been president of the Trust Company of Cuba. In fact, Davis had been under consideration by FDR for the post of secretary of state, and the intimate involvement of his bank in the scandal concerning a harbor-dredging concession granted by the Cuban government may have caused him to be passed over for Cordell Hull. Hull himself had served briefly in the Military Government of Cuba just after the Cuban-Spanish-American War and had lobbied in favor of Cuban sugar interests in the 1920s.[3]

The Welles Mission to Cuba

Sumner Welles had been appointed assistant secretary of state early in April, and on April 24 Roosevelt announced that he was sending him to Cuba as ambassador. Accompanying his old friend on his mission was a detailed set of official instructions (apparently written largely by Welles himself) which reflected the growing recognition in Washington of the seriousness of the political and economic situation in Cuba and of the need for forceful U.S. action.

In order to wield effective influence over internal Cuban affairs, the new ambassador was armed with two powerful weapons: the stick of the Platt

Amendment and the carrot of a new trade treaty. With these Welles hoped to enjoin the cooperation of the contending political factions in constructing a compromise settlement which would pave the way for stable government and form the basis of a revitalized economic relationship between Cuba and the United States.

The instructions he carried traced the history of the Machadato and concluded that the constitutionality of Machado's second term was doubtful. They attributed the political unrest in the island to the depression and decried the fact that governmental repression was leading the younger generation to conclude that constitutional change of government was no longer possible. As a result, the document read, "the Government of the United States is forced to view with the gravest concern the situation now existing in Cuba."

While taking no steps "which would tend to render more likely the need of the Government of the United States to resort to formal intervention," Welles's instructions urged that in view of the possibility of "open rebellion against a Cuban Government," the new ambassador take "measures intended to prevent the necessity of intervention." He was requested to "point out to President Machado in the most forceful terms" that the state of terrorism by both sides must end, and to offer "friendly mediation" for an agreement between Machado and "the responsible leaders of the factions opposed." Moreover, in view of the fact that "a speedy improvement in the economic and commercial conditions in Cuba would result in an immediate allaying of popular unrest," Welles was instructed to profess that the United States was "particularly desirous of considering the bases of a reciprocal trade agreement."[4]

These instructions reveal the policy connection between stability and economic recovery. Moreover, they express Welles's preoccupation with the establishment of a constitutionally based legal order as the source of social cohesion and economic development. This concern with social bonding and the belief that legitimacy derived from the functioning of a constituted legal system was to lead Welles to focus inordinately on the reconstruction of constitutional procedure in Cuba. This meant that his influence would be essentially conservative, and that while it would be used to stem the irregular practices of the Machadato, it could hold out no more adequate solution to the deep social and economic tensions in Cuba than that of "honest" elections. Such a solution, while consistent with U.S. goals of stability and enhanced economic presence, was not compatible with antihegemonic Cuban nationalism, for it was to be achieved through greater interference by the U.S. embassy in the internal affairs of the island. Indeed, Welles's "preventive" policy may have ultimately deepened the Cuban revolution of 1933. In any event, some action had to be taken and risks run.

Welles and Machado

Because of his preoccupation with legitimacy, Welles landed in Cuba with a predisposition to uphold the incumbent president—provided he was willing to help bring about a legitimate succession to his rule. In his first interview with Machado, Welles said that "the prime requisite to insure the permanent welfare of Cuba was the maintenance of constitutional government and the fortification of the tradition of orderly procedure." He urged Machado to end "this state of political agitation" because "steps toward any permanent basic economic improvement in the Republic of Cuba could not be taken with complete success until political quiet once more existed." Welles made no move to terminate the Machadato, asking only that the end of Machado's extended second term in May 1935 be preceded by "uncontrolled" national elections, which were scheduled for autumn 1934. To Welles's surprise, Machado declared that he had absolutely no desire to serve another term and that he might even be willing to resign prior to election time to demonstrate his impartiality as to a successor.[5]

As a result of discussions on economic policy which had been held prior to Welles's departure from Washington, the new ambassador to Cuba also indicated to Machado the possibility of an increased tariff preference for quota allotments of Cuban sugar. The Cuban president, having by now completely abandoned even the business nationalism of the twenties, assured him that in return for a stable market for sugar in the United States, Cuba would, as Welles reported, "grant us a practical monopoly of the Cuban market for American imports."

Summing up his interview for the State Department, Welles urged the initiation of negotiations for a reciprocal trade agreement with Cuba because it "will give us practical control of a market we have been steadily losing for the past ten years," and because "the negotiations leading toward such an agreement will assist in part in distracting public attention from politics." The new ambassador concluded that the United States should, for the present, sustain the cooperative Machado because he "is well aware of the fact that [he] could not for long remain in power were the support of the United States to be even negatively withdrawn." Machado's rule was also acceptable to the United States because he alone possessed the loyalty of the army, and his fall might bring about a "general chaos" which could force the United States to intervene.[6]

This policy of luring Machado toward a legal succession with the hope of closer trade relations, while stage-managing the gradual reopening of the political arena to the moderate opposition, was the basis of Welles's policy for the next two months. Nevertheless, such factors as the mutual hostility between Machado and the political opposition, the anti-U.S. nationalism of the students and the Partido Comunista de Cuba, and the militant response of the proletariat and the petty bourgeoisie to the worsening depression all worked against the essentially conservative U.S. policy. For a while, however, Welles appeared to be having success.[7]

Welles initiated exploratory discussions of political and economic matters with the Cuban government in mid-May and began separate meetings with opposition leaders shortly thereafter. He told Cosme de la Torriente, one of the leaders of the moderate opposition, that he disagreed with the opposition's desire to depose Machado and to replace him with what Welles termed "a provisional and unconstitutional government." He added that a proper solution to the crisis should "be based upon the preservation of the structure of constitutional government and upon the utilization of the existing Congress" to make legitimate an agreement between Machado and the opposition.[8]

This insistence on retaining both Machado and his subservient Congress, the product of an election in which the opposition had been effectively barred, was anathema to the opponents of the president. They were further upset by the trade discussions because they feared that any economic recovery might help to entrench Machado in power. The more moderate opposition, however, had by this time despaired of their ability either to force U.S. intervention or to oust Machado on their own. Moreover, because of the rising labor insurgency, they now perceived the possibility of a radical upheaval and thus were willing to cooperate with Welles, who alone could force their reentry into the mainstream of Cuban politics while at the same time suppressing revolution. The major difficulty with this strategy was that, despite their public rhetoric, it would identify them with U.S. policy and thereby damage their nationalist credentials.[9]

While the opposition was coming to terms with its fears concerning continued U.S. support for Machado, Welles began to appreciate the depth of the hostility toward the Cuban president and reluctantly concluded that he might have to ask Machado to step down even before the next presidential election. However, such early resignation would raise legal questions which would have to be dealt with in advance so as not to disturb the constitutional fabric so dear to the U.S. ambassador. He thus resolved to go along with Machado until the Congress had passed a new electoral law (drawn up, as usual, by a U.S. "expert") allowing the moderate opposition to run for office, and until a legally constituted constituent assembly could approve such amendments to the Cuban constitution as would regularize the successor regime to the Machadato. This delicate Wilsonian construct was to be put together while Welles employed carrot, stick, and artful compromise to keep the contending political factions from each other's throats. In addition, to support the mounting professions of nonintervention, Good Neighborism, and cooperation coming from Roosevelt, Welles also had scrupulously to avoid the need for military occupation. Finally, though he did not fully appreciate the extent of the task, he had to avert social revolution.[10]

Welles was pretty much on his own in Cuba. Secretary of State Cordell Hull had not been part of the formulation of Cuban policy and had left for the London Economic Conference at the end of May, not to return until August. The president, whose confidence in Welles allowed the latter a great deal of discretion, was hurtling through the legislation of the Hundred Days and, while copies of many of Welles's cables were sent to him, he saw no reason to intervene in Cuban policy at this time.[11] Roosevelt did inform his ambassador to Cuba, however, that congressional approval of executive authority for making reciprocal trade agreements would not come during the current session. Welles was at first disturbed that the weapon of a trade agreement would be removed from his arsenal, but he soon came to feel that too rapid progress on a new trade treaty might reduce Machado's incentive to cooperate. Indeed, by late May his attitude toward the Cuban president had cooled further, and he wished to retain a firm grip on economic developments to ensure that they would be used most effectively in bringing about political compromise. Welles's position was supported by Taussig and Lawrence Duggan (of the Division of Latin American Affairs), who felt that "the prospect of increased economic advantages is a plum which will not be granted until the Cuban Government has taken positive and satisfactory steps to conclude the present unrest."[12] Thus, the delay of trade legislation was not a serious problem.

Preparing the Mediation

By early June, Welles judged that he had maneuvered both the moderate opposition and Machado into a position where they would accept his "friendly and unofficial" mediation. The ambassador, contrary to his public protestations, was to be an active and at times dominant participant in the negotiations. In answer to the opposition's desire for Machado's immediate resignation, Welles argued that this would lead to chaotic conditions. The U.S. ambassador insisted instead on a program by which the electoral code would be reformed, new political parties allowed to organize, and the constitution amended both to allow election of a neutral vice-president and to revoke the "irregularly" extended mandates which formed the basis for Machado's second term. The whole preparatory process, he believed, would take six months, at which time a neutral vice-president would be selected and Machado would resign. The vice-president would then prepare "free" presidential elections for the fall of 1934. While the ambassador now felt that no election could serve its legitimating function as long as the hated Machado was in office during the preelection period, he nevertheless feared that a premature announcement that Machado would step down before elections would destroy the Cuban president's ability to maintain control of the country. Welles thus supported Machado's public statements that he would remain in office for his full term.[13]

To set the basis for the mediation, Welles "suggested" that the Cuban president announce his desire to have all political factions participate in a reform of the constitution and that a neutral vice-president should be chosen. Machado, acting very cooperatively at this point, issued a statement to that effect on June 8.[14] Lining up the opposition, however, was a less tidy operation. Division arose among these groups over whether it was destructive of their nationalist credentials to accept the mediation of the U.S. ambassador. With the exception of the anti-Machado Conservatives led by Menocal, all of the moderate political opposition eventually accepted the offer. However, the mass-based, middle-class action groups, the ABC and the student Directorio, underwent serious ideological disputes. The "realist" majority of the ABC leadership, after a flourish of patriotic statements and the defection of minority wings, conditionally accepted the mediation. This was the first of several steps, now toward the center and later toward the right, which presaged the slow decline of this group. Indeed, of the major parties created out of the social upheaval of the thirties, the ABC alone failed to establish itself as a viable electoral organization in the following decades.[15]

The Directorio Estudiantil, despite its anti-interventionist attitude, engaged in several days of intense debate on the mediation issue. Eventually the more militant exile wing of the organization prevailed, and the mediation offer was rejected. The Directorio majority held the mediation to be diplomatic intervention. They considered the Machadato as totally without legal foundation and thus felt that there could be no legal way of ending it. Moreover, the Marxist wing of the student movement, the Ala Izquierda Estudiantil, attacked the mediation and the Welles mission as an alliance between the Cuban bourgeoisie and U.S. imperialism, as did the Cuban Communist party.[16]

Even some of the moderate opposition created difficulties for Welles. A group within the New York Junta was still holding out for their original demand of the resignation of Machado, his cabinet, Congress, and local officialdom. This group, made up mostly of exiled members of the faculty of the University of Havana, was not anti-Yankee but withheld cooperation from the U.S. ambassador because he would not press for a clean sweep of the Machadato. Their aim thus ran counter to the stability-oriented program of Welles whereby the nine-year Machadato would end with a peaceful and constitutional succession of the presidency while leaving legislative and appointive supporters of the regime to be gradually replaced in subsequent "free" elections.

What Welles failed to understand was that even the immense power of the United States could not overcome the destruction wrought upon the electoral and party system under the Machadato, or erase the hatreds engendered by hundreds of political murders. A situation had been created in which the political and police structure of the dictatorship must either prevail or be destroyed. Welles himself recognized an element of this dilemma by acknowledging to Roosevelt that "the situation here is both more precarious and more difficult than I had anticipated." He further stated that Machado's "pathological obsession that only repressive measures, culminating in acts of hideous cruelty, could stifle the opposition, [has] fanned the flames of opposition into a detestation of the President's person which is unparalleled, I think, in Cuban history."[17] The U.S. ambassador showed recognition of the other horn of the dilemma as well when he supported Machado's refusal to make any public concessions regarding his tenure or that of his Congress.

The only weapon Welles possessed which could both resist opposition demands that the core of Machado's power be excised immediately, and simultaneously force Machado to relinquish enough of that power to draw the opposition into dialogue, was the threat to cast the full force of U.S. strength against one side or the other. This approach, however, involved further dilemmas. Welles's threats (or promises) had to be credible, and credibility could come only through strong public support by the top State Department spokesmen and the president. The problem was that Hull and Roosevelt had both announced a new policy of nonintervention in Latin American affairs. How could they at the same time publicly support an effort in Cuba which was developing into one of the most far-reaching political interventions ever engaged in by the United States?

To convince the prospective members of the mediation that he meant business, Welles began an effort to enlist Roosevelt's support. As early as mid-May, he had laid out his constitutional balancing act to FDR and asked for specific approval of his policy. Roosevelt had answered with assurances of confidence, but no explicit approval. On June 20, with the prospect of mediation drawing closer, Welles asked Roosevelt to make a statement to both sides urging compromise and "peaceable adjustment of Cuban problems through orderly procedure of Constitutional Government." The president authorized the statement but warned Under Secretary William Phillips that "it should of course be made clear that request for any assistance from Welles originates from Cuban Government and people and is not suggested in first instance by Washington." Despite the euphemisms in Welles's cables, Roosevelt had read enough of them to know the amount of knocking of heads Welles had engaged in. His words were thus a way of telling the ambassador that *public* appearances would have to conform to Good Neighbor Policy standards.[18]

Machado understood this pressure on Welles, and when he announced official government acceptance of the mediation on June 21, he referred to the offer of "good offices" and assured Cubans that the offer in no way infringed on Cuban sovereignty and was in accord with the Good Neighbor policy. The opposition factions which accepted the mediation all made similar statements.[19]

The Mediation Begins

On July 1, 1933, the mediation proceedings commenced. Each side met separately with Welles, who read a statement by Roosevelt and one of his own which noted that his "good offices" had been requested by both parties and that he considered his role as one of a "disinterested and impartial friend."[20]

Welles believed that all of the important political forces in the island were represented in the mediation and that the absence of the Marxist, student, and labor movements would in no way affect the outcome. The ambassador generally ignored or deprecated the strength of these forces and considered that his most worrisome problem would be that Machado and the moderate opposition would fail to compromise and would return to a state of warfare.

Because they were the bearers, however besmirched, of constitutionality, Welles treated the government parties (Liberal, Conservative, and Popular) with respect and generally overestimated their popular following. Among the opposition forces in the mediation, Welles considered the ABC the most radical. He made a special effort to keep close to the ABC leadership, which was generally more accommodating than its membership. The other opposition groups Welles considered "decidedly conservative."[21]

Mediation sessions did not concern themselves with the strength of the left in Cuba or the economic crisis; their main preoccupation was the working out of a modus vivendi for restoring moderate and legitimate party politics in Cuba. In the early sessions, Welles expressed disagreement with the opposition's desire that civil guarantees be restored immediately. He feared that the unleashing of "irresponsible" editors and revolutionaries would destroy the effort at compromise. He favored a lessening of press censorship but gathered written statements from all the newspapers promising not "to disturb public order or interfere with the successful course of the mediation negotiations." In his dealings with the government representatives, Welles tried to obtain freedom for the nonleftist oppositionists who were being held as political prisoners, and to gain a partial restoration of constitutional guarantees. Welles agreed that these concessions would apply to those who accepted the mediation, but not to those (such as the Directorio and Menocal) still actively opposing the regime.[22]

By mid-July, the mediation had gotten around to the thorny question of when Machado would step down and how the neutral, interim vice-president would be selected. Up to this point, Machado had been generally cooperative, having accepted a diminution of his police powers in return for an end to antigovernment acts by the opposition. The Cuban president, though suspicious of Welles's extensive contacts with the moderate opposition, had not wished to incur the displeasure of the United States by rejecting the mediation offer. He was confident, however, in view of the support his regime had formerly received from the Republican administration in Washington, and in view moreover of the clear noninterventionist and Good Neighbor pronouncements of the new Democratic administration, that no concerted effort to remove him from the presidency was contemplated.[23]

As the question of presidential succession and constitutional reform arose in the mediation, Welles began to press Machado on his earlier statement of willingness to resign prior to the elections. To gain the leverage needed, he once again wrote directly to Roosevelt asking for "specific authorization" to ask the Cuban president to step down around May 1934, pursuant to the selection of a neutral vice-president. Welles explained to FDR that the opposition forces would not participate in the regular November 1934 elections if Machado remained in office during the campaign. The ambassador felt that Machado, if properly approached, would be willing to make this sacrifice. Welles did not consider that such a resignation would destroy the political power of Machado's (Liberal) party, and indicated that the Liberal party candidate might even win the 1934 presidential election.[24]

It was also necessary at this time for Welles to pressure Machado regarding his delay in restoring constitutional guarantees. The opposition was threatening to break off the negotiations unless martial law was ended. Welles obtained the agreement of the State Department to tell Machado that negotiations would be broken off if he did not act. To induce Machado further, Welles agreed that the police actions (the opposition considered them murders) taken under the late Machadato would be protected from legal redress by the passage of an amnesty bill, and that the Cuban armed forces were to be left unimpeded to handle any disorders accompanying the return of constitutional liberties. The fact that Machado's police and army would go unpunished for their acts incensed the opposition, but Welles managed to overcome their resistance.[25]

As Welles's pressure on Machado began to grow, the Cuban president maneuvered to gain relief. Realizing that by accepting the mediation the political opposition had lost some of their nationalist image, he began to construct a public anti-Yankee position for himself. He accused the opposition of favoring U.S. intervention and swore that he would not allow Cuban sovereignty to be compromised.[26]

The Cuban president also attempted to drive a wedge between Welles and the State Department. The Cuban ambassador in Washington had been reporting to Havana that Hull and Roosevelt were adamantly opposed to the use of force in Cuba and that the veiled threats of intervention which lay behind Welles's various demands were mere bluff. In the belief that Welles's interference went beyond his instructions, on July 25 Machado had Ambassador Oscar Cintas tell Acting Secretary of State Phillips that Welles had threatened Machado with a landing of U.S. Marines if he did not cooperate and had maintained that Roosevelt had authorized such an act if necessary.[27] The next day, the Cuban president made a rare and unscheduled appearance before both the Cuban Senate and House of Representatives. He stated his intention to serve out his full term and said that he had accepted the mediation only because it was a spontaneous act of generosity by the U.S. ambassador and not based upon instructions from the U.S. government.

Welles countered swiftly, rushing one cable to Washington asking Assistant Secretary of State Jefferson Caffery to do what he could to deter publication of Machado's remarks about the mediation, and sending another to the acting secretary of state (Phillips) requesting a statement that the department had given full authorization for the mediation offer.[28]

On July 28, Phillips, at a press conference, stated that the U.S. government had authorized the mediation effort. Welles followed up the offensive the next day, declaring before the mediation parties (who had now reached the stage of sitting as a single body) that he was acting in an official capacity and as "the representative of the President of the United States." Welles did, however, try to assuage Machado's Congress by stressing the conservative nature of the mediation, whose reform proposals would have to be ratified by that body and by a constituent assembly.[29]

Although the mediation sessions continued into early August, the main arena of political struggle was now between the U.S. ambassador and the Cuban president. As August began, both of the contestants cast about for new allies. Each now attempted to utilize the Cuban proletariat and the Cuban Army to destroy the other. In their desperation they tampered with the basic elements in the power equation of Cuban society. This gamble eventually brought grief to both men—costing Machado his presidency and Welles his precious constitutionality.

The General Strike

While Machado and Welles were intensifying their contest over the Cuban presidency, the base of Cuban society had been shifting under their feet. The efforts of the early Machadato to destroy the power of the noncollaborationist labor unions (see chapter 4) had turned these organizations into active opponents of the dictatorship. Moreover, the stark economic conditions which coincided with (and were partly responsible for) the brutality of the late Machadato led their anger beyond the Cuban president and into a desperate assault upon the owning class (both native and U.S.) of Cuban society. Ultimately, it was this force rather than the political opposition, the army officers, or the U.S. ambassador that would release Cuba from the nine-year grip of the Machadato.

By the spring of 1933, daily wages for agricultural field workers—which had averaged above one dollar in the late 1920s—had fallen to twenty-five cents or less for a ten- to twelve-hour day. These wages were said to be the lowest in Cuba since the days of slavery. Many workers were receiving no pay at all, selling their labor merely for food and lodging. Even the skilled laborer was on the edge of poverty. Locomotive engineers who had earned $200 to $275 a month in the mid-twenties were making $30 to $75 a month. Clerks in the mill offices had experienced a similar decline. [30]

For the first time in the history of the industry, massive sugar workers' strikes had occurred during the 1931–1932 and 1932–1933 harvests. The Communist-directed Cuban National Workers' Federation (CNOC) had organized the first union of sugar workers in December 1932. CNOC unions, and others as well, carried out a series of strikes during the spring and summer of 1933 to resist wage reductions and to obtain better wages and conditions of employment. The CNOC unions often added demands concerning the treatment of blacks and women workers, as well as attacks upon the policies of the Cuban and U.S. governments. The CNOC also attempted to broaden the base of the economic struggle in the countryside by supporting the grievances of the small sugar planters against the mill owners. [31]

Economic conditions and labor repression had become so severe by the summer of 1933 that even the collaborationist unions had begun to criticize Machado. As wages continued to fall, work stoppages by even the most politically conservative unions became commonplace, and hostility to the government's attempts to break these strikes turned them in many cases into anti-Machado demonstrations. [32]

On July 25, one of many such strikes was begun by the Havana bus drivers, whose unions were politically moderate. The drivers struck over a tax levied upon them in the garages where they bought their gasoline—a tax collected by the Machado-appointed mayor of Havana. By August 1, the striking bus operators had clashed with police and soldiers, and sympathy strikes broke out among truck and taxi drivers and later among streetcar drivers, stevedores, and newspaper employees. Transportation in Havana came to a standstill, and the strike began to spread to the transport network throughout the island.

Though begun without political design, the walkout by the drivers, as an expression of hostility toward the corrupt officialdom of the Machadato, was now joined by many shop and even factory owners who closed their doors. By August 5, all the Havana unions were out and only banks and government offices functioned. Almost before the full political import of the event could be assessed, the economy of the capital had come to a halt; the long-threatened general strike had occurred. [33]

The general strike, coming as it did amidst the final stages of the conflict between Welles and Machado, became the backdrop for the maneuverings of the four most powerful forces in the island—the U.S. ambassador, the president, the opposition, and the CNOC.

At first Welles did not seem to appreciate the political dimensions of the strike. He was engrossed in the work of the mixed commission of the mediation, which had finally agreed on the first of the constitutional reforms to be presented to the Cuban Congress. The electoral code reform drawn up by Professor H. L. McBain of Columbia University was also ready to be presented to that body. On August 4, when Welles first took notice of the extent of the stoppage, he felt that Machado might be trying to use the strike to obtain the reinstallation of martial law as a way of inhibiting or possibly ending the mediation. On that day, the representatives of Machado's (Liberal) party in the mediation requested a suspension of the negotiations until the strike was settled. Welles responded that "if they persisted in their intention [of withdrawing] they themselves would be directly responsible for the downfall of the Government and for disaster to the Republic of Cuba." He did not elaborate on this, but the Liberal delegates withdrew their suggestion.[34]

By August 6, concluding that only the removal of Machado would end the now island-wide strike and avert a total breakdown of social order, Welles formulated what amounted to an ultimatum to the Cuban president. The formula that Welles took to Machado that day asked him to: (1) appoint an impartial secretary of state; (2) ask the Congress for a leave of absence; (3) authorize the secretary of state to appoint members of the opposition to the other cabinet posts; (4) request immediate passage by the Congress of the constitutional reforms suggested by the mediation (including the shortening of the terms of existing members of the House and Senate); and (5) request the creation of a vice-presidency, the appointee to which would serve as president until the November 1934 elections.[35] Machado resisted Welles's plan, but did not reject it.

The imminence of social insurrection had forced Welles's hand. He was now impelled to require that Machado step down immediately rather than after the selection of the vice-president in 1934. The face-saving substitution of a leave of absence for a resignation was to make it easier for Machado to consent and to satisfy certain legal requirements. The vehicle for retaining the constitutional thread in this instance was to be the neutral secretary of state, who would serve (according to the constitution) as president during Machado's "leave" and until a vice-president could be legally provided for and chosen. Welles was now forced to take much the same position as that which the opposition had proposed in the spring (and which Welles had rejected). However, even now, he did not go so far as to support the opposition desire that the members of Congress resign as well. By this time Welles had become convinced of the absence of any popular support for the legitimate political parties (only 5 percent of the eligible voters went to the polls in the supplementary election of July 16), but he could not accept their removal, since they were the only body which could sanction a legal succession of the Machadato.[36]

To put teeth into his demands, Welles once again asked Washington for support. He requested presidential authorization of the leave-of-absence formula and obtained it on August 7. That evening, he went to see Machado with this authorization in hand. However, in an almost unheard-of action by a Cuban president toward the U.S. ambassador, Machado refused him admittance.[37]

Concluding that his only hope of staying in power was to don the mantle of Cuban nationalism and pose as the defender of Cuban sovereignty, Machado had for several days been planning a counterattack against the U.S. ambassador and the opposition. In addition to a press campaign by loyal editors denouncing U.S. intervention, the president embarked upon a major effort to conciliate the general strike leaders in the hope of turning the force of Cuban labor against Yankee interference. From the outset of the strike, police action had been moderate, possibly resulting from a hope by Machado (as Welles suspected) that a full general strike would give him an excuse to declare martial law. In any event, on August 7, Machado invited to the palace the strike leadership, in which the Communists of the CNOC were dominant.[38]

The Cuban Communist Party and the General Strike

The year 1933 was a difficult one for the Cuban Communist party. Machado's invitation to the CNOC came when the party was only just recovering from its purge of the "tailist-Trotskyist" minority and its termination of a program of cooperation with reformist labor and political leaders. It had embarked instead upon a serious effort to organize peasants, agricultural workers, blacks, and the urban petty bourgeoisie. Finally, alone among the groups opposed to Machado, it had participated in the elections of 1932. All of these developments had been controversial, and the central committee by early 1933 found itself in the midst of a rapidly developing revolutionary situation, without either the ability to exert its authority fully over the various revolutionary organizations or a strong conviction as to the proper political line to promulgate.

Like most observers, the party had been surprised by the rapid development of the general strike in the first days of August. They had supported the strike, making the crucial decision to define it, not as a mass revolutionary movement of the proletariat, but rather as the culminating political expression of the multiclass opposition to the dictatorship. Believing the general strike to herald the overthrow of Machado but not the proletarian revolution, the Communist party was in a frame of mind to sacrifice the strike to gain concrete advantages for the coming revolutionary struggle. They saw the opposition to Machado as representing the same bourgeois-landlord faction that had backed the president until recently, and thus the party had no desire to see the "nationalist" revolution succeed. Furthermore, they reached the more obscure conclusion that nothing—not even a continuation of the Machadato—would represent a greater setback to the final development of the proletarian struggle than military intervention by the United States. Thus, with a pragmatic attitude toward the general strike and a fear of a U.S. intervention which would destroy all radical organizations, the party accepted, in the name of CNOC, Machado's invitation to conciliate.[39]

On August 7, the same day that Welles had tried to see Machado to press his demand for an immediate leave of absence, the president met with the strike leaders. Since the CNOC represented the largest group of striking workers, only a deal with that organization could end the strike and possibly save the regime. Machado held several cards in regard to the Communists. While the mediation had obtained the freedom of the jailed members of the political opposition, Machado still held many leaders of the Communist-led unions. Moreover, both the PCC and the CNOC were illegal organizations and suffered from the necessity of working underground. After much wrangling, the deal was consummated. In return for a promise to have the strikers return to work, Machado agreed to free the Communist prisoners, legalize the PCC and the CNOC, and meet some of the strike's economic demands.

The agreement caused a bitter debate in the central committee of the party. Though the Comintern representatives and the party's secretary general opposed the pact, they were overridden by the majority of the PCC, led by Rubén Martínez Villena, the party's charismatic leader. He maintained that the coming to power of the bourgeois opposition or the military intervention of the United States—the two most likely outcomes if the general strike continued—were both more detrimental to communist revolution than the continuation of the Machadato.[40]

Both the pact with Machado and its ideological rationalization, however, were quickly overtaken by events. First of all, the Trotskyist leaders of the Havana Workers Federation—the only other major labor organization in the city—denounced the back-to-work order of the PCC, as did the ABC and the student Directorio. Even among the CNOC-controlled unions, few workers were willing to accept a deal with the dictator.[41] Having considered the strike to be anti-Machado in nature, the party failed to realize that that very fact precluded a deal with Machado to end it. Even more damaging to the PCC strategy, and ultimately fatal to Machado, was the false announcement, also on August 7, of the president's resignation.

The Fall of Machado

The political opposition to Machado had at first feared that the president would use the general strike to revoke the concessions that the mediation had obtained from him up to that point. They called for calm and for continuation of the negotiations with the government. However, as the strike spread, and as its anti-Machado component became manifest, the opposition, especially the ABC membership, sought to spread the strike so as to force Machado from office. The directors of the ABC, nevertheless, still hoped to use the mediation as the basic vehicle for removing Machado, seeing the strike as creating the necessary circumstances to wrest from the president a more speedy and complete vacation of office. Thus, while working to sustain the strike, they urged Welles to press Machado for an immediate leave of absence. [42]

The militant wing of the ABC, the ABC Radical, had rejected the mediation, and it saw the general strike as a direct weapon of destruction against Machado. On August 7, the same day that Machado met with the strike leaders, the underground radio station run by the ABC Radical broadcast a false report of Machado's resignation. This report brought large celebrating crowds into the streets of Havana, and when a group of several thousand approached the presidential palace the troops fired upon them, killing twenty and wounding over one hundred. The Congress went into special session and suspended all constitutional guarantees. [43]

Welles now considered his position to be even stronger. Temporarily blocked from seeing Machado, but now in possession of a fresh statement of approval by Roosevelt for the demand that the Cuban president take an immediate leave of absence, Welles tried another tack. He asked Acting Secretary of State Phillips to tell the Cuban ambassador to the United States, Oscar Cintas, of FDR's support for Machado's speedy withdrawal. Phillips did speak to Cintas on August 8, but when the Cuban ambassador brought up the subject of pressure by Welles for Machado's resignation, stating that Machado would not be "pushed out by the United States," the acting secretary of state made no comment. That evening, Welles once again requested a statement of support, this time directly from the president of the United States. He informed Roosevelt that Machado was being told by his advisors that Welles's demand for an immediate leave of absence did not have the backing of the U.S. president. He asked Roosevelt—who had agreed to see Cintas in the next day or two—to tell the Cuban ambassador that "I [Welles] am acting in every detail with your fullest authorization and approval," and to imply that if the situation in Cuba became anarchic the United States would be forced to intervene. [44]

On the evening of August 8, Welles finally did get to see Machado. Despite the relation of Roosevelt's support for a leave of absence, the Cuban president, who now appeared determined to resist to the last, refused. He did agree, however, to make a counterproposal. Welles consented but stated that it must come quickly.

The resourceful Welles was now pressing Machado from other directions as well. In an attempt to weaken the president's base of support, he had met earlier on August 8 with several of the most influential members of the Cuban Congress. He told them of FDR's support for a leave of absence by Machado and implied that Roosevelt was willing to intervene if necessary to secure the removal of the Cuban president.[45]

To add another turn of the screw, Welles also suggested to the State Department that if Machado did not step down the United States should consider withdrawing diplomatic recognition. To bolster his point, Welles told the State Department, with some exaggeration, that most of the members of the Cuban cabinet, Congress, and army agreed to the leave-of-absence proposal. To allay possible fears on the part of the State Department that all of this pressure might force the United States into a position where it would have to intervene, Welles noted that nonrecognition or even its threat would itself force Machado's removal. In the circular logic of the "preventive" versus "remedial" policy debate, Welles concluded that only the threat of intervention could remove Machado and thereby resolve the growing state of anarchy whose continuation would force intervention. Finally, Welles asked that he be authorized to give an ultimatum with a deadline for Machado's removal, after which time recognition would be withdrawn.[46]

Though the attack upon the crowd celebrating Machado's supposed resignation had removed the last shred of popular support he may have had, the dictator still retained the loyalty of the Congress and the army. Depending upon these last resources, the president, on August 9, counterattacked once again. He declared a state of war and introduced before the Congress a resolution of censure against the U.S. ambassador. In addition, the Liberal party made a public statement calling Welles's proposal that Machado request a leave of absence unwarranted interference. The other two parties made similar, though weaker, statements. The politicians of the Machadato were showing no serious signs of defection.[47]

The other pillar of the dictatorship, however, was beginning to show the strain. The Cuban armed forces, whose troops were now the only real power standing between Machado and the wrath of the Cuban people, were becoming nervous over the hostility toward the president and the growing talk of U.S. intervention. Indeed, for some time, a portion of the officer corps had opposed the army's role as the enforcer of the terrorism of the late Machadato.

Since the spring of 1932, a small group of officers, led by retired Colonel Horacio Ferrer and Colonel Julio Sanguily, had been working within the officer corps to secure Machado's removal. These officers resented the politicization of promotions under Machado and the association of the officer corps with the killings of Machado's enemies by special police and military units. By the fall of 1932, these men had gained a following among the junior officers, especially in the Aviation Corps, but they were unable to convince the heads of the major Havana military installations at Camp Columbia and Cabaña Fortress, or the chief of the general staff, General Alberto Herrera.[48]

The general strike was a disquieting experience for the army. The return to martial law had made them, more than before, the symbols of the hated Machadato. Sanguily and Ferrer began new explorations with their fellow officers, spurred also by the possibility of a U.S. military occupation which, many officers feared, would lead to a reorganization of the Cuban armed forces. Furthermore, if Machado resigned, a new government might itself purge the officer corps; if the army itself acted to overthrow the dictator, it would gain a measure of popularity, and only those officers most closely tied to the Machadato would face danger. By August 9, Colonel Erasmo Delgado, second in command of Cabaña, joined the movement, as did Captain Mario Torres-Menier, head of the Aviation Corps. Approaches were now made to Colonel Demetrio Castillo, commandant of Camp Columbia, and Colonel Juan Cruz Bustillo, commandant of Cabaña Fortress. While neither of the two commandants was willing to act, it was agreed that General Alberto Herrera, now secretary of war, should be told of the desire of many officers that Machado resign. Ferrer was chosen to see Herrera, but when he arrived at his home on the evening of August 10, he found the latter already engaged with another caller—the ubiquitous U.S. ambassador.[49]

Sumner Welles had indeed been busy. He was strongly pressing his latest plan for obtaining the removal of Machado—withdrawal of U.S. recognition—upon the State Department. He had been able to convince Roosevelt that Machado's advisors were still maintaining that Welles's demand for his removal and the hints of intervention were not supported in Washington. He further pressed FDR to tell Ambassador Cintas that this was not the case. As a result, Roosevelt had scheduled an interview with the Cuban ambassador for August 9. Welles desired that Roosevelt use the interview not only to affirm full support for Welles's actions but to convey the president's own desire for Machado's removal, and to make reference to the possibility of U.S. intervention if that did not occur.

As Welles's intervention had grown more blatant, the State Department became concerned over the attitude of other Latin American countries. Acting Secretary of State Phillips cautioned the president not to use language with the Cuban ambassador which directly requested Machado's removal or threatened U.S. intervention. Roosevelt showed his own sensitivity to the matter during a press conference on the morning of August 9. The president denied that Welles had given Machado an ultimatum, stating that the requests for his removal were coming from the opposition and that Welles was merely offering his good offices. Roosevelt added, off the record, that "I have to be terribly careful not to be in a position of intimating that the Cubans get rid of their President."⁵⁰

Roosevelt saw Cintas that afternoon, telling him, in proper diplomatic circumlocution, that he fully approved Welles's actions and that Machado "can go down in history as a great... patriot if he will take the step recommended by the representatives of all the Cuban political parties." The president made no mention of withdrawing recognition or of intervention. He did suggest that in view of Cuba's economic crisis, Machado might say that he was stepping down to "save the Cuban people from starvation," and that in such an event the United States could send a boatload of foodstuffs to Havana. The apparently chastened Cuban ambassador indicated that if the intense pressure on Machado were removed, he might be willing to step down of his own accord, and that the ambassador would have some word for Roosevelt from the Cuban president by the next day. The two then agreed on a face-saving joint public statement which emphasized that "the problems of starvation and of depression are of such immediate importance that every political problem should be met in the most patriotic spirit." In the light of this progress, Welles was told that "it would be desirable for you not to press him [Machado] further at the moment."⁵¹

However, the extent of Welles's involvement in Cuban politics precluded any cessation of his interference at this climactic moment. On the morning of August 10, Welles took Roosevelt's latest statement of support—given in the Cintas interview—to Orestes Ferrara, the Cuban secretary of state. Welles was worried about another counteroffensive begun the day before by Ferrara who, like Hull, had just returned from the London Economic Conference. The confident Ferrara had reassured the wavering congressmen that there would be no U.S. intervention and had elicited from them new public statements of support for Machado. Ferrara now told the U.S. ambassador that only if the United States agreed to an interest-free loan and a more favorable trade treaty would he advise Machado, after an appropriate period, to step down. Welles, in no mood to bargain, refused to consider such an offer.⁵²

In a desperate bid to ease the pressure upon him, Machado had Cintas see Phillips, this time to ask that Welles be recalled to Washington "for consultation." Cintas met with Phillips on the morning of August 10 and explained that Welles's interference was making it more difficult for Machado to step down and that conditions were becoming very serious. Phillips, who by now had doubts of his own about the wisdom of Welles's activities, conveyed the request to Roosevelt. The president, however, refused to call Welles to Washington, stating for the benefit of the Cuban ambassador that "the next move was up to President Machado" and that time was of the essence.⁵³

Despite State Department doubts as to the propriety of some of his actions, Welles had spent the day of August 10 in attempts to convince the remaining supporters of the dictatorship that Machado must go, and in the consideration of a possible successor. That night, possibly unaware of the extent of the anti-Machado conspiracy among the officer corps, he went to see Secretary of War Herrera. By that time Welles had concluded that Herrera, as a member of Machado's cabinet, and thus constitutionally able to succeed the president, was the best available choice for provisional president. Since Machado showed no willingness to appoint a new secretary of state acceptable to the opposition (who would then constitutionally succeed to the presidency), Welles hoped that the president might step down for Herrera, who had been his trusted supporter for many years and whom Machado had favored as his party's candidate in the 1934 elections. Moreover, because Herrera, Welles believed, controlled the armed forces, his defection might be extremely persuasive in convincing Machado that the game was up. His position would also aid in controlling any post-Machado violence.

Welles had come to know General Herrera during the mediation, in which the latter had served as a member of the government delegation. Welles described him to the State Department as having the absolute loyalty of the army and as having "unswervingly supported my efforts to bring about a peaceful solution of the political problem." Perhaps most important of all, Welles stated that "he is exceedingly amenable to suggestions which represent the interest of the United States Government."[54] When Welles met with Herrera on the evening of August 10, he gained the agreement of the secretary of war to act as president ad interim upon Machado's taking a leave of absence, and to serve in that capacity until a neutral vice-president was selected to oversee the 1934 presidential election.[55]

However, before Herrera could determine Machado's reaction to this new proposal, his plans were suddenly altered. Like Welles, Herrera seemed unaware of the extent of anti-Machado feeling among the officers. The existence of the conspiracy now arose to complicate this latest maneuver to achieve a constitutional and conservative replacement of the Machadato. Immediately after Welles's departure, Colonel Horacio Ferrer, on behalf of the anti-Machado officers, met with Herrera. As noted earlier, the purpose of the visit was to enlist Herrera's support in the demand for Machado's removal, a demand which by that time had gained extensive support among the officer corps. Ferrer pleaded with Herrera that the removal of Machado was the only way to avoid revolution or U.S. intervention. Herrera, either out of loyalty to Machado or in hope of securing his own succession (which now had the support of the U.S. ambassador), refused to be a part of the coup. However, now realizing the extent of the conspiracy and the fact that a move was imminent even without his concurrence, Herrera determined on a daring plan both to thwart the coup and perhaps to secure his own elevation to the presidency. To implement his plan, Herrera agreed to see Machado and inform him of the wishes of the rebellious officers, but only if Ferrer would hold off the coup for forty-eight hours. Around midnight, Ferrer reported to Sanguily and it was agreed to defer action until they heard from Herrera.[56]

On the morning of August 11, Herrera, hoping to quash the revolt and thus remove an obstacle to his own succession, gave orders for the disarming of the disloyal units and the transfer of suspected officers. The effort to suppress the coup, however, led to resistance. By midday many units had fortified themselves in their barracks, and anti-Machado officers had taken over the general staff headquarters at the Castillo de la Fuerza. Shortly thereafter, Machado himself learned of the rebellion, but Herrera and Colonel Demetrio Castillo (commandant of Camp Columbia) assured him that it could be contained. Herrera then went to the general staff headquarters, where the rebellious officers again demanded Machado's removal. The secretary of war once more agreed to convey the demand to the president and, apparently without informing the officers of his discussion with Welles, expressed his willingness to become president in place of Machado. There was some opposition among the officers to Herrera's candidacy, but either to gain time to consolidate their forces or as a bloodless way of removing the dictator, they agreed with Herrera's suggestion.[57]

Herrera met with Machado later that afternoon and told him that the *insurrectos* had agreed not to act, but from all evidence he did not inform the president that the condition was his own removal or that Herrera was his expected replacement. Later in the day, when Machado was informed by others of the extent of the rebellion and of the plan for Herrera to replace him, the president, now resigned to his fate, retired to his estate. When Herrera called later and finally told him the truth, Machado lamely wished him well, requesting only that he be given safe conduct out of the country. Herrera, however, was having troubles of his own. During the day, resistance to the secretary of war as a replacement for Machado—because of his close identification with the dictator—had arisen in the ranks of the *insurrectos* and among sectors of the opposition who were becoming aware of the military conspiracy. That evening Sanguily informed Herrera that he was no longer acceptable to the rebellious officers.

By this time both the political supporters of the Machadato and the conservative opposition had come to accept the replacement of Machado by Herrera as the best possible alternative. That evening, at a meeting attended by Cosme de la Torriente (for the conservative opposition) and Orestes Ferrara (secretary of state), there was consternation when Herrera arrived and reported that he was no longer acceptable to the army. Ferrara had just come from informing Welles that Machado had finally agreed to ask Congress for a leave of absence. He now returned to tell the U.S. ambassador that with Machado's leave of absence in hand, the only person legally capable of taking his place had been rejected by the army. When Welles heard the news he refused to accept the loss of his last legal recourse. He went to see Sanguily and reportedly threatened intervention if Herrera was not accepted. Sanguily protested that the army wanted an impartial civilian to replace Machado, but finally agreed to reconfer with the officer corps on the subject. The U.S. ambassador then asked Ferrara to call all the commanders of military districts throughout the island and to have those who were favorable to Herrera call him at the embassy. Welles then went into conference with Herrera to rally the political forces around the secretary of war. Nevertheless, by late that evening, the ABC, Menocal, and the less conservative opposition in general, heedless of constitutional niceties, had come to agree upon the candidacy of the retired head of the Medical Corps, Colonel Horacio Ferrer. Ferrer declined, however, feeling that Welles had settled on Herrera and could not be moved.[58]

Early on the morning of August 12, Sanguily returned to the U.S. embassy to report on his poll of the rebellious officers. Welles was upset at Sanguily's reply that Herrera was still unacceptable to the *insurrectos*. By that time Welles also had reports from several area commanders that, despite their loyalty to Herrera, they felt that public opposition to him as a Machadista would be too great. The last thread of Welles's carefully contrived plan of constitutional procedure was coming unwound. The redoubtable U.S. ambassador, however, was not to be denied. With hints of the dire consequences of refusal, he suggested that the officers accept Herrera as president only for the few hours necessary for the latter to name a neutral secretary of state, in whose favor he would immediately resign. Sanguily agreed, and Welles set about to line up the opposition. By eight o'clock he had gained adherence to the new proposal by Herrera, who agreed to replace Machado as soon as the Congress had granted Machado's request for a leave of absence.[59]

At 11:30, the busy ambassador was in conference with Cosme de la Torriente and Machado's ambassador to Mexico, Carlos Manuel de Céspedes. The latter had been mentioned during the mediation proceedings as a possible appointee as neutral vice-president to hold the November 1934 elections. Welles favored Céspedes, but the general strike and Machado's resistance to Welles's earlier proposals had forced the U.S. ambassador to adopt the expedient of Herrera's candidacy. Now that Herrera himself was unacceptable, the final plan was to have the secretary of war, upon Machado's leave of absence, become president and immediately appoint Céspedes as secretary of state. Herrera would then immediately resign, at which point Céspedes would become president. Though he was by no means a popular figure (except perhaps with Welles), neither the political parties, the opposition, nor the armed forces had strong objections to Céspedes. For Welles, the situation was almost perfect. He had known Céspedes and considered him "a most sincere friend of the United States" and very open to advice. Furthermore, Céspedes had agreed to inform Welles of his proposed cabinet appointments. Finally, by means of constitutional slight-of-hand, Céspedes' succession would be "legal."[60]

The Cuban people, however, did not share Welles's concern with constitutional procedure. On the morning of August 12, when word was broadcast that Machado had put his request for a leave of absence before the Congress, crowds motivated by both joy and vengeance surged through the streets of Havana. It soon became apparent that the mass of Habaneros were directing their pent-up emotions not only against the dictator (who had fled the palace and later in the day flew to Nassau), but against a larger system of repression that he was felt to represent. Unfortunately for Welles, that essential link in his constitutional chain—the Cuban Congress (which alone could accept Machado's resignation)—became one of the targets of the mob. With the houses of many of the congressional leaders being sacked and burned, and with most congressmen in hiding, it was not possible for the Congress to meet.

That afternoon, a few members of Machado's cabinet had met in the now besieged presidential palace to prepare the documents of succession for congressional approval. By telephone, Welles told them to bring the documents to the house of General Herrera, where Welles, Céspedes, Sanguily, and Cosme de la Torriente would meet them. At Herrera's, documents attesting to Machado's desire to resign, the naming of Herrera as interim president, the naming by Herrera of Céspedes as secretary of state, the resignation of Herrera, and the naming of Céspedes as provisional president were all put in final form for congressional approval. Céspedes' cabinet appointments were also reviewed by Welles, who found them "excellent in every sense." The only remaining problem was to obtain the necessary quorum for a session of the Congress to put the measures into law.

Later in the day, it having been impossible to locate more than a handful of congressmen, an "official" meeting of that body was declared in session, which quickly ratified the documents prepared for them and additionally repealed an executive statute which stood in the way of Céspedes' presidency. Thus on August 12, 1933, Carlos Manuel de Céspedes became the "constitutional" president of Cuba. Welles assured a relieved State Department that this solution to the crisis of the Machadato "has been worked out solely by the Cubans themselves."[61]

Wielding the implements of U.S. hegemony, the ambassador to Cuba achieved what appeared to be a conservative outcome to the passing of the Machadato. Welles's policy toward the Cuban crisis exhibited an understanding of the tensions attendant upon social change. What he did not realize, however, was the extent to which the United States' desire for stability in Cuba precluded a meaningful resolution of those tensions.

Welles did appreciate the seriousness (though not necessarily the nature) of the Cuban crisis. He had removed U.S. backing from the dictator and had begun the process of alignment with nontraditional forces such as the ABC. However, his method was extremely cautious, and his actions fell far short of establishing a new domestic basis for U.S. hegemony. Indeed, because he required too much of them, he tainted those forces which worked with him.

The moderate opposition groups which cooperated with the ambassador tended to lose, by that very act, much of their ability to serve as effective allies of U.S. predominance. Yet they seemed to have no choice. They could not, by their own effort, remove a dictator sustained by the U.S. political and economic presence and the loyalty of the Cuban Army. While their movement was popular, it did not enlist active involvement outside the ranks of middle-class youth. The only true mass movement—organized labor and its general strike—developed in great measure separately from the middle-class political opposition to Machado, and in many ways threatened it. Thus, the political opposition was forced by its own weakness, by its fear of revolution from below, and by its proclivity to accept U.S. tutelage to ally itself with the policy of the U.S. ambassador. In doing so it sacrificed much of its nationalist image and was led to accept U.S. requirements for legal continuity and social stability. In the process, the original antihegemonic thrust of many elements of its program were submerged. Indeed, the experience of working closely with U.S. representatives became so influential to its thinking that its later ideological formulations took on a conservative and sometimes annexationist flavor. Subsequent expressions of Cuban nationalism were thus to come from the dissident wings of these groups and from proletarian organizations.

Welles's attempt to subdue the violent emotions which underlay the pressure for social change in an oppressive environment, and to confine such change within constitutional procedure, was undercut by the basic response to that oppression—the general strike. This strike, representing as it did the imminence of social revolt, forced Welles to move precipitously and overbearingly, in a manner which mocked his pretensions to noninterference and orderly procedure. The result was the artificial creation of a regime with neither social base nor nationalist appeal. Its rule was to be ineffective, its demise swift.

CHAPTER SEVEN

The New Deal and the Search
for Cuban Stability—Part 2

UNLIKE THE POLITICAL STABILIZATION PROGRAM for Cuba, the plan for economic stabilization involved problems beyond those presented by Cuban social tensions. Rival economic interests within the U.S. and international economies and among the various bureaucracies of the U.S. government had to be taken into account. As noted in chapter 6, the emerging goal of New Deal economic policy toward Cuba in the spring of 1933 was to obtain more favorable access to Cuban markets and to grant in return a more stable market for Cuban sugar in the United States as part of a larger program of rationalization in that industry. This rationalization was also expected to salvage the large U.S. investment in the island's sugar production. Because of the overriding importance of the worldwide economic collapse, Cuban policy would be hammered out as a component of broader programs designed to lift the U.S. economy out of depression. The struggle within the New Deal between outward- and inward-looking solutions to the depression would thus be reflected in the search for Cuban stability.

The Contradictions of Trade Promotion

Ever since the latter part of the nineteenth century, when the economy of the United States developed a productive capacity and a fund of liquid capital in excess of effective domestic demand, programs of export promotion and foreign investment have been central elements of the government's foreign economic policy. Nevertheless, economic forces favoring the development of foreign markets, raw materials sources, and other capital investments were generally challenged by "isolationist" forces which denigrated the advantages of the international movement of the factors of production and which often favored inhibiting such movement by the use of tariffs and other means to protect domestic producers from foreign competition.

By the end of World War I the U.S. balance of trade was so heavily positive that efforts to promote exports confronted the growing inability of foreign nations to finance their imports from us. While overseas lending and investment temporarily supported the capacity of foreign states to purchase goods from the United States, foreign trade interests worked to supplement foreign buying power by increasing the level of U.S. imports. However, the interwar period saw a growing resistance by protectionist forces to any program of expanding U.S. purchases of foreign goods. This struggle climaxed periodically during the passage of tariff legislation by the U.S. Congress, which on balance still reflected the political influence of small farmers and producers rather than the growing economic power of mass producers with foreign markets and inputs.

The various tariff debates of the 1920s were complicated by the results of previous decades of foreign investment, which had led many large corporations to desire not only to export their domestic production freely, but to enhance the importation of raw materials and semifinished products which they controlled abroad. Inasmuch as the U.S. investment in Cuban sugar production was the largest single block of U.S.-owned imports, the sugar tariff became a particular center of controversy.[1]

The industrial depression of the 1930s complicated and intensified the struggle between international traders and protectionists within the United States. Export interests, now in desperate need of both foreign *and* domestic markets, faced the additional difficulty of the cessation of private foreign lending. With much of their paper either insecure or in default, the international investment banking houses had little desire—and greatly diminished capacity—to support foreign trade. This forced the exporting community to press ever more sharply for alternative methods of promoting foreign commerce. At various times during the 1930s, they turned to programs of tariff reduction, export subsidization, barter agreements, and government lending.[2] It was the attack upon the tariff, of course, that most upset economic interests which bought and sold exclusively in the home market. Their concern was to protect what was left of the domestic market from low-priced foreign goods and to return their operations to a profitable basis by achieving an increase in domestic price levels.

Protectionist forces had long been effective in influencing tariff legislation. They were now aided by the fact that the worldwide depression, which heightened autarkic sentiments in most industrially developed states, caused a large group of intellectuals and business leaders in the United States to defect temporarily from their traditional allegiance to internationalism. This group, and the political leaders who were influenced by them, sought some new way of dealing with the threatening social and economic tensions caused by the depression. Their immediate concern was to end the condition of unprofitable sales, unused capacity, and unemployment in the domestic economy, and with this focus they were less willing than in the past to support programs of export promotion, especially if such programs appeared to work against domestic recovery. Though most of this group would return to an international orientation later in the decade, in this period export schemes were granted consideration only if they were seen as extensions of, and not threats to, what was then considered a viable national recovery program. Thus, as noted earlier, the program to aid the importation of Cuban sugar and to revive U.S. exports to the island had to be designed to fit such criteria. It is an indication of the strength and profundity of the expansionist impulse within the U.S. economy (as well as an expression of U.S. hegemony in regard to Cuba) that such a program was designed and actually carried out during the depths of the depression.

The Survival of the Export Impulse

The clear thrust of New Deal economic programs during 1933 was "intranational," that is, they focused primarily, though not exclusively, on inward-looking solutions to the economic crisis. Roosevelt's most influential advisors accepted the proposition that domestic recovery necessitated a temporary disengagement of the U.S. economy from international economic influence. While trade promotion was deemphasized, however, it was not discarded, and trade deals which were supportive of recovery efforts were eagerly pursued.[3]

When trade promotion was expounded on ideological rather than pragmatic grounds, it met strong opposition from both the New Deal intranationalists and the traditional protectionists. But even here the struggle was not totally one-sided. The economic base of the capital- and goods-exporting sector of the economy, though diminished in status and influence, still retained great strength. Moreover, the internationalist sector of both major political parties could still command a hearing in the centers of governmental authority. The forces of this persuasion within the Democratic party were able to establish themselves in the State Department and were allowed to develop the outline of a program of trade expansion. Roosevelt, himself a liberal internationalist until the economic crisis, had appointed the Democratic party's free-trade leader, Cordell Hull, as secretary of state, and retained Norman Davis, a strong Wilsonian, as an advisor on European economic and disarmament affairs. He also appointed Sumner Welles, an advocate of lower tariffs and increased imports from Latin America, as assistant secretary of state. Hull eventually brought in Francis Sayre, a convinced free-trader, to administer the trade program and retained such high-level State Department internationalists from the Hoover years as Herbert Feis, William Phillips, and Stanley Hornbeck.[4]

It was from this liberal internationalist base in the State Department, with the cooperation of U.S. firms having an interest in the island's economy, that much of the initiative for a new Cuban policy was developed. The depth of the U.S. economic presence in Cuba inevitably involved this policy in the ongoing domestic economic debate. In the final analysis, the extent of this presence made manifest the relationship between U.S. and Cuban recovery and led elements of intranationalist and protectionist forces to conclude that Cuban purchasing power and thereby U.S. trade could be revived without introducing any uncontrollable influences into the U.S. economy. U.S. hegemony in Cuba held out the possibility that such a solution, acceptable to both nationalists and internationalists, was possible.[5]

The Cuban Bridge Between Autarky and Internationalism

The main thrust of the New Deal recovery effort was centered at this time in the National Recovery Administration (NRA) and the Agricultural Adjustment Administration (AAA). In addition to the distinct nationalist and even autarkic nature of these programs, they reflected another theme of the early New Deal as well—the collaboration of government with the largest producing and processing units in agriculture and industry in programs of production and distribution planning.[6] Such planning mechanisms could be harnessed to a Cuban recovery program because of the integration of the Cuban economy with that of the United States. For example, because of the large amount of Cuban sugar sold in North America, no rationalization of the U.S. sugar industry was possible without some control over Cuban production. Moreover, business-government cooperation in the domestic economy could easily lead to business-government cooperation in international trade. An important illustration of this tendency was the close liaison between the State Department and the leading U.S. firms doing business in Cuba, a liaison which arose during the study of a new trade agreement.

Even as the industrial codes and marketing programs were being hammered out in Washington, foreign trade forces were making renewed claims upon government attention. The April 1933 convention of the National Foreign Trade Council called for the reciprocal lowering of tariffs, loans to facilitate trade, and the use of government leverage to break down foreign barriers to U.S. goods. The American Manufacturer's Export Association took a similar position.

One of the most audacious efforts made by U.S. export interests at this time was specifically related to the Cuban trade. In the spring of 1933, at the instigation of Juan T. Trippe, president of Pan American Airways, a group was formed of the presidents or chairmen of the board of the ten largest nonsugar corporations involved in the Cuban market. This group, expecting that a revision of the trade treaty with Cuba would be undertaken by the new administration, commissioned Phillip Jessup, the economic advisor of outgoing Ambassador Guggenheim, to conduct a study of U.S. exports to Cuba. The group expected that such a study "would aid in restoring the Cuban market to United States exporters." In addition, the influential "Cuban

Chamber of Commerce in the United States" asked Roosevelt for a new Cuban trade treaty to restore the market for U.S. goods in the island. During this period, moreover, the State Department received numerous complaints from individual exporters, both large and small, describing the decline in their sale of goods to Cuba and urging that some action be taken. The State Department at this time had developed its own concern for reviving and recapturing the Cuban market, and proposals to achieve such a goal were already under serious consideration.[7] What remained was to cast these proposals in a form acceptable to those forces which clung to narrower concepts of economic recovery.

Cuba and the Reciprocal Trade Agreements Program

Owing to the strength of protectionist forces in Congress, and Roosevelt's desire to raise domestic price levels, trade expansion forces had to develop a procedure which would lower foreign barriers to U.S. trade without exposing the U.S. market to a flood of low-priced foreign goods. Such one-sided sacrifice could only be expected from nations over which the United States exercised dominant political influence, or whose economies were heavily dependent on access to the U.S. market. Inasmuch as Cuba fit both descriptions perfectly, the State Department placed great hope in a new trade treaty with the island. Moreover, the expectation of reviving what had been the sixth largest market for U.S. goods was of great material interest to that nation's exporters.[8]

Reciprocal trade agreements, under controlled circumstances, had been accepted by Roosevelt's advisors as the best way to find markets for U.S. production abroad without disrupting domestic inflation programs. Interdepartmental meetings to draw up trade legislation had begun even before inauguration day and centered around suggestions for granting the president authority to make bilateral reciprocal tariff reductions with foreign states by executive agreement. In April, Roosevelt announced that a bill to initiate "practical tariff agreements to break through trade barriers and to establish foreign markets for farm and industrial products" would soon be sent to Congress. The president had not yet concluded that a program of domestic inflation was incompatible with some tariff reduction, and he hoped to display the willingness of the United States to join in an attempt to lower trade barriers in the light of the upcoming London Economic Conference, which was seen as a last-ditch effort to arrest the growing international monetary and trade chaos.[9]

The expectation that Congress would grant the president powers to make reciprocal trade agreements heartened the formulators of Cuban policy. Welles's mission to Havana was publicly described as an effort to solve the problem of depression in Cuba by renegotiation of the 1903 trade treaty. As noted in chapter 6, the U.S. ambassador was to hold out the possibility of a new treaty as a way of gaining agreement to a political settlement from the contending Cuban factions. A new treaty was also expected to capture for U.S. firms an even larger segment of Cuba's imports than had resulted from the preferential position granted them in the original document. Even before Welles arrived in Havana, the U.S. commercial attaché was reporting the "considerable time" spent in determining "how much our duty preferential should be increased to enable the United States to secure a greater share of the available business." In April, an extensive study was begun which examined the lines of Cuban production that had grown up behind the tariff of 1927 and the related customs charges of the late Machadato. Embassy researchers found many Cuban industries to be "artificial," and it was expected that Cuba's desperate need for access to the U.S. sugar market could be used to break down the tariff protection behind which they operated. [10]

In the period prior to the initiation of the mediation on July 1, Welles maintained tight control over the discussions of the new trade treaty. He kept in touch with the formulation of the trade bill in Washington and hoped for speedy presentation and passage by Congress to enhance the attractiveness of the lure he was employing. Meanwhile, informal discussions of the increased tariff concessions which Cuba would make, if and when the U.S. president received authority to make reciprocal concessions, went forward. Machado was pushing hard for a trade agreement in the hope that some economic recovery might strengthen his position. Welles, on the other hand, wished to delay the consummation of such a treaty until Machado had made the necessary political concessions. [11]

Inasmuch as the 1903 preferential trade treaty with Cuba was the only such agreement with a self-governing state, its legal position was different from that of all the other trade treaties of the United States, which were negotiated on the basis of most-favored-nation treatment. Thus, special provision had to be made in the trade bill being prepared for Congress both for the special status of the preferential rates granted to Cuba and for presidential permission to raise these rates of preference if Cuba reciprocated. Taussig feared that the New Deal program for achieving stability in Cuba would be defeated if such special legislation were not forthcoming, and Roosevelt himself requested that the provision of special authority to increase Cuban preferences be written into the proposed legislation. Increased preferences for Cuban imports meant, however, an effective lowering of the sugar tariff, and therefore there was strong opposition to this idea from beet sugar forces in Congress. [12]

By June, however, beet growers' opposition to increased importation of Cuban sugar was the least of Roosevelt's worries. The momentum of the fundamental legislation of the Hundred Days had swept away conservative opposition, and the president's problem by the closing days of the congressional session was that legislation more radical than what he was proposing might be passed. Rather than ask for an extended session to take up the trade bill, Roosevelt preferred that Congress adjourn. Thus, he was not able to get his trade proposal before the legislature and informed a saddened Cordell Hull (en route to the London Economic Conference) that while the secretary could offer to negotiate reciprocal trade treaties with other states at the conference, congressional authorization would have to await the next session of Congress. The bad news was also passed to Welles, whose initial reaction was that this would greatly complicate his task. To counter any public relations disadvantage, he asked for permission to begin official negotiations nonetheless and urged Washington publicly to announce their initiation so that the "plum" of prospective economic improvement would not be taken from him. Permission was granted, and the unofficial discussions which had been going on for months now received official blessing. [13]

The decision to move ahead on the Cuban trade treaty reflected the importance of the Cuban trade (27 percent of all U.S. trade with Latin America by value in 1927) and of the U.S. investment in the island (24 percent of all direct investment in Latin America). It also reflected an appreciation of the deep social conflict that the depression had spawned there. The need to conclude a treaty with Cuba, however, might not be frustrated so much by Cuban demands, it was felt, as by those of competing sugar interests in the United States and its insular possessions. [14]

Those who urged a reciprocal trade agreement program were extremely wary of protectionist and nationalist opposition and therefore carefully chose those states with which negotiations were begun. In general, the foreign nations to be granted reciprocity were to be those which traded a product not produced in significant quantity in the United States and which were the chief supplier of that product in the U.S. market. In this manner, confrontation with a major protectionist lobby would be avoided, and the extent of most-favored-nation concessions would be severely restricted. As Francis Sayre, chairman of the Interdepartmental Committee on Commercial Policy, put it: "Our whole program was based upon finding places in the tariff wall where reductions could be made without substantial injury to American producers." This defensive position by the internationalists was a sign of the strength of protectionism as well as of the general desire to produce short-run gains in exports. Accordingly, the presidential message on the proposed trade bill described the program as "highly beneficial to our export industry, especially agriculture, [and] entirely harmonious with reasonable safeguards for those of our producers who are subject to the competition of imports." [15]

While a reciprocal trade treaty with Cuba was almost ideal in terms of its capacity to increase U.S. exports and to limit third-country concessions (almost all duty-paying sugar came from Cuba), it was potentially explosive because it threatened to enhance the competitive position of imports (sugar and, less significantly, tobacco and certain tropical fruits) which were in direct competition with a large domestic industry. Thus, the State Department effort to achieve a new trade treaty with Cuba faced its greatest difficulty, not in Cuban nationalism (which was finessed by the operation of U.S. hegemony—see chapter 10), but in the political influence of the non-Cuban suppliers of the U.S. sugar market.[16]

Cuba and the New Deal Sugar Program

While domestic sugar producers had raised the tariff against Cuban sugar successively in the 1920s, their effort to keep the low-cost Cuban product off the U.S. market had become by 1933 an act of self-destruction. Though the Cuban share of the market had been reduced from 57 percent (1922) to 28 percent (1932), and though the sugar tariff now stood at a level higher than the price of the commodity itself, world overproduction—which the U.S. tariff (actually a subsidy to nonduty producers) had encouraged—so depressed the international price that even sales in the protected U.S. market were becoming unprofitable. Thus, by 1933, all segments of the sugar industry which supplied that market were in the mood for some plan of market control which would raise prices. Because Cuba still sold enough sugar in the United States to affect the domestic price, and because the influence of the State Department and the U.S. sugar companies in Cuba could not be discounted, no rationalization of the domestic market could succeed without some provision for the massive low-cost production of the island.[17] Thus, even protectionists were forced to consider a new policy toward Cuba.

The new administration had before it several precedent-setting proposals for reorganizing the U.S. sugar market. For several years now the Machado administration had been pressing for a lowering of the sugar duty and had even shown a willingness to accept quota controls on Cuban sales to the United States. U.S. sugar companies in the island and continental cane refiners looked with favor upon the proposal of Samuel Bertron, which would stabilize sugar purchases for the U.S. market on a regional basis. Roosevelt's advisors were contemplating a program much like the colonial policies of European states which imported tropical sugars, which would define and regulate a U.S. sugar supply area and establish import quotas within that area, including one for Cuba sufficient to restore the island's economy.[18]

The U.S. Tariff Commission had been conducting a study of the sugar tariff for almost a year. The study focused on the inability of the tariff to maintain domestic sugar prices. A field study in Cuba had indicated that the depression in the island had so reduced the normal cost of production that Cuban sugar would continue to enter the U.S. market even under a greatly increased tariff level. In April 1933, this view was communicated to the president by Robert L. O'Brien, the chairman of the Tariff Commission. O'Brien concluded that the tariff could not protect the price of sugar in the United States and that the best policy for raising that price would be to limit supplies entering the domestic market. The Tariff Commission generally endorsed the quota system to control imports and suggested an annual quota of 2 million tons for Cuba.[19]

The small band of free-traders in the State Department winced at the use of that most evil of trade barriers—the quota. Nevertheless, they came to accept it because it held the promise of restoring the Cuban market for U.S. goods and because trade agreements with Cuba had always been treated as being in a special category. Thus, a quota for Cuban sugar might not set a precedent for later trade agreements. Beet sugar interests, for their part, feared that the State Department and Cuban interests would have more influence over the level of a Cuban quota than they had over the tariff. Like autarkists in general, they found the quota concept appealing. Yet they recognized that it could be used to undermine as well as to strengthen protection of their market. Nevertheless, with the tariff now useless as a weapon, they had no alternative to bargaining with the other producing interests for some form of market control.[20]

The various rationalization schemes under discussion in the spring of 1933 were to be funneled through the basic agricultural agency of the early New Deal—the Agricultural Adjustment Administration (AAA). Like its industrial analogue, the NRA, the AAA represented a close working relationship between government and the nonmarginal commercial farmer. Because processors and traders rather than numerous small growers were the dominant force in domestic sugar production, it was they who utilized AAA machinery to reverse, in part, the twelve-year record of high tariff protection for beet agriculture.

When the Agricultural Adjustment Act was passed in May 1933, its production control measures did not provide for sugar, because it was not in domestic surplus. However, sugar did fall under the provision for voluntary marketing agreements which could be licensed by the secretary of agriculture. At the request of the secretary, a conference of U.S. sugar industry representatives was convened in June 1933 to work out such an agreement.[21]

Throughout the summer of 1933, the planters, millers, and refiners of sugar met and heatedly contested for their share of what was to be a closed sugar economy for the United States. As a foreign state, Cuba could not legally be represented in a meeting of domestic producers. However, the major East Coast refiners having strong connections with Cuban sugar were present, and several spokesmen for the AAA, sensitive to the ability of low-cost Cuban sugar to upset any price-raising efforts which did not stabilize the island's production, argued in defense of Cuba during the meetings. One of the latter, the counsel of the AAA, Adolf Berle, was accused—

because of his connection to the American Molasses Company—of favoring Cuban interests. Roosevelt himself was partial to Cuba and supported a quota of 2 million tons, as did Assistant Secretary of Agriculture Rexford Tugwell. Secretary of Agriculture Henry Wallace, a moderate inter-nationalist, looked askance at the highly protected beet industry. Finally, the major government negotiator in the meetings was Tariff Commissioner John L. Coulter, who favored an adequate quota for Cuba and was consid-ered by the State Department as a strong defender of Cuban stabilization.[22]

As part of its activist Cuban policy, the State Department was pressing for a quota on Cuban sugar of 2 million tons a year or higher and a doubling of the preferential (discount) rate on the island's sugar from the current 20 percent to a level of 40 percent below the full tariff. The other producing areas resisted. Since the total of all quotas could not exceed the consumption estimate for the U.S. market, a larger quota for one producing group au-tomatically lowered that of the others. After weeks of arguing and constant threats of withdrawal by one group or another, a tentative agreement was reached which pleased none of the parties, least of all Cuba, which was granted only 1.7 million tons. Furthermore, quotas of all parties totaled more than the estimate of demand. Production at that rate would have failed to achieve the one goal on which all parties were agreed—raising the price of sugar.[23]

The failure of the industry in the United States to stabilize itself worked further injury to Cuba because it forced the delay of programs for interna-tional sugar control. A subgroup of the London Economic Conference had taken up a Cuban proposal to stabilize the world sugar industry by reducing production, subsidies, and tariffs over several years. There was strong sup-port for this proposal at the conference, but, as with the more prominent monetary question, Hull was advised to delay any action on the proposal until the meetings of the domestic industry had reached a final conclusion. Thus, while the United States was willing to aid Cuba by granting security to that portion of its sugar production sold in the United States, the price to Cuba might have to be the failure of its attempts to raise sugar prices, which in the long run were the only hope the island had of selling on a scale even approaching its capacity to produce. New Deal philanthropy, as frugal as it was, would have to be paid for by increased dependence on the U.S. market and a consequent reinforcement of U.S. hegemony.[24]

While Cuba's hopes for returning her cane fields to full productivity hung in suspension, the U.S. secretary of agriculture called for public hearings on the sugar industry proposal for August 10 and 11. These hearings were vigorously partisan, with each producing area and processing association sniping at all the others. With the collapse of what was left of the U.S. sugar market imminent, however, another quota allocation was hammered out, but it still left Cuba at 1.7 million tons. Fearing that Cuba might do even more poorly in another round, the State Department reluctantly prepared to accept the result. This was due in part to their great desire to afford some hope of immediate economic relief to the regime of Carlos Manuel de Céspedes that had been erected upon the fall of Machado on August 12.[25]

The advent of the Céspedes regime added a new urgency to Cuban policy. The "plum" of economic aid was to be withheld no longer. The "legal" successor to the Machadato was to be granted immediate economic relief which, it was hoped, could head off radical nationalism and possibly even social revolution. Before studying the effort to sustain Céspedes, however, we must gather up another strand of the fiber which bound Cuba in its hegemonic relationship with the United States—the Cuban debt.

The New Deal and the Cuban Debt

Complementary to trade and tariff renegotiation, New Deal Cuban policy contained a program for debt renegotiation. There was no prospect of Cuban stability unless debt repayment could be made consonant with the greatly decreased revenues of the island's government. On the other hand, as a creditor nation with a capitalist economy, the United States could not countenance debt repudiation or default. The State Department had to steer a narrow course between Cuban bankruptcy and the "legitimate" demands of the U.S. bankers who had underwritten $150 million in Cuban securities.

By the end of 1932, Machado, the ever faithful debtor of the National City Bank and the Chase National Bank, had been driven to the wall. Unpaid government salaries and pensions totaled more than the entire yearly revenue of the Cuban government, and even the last buttresses of the regime, the army and police, were threatened with empty pay envelopes. The bankers, supported by the State Department, refused to countenance any additional borrowing to ease this internal debt for fear that the bonds they held would drop further in value. Nevertheless, by the spring of 1933, after every current asset had been mortgaged and future revenues pledged, Cuban default seemed inevitable. To protect the value of their securities, the banks agreed to another short-term credit and a juggling of the repayment schedule to buy time.[26]

Public opinion in Cuba overwhelmingly opposed any further payments to the Wall Street banks, and Machado was constantly vilified for his subservience to the "Yankee" bankers and his lack of concern for the poverty of the former middle classes and the actual starvation of the unemployed working class. By March, the Cuban Congress had passed a partial moratorium on private debts and asked Machado to seek a delay of amortization payments on the foreign debt.[27]

In preparation for his mission to Cuba, Sumner Welles had interviews with representatives of the National City Bank and the Chase National Bank. Although he had seriously considered a banking career in the twenties, Welles shared the disappointment of many early New Dealers in the lack of discretion shown by the bankers in their international lending. He was not greatly concerned with salvaging their fortunes in Cuba except as part of a larger policy of Cuban stabilization. Nevertheless, he too opposed a moratorium by Cuba, in great measure because it would remove the debt as a tool to be utilized in obtaining a political settlement from Machado.[28]

When Welles arrived in Havana, he was shocked by the prevailing poverty and economic chaos and asked Hull to determine the bankers' views on a partial moratorium so that some government salaries could be paid. When Machado threatened a complete moratorium, however, Welles cabled Washington to stand firm, requesting that "no concessions of any character be made to the Cuban Government until a final decision has been reached by the President [Machado] regarding a solution of the political problem." The State Department was unwilling to intervene with the bankers over the matter, but eventually discussions between the Chase Bank and the Cuban government did lead to a debt settlement on June 27 which eased the repayment schedule. The new arrangement was not generous enough to alter the impoverished condition of the Cuban civil servants, but the bankers hoped that it was sufficient to get Machado through to the end of the year without default.[29]

The Céspedes Regime and the Cuban Debt

The Chase Bank settlement notwithstanding, Machado did not last the year. His overthrow on August 12 caused an abrupt change in Welles's attitude toward Cuban finances. While the U.S. ambassador had supported only enough relief to stave off disaster under Machado, he was eager to grant swift and substantial economic aid to his "legal" successor, Céspedes. Indeed, the path-breaking forms of financial assistance put forward at this time reflect the sophistication of a later period and mark Cuban policy as a forerunner of large-scale government-to-government assistance programs on the part of the United States.[30]

After assuring himself that the Céspedes regime was cooperative and worthy of support, Welles cabled the department forebodingly that "if steps are not taken immediately to make the Cuban people confident that their distress will in some measure be relieved in the not distant future, a condition of chaos will unquestionably ensue which will . . . make stable and constitutional government in Cuba impossible." He then proposed drastic and unprecedented action. He suggested, in effect, that the U.S. government take over the financing of the Cuban state from the bankers. Welles deemed a moratorium on the Cuban debt to be essential both economically and politically. Because such an act would preclude any further cooperation from the bankers, and because the entire civil service was threatening to walk out if not paid some of their back wages, Welles stated that a loan from some other source to meet these salary payments must be forthcoming immediately or the government would fall. Where could the money come from? At a time when the U.S. government had not yet learned to use its tax revenues in direct support of foreign policy objectives, the early Good Neighbor diplomats had to rack their brains for a legal way of keeping Céspedes afloat.[31]

Various emergency financing proposals were aired in late August 1933. Welles relayed a scheme whereby the U.S. government would transfer title to Cuba of a sum of U.S. Treasury notes which would be held by a U.S. bank in Cuba as trustee. The bank would discount the notes with the Federal Reserve and deliver the cash to the Cuban government. Cuba would pay for the bonds over a period of time. The Treasury Department, which had no authority to make foreign loans, found the measure "of most doubtful legality," but promised to study the matter. The U.S. banks involved in Cuba, while dubious of any proposal that was merely a cover for default, were willing to consider this plan for "lending" U.S. Treasury bonds to Havana. They eventually agreed with the proposal, but only on the condition that Washington guarantee them against loss.

Another ingenious device, proposed by Charles Taussig, was for U.S. silver producers to accept Cuban bonds in return for the sale to the Cuban government of $5 million in silver. The producers could then discount the bonds for a $5 million loan from the Reconstruction Finance Corporation. With the silver, the Cubans could create $15 million in coinage to pay its internal debts. Roosevelt was intrigued with this solution, and several versions of it were under study at the State and Treasury Departments.[32]

To work out the details of a financial aid program, Céspedes called for the immediate dispatch of a team of U.S. financial experts. However, so as not to appear too dependent upon the United States, and in view of inflamed Cuban nationalism, the Cuban president asked that delegation members do their work quietly as experts attached to the U.S. embassy staff rather than as official government representatives. On August 31, Adolf Berle (on this occasion as special counsel for the Reconstruction Finance Corporation) and two Treasury officials left for Havana. Their report, submitted on September 5, set out a broad program of debt refinancing, proposing that Cuban government revenues be allocated first to general expenses and back salary claims and only later to debt repayment. This proposal, reflecting the new priorities, placed Cuban stability ahead of the interests of the bankers. It did not come in time, however, to save the Céspedes regime, which succumbed on the night of September 4–5, 1933.[33]

U.S. Cuban Policy at the Fall of Carlos Manuel de Céspedes

The demise of the Céspedes regime (whose overthrow will be discussed in chapter 8) not only ended the hope for a constitutional and moderate government in Cuba, but left U.S. economic policy up in the air. The State Department would spend the next six months trying to work out the U.S. side of the proposals for financial, trade, and sugar market reform, while waiting for the return of a regime in Cuba which was willing to negotiate "reasonable" agreements along these lines. It is expressive of U.S. hegemony in Cuba that, despite the temporary absence of a cooperative government on the island, the development of Cuban policy within the U.S. and Cuban bureaucracies went forward much the same as before.

We have seen that by the fall of Céspedes debt policy had reached the stage where the State Department was considering the report of the Berle mission, which called for a partial default to relieve some of the pressing needs of the domestic economy. Sugar policy, at the end of the Céspedes interregnum, was less clear. Nobody, least of all those advocating Cuban interests, was satisfied with the proposals which issued from the industry conference and subsequent public hearings in Washington in the summer of 1933. By September, the decision on a sugar program, including quota allocations, was back in the hands of the secretary of agriculture for approval. Though the beet interests put great pressure upon him, the secretary finally decided that the program would not cause production to be held to expected demand, and thus would fail to stem the chaos in the sugar industry caused by abysmally low prices. Moreover, the program favored processors and refiners in such a way that any price increases which did occur would be absorbed before they reached the growers. On October 9, Wallace rejected the agreement. The demise of the industry's plan of rationalization saved Cuba from a program less benign than that favored by the State Department, and gave that department the opportunity to lobby once again for a stabilizing quota for the island. When the new U.S. government–inspired proposal appeared in February 1934 (after the fall of the nationalist regime of Ramón Grau San Martín) the island's sugar industry received somewhat better treatment.[34]

In the area of trade policy, the fall of the Céspedes government ended the discussions of a new trade treaty. However, it did not halt the formulation by U.S. exporters and the Departments of Commerce and State of the price they were eventually going to ask in return for granting Cuba a secured share of the U.S. sugar market. By the early autumn of 1933, Department of Commerce figures—which had been showing over the previous four years an immense decline in the *value* of U.S. trade with Cuba—began for the first time to show a decline in the U.S. *share* of the Cuban market. Devaluation of European and Japanese currencies had preceded that of the dollar, and their goods—despite the preferential tariff rates on U.S. products—were biting into the traditional U.S. domination of the Cuban market. Moreover, the dismally low level of purchasing power in Cuba put many U.S. products out of the reach of the island's consumers. The trade treaty formulators therefore desired not only to restore Cuban purchasing power by easier entry of Cuban sugar into the United States, but to arrange the island's tariffs, tariff preferences, and customs taxes so that the United States would reassert its dominance in most lines of Cuban imports. Because there were also certain U.S. products for which Cuba itself—under the protection of Machado's 1927 tariff—was the main competitor, the trade negotiators also set their sights on some of the island's domestic lines of production.

The major studies produced during this period by both the U.S. export community (Phillip Jessup's 247-page "Analysis of the United States Export Trade with Cuba") and the U.S. consul in Havana (the four-month, 21-part "Effects of Increased Cuban Tariffs upon Imports from the United States") concluded that the United States was losing its share of the Cuban trade. To restore its "competitive" position, the studies reported, the precise impediment (tariff, preference, classification, customs charges, internal taxes, and so on) for each line of U.S. exports would have to be determined and then remedied in a new treaty.

Among other things, the studies envisioned increased interference by the United States in the domestic Cuban economy. They proposed such things as the binding of tariff rates and product classification against alteration by the Cuban government and the restriction of the rights of internal taxation. The Jessup Study, in referring to Cuba's tariff-protected industries, spoke of the "difficulty" on the part of the United States "in determining which of these industries are entitled to persist" (p. 28). In a reference to Cuba's internal taxes, Jessup concluded that "it would not appear to be a disservice to Cuba to induce her to abandon the complicated system of taxes bearing indirectly on imports" (p. 73). As an indication of the place of Open Door doctrine in the context of the Caribbean, Jessup, upon observing that many items of U.S. export would remain uncompetitive even with a higher rate of preference, unselfconsciously concluded that in such cases it might be necessary to *raise* the Cuban tariff (pp. 74, 79).

The study by the U.S. consul sounded even less Good Neighborly. Speaking of salt: "Should the import duty be reduced and the preference of thirty percent be retained, the United States would still have a monopoly in this trade and be able to compete again with Cuban salt" (637.113/42). Speaking of automobile tires: "While no greater preferential than twenty percent is needed at this time, it would not be inappropriate to increase this preferential to a point which would maintain this quasi-monopoly" (637.113/47). On glassware: "A fifty percent decrease in duty will allow American manufacturers again to dominate this very important bottle trade." The villain in this latter case was not foreign competition, because there was none; the only other producer was "one large factory in Havana" (637.113/49). Thus, in this instance, the point of attack was the Cuban tariff. When it came to light bulbs, however, the competition was Japanese, and here the consul concluded that "only a sharp increase in the present tariff rate . . . will be able to restore this very important trade in this article to the United States" (637.113/49). Indicative of the close working relation between the export group which employed Jessup and the State Department was the fact that the consular reports were made available to Jessup, and his study in turn was closely read by the Commerce and State Departments and by the U.S. embassy in Havana.[35]

Just as in the quest for political stability Welles acted to strengthen U.S. direction of Cuban politics, so in the name of economic recovery the State Department sought to increase U.S. domination of the Cuban economy. The rhetoric of political and economic liberalism notwithstanding, Cuba was being bound ever more tightly in its relationship to the United States.

Such was the stage of development of Cuban policy when once again the Cuban president was swept from the scene. To understand the origins of this event we will have to return to a study of Cuban politics and social struggle and examine what the State Department perceived as the collapse of Cuban stability and what most Cubans refer to as the "Revolution of 1933."

CHAPTER EIGHT

The Cuban Revolution of September 1933

THE STRUGGLE AGAINST MACHADO, while it focused upon the tyranny of the regime and united diverse groups in Cuban society in the struggle against it, was also an expression of class conflict and antihegemonic nationalism. While the class and national struggles threatened U.S. interests, they cut across one another and offered U.S. diplomatic representatives the opportunity to exchange U.S. support in removing the dictator for cooperation from the moderate elements of each struggle—the conservative classes and the less militant nationalists. The U.S. ambassador, as we shall see, was able to promote a government of these forces, and sought to provide it with economic assistance and an image of sovereignty so as to remove the basis for proletarian and radical nationalist agitation. However, the historical weakness of the conservative social base, the top-down nature of U.S. economic relief, and the tainted origins of the new regime rendered it incapable of securing relief from radical pressures.

In the end, the conservative-moderate solution to the Machadato did not hold. It was succeeded by a period (however brief) of nationalist rule which, while it developed no effective program, did respond to the deep-seated resentment of *dependencia* felt by large segments of the Cuban people.

The Céspedes Interregnum

The Céspedes government was composed mainly of those elements of the opposition to Machado who had joined the mediation conducted by the U.S. ambassador. Its membership was strongly pro–United States, and its relationship to Welles so close as to cause even the latter some embarrassment. Céspedes himself had been born and educated in the United States, had served with the U.S. Army and later the Military Government, and had known Welles during his ministership to the United States at the time of the Wilson administration. His cabinet was dominated by moderate, middle-class nationalist leaders of the ABC, the UN, and the OCRR, plus several "nonpolitical" figures. He also appointed to high municipal office in Havana two "respectable" members of Machado's Liberal party.[1]

Though the government and its patron in the U.S. embassy desired a period of calm, from the outset they were under public pressure to carry out a far-reaching purge of the personnel and institutions of the Machadato. Indeed, the level of civil unrest did not diminish after the fall of Machado. For a week after the overthrow of the dictator, mobs hunted his closest supporters and murdered several members of the hated death squad of Machado's terrorist police organization, the Porra. The general strike, because it was both a political and an economic movement, did not immediately cease after August 12. Many groups returned to work, but some unions stayed out for weeks afterward, and new strike waves, though on a lesser scale, broke out under Céspedes, especially outside Havana. The proletariat seemed hardly to notice the end of the Machadato.[2]

The continued unrest forced the government to present a "nationalist" program, though its commitment to stability kept this program from having any effective political content. Nor could the regime meet the public demand that all appointed and elective high officials of the late Machado period be dismissed and that summary trials be held for the hundreds of Machadistas accused of crimes. The amnesty law of July, which Welles had sanctioned, stood in the way of such a move, and Welles continued to declare publicly "that only legal methods and civil tribunals" should be used to enforce the laws. Indeed, the legal basis of the Céspedes regime itself was the constitutional amendments and legislative acts of the late Machadato. A situation was fast approaching in which either the regime's remaining popular support or constitutional procedure would have to be sacrificed.

In the face of continuing proletarian agitation and declining middle-class support, the government, on August 24, annulled the constitutional amendments of 1928 and declared in force the original 1901 constitution which those amendments had largely revoked. Céspedes dissolved the Machado Congress and dismissed most of the office holders of the second Machado term. With the dissolution of the Congress, there disappeared the last vestige of the constitutional legitimacy for which Welles had maneuvered so unceasingly in the last weeks of the Machadato. Even with these acts, however, the Céspedes regime was still only a pale reflection of the forceful new departure which much of the middle class and even the ABC members of the government were demanding. Because of its desperate need for U.S. approval, the Céspedes regime could not invalidate the *acts* of the Machado government—even though they had declared its legal basis invalid. To do so would have dissolved many of the "international obligations" (especially state and private debts) which bound Cuba to the United States—and this the U.S. embassy would have found unacceptable.[3]

By returning to the 1901 constitution, which only the conservative opposition had made a central demand, the government did not actually regain much support. In effect, its only major backing throughout its entire twenty-three days of existence was the U.S. embassy.

Sumner Welles and the Céspedes Regime

The creation of the Céspedes government on August 12 had seemed to herald the complete success of Welles's program. Roosevelt and Hull cabled their congratulations to the Havana embassy, and recognition of the new regime was automatically extended since, as Hull put it, "the change of Government had been achieved by constitutional process." Welles described various members of the new cabinet (which he had approved in advance) as "conservative," "non-partisan," "outstanding," and concluded that the body was "of a high-class, representative character." The U.S. ambassador was pleased that "the military have taken a very determined attitude" toward the vengeance-seeking crowds that were filling the streets, and he was confident that the striking unions, as a patriotic act, would soon return to work.[4]

Yet all was not well, and on the very day Céspedes took office, Welles asked that two U.S. destroyers be sent to Havana in case post-Machado rioting should get out of hand. The public announcement of the dispatch of the vessels was made by Roosevelt on August 13. To help square this act of gunboat diplomacy with Good Neighborism, the president declared that the warships were sent "solely for the purpose of safeguarding and protecting the lives and persons of American citizens in Cuba" and that "no possible question of intervention or of the slightest interference with the internal affairs of Cuba had arisen or is intended." Welles, for his part, told Hull that "if the [general] strike is broken today [August 14] as I anticipate conditions may become normal rapidly and in that event the two ships might well leave after forty-eight hours."[5]

Welles pinned his hopes for the new government on the popularity and reform program of the ABC, for whose presence in the cabinet he was responsible. Although he considered their program "radical," he worked hard at gaining their confidence because their willingness to join a government of more conservative leanings might give that body the nationalist legitimacy it sorely needed. Such legitimacy might stem the growing demands for the ousting of the Congress (which could not meet in any event, as its members had fled the country or were in hiding) and for other unconstitutional acts the prospect of which so disturbed the U.S. ambassador.[6]

On August 15, however, just three days into the new government, the secretary of war visited Welles and told him that public pressure (including that applied by the younger army officers) for the removal of all office holders of the Machadato was becoming unbearable and that some action was necessary. Welles immediately went to see Céspedes and "suggested" that the president declare that all those guilty of crimes would be brought to trial "through legal channels" and that until then the public should halt all forced displacement of office holders. Céspedes agreed to do so.[7]

At this point, though still underestimating the radical forces at work, Welles began to conclude that despite the backing of the old political parties, the conservative opposition, and the ABC, the new government might not be able to create stability in Cuba. In addition to growing labor and student unrest, Welles was slowly coming to perceive the effect which his own relationship with the regime was having on its ability to govern. On August 19, Welles told Hull that "after considerable reflection I feel that in the best interest of our Government I should be recalled . . . not later than the first of September." Welles explained:

> My personal situation is becoming increasingly difficult. Owing to my intimate personal friendship with President Céspedes and the very close relationship which I have formed during these past months with all of the members of his Cabinet I am now daily being requested for decisions on all matters affecting the Government of Cuba. These decisions range from questions of domestic policy and matters affecting the discipline of the Army to questions involving appointments in all branches of the Government.

Welles suggested that his designated successor (Jefferson Caffery) remove himself as much as possible from open involvement in internal Cuban affairs. He considered it damaging to U.S. relations with Latin America "for the American Embassy here to possess the measure of control over the Government which it now does possess." However, Welles's Good Neighbor attitude remained more image than substance, for he added that "Caffery unquestionably will obtain all of the needed influence immediately after his arrival but it will be an influence exerted behind the scenes and not apparent to the public." Welles further evidenced his reluctance to diminish U.S. control over Cuban affairs by concluding that should a crisis arise "it would presumably be best for me to remain until it is straightened out because of the contacts which I now have." Thus, Welles's self-consciousness was rather circumscribed. Roosevelt agreed to the request, and Welles's return was scheduled for September 15.[8]

By the third week of August, Welles had turned even more pessimistic. He noted the growing desire to "transform the present government of Cuba into a purely revolutionary *de facto* government." This move he continued strenuously to resist, feeling that such a "form of government would in all likelihood result in general chaos." However, on August 24 he had to report to Hull that such a condition already existed. He noted the "almost anarchic condition throughout the country" and concluded that "my original hope that the present Government of Cuba could govern as a constitutional government for the remainder of the term for which General Machado had himself elected must be abandoned." Nevertheless, the resourceful Welles had yet another plan. The Supreme Court would declare the 1928 Machado constitution invalid and restore the 1901 charter. The incumbent Congress (in office by virtue of the 1928 Act) would thus be dissolved, and Céspedes would then call national elections for three months hence. Welles had discussed this new plan with Céspedes and with all the major political leaders outside the Marxist and radical nationalist movements, and judged them to be in agreement. The day after this meeting Céspedes issued a decree which generally followed the program that Welles had worked out with the Cuban leadership.[9]

This new dispensation allowed the Céspedes government to rule by decree, but as a client of the United States it still could not take the steps necessary to satisfy growing popular demands for sovereignty and economic security. Just a few days before the demise of the regime, Welles finally took notice of the "epidemic of strikes which have swept the Republic" and began to interpret the economic demands of the Cuban proletariat as central to the condition of unrest in the republic. On August 30, a delegation of prominent U.S. businessmen in Cuba expressed to the ambassador their great concern with the labor situation. Welles disagreed with their fears of a Communist revolution, not believing that "Communist theories as such have as yet any support among the laboring classes." He did, however, acknowledge to Hull that "the conditions of distress and actual destitution which exist cannot be exaggerated." As a New Deal liberal, Welles had a paternalistic sympathy for downtrodden labor, and he acknowledged that their impoverished condition and the suppression of their organizations had made them "ripe for agitation" and that many of their demands were reasonable. Since business was unprofitable, the only way to forestall some manner of revolutionary disturbance, according to the ambassador, was to initiate a program of economic relief from the United States in the form of loans, sugar quotas, and increased trade.[10]

However, the economic arrangements that the U.S. ambassador thought would pacify the Cuban proletariat and make the middle class a conservative force once again did not come in time. The radical forces built up in Cuban society through nine long years of economic decline and political repression would finally find their outlet. For the first time in Cuban history, a regime was to be created in the island in contradiction to the wishes of the United States.

The Origins of the Overthrow of Céspedes
Labor

The general strike of early August which led to the removal of Machado was in part a multiclass assault on dictatorship and in part a syndicalist labor offensive. While the middle class quickly reopened their shops and took up their professions once the tyrant was removed, many unions remained on strike to obtain specific economic demands. Other more radical unions continued to agitate for both economic gains and political power. The port workers in Havana did not return to work until August 22, when their union recognition and other demands were met. While most Havana unions were back at work by late August, this was only because owners had agreed to workers' demands. When it became apparent that these new contracts could be honored only by a return of prosperity, new walkouts occurred.

The strike wave in the interior actually expanded after August 12. In Santiago, the second largest city, radical and Communist unions called for the overthrow of Céspedes as well, and about half of the workers stayed on strike. By the end of the month a new general strike was impending there. The railroad workers' strike in the eastern provinces continued throughout August, attended by conditions of worker starvation and sabotage of rail facilities. There were also strikes by tobacco workers in Pinar del Río and by coffee workers in Oriente. The government declared the continuing walkouts "counter-revolutionary," but because it was loath to use Machado's brutal antilabor methods and because the army also had no desire of being accused of Machadista tactics, no concerted antistrike effort was mounted.

The most significant stoppages were occurring in the sugar mills and fields. In the sugar harvest strike of 1932–1933, workers for the first time had seized a mill. On August 21, under the leadership of Communist labor officials, *central* Punta Alegre (a large U.S.-owned mill) was seized and a "soviet" was organized. The next ten days brought strikes at dozens of mills, with the most significant ones occurring at *centrales* Preston and Boston, the huge mills owned by the United Fruit Company. As August ended, it was becoming clear that the agricultural proletariat, the backbone of the Cuban economy, had reached the end of its endurance. No government which ignored their desperate situation or which had no viable alternative to the socialist doctrine of their leaders could long stand. [11]

Students

Another force in the struggle against Machado which was not part of the mediation or the Céspedes government was that of student groups. In most cases, they did not return to their classes after August 12. They considered Céspedes a tool of the U.S. government and saw his regime as an effort to compromise the victory of reformist forces over the dictatorship.

With the exception of the small group of Marxists among them, the activist students envisioned their struggle as a continuation of the efforts of José Martí to forge a national unity and to complete the struggle of the 1890s for sovereignty, frustrated in the intervening years by the United States. Their politics were Jacobin, with a strong attachment to Martí's vision of a just society. By 1933, after many had endured exile in Europe and in North and Latin America, the student leaders had incorporated elements of fascism, communism, Spanish Republicanism, and even the New Deal into their ideology. In the struggle against Machado, they espoused the complete uprooting of the personal and institutional foundations of the dictatorship, including the political parties, the army, and the university. They also stood for an end to political and economic dependence on the United States.[12]

Student thinking became isolated from both middle-class and proletarian ideology in the summer of 1933. Up to that time, a significant number of student activists had participated in the terrorist activities of the ABC, and there was a growing influence of ABC doctrine among students. At the same time, a small but growing number of students were attracted to communism, and some young recruits entered the CCP or the Marxist student organization, the Ala Izquierda Estudiantil. However, the acceptance of U.S. mediation by the ABC ended the influence of that body on student organizations, while the CCP's attempt to make a deal with the dictator for ending the general strike created a long-lasting distrust of Cuban communism within mainstream student politics. In the months to come, some of the most biting criticism of the ABC and the CCP came from the Directorio Estudiantil, which reflected the position of the largest number of activist students, especially at the University of Havana.

The student movement treated the Céspedes regime as transitional, and as early as the middle of August rumors circulated that the students were attempting to bring about a revolt within the army. The desperate effort by the Céspedes government to achieve a "revolutionary" stance by restoring the 1901 constitution and declaring the late Machadato illegal in no way satisfied the students. They considered the 1901 charter, closely modeled on that of the United States, as itself a symbol of dependence, and on August 24 the Directorio put forward its own program. The manifesto denounced the government and especially the ABC as having betrayed the anti-Machado struggle by accepting U.S. interference. It demanded the liquidation of all the political forces which supported the Machadato and called for a new government to promulgate a new nationalist constitution which would include full democratic rights, social legislation, educational reforms, alienation of foreign land holdings, and taxation of native latifundia. It called upon all Cubans to fight against oppression, latifundism, and intervention. A special appeal of the Directorio manifesto was directed toward the Cuban Army, and in the latter part of August there were increased contacts between the two organizations. Recognizing the decisive part played by the army in the removal of Machado, the students, like many other groups in Cuba, were reassessing their relations with that body.[13]

The Army

Though the officer corps of the Cuban Army had struck the final and decisive blow against Machado, its members were very uneasy about having done so, and throughout the Céspedes regime they remained ambivalent as to their role. The officer corps above the rank of captain was made up of several groups with differing attitudes toward the dictatorship. There were those who had supported the Machadato actively, those who despite their dislike of the dictator had refused to join the movement against him, those who joined only when the movement was inevitable and whose motives were self-serving, and finally those who actively opposed Machado and moved to overthrow him because of fidelity to their honor as soldiers or to one or another political creed current among the civil opposition. The principal division within the officer corps, however, was that between the younger officers, who suffered in their advancement from the reappointment of retired officers for political reasons (especially under Céspedes), and the older officers, whose loyalty to Machado (or now to Céspedes) took precedence over their professional concerns. To gain relief, the junior men, aligning themselves with the popular hostility to the top officers, called for a reorganization of the corps and for their right to participate in the process. Another fracture separated the junior officers from the noncommissioned officers, whose advance to commissioned status had been greatly accelerated under Machado. This competition was resented by the graduates of the service institutions.

Civilian efforts to politicize the military were common in the republican period, and thus the anti-Machado struggle had its reflection within the Cuban Army. Supporters of ex-President Menocal could be found among the senior officers, while student and ABC influence was strongest among junior officers. Radical youth had contacts, though not extensive ones, with noncommissioned officers and enlisted men.[14]

Whereas senior officers had dealt the coup de grâce to Machado, the termination of the Céspedes regime was the work—albeit inadvertent—of the noncommissioned ranks. The sergeants and corporals were dismayed by the barriers raised by the post-Machado general staff to the entry of enlisted men into the officer corps. Their hope of gaining officer status was accentuated because, despite the economic depression, officers managed to maintain many of the amenities of middle-class civilian life, whereas the noncommissioned rank shared the great privation of the common soldier and worker. Differences in life-style between the commissioned and noncommissioned officers were not only a matter of pay. The day-to-day business of commanding the troops was left to sergeants, who lived a typical barracks life; the officers rarely spent a night on an army post, retiring instead to their residences in the city. Thus, the noncommissioned officers acted as foremen for the absentee officer class. This role of responsibility without reward was resented by the noncommissioned officers, but it did put control of the garrisons (especially at night) in their hands. This fact was to assume paramount importance.[15]

By mid-August, rumors of impending reductions in military force levels and salaries were rife. Against this background, and acting from a desire both to facilitate their own advance into the higher ranks and to adopt the protective coloration (and in some cases the substance) of "revolutionary" politics, the sergeants began to organize a movement to gain support for redress of their grievances. The interest-group organizing of the junior officers no doubt influenced this process. Sergeant Pablo Rodríguez organized a series of meetings with some of his fellow noncommissioned officers, including José E. Pedraza, Manuel López Migoya, and a sergeant stenographer then assigned to the office of the chief of the Army Secret Service—Fulgencio Batista. While radical nationalist groups were attempting to turn the officer corps against Céspedes, this small group of sergeants was meeting to discuss such mundane matters as protecting sergeants accused of collaboration with Machado, demands for the restoration of clothing and food rations, complaints of having to ride in third-class rail coaches, domestic service for officers, and the lack of opportunity to enter cadet school.[16]

By late August, the circle of sergeants had expanded and had formed a "Junta de Defensa." Because of their focal position in regard to the troops and armament stores, the sergeants were in a favorable position to launch a coup against the officers. The officer corps was especially susceptible to a revolt from below at this time because their association (especially in the higher ranks) with the Machadato had undermined their authority over the troops and because they were under great pressure from civilian forces to prove their loyalty to the "people." Therefore, they found it necessary to ignore signs of insubordination coming from the hardly secret meetings of the sergeants' Junta.[17]

Toward the end of the month, there began a process whereby the status-conscious *sargentado* was maneuvered into the current of radical nationalism. It was this combination that produced the coup of the night of September 4–5 and initiated the "Cuban Revolution of 1933."

The Coup of September 4–5

As noted above, the general staff had become aware of the meetings of the sergeants' junta which were taking place at the Enlisted Men's Club at

Camp Columbia. However, in view of the larger problems posed by the wave of militant strikes and the occasional fraternization of soldiers with strikers, the officers were not especially alarmed by a movement of sergeants whose main concern was the defense of their rights. They did act, however, to allay the fears of dismissals and pay reductions that were eating into army morale at all levels and of which the Junta de Defensa was an expression. To deal with the growing civilian strike threat and with the failing discipline in the ranks, Céspedes named the anti-Machado conspirator Colonel Horacio Ferrer as secretary of war on August 29. Ferrer acted on both fronts, ordering on September 1 both the arrest of all armed civilians and army intervention into serious strike situations. In addition, on September 3 he announced there would be no reduction of pay or force levels in the armed forces.[18]

These actions, however, did not deter the sergeants' movement, which by this time had gained a favorable hearing from many of the privates and corporals and was beginning to appreciate its own strength. They pressed on, holding more meetings, hoping to gain enough support to present their promotion and pay demands effectively to the general staff.[19]

On September 1, a severe hurricane had hit the provinces just east of Havana, and the following day President Céspedes and the chief of the general staff had left on an inspection tour. The confusion caused by the storm and absence of the chief of staff led to rumors of an impending coup by Menocalista officers. It is probable that the sergeants' junta, though still not fully sure of purpose or even methods, now decided to take action to force agreement with their demands. There is no clear evidence, however, that they intended to mutiny, much less bring down the government. A meeting of sergeants and enlisted men was called for the morning of September 4 at Camp Columbia.[20]

Colonel Julio Sanguily, acting chief of staff, learned of the September 4 meeting and asked a popular young officer, Captain Mario Torres-Menier, to attend as an unofficial spokesman for the general staff. Though now aware of the unrest in the ranks, the officer corps still took no action to suppress it. The sergeants had not expected a member of the general staff to be at the meeting, and Torres-Menier, for his part, was surprised by the size of the meeting and the combativeness of the speakers. The young captain spoke to the meeting, again denying the rumors of reductions in pay and forces, stating further that actions would soon be taken to improve the conditions of the enlisted men. He was then barraged with complaints of past ignoring of enlisted men's requests. Batista's contribution to the meeting was more high-minded and political, possibly with a view to the potential of the sergeants' movement. He spoke of the rights not only of soldiers, but of all citizens, and of the sacrifices which the group was willing to make for the nation. By the end of the meeting tempers were short. Torres-Menier agreed to carry their grievances to the general staff, and the sergeants called another meeting for that afternoon to formulate specific demands.[21]

To strengthen themselves further, the leaders of the movement spent the rest of the day contacting all nearby installations, gathering support for their demands. The officer corps, however, still did not appreciate the seriousness of the situation and decided to await the formal list of demands which was expected later in the day. At eight o'clock that evening, in the movie theater at Camp Columbia, a large meeting of noncommissioned officers and enlisted men was held. Though accounts do not agree, the outcome of the meeting was a conviction that the general staff had rejected their demands and that they would seize the military installations and some of the officers to force compliance.

Toward midnight, while sergeants set out to take command of all the major military facilities, the civil opposition began to hear of the events at Camp Columbia, and soon members of the Directorio and assorted other radical nationalists arrived. In a decisive development, the student leaders convinced the sergeants to broaden their protest/revolt, and then sat down to write a political manifesto. This document declared the replacement of the Céspedes regime by a "Provisional Revolutionary Government," thus initiating the first Cuban regime ever formed against the wishes of the United States. An executive commission of five, usually known as the Pentarchy, was chosen to run the country.[22]

Sumner Welles and the Coup of September 4–5

Though by late August Welles was pessimistic about Céspedes' chances for survival, he seemed unaware of the forces that would topple the president. As early as August 20, Welles had received word of a possible revolt against the army officers, but he discounted it. Military Attaché Gimperling saw no trouble brewing in the army. He reported that the post-Machado general staff was handling its task well, and that he was making "tactful and helpful suggestions," especially regarding the handling of "the communistic elements."

By the end of the month, however, Gimperling concluded that the government was not backing the army in the effort to control labor unrest and that communism, chaos, and anarchy were likely, in which case he suggested U.S. military intervention. Welles was not as panicky, but from the daily reports on conditions in the island which the Cuban secretary of war was generous enough to supply, he knew of the breakdown of public order. When the hurricane struck on September 1, Welles telephoned Hull to say that "I am afraid this may be the last straw." It was.

Late on the evening of September 4, Welles was called back to the embassy and told of the sergeants' action. Almost immediately, and throughout most of the night, representatives of the Céspedes government came to the embassy, where Welles urged them to stand firm. About 1:00 A.M., however, Secretary of War Ferrer arrived and informed the ambassador that all major military installations throughout the island were in the hands of the noncommissioned officers. Welles then cabled Hull of the "complete collapse of government throughout the island" and recommended the return of U.S. warships to Havana.[23]

Early the next morning, Welles called Hull to report that "a revolutionary government has been set up, composed of the most extreme radicals in Cuba."[24] This was either a misjudgment or a deception by the ambassador, which, in any case, reflected his innate hostility to unconstitutional regimes, especially those not of his own choosing.

The First Days of the "Revolutionary Government"

While the rhetoric of the forces that came to power on September 4–5 was more militant and nationalistic than that of the conservative Machado opposition which comprised the Céspedes regime, the "revolutionary government" acted very warily and without any definitive program. Like any political movement in Cuba, the coup of September 4–5 had to make its peace with U.S. hegemony. Batista's first public statement contained vague promises of honest revolutionary leadership and an end to the old corrupt politics of the parties, combined with specific assurances that order would be maintained and the life and property of foreign nationals protected. Sergio Carbó, a civilian leader of the revolt (described by Welles to the State Department as a "communist"), declared the new government to be neither communist nor socialist but a "pure revolutionary government of all classes."[25]

By the early morning of September 5, the civilian groups now allied with the sergeants' movement had put together a political program. Calling themselves, appropriately, "Agrupación Revolucionaria," they proclaimed to the Cuban people that they stood for "modern" democracy, national sovereignty, and "a new Cuba." They promised to call a constituent assembly, to cleanse the crimes of the Machadato, to protect foreign nationals and their property, and to "strictly respect" the debts and treaty obligations of the republic. There was no reference to ending Yankee domination.[26]

The Agrupación Revolucionaria, composed of the Directorio Estudiantil, ABC Radical, and several other radical nationalist factions and individuals, elected a Pentarchy to run the country until the forthcoming constituent assembly could name a government and set a date for general elections. The Pentarchy members were: Sergio Carbó (left nationalist, a publisher), José Irizarri (moderate, professor of finance), Guillermo Portela (moderate, professor of law and lawyer), Porfirio Franca (conservative, banker and business leader), and Ramón Grau San Martín (nationalist, professor of medicine and doctor). Of these, only Carbó even came close to deserving the description of "extreme radical" which Welles used to describe all but Porfirio Franca in his cable to the State Department. The U.S. ambassador referred to Franca (who had been manager of the Havana branch of the National City Bank and director of the Banco Nacional) as "window-dressing."[27] The first public statement by the Pentarchy called for the cooperation of all citizens in maintaining public order, and exhorted civil servants to remain at their posts.[28]

If the Pentarchy was proceeding with great moderation, the sergeants were showing signs of actual regret. Even when they took command from their superiors on the night of September 4, the sergeants' junta had not contemplated actual revolt, much less revolution. Batista, for example, most likely wished only that the Agrupación Revolucionaria adopt the enlisted men's grievances. However, he was convinced by his friend Carbó, with whom he had a long private talk that evening, to put his name (and indirectly that of the army) to the broad political statement which proclaimed the "Provisional Revolutionary Government." Most other members of the sergeants' movement preferred to ignore the "Revolutionary Government" and to do no more than use their new and more powerful position as a way of gaining adherence to their demands from the old general staff. The preponderant thinking among the group seems not to have gone beyond a proposal calling on the general staff to set up a "Junta Militar" headed by the chief of the general staff but to include some sergeants. In return, the rebels expected to reinstate the officers in their commands and continue to recognize the Céspedes government.[29]

Though fast becoming the most politicized of the army coup leaders, Batista was still uncertain as to how he should proceed. Indeed, at ten o'clock on the morning of September 5, he paid a call on the U.S. ambassador. Apparently he hoped to get a clear sign from Welles that the "revolutionary government" would be acceptable to the United States. However, Welles would give no assurances and was most interested in the measures the sergeants would take to "preserve the maintenance of public order."

While he does not seem to have committed himself at this point, Batista was nonetheless being forced in the direction of militancy because the meetings with the officers indicated their unwillingness to accept anything less than the complete restoration of their authority. In the next two days, Batista's position as de facto head of the army was consolidated, but his official statements still referred to the possible return of the officers, and he alternately signed his public statements as "Chief of the Movement" or "Sergeant Chief of the Revolutionary Forces" rather than appropriating the title of commander in chief of the Cuban Army.[30]

The radical nationalist forces which had attached themselves to the noncommissioned officers' mutiny were acting with somewhat greater resolve.

Nevertheless, they too were keeping one eye on the U.S. embassy and the warships which, pursuant to Welles's request of September 5, were returning to Cuban harbors, this time in greater number. For their part, the Directorio Estudiantil bravely announced that with the fall of a government designated by the U.S. ambassador, Cuba was now a truly sovereign state. They urged a take-over of the government apparatus by the "revolutionary" forces and an implementation of their nationalist manifesto of August 24. The Pentarchy, however, was more concerned with the hostile attitude Welles was manifesting and preoccupied with its fear of U.S. intervention to restore Céspedes. Thus, the five men spent most of their time during the first days of the revolt negotiating with the government they had overthrown. Like many of the sergeants, they were trying to put part of the omelet back into the eggshell. Thus, while the noncommissioned officers were negotiating conditions for a partial return of the authority of the general staff, the Pentarchy was discussing with Céspedes' cabinet the creation of a coalition government. Eventually, however, this attempt at negotiating the extent of the "revolution" was to fail, partly because the rebels' sense of mission made them loath to give up the opportunity to create a "new Cuba," but also because the U.S. ambassador encouraged the Céspedes forces to believe that his country would help them to return to full power.[31]

Sumner Welles and the Revolutionary Pentarchy

While Sumner Welles was not totally surprised by the fall of Céspedes, he was unprepared for the army mutiny. Moreover, he resented the new Provisional Revolutionary Government because it represented those forces which opposed his mediation and because it destroyed the conservative outcome to the end of the Machadato for which he had labored so strenuously. At times this resentment led him to make emotional judgments, but, as we shall see, there was usually some method to his madness.

Welles's initial response to the new government, as noted above, was to describe it as radical and illegitimate and to call for the return of U.S. warships to Cuba. He understood the disinclination of Roosevelt and Hull to intervene, and from the outset his bleak picture of conditions in Cuba was likely meant to prepare Washington in case he should request that strong measures be taken. Less than twenty-four hours after the revolt, Welles cabled Hull: "It appears hardly likely that a so-called revolutionary government composed of enlisted men of the Army and radical students . . . can form a government 'adequate for the protection of life, property and individual liberty.'"

By using the exact language of the intervention clause of the Platt Amendment, he was telling Hull, in effect, that the legal basis for U.S. intervention was about to be established. Indeed, Welles suggested that this possibility be explained to the Latin American diplomatic corps so as to minimize possible damage to the new Good Neighbor image in the event such action was undertaken. In that there was little violence attendant upon the fall of Céspedes, Welles was hard pressed to substantiate the image of growing anarchy conveyed by his messages to the State Department. Phrases such as "I anticipate a renewal of the general strike," and "It is highly problematical how many hours or days will elapse before violence and open dissensions take place throughout the Republic," recurred in his dispatches.[32]

While preparing the State Department for the worst, Welles began almost continuous conferences with the supporters of the Céspedes government in an effort to convince them that the United States favored their return to power. After seeing Batista at ten o'clock on the morning of September 5, the U.S. ambassador received the members of Céspedes' cabinet together with all the major conservative and moderate political leaders on the island. Welles told them of his view that the Pentarchy could not govern effectively and that chaos would result. In the light of later events, it is likely that he explained some of the difficulties involved in obtaining agreement from Washington for a military intervention. Possibly hoping that a proposal for U.S. help coming from "responsible" Cuban leadership would gain a sympathetic hearing from Roosevelt, Welles asked the group to devise a plan "to prevent the utter breakdown of government." These "responsible" Cuban leaders agreed to formulate such a proposal and present it to him later in the day. The discussion then turned to an imminent meeting between Céspedes and the Pentarchy. It was proposed that Céspedes offer one or more posts in his cabinet to the "revolutionaries" in return for their recognition of his presidency.[33]

At noon the cabinet and the U.S. ambassador went to the presidential palace for the meeting with the Pentarchy. While the rebels, because of their concern for U.S. approval, were willing to form a coalition with the more conservative anti-Machado forces, they could not accept Céspedes, who had become the symbol of U.S. interference in Cuban affairs. They thus turned down the offer made by the cabinet. In the face of this rejection, and in the light of reports from across the island that the noncommissioned officers were in full control of the armed forces, the cabinet did not resist Céspedes' decision to resign. (Céspedes had been a reluctant president from the start, and the conclusion even of his supporters was that his leadership had been extremely weak.) The resignation of the Cuban president, immediately followed by that of his cabinet, must have been a blow to Welles. These developments suggested that a potential U.S. intervention could not be based on the restoration to power of an incumbent regime. This was sure to make the Washington officials even more leery of invoking the Platt Amendment.[34]

Despite this turn of events, the "responsible" leadership returned to the U.S. embassy late in the afternoon and presented their plan to restore a moderate regime. As Welles relayed the plan to Hull, it involved "the installation of a government composed of the chiefs of the [moderate] political groups," with Carlos Mendieta as president. The only problem was what to do about the rebel-controlled Cuban Army. Welles informed Hull that "it was the unanimous opinion [of this group] that the only way in which a government of the character proposed could be maintained in power, until a new Army could be organized under the Cuban Army officers, was for the maintenance of order in Havana and Santiago and perhaps one or two other points by American Marines." For added measure, the ambassador reported that Cuban leaders felt that in a day or two the Pentarchy would itself be replaced by "an out and out communist organization." Welles suggested that, until this group received the expected commitment from the army officers and was ready to act, a small number of troops be landed to guard the U.S. embassy and the National Hotel, which served as home for a large segment of the North American community in Havana. When asked by Hull how the United States would explain such action, Welles replied that its purpose was to protect U.S. citizens. Earlier in the day, Hull had indicated that if intervention were necessary it might be best for the United States to seek the cooperation of Argentina, Brazil, Chile, and Mexico. However, since only fifty marines were available on the ships already in Havana harbor, and since the battleships Richmond and Mississippi, with their large marine contingents, were not due for another day or more, the question of intervention was still moot. In a later telephone conversation that evening, Hull told Welles that Roosevelt had decided that the small group of marines on hand should be landed only in case of an attack upon the embassy and that "a broader policy" could be worked out by the time an intervention-sized force was expected to arrive.[35]

By the morning of September 6, Hull called Welles to say that the question of intervention had been discussed at the department and that the consensus was that short of complete anarchy no U.S. troops should be landed. Welles was urged to adopt a policy "of absolute neutrality towards ... the group in power." Hull concluded that "the army, as now constituted, for the time being is in supreme control," and that if the moderate forces "give such cooperation as the dominant forces are willing to receive" they might act as a moderating influence and calm things down to the point where the possibility of intervention would be removed. This position of the secretary of state was almost totally at odds with the actions taken by Welles since the coup. Where Hull was urging compromise and the necessity of avoiding intervention, the U.S. ambassador had been working day and night for almost thirty-six hours not only to overthrow the Pentarchy but to employ U.S. intervention to do so. Despite his diametrically opposed position, however, Welles responded to Hull that "I agree absolutely with everything you have said." Given the above interpretation of Welles's policy, this statement can only be described as an attempt to pacify or even deceive the secretary.[36]

President Roosevelt was concerned about the public discussion of possible intervention in Cuba. A force of 1,100 marines had been assembled at Quantico, Virginia, and the number of vessels sent to Cuban waters, from Coast Guard cutters to battleships, was approaching two dozen or more. At a news conference on September 6, the president insisted that the flotilla was being sent only for the protection of American lives and that intervention was "absolutely the last thing we have in mind." He did stress, however, that U.S. actions in regard to Cuba, because of the special treaty relationship existing, should not be taken as an indication of general Latin American policy. That afternoon, Roosevelt called in the ambassadors of Argentina, Brazil, Chile, and Mexico. He told them of his desire not to intervene and of his hope that the Cuban people would obtain a government "of their own choosing" and one "able to maintain order." In that case, he said, any thought of intervention would end.[37]

Though the U.S. ambassador claimed agreement with the noninterventionist desire of Hull and Roosevelt, his actions indicate that, with growing circumspection, he was still pursuing the possibility of a U.S. landing which would neutralize the Cuban Army long enough for Céspedes or another moderate to return to power. Late on the evening of the sixth, Céspedes' secretary of war, Horacio Ferrer, outlined a new plan to Welles. Ferrer believed that a sizable segment of the garrison at Cabaña Fortress supported the return of Céspedes. In a day or two, he stated, a large number of the officer corps, together with Céspedes and his cabinet, would go to Cabaña, expel the sergeants, and proclaim Céspedes the legitimate president. He expected that this would spark revolts at other garrisons, but to assure success, he hoped the United States might consider landing troops "to assist the Céspedes Government in maintaining order."

As a result of this meeting Welles sent a long dispatch to Hull in which he argued that Céspedes had headed a de jure government, duly recognized by all nations, and that this regime had not actually resigned but rather had been deposed. It was therefore in the United States' interest to support its return to power by "landing of a considerable force at Havana and lesser forces in certain of the more important ports of the Republic," until such time as the Cuban Army could be reorganized under the old officer corps.

Realizing that a condition of total anarchy was the only circumstance which Roosevelt and Hull had implied might warrant intervention, and inasmuch as there was actually *less* unrest in Havana now than during the three weeks of the Céspedes regime, Welles had to provide some new bases for intervention which would convince an unwilling State Department and at the same time protect the United States' Good Neighbor image. He thus proposed a "strictly limited intervention," which he described as "the lending of a police force to the legitimate Government of Cuba." His definitive defense of such an action, which might be characterized as the Welles Corollary, went as follows:

> When the recognized and legitimate government of a neighboring republic, with which republic we have special contractual obligations, is confronted by mutiny in the army and can only maintain order and carry through its program of holding election for a permanent constitutional government through the assistance of an armed force lent by the United States as a policing power, it would seem to me to be in our best interest to lend such assistance.

Welles conceded that such an action would "incur the violent animosity of the extreme radical and communist groups in Cuba," but added that these forces would oppose *any* action by the United States and that the other countries of Latin America, having knowledge of the true situation in Cuba, would construe the landing of troops "as well within the limits of the policy of the good neighbor."[38] Had Welles known in detail the strong nonintervention pledge which had been made in the recent consultations with the Latin American diplomats in Washington, he perhaps would have realized how anachronistic his "corollary" actually was. Such a statement is nevertheless illustrative of the interpretation of Good Neighbor doctrine by one of the United States' leading Latin American diplomats in 1933.

That evening, Roosevelt informed Welles that any promise of support to Cuban factions would be "regarded as a breach of neutrality" (which attitude Welles had supposedly been pursuing) and would "set up a government which would be regarded by the whole world, and especially throughout Latin America, as a creation and creature of the American Government." Hull added that any action contrary to Roosevelt's policy as outlined in the meeting with Latin American representatives, which had received wide public support, "would have disastrous effects." The secretary of state concluded diplomatically: "All of us appreciate the heavy load you are carrying and hope you may bear up well."[39]

Had Welles been out of touch only with the mood in Washington, this clear rebuff would most likely have caused him to give up the idea of a marine-backed restoration of Céspedes. But the U.S. ambassador had also lost touch with events in Havana. Believing reports from Céspedes' supporters that Batista was on the verge of placing the army behind Céspedes and that only a handful of radical students were blocking the plan, and expecting the Ferrer countercoup at any moment, Welles concluded that the most minor policing effort by the United States was all that was necessary to return the former government to power. While the situation in Havana was indeed very fluid, with both Batista and the Pentarchy still in discussions with Céspedes' backers and the officers as to how much "revolution" was to be traded for how much "stability," Welles's expectation of an imminent and total victory for the forces of "stability" was without foundation. Nevertheless, being so convinced, the U.S. ambassador decided on one more attempt to sell intervention to Washington.

On September 8 Welles cabled to Hull that the limited intervention he had proposed was no more than the lending of a police service to Cuba, more or less as we might facilitate a loan to the island. He was sure that such an act would not be interpreted as non-neutral by others, since all but a tiny fraction of Cubans supported Céspedes. Welles described the Pentarchy as supported only by a few university professors, some students, and a "heterogenous mass of extreme radicals of every shade." (Welles consistently underestimated the popular strength of the forces that overthrew Céspedes, but it is unlikely he was unaware of the broad sympathy, if not support, they received from a wide range of Cuban nationalist opinion.)

While painting the new regime as radical and unpopular, Welles depended most heavily on his dire predictions of future chaos and communism to win his point. He told the secretary of state that the army mutiny was originally organized by the Cuban Communist party and that the new government "was secretly committed to the semi-Communist program published by the extreme radical students two weeks ago." He concluded that "if this government continues much longer and no counterrevolt is successfully staged by the conservative groups it will be replaced by a soldier workman [government]," in which case complete anarchy would prevail and a full-scale military occupation would be forced upon the United States.[40]

There is no record of a specific response to Welles's third request for intervention. He did speak to Roosevelt by phone that evening and thereafter never mentioned the subject in his dispatches.[41] For the remainder of his ambassadorship, his principal tools for restoring conservative constitutional leadership to Cuba would no longer be intervention but nonrecognition, economic sabotage, and political interference. The expression of hegemony under the Good Neighbor era would thus be characterized by a more protective coloration.

The Dissolution of the Pentarchy

Welles's failure to achieve a U.S. intervention was paralleled between September 5 and 10 by the failure of the Pentarchy to consolidate itself. Caught between its fear of U.S. disapproval and the demands of both its constituents and opponents, the revolutionary junta never actually ruled Cuba. Its sessions were informal, to say the least. Members were often absent, and those present conducted business while surrounded by student adherents urging them against any compromise with the U.S. ambassador and Céspedes' supporters. Moreover, the Pentarchy had to keep close to the negotiations between the sergeants and the officers so that the two rebel movements, still distinct at this point, did not compromise on different bases.

The Pentarchy made only one significant decision throughout its entire life, but it was of momentous importance. On September 7, fearing that a breakdown of order would lead to U.S. intervention and the end of any "revolutionary" program, Sergio Carbó (Pentarchy minister of war) decided that the Cuban Army could not continue to maintain order unless it had a recognized chief of staff. At first he offered to allow the old officers to name the chief in return for accepting a five-man commission to govern army reorganization, three members of which would be from the sergeants' junta. When this was rejected, Carbó took the fateful step of naming Batista (his close friend) to the post, with the rank of colonel. He also promoted the other members of the sergeants' junta to the ranks of captain and lieutenant. As Carbó may have realized, this effectively ended the possibility of achieving a compromise with the old officer corps, though negotiations continued nevertheless. Batista's statements as chief of staff were more self-assured, but he still maintained the position of offering to return at least those officers not tainted by the Machadato. He remained sensitive as well to the possibility of U.S. intervention, continuing to declare that the army would maintain order.[42]

The Pentarchy also tried to improve its image in Washington. It sent a memorandum to the Department of State in which it denied any communist program or affiliations, declared itself effective in preserving public order, and stated its desire to reach agreement with the officers and the other anti-Machado forces. It even promised the creation of a coalition cabinet in the immediate future.[43]

Indeed, September 7 and 8 were days when negotiations seemed most intense. This is what led Welles to believe that either the Pentarchy or Batista was on the verge of breaking and to his determination to call on Washington one last time for a troop landing. On the eighth, it is likely that Batista actually offered to back the return of Céspedes to the presidency in return for his own confirmation as army chief of staff. This offer was rejected, as the notion of serving under a mutinous sergeant was anathema to the general staff. The search for a coalition cabinet fell through as well. At this point both sides began to pull apart, as the officers sought to carry out the Ferrer conspiracy to seize Cabaña Fortress and the student supporters of the Pentarchy called for an end to negotiations and the implementation of a nationalist program.[44]

The Pentarchy, however, was by now hopelessly divided over the issue of possible U.S. intervention. At a meeting on the night of the eighth, the two more conservative members, Portela and Irizarri, suggested that the body dissolve itself and hand power to a council of notables composed of men acceptable to the United States.[45] The Directorio leaders present violently objected to this proposal. Grau San Martín took the position that Roosevelt's Good Neighbor pronouncements would deter the United States from a military intervention and that Pentarchy members had an obligation to carry out their "revolutionary" program. Portela and Irizarri countered that the Pentarchy had not enough political support to govern and that any attempt to do so would bring immediate intervention. Carbó, while less optimistic than Grau that Roosevelt would not order an intervention, agreed that an attempt to govern should be made. One of the Directorio leaders, Eduardo Chibás, proposed that the Pentarchy choose a provisional president to govern in its place, arguing that such a move would obtain recognition from enough Latin American countries to stay the hand of the United States. The motion was debated all night and apparently rejected. However, when Portela and Irizarri announced their desire to resign, the Directorio leaders pressed the question again.

On the evening of September 9, the Pentarchy met again to discuss the question of its future. One floor above its meeting room in the presidential palace, the Directorio leadership was also meeting. Those present at this latter session concluded that a move, supported by Pentarchy members Portela and Irizarri, to return power to the officers and conservative politicians was imminent. They decided to name a president themselves and then inform the Pentarchy of their decision. Their choice was Grau San Martín, whose name they proposed at the meeting downstairs. After a brief and violent debate with the conservative Pentarchy members, that body was dissolved and Grau was named provisional president of the Republic of Cuba.[46] Despite the fears even of its supporters, Cuban nationalism was finally to have its opportunity to rule the island.

Sumner Welles and the Crisis of Cuban Nationalism

The totalitarian and brutal nature of the late Machadato was unprecedented in Cuban history. This fact moved Sumner Welles to treat it as an aberration rather than as a sign of contradictions in Cuban society heightened by economic dependence and political impotence. Thus, the ambassador believed that the constitutional succession of a moderate regime, afforded a measure of economic relief by the United States, would be sufficient to return the island to political and social peace. He did not appreciate the extent to which the depression had jarred the social position of the middle class or the social consciousness of the proletariat. Nor did he understand that the economic priorities and political violence of the

Machadato had undermined the legitimacy of the old landed and trading forces for which the traditional political organizations spoke.

As a result, Welles's understanding of the Céspedes regime was predicated on his assumption that the middle-class elements of the movement against Machado, once in possession of executive authority, and sustained by the legitimating forces of the old judiciary and legislature, would provide Cuba with a government which would regain the allegiance of the Cuban electorate. He expected the major anti-Machado groups to organize themselves into legitimate political parties, one of which would provide the next Cuban president to be elected in 1934. This interpretation was seriously flawed, and had not the ambassador been able to call upon the power he held by virtue of U.S. hegemony in Cuba, his faulty understanding would have rendered him incapable of defending his nation's interests.

As the representative of a nation founded upon antityrannical principles, Welles saw the Cuban upheaval of 1933 as a struggle for legitimate representative government. It was this, in his paternalistic way, that he was determined to give the Cubans. Yet because his fight was directed against the tyranny of the palace and not of the marketplace, he took little note of the militant mood of Cuban labor or the revolutionary ideology of its leadership. He did not perceive capitalism as an oppressive system and thus discounted the chorus of complaints against economic exploitation that was rising around him. Furthermore, because he saw the U.S. role in Cuba as benign, he did not understand the extent to which radical nationalists among the middle class and especially the students held the United States responsible for the Machadato. For all these reasons, the regime Welles helped create was not capable of answering—or even expected to answer—the demands for economic justice which had accumulated in Cuban society since the sugar depression of the mid-1920s. When its army was taken from it on the night of September 4, there was nothing to sustain it.

From the outset of the Cuban Republic, the intended source of stability had been the Platt Amendment. In its broadest sense, Welles's policy was an effort to transfer such a role to the Cuban constitution. The actual recipient, however, was the "revolutionary" army created out of the enlisted men's revolt. For four months after the coup against the officers, this army, led by Fulgencio Batista, sustained the nationalist government of Grau San Martín during its nervous experiment in antihegemonic government. Eventually, the pressure from Washington (and from the radicalized Cuban working class) would prove too great, and Batista, tutored by Welles for his role as the latest incarnation of stability, would move the legitimating hand of the army back to the shoulder of the moderate anti-Machadistas. In those brief four months, however, Cuban nationalism would have its turn to grapple with the colossus.

CHAPTER NINE

The New Deal and the Collapse of Cuban Stability

BY THE TIME of the inauguration of Ramón Grau San Martín as provisional president of Cuba on September 9, 1933, the United States had
turned away from military intervention as the means for bringing stability to
the island. During Grau's four-month incumbency, U.S. hegemony expressed itself, not through the marines, but rather through political and
economic interference. This chapter will record the major forms of *political*
pressure brought to bear against the Grau regime.

U.S. policy toward Cuba, guided by Sumner Welles (but supported or at
least not challenged by policy makers in Washington), was one of loud protestations of Good Neighborliness combined with an attempt to moderate or
overturn the nationalist government in Havana by withholding vital political
support and (as will be shown in the next chapter) economic relief. Because
this policy of interference by deprivation required at certain crucial periods
the complementary exercise of physical force, and because the United States
preferred not to use its own enforcement apparatus, it was necessary to
establish a close relationship with Cuban groups capable of acting decisively
against the weakened regime and of providing stability for a successor regime. Thus, the United States eventually sought an alliance with Fulgencio
Batista who, as chief of the "Revolutionary Army," came to hold the key to
the internal power equation. This alliance, based upon U.S. assurance of his
position, led Batista, after some hesitation, to throw the weight of the army
behind the conservative-moderate coalition which had supported the Céspedes government, and to drive Grau into exile.

The ripening of the process of external deprivation and internal co-
optation, however, required four desperate months during which the island's economy bordered on chaos and certain rural areas experienced social
revolution. This period, while it did not witness the development of an
effective antihegemonic party or program in Cuba, established the rhetoric
of Cuban nationalism as the only acceptable form of political discourse. All
subsequent regimes were to pay homage to the "Revolution of September 4"
even as they labored to render its accomplishments consonant with continued U.S. domination.

150

In its awkward effort to develop a new manner of expressing its power in Cuba, the United States learned many important lessons. Most important, perhaps, the policy makers in Washington came to appreciate both the punitive and co-optive potential of the politico-economic instruments which the depression and New Deal reforms were placing in their hands. In the context of rising anti-U.S. nationalism in Latin America, the centralized control of the granting and withholding of political and economic benefits—a form of interference much less palpable than the marines—was to become the new basis for U.S. hegemony. Furthermore, by adding political and economic manipulation to the structural bonds that favored U.S. interests, and by eliciting the cooperation of newly rising dependent groups in the island, U.S. policy makers groped their way toward an understanding of the interconnected social and material strategies needed to maintain the system.

The Bases of U.S. Attitudes Toward the Grau Government

While almost all studies acknowledge the United States' effort to overthrow the government of Ramón Grau San Martín, many attribute that effort to a repugnance for illegitimate and unstable regimes, or to the personal hostility of Welles toward Grau and his supporters for causing the demise of the ambassador's carefully created Céspedes government.[1] My study of the evidence, however, indicates that it was not Grau's illegitimacy, his inability to rule effectively (social unrest and violence were no greater than under Céspedes), or the personal hostility of the U.S. ambassador that led the United States to use its power in Cuba to bring him down. Rather, his demise was sought because his government (1) would not act with sufficient resolve to suppress the radical nationalist and Marxist insurgencies which were attacking U.S. property, (2) passed legislation which inhibited the wealth-producing capacity of U.S. investments in the island, and (3) blocked the return to power of the conservative-moderate coalition which had formed the basis of the Céspedes regime and with which the United States hoped to arrange a new and closer economic relationship.

During the four months of the regime, the goal of U.S. policy was to use its economic and political power to divide Grau's supporters, encourage his opponents, and thus set the stage for the return of a regime with the ideological resolve to suppress proletarian insurgency, restore "constitutional" legitimacy and order, and cooperate with Washington policy by accepting new economic arrangements rationalizing the relationship between Cuban sugar production and its traditional market and providing increased access to the Cuban market for U.S. goods. There was no vendetta against Grau himself, and on those occasions when the "realists" (that is, those who acknowledged the need to accommodate U.S. wishes) bested the nationalists among Grau's closest advisors, Welles readily entertained compromise settlements which would have retained Grau in office, albeit with greatly diminished power. While it is true that Welles worked diligently to head off any State Department consideration of the possibility of recognizing Grau, this was because he had concluded that a workable arrangement to secure U.S. interests and end unrest in Cuba could only be obtained through the return of more moderate forces. Despite occasional doubts, Welles concluded that these forces were not strong enough to remove Grau unless U.S. pressure placed his regime in an untenable position. Furthermore, the ambassador's constant advocacy of nonrecognition stemmed from his belief that this particular weapon in the arsenal of U.S. hegemony was at once the least damaging to the Good Neighbor image and the most likely to bring about the Havana regime's demise. While embarrassed by the more overt forms of interference in which Welles engaged, Roosevelt, Hull, and most State Department policy makers went along (however reluctantly) with Welles's conclusions regarding the unacceptability of the Grau regime.[2]

The Policy of Nonrecognition

During a September 5 telephone conversation with Secretary of State Hull, Welles, realizing the growing resistance in Washington to his proposals for intervention, had set out a more moderate position based upon nonrecognition of the Pentarchy. Hull agreed to nonrecognition until the Pentarchy "has shown its ability to preserve law and order." However, given the effect of nonrecognition by the United States upon a Cuban government, such a position was not materially different from one of outright opposition.[3]

On September 8, at Welles's urging, Roosevelt allowed his ambassador to state publicly that the question of recognition was not even under consideration by the U.S. government. In the context of U.S.-Cuban relations, this was a stern rebuff to the Pentarchy, though less severe than that desired by Welles, who preferred a clear statement that the United States would never recognize the group then in power in Havana.[4]

Welles's desire to use nonrecognition to unseat the Cuban government was a logical extension of the evolution of U.S. recognition policy. The general trend of this policy as applied to Latin America had moved from de facto to de jure recognition by the early twentieth century, reflecting an increased concern for establishing political and economic stability in the area on a more permanent basis. To reinforce the "stabilizing" effect of such a policy, especially within the Caribbean area, both political and economic conditions were often made a part of recognition bargaining. Such conditions usually included an expression of willingness by the Latin American regime to fulfill certain "international obligations."[5]

After the Wilsonian experiment with rigid constitutional criteria, the Republicans reverted (except for the states of Central America covered by a separate treaty) to a modified de facto policy which retained the bargaining feature. Nonconstitutional regimes which evidenced ability to control the population were generally recognized, but only after they had pledged to fulfill their "international obligations" and to prepare elections. Because most regimes in monopoly possession of physical force could arrange to "win" subsequent elections, the only real concession was the de facto governments' agreement to meet international obligations, which consisted in most cases of recognizing the international legal rights of the industrialized states, particularly those concerning private property and debt service. Thus, the return to a modified de facto policy continued to inhibit unconstitutional changes of mandate, but only when the new regimes might wish to challenge dependent international relationships.[6]

Given the development of a pragmatic de jure policy, the United States was able to substitute nonrecognition for physical intervention as the major tool for bringing down the Cuban government. It was still necessary, however, to make the active use of nonrecognition consonant with the new Good Neighbor dispensation, which precluded "interference" in Cuban affairs. Thus, Secretary of State Hull informed U.S. diplomatic posts that the policy toward the island involved "not the slightest intention of intervening or interfering in Cuba's domestic affairs." He defended the newly announced withholding of recognition from Grau as noninterference and expressed the hope that the Cubans would soon "be able to form a government capable of maintaining order."[7]

The conditions to be attached to recognition were worked out by Sumner Welles. The ambassador, who from the very outset of the regime was reporting to Washington that Grau represented only "a small number of insignificant radical groups," urged that Hull or Roosevelt proclaim publicly that recognition would be granted only if the regime met certain (and, as he believed, impossible) conditions. Going well beyond the criteria used under Republican Secretary of State Henry Stimson (de facto control, recognition of international obligations, eventual elections), Welles suggested that a Cuban regime be asked to meet the following conditions: (1) conclusive demonstration of the effective representation of the will of the majority of the people; (2) capability of maintaining order and guaranteeing life, property, and liberty; and (3) capacity to meet its international obligations.[8]

These criteria were so stringent, and the first of them so elusive of definition, that they clearly revealed Welles's desire that recognition be permanently withheld. Roosevelt toned down his ambassador's request, declaring publicly only that recognition would be granted a Cuban regime which: (1) represented the will of the people, (2) was capable of maintaining law and order, and (3) was competent to meet its obligations.[9] Nevertheless, given the economic chaos and near civil war in Cuba, no government, especially one not backed by the United States, could meet such conditions; indeed, U.S. recognition was itself the one element which could have enabled Grau to fulfill them. Furthermore, because Roosevelt retained Welles's unique requirement of representing the "will of the people," and since the ambassador, who had already declared that the regime represented almost no one, would be his government's main source of information concerning the meeting of that requirement, there was little likelihood that the United States would ever recognize Grau. As Grau (as well as Batista and the opposition) came to perceive this, the destabilizing process of political realignment within the island gathered momentum, further undermining the regime's ability to govern.

Welles's dispatches appear to have had as their main purpose the disparagement of the Cuban government. They consistently characterized Grau as impractical, vacillating, radical, and easily swayed by his more militant student advisors. Within twenty-four hours of the establishment of the regime, Welles had already concluded that "the possibility of general popular support is now in my judgement out of the question." For the remainder of his tenure as ambassador (his mission ended on December 13), Welles consistently argued for continued nonrecognition and regularly sought strong public reiteration of that policy from Washington.[10]

Nonrecognition was, of course, meant to be not merely a punitive device, but a method of altering the character and actions of the nationalist regime. To achieve this, Welles actively engaged in influencing the domestic political dialogue. He continued to meet both with representatives of the opposition and with those members of the regime who wished to keep open the possibility of U.S. recognition. The ambassador pressed for a "concentration Cabinet" which would substitute many of Céspedes' supporters for the more nationalist forces advising Grau. Despite his supposed hostility to Grau, however, Welles did not make the latter's removal a condition for compromise. The ambassador, his military attaché, and Adolf Berle (who was in Cuba from September 1 to September 16) met not only with the conservative opposition, but on several occasions with Grau, Batista, and even the leaders of the Directorio. Welles went so far as to tell Hull—in a statement which revealed the purely pragmatic character of the recognition weapon— that if a more moderate cabinet were agreed upon, "I think we could safely waive the maintenance of order question, because no government here will be able to maintain absolute order for some time to come."[11]

While using nonrecognition to weaken the nationalist government and alter, in part or in whole, its political direction, the U.S. ambassador had to hold at bay those in Washington and Latin America who argued for immediate de facto recognition as the means to stabilize the situation in Cuba. Secretary of State Hull, contemplating possible attacks on the United States at the Inter-American Conference set for December in Montevideo, wanted the Cuban question settled as quickly as possible. Other Latin American states, particularly Mexico, called for U.S. recognition of Grau and communicated to Washington their conviction that, contrary to Welles's reports, the Cuban government was generally effective and popular. Indeed, the State Department eventually accumulated information from the military attaché in Havana, from the commanders of the many U.S. destroyers stationed in Cuban harbors, from U.S. Ambassador to Mexico Josephus Daniels, and from the liberal media and intellectual community in the United States to the effect that unrest had subsided from a high point during the Céspedes interregnum, that Grau's nationalistic decrees were looked on with favor by most Cubans, and that most members of the government were not radicals.[12]

Nevertheless, the revolutionary unions under the control of the CNOC and the CCP continued to threaten and, on occasion, to occupy U.S. establishments on the island. These actions, combined with indications of the growing strength of anti-Yankee radicalism, enabled Welles to convince the State Department that the incumbent Cuban government was unable or unwilling to protect U.S. interests.

On the question of communism, Hull and Under Secretary Jefferson Caffery were actually much more sensitive than Welles, who appreciated the hostility between the Marxist left and the nationalist radicals who supported Grau. In their first conversations, during early and mid-September, Hull often raised the question of the strength of communism in Cuba and its relationship to the new government and to the international Communist movement.[13] This concern with communism in Cuba, and the consequent belief that only a strong and more conservative Cuban government could suppress it, undercut pressure on Washington to recognize Grau.[14]

While in later years a more sophisticated policy would lead to instances of U.S. support for anti-Communist nationalist movements in Latin America, the early Good Neighbor policy was only slowly moving in this direction. In the case of Cuba, such an alliance would not develop fully until 1935–1936, when a populist but reliable Batista moved to destroy the Marxist organizations and their labor movement.[15] In 1933, however, the United States still preferred conservative restoration to nationalist compromise, though it was willing to be somewhat flexible concerning the balance of forces in a new Cuban government.

The Policy Toward Communism in Cuba

The Grau regime coincided not only with the high tide of Communist agitation on the island but with the climax of the movement by the New Deal for U.S. recognition of the Soviet Union. Thus, the question of Soviet direction of revolutionary activities by the CCP was inserted into the domestic debate on the recognition of both Grau and the USSR.

Soviet fears concerning its Asian borders, combined with U.S. needs to find new outlets for a shrunken foreign trade, had led both states to initiate a study of diplomatic recognition.[16] When Soviet purchases in the U.S. market declined in 1932–1933 and the Nazi party rose to prominence in Germany, pressure grew on both sides for closer ties. In the early autumn of 1933, President Roosevelt had begun to explore the question of recognition. While most of FDR's advisors favored recognition, the State Department felt that certain guarantees concerning subversion should be made a part of any agreement.[17] The head of the East European Affairs Division, Robert F. Kelley, whose department had been charged with monitoring international Communist activities from its listening post in Riga, wrote a lengthy memorandum which, while it did not oppose recognition, elaborated upon the dangers of political intercourse with the Soviet Union. In reciting international Communist propaganda concerning the overthrow of capitalism, Kelley's memorandum touched upon the association of the Cuban and U.S. Communist parties and made reference to the anti-U.S. activities of the CCP during the summer and early fall of 1933.[18]

As noted earlier, Hull had been asking Welles about communism in Cuba since early September and referred to "very persistent reports that there are more or less communistic influences in there." On September 8, Assistant Secretary of State Jefferson Caffery had mentioned his own concern over Communist activities in an interview with the Cuban ambassador in Washington. Three days later, Hull asked Welles if he could obtain any evidence that Cuban Communists were "getting instructions from some other country." The ambassador, on September 15, relayed the text of a message from the executive board of CNOC to Profintern headquarters in Moscow. The cable stated (indeed overstated) the strike activities of CNOC unions, announced the resistance of the "revolutionary movement" to U.S. intervention, and requested the "immediate solidarity of [the] international proletariat."[19]

This cable was apparently used by forces within the State Department uneasy about U.S. recognition of the Soviet Union. In October, Assistant Secretary of State Jefferson Caffery leaked a version of the telegram to the United Press. His purpose was to link (rather tenuously, it would seem) the Comintern to unrest in Cuba. Caffery told the United Press reporter that the State Department had evidence that Moscow was "directing communist leaders engaged in fomenting labor disorders in Cuba." The story was never printed, however, because Caffery would not allow his name to be used and because the vice-president of United Press concluded that it was an effort to sabotage the beginning of negotiations with the Soviets which had been set for early November.[20] It is possible that Caffery and, as one source claims, Hull himself may have used the question of communism in Cuba to harden the U.S. negotiating position vis-à-vis the Soviet Union. For our purposes, however, it is sufficient to note that both men were disturbed by the extent of Communist strength in Cuba.[21]

As long as Grau was seen to be either an ally of communism or (more realistically) its ineffective opponent, the United States was unlikely to deem him worthy of support. For his part, Grau failed to accommodate to this basic anti-Communist aspect of U.S. foreign policy. In need of labor support, he refused to adopt anti-Communist rhetoric and for a long time resisted cracking down on militant labor. During his regime, in fact, the newly created Ministry of Labor was generally sympathetic to workers' economic demands.[22]

In an effort to show that the Grau regime could not control events, Welles's dispatches emphasized the labor "disorders" which were forcing the shutdown (and occasionally the occupation) of sugar mills, mines, and commercial and service establishments. The ambassador also reported the numerous demonstrations organized by the CCP and instances of fraternization between striking workers and police and soldiers. By mid-September, a clear theme of Welles's dispatches was that Grau must be replaced because his general sympathy with worker demands prevented him from using the full force of police power against proletarian revolt.[23]

In some eyes, Grau was to be opposed not merely for his incompetence, but on the basis of the radical nationalism of his regime. Most U.S. businessmen in Cuba, for example, drew little distinction between radical union activities and the nationalist decrees of the government. These decrees provided for an eight-hour day, compulsory mediation of labor disputes, control of utility rates, tenant rights, an enlarged jurisdiction for the Department of Labor, including certain traditional management prerogatives, workmen's compensation, controls on interest rates, and so on. They further provided that 50 percent of all workers in each establishment be Cuban nationals.

The prolabor aspects of many of the decrees were criticized by Cuban as well as U.S. businesses, even though the general thrust of the legislation was the attempt to favor not only labor, but national as opposed to foreign entrepreneurs. Not surprisingly, the loudest cries came from the association of U.S. businessmen on the island, the American Chamber of Commerce of Cuba. From the first day after the fall of Céspedes, its board of directors called for U.S. protection and warned of the strength of communism in Cuba. They considered Grau's nationalistic decrees to be as damaging as the program of the CCP and, in themselves, a form of communism. Many of Grau's supporters were labeled as crypto-Communists. Among others, the United Fruit Company, Bethlehem Steel Corporation, Standard Oil Company, and the New York banks which held the bonds of U.S. sugar companies in Cuba labeled worker demands "communistic" and sent the State Department innumerable reports of attacks on their properties by "mobs" led by "agitators."[24]

Though Grau's ministers eventually responded to the threat to their middle-class nationalism and moved against the CNOC unions with military force, much of the rhetoric of the regime continued to attack U.S. business interests and generally sided with labor's economic demands. For their part, U.S. businessmen rarely drew a distinction between the revolutionary acts precipitated by the CCP (confiscation or occupation of property and assaults upon managers) and the ameliorist economic demands of workers that were supported by the more nationalist and populist cabinet ministers. Thus, the nationalism of the regime and the revolutionary socialism of certain labor organizations were often fused in the minds of those in Washington assessing reports on conditions in Cuba. Welles's dispatches generally separated the actions of the two movements, but, as noted earlier, the ambassador nevertheless considered Grau's unwillingness or inability to suppress radical labor to be a major reason for his removal. Moreover, Welles considered most labor demands, even those of nonradical unions, as irresponsible given business conditions on the island, and he wanted a regime that would resist them. The workers, as Welles saw it, could only gain rewards after the return of normal business activity, which must await the installation of a cooperative government in Havana.[25]

In the final analysis, incipient Communist revolution in Cuba did not in this instance give rise to a policy of supporting liberal nationalism as a defense of U.S. rights in the island. Most policy makers in Washington, while they were embarrassed by public reports of Welles's efforts to oust Grau, agreed that their country should withhold support from a regime which offered no way out of the crisis other than a diminution of the traditional benefits of U.S. economic relationships with Cuba.

Internal Cuban Contradictions

Nonrecognition and anticommunism set the stage for the attempt to force compromise or resignation upon Grau San Martín. While Welles had originally urged intervention and a countercoup by Céspedes' supporters, he eventually settled, as we have seen, for a slower process of unseating Grau or at least moderating his regime. The theme struck by Welles in his meetings with the opposition was that they were the only hope for Cuba, that the United States, although it would not force their return to power, would not recognize the present regime, and that the best outcome was for them to negotiate their entry into the present government so as to moderate and if possible replace it. Welles's attitude with Grau's supporters was to emphasize the political significance of nonrecognition, and to impress upon them the imminence of economic collapse (Welles kept close tabs on the Treasury balance and food stocks) and Communist revolution. His purpose was to convince the government of the impossibility of continuing in office unless it compromised with or made way for a more moderate group with whom the U.S. economic interests and government would do business.[26]

With the United States pressing for removal of the nationalist regime, the negotiations between the Grau government and the opposition stalled over several questions related to internal Cuban politics and social structure. First of all, there was the question of Cuban nationalism. The anti-U.S. pronouncements and nationalist decrees of the regime were, contrary to Welles's reports, generally popular with most Cubans. Because of this, the opposition had to portray themselves, not as opponents of the "Revolution of September 4," but rather as more "responsible" nationalists who, being untainted by Marxist influence, were capable of restoring stability and prosperity to the island.

Meanwhile, as the regime continued to pronounce decree-laws, there came into existence a body of legislation which, however superficial or utopian its content, became associated in the public mind with true Cuban independence. Any attempt by a successor regime to alter it would inevitably be seen as a sign of domination by the United States. Nevertheless, capitalist reconstruction based upon closer ties to the U.S. market was not possible unless the prolabor legislation, market controls, business taxes, and government take-overs of private property which accumulated during the four months of the Grau regime were in some measure reversed. Because of this, the opposition and its U.S. supporters, despite their public pronouncements, privately took the position that certain of the nationalist decrees must be rescinded. This position aroused the ire of the student supporters of the regime who, branding the opposition as reactionary, opposed any coalition which would weaken the "purity" of the "revolution." In these circumstances, Grau's opponents were weakened by the necessity of espousing the "revolution" publicly while working privately to undermine it.

Another difficulty arising during the negotiations was the question of Batista's future and the control of the Cuban Army. On class, racial, and political grounds, the opposition was unwilling to accept the demise of the traditional officer corps and the turning over of the only organized military force on the island to an ex-sergeant of noncriollo heritage and dubious political beliefs. Lower-class control of the military was further unacceptable because the sergeant-led army continued to stand between the opposition and the presidential palace and because Batista would make no public criticism of the revolution. The opposition doubted that the army could again be made a source for stability until it was returned to upper-class control. If left to Batista, they feared it would remain a bulwark of radical nationalism, or become the basis for renewed military dictatorship.

The anti-Batista attitude of the opposition cut across the main lines of force within the negotiations and caused them at times to take on a Byzantine character. As Welles began to conclude that Batista could be separated from Grau and used against him, the U.S. approach and that of the opposition began to diverge, thus weakening the conservative-moderate position. In the absence of a viable alternative, Welles convinced himself that Batista would be "reasonable" as long as his position within the military and the official rhetoric of the Revolution of September 4 were maintained by a successor regime. Welles scoffed at the opposition's fears of military dictatorship, while endeavoring to gain from Batista assurances of his desire for stability and good relations with the United States.

With the U.S. position beginning to swing toward Batista, the anti-Yankee students began to suspect that the army might depose the revolutionary regime. This caused them to consider potential alliances with the more moderate opposition so as to thwart the aims of the U.S. ambassador and preserve the revolution. Fearing the emotional and impractical students less than a military led by the lower class, portions of the opposition responded. Though these two groups, because they clashed over the retention of Grau and his nationalist legislation, never came together, their maneuverings confused the negotiations and caused Batista to be very leery of jumping to either the opposition (who would not guarantee his position) or the nationalists (who desired to use the army as a weapon of the revolution).

A final factor in the uncertain equation was the mercurial Grau San Martín. Grau seems to have believed in the national, capitalist, anti-U.S. "revolution," though he was less uncompromising than his student supporters. Groping desperately for a viable policy, he wavered between attempts at pursuing the "revolution," appealing over Welles's head for U.S. recognition, compromising with the opposition, keeping the army loyal to the revolution, and building a revolutionary militia beyond the control of Batista. Never able to consummate the alliances he sought, he finally alienated the nationalist students (for having failed the revolution), the opposition (for stubbornly blocking the return of the moderates), the United States (by failing to be "realistic" in his nationalism or to suppress Marxism), and Batista (for trying to politicize the army). What kept Grau in office so long was that his name had come to represent the "revolution" in the minds of most Cubans. Also maintaining his power was the fact that his enemies feared one another more than the president. Indeed, when a coalition (in this case between the army and the opposition) was finally arrived at, Grau was quickly dispatched.[27]

The Policy of Befriending Batista

By late September, Welles began to perceive that Batista might become the vehicle for emerging from the impasse between those who had supported Céspedes and those who overthrew him. At first, Welles, like the opposition, considered the ex-sergeant and his "mutinous" army as strong supporters of anti-Yankeeism and as a radical element that could only be controlled by returning the old officer corps to power. Welles seemed not to understand the essentially conservative nature of the sergeants' movement or to appreciate the fact that Batista's support for Grau derived from the belief that his command over the army depended upon legitimating the coup of September 4. Eventually, though, the ambassador came to perceive that Batista was molding the army into a loyal if not yet efficient instrument, and that only he had the power to disarm the various student militias and to suppress the labor insurgency. In an important interview with Batista on September 21, Welles (who in his encounter with the ex-sergeant in early September, had seen fit to comment to the State Department only upon the latter's non-Caucasian appearance) found him "extremely reasonable" and in "rigorous opposition to all communist propaganda and activities," and noted that he had "increased his control over the troops."[28] At this point, the ambassador was actually closer to Batista (still the basis of strength of the Grau regime) than the opposition forces, who were strongly backed by the ex-officers and thus as much opposed to Batista's control over the army as they were to the nationalist Grau's hold on the presidency. Indeed, the coalition discussions broke down in late September over the issue of nonelite control of the army and the refusal of the students to agree to non-"revolutionary" men being admitted into the cabinet.

On October 2, a long-impending showdown took place between the ex-officers, most of whom had barricaded themselves in the Hotel Nacional, and Batista's troops, which had surrounded it. Despite a ragtag performance by the army, a day and a half of siege led to the officers' surrender and, in effect, a consolidation of Batista in his position as commander in chief of the revolutionary army. The defeat of the officers, who up to that point had formed the prime base for any armed attempt to overthrow Grau, demoralized the opposition and enhanced Welles's effort to separate Batista from the regime, for it was now apparent that this was the only way of bringing the government down.

The day after the officers surrendered, Welles told Batista that he "was the only individual in Cuba today who represented authority." Welles intimated that by taking a firm stand against "the communistic and extreme radical elements" Batista could rally "to his own support the very great majority of the commercial and financial interests in Cuba who are looking for protection and who could only find such protection in himself"; he told Batista that the main opposition leaders were now willing to support him as chief of staff. To drive his point home, Welles concluded by informing Batista that "the present government of Cuba did not fill any of the conditions which the United States Government had announced as making recognition possible" and that the only force blocking an acceptable compromise was the "unpatriotic and futile obstinacy of a small group of young men who should be studying in the university instead of playing politics." The ambassador left him with the admonition to use "the force of authority which he represented" to resolve the political impasse.[29]

Before there was time to assess the effect his advice had upon Batista, however, Welles was saddled with the problem of convincing Washington that the defeat of the old officer corps did not represent a significant strengthening of the Grau regime, which in most circles (and in Welles's mind as well until late September) was closely identified with the fortunes of the sergeants' revolt. If Washington could not be disabused of its growing belief that Grau might weather nonrecognition, then pressure for recognizing him, and thereby lessening the damage to U.S. policy overtures toward Latin America, might increase just when Welles believed that Batista was about to act.

On October 5, Hull relayed to Welles Roosevelt's opinion that in the light of the events at the National Hotel, and of Grau's willingness, in principle, to broaden the base of his government, a less strict application of the recognition criteria might be called for.[30] Welles cabled back within the hour that the army revolt and the civilian coup were now moving in separate directions (not explaining that this was due in part to his own efforts) and that the victory at the hotel strengthened Batista, but not Grau. The ambassador declared that recognition would only sustain an unpopular, inept, and radical regime, and avert its imminent demise. No rebuttal to Welles's judgment of the situation was forthcoming and, in expectation of the creation of a moderate coalition, any thought of changing policy was set aside.[31]

Sumner Welles's expectations notwithstanding, negotiations for a new Cuban government broke down once again. The opposition perceived Batista's increasing control over the army not as a source of stability, but rather as the basis for military dictatorship. Moreover, the students, who had been the strongest opponents of diluting the revolution through a coalition with Céspedes' supporters, now began to perceive Batista and his closeness to Welles as a greater danger to the "revolution" than the conservative politicians. As a result, the dance of realignment began once again, with the students now beginning to meet with the ABC to consider ways of eliminating the army chief.

Batista, by now a skilled political performer, sought to cover himself on all sides. He met again with Welles and agreed that Grau had to go before business confidence and recognition could be restored, and that the Communist leadership of the striking sugar workers should be arrested. Next he conferred with business and opposition leaders and agreed to support Carlos Mendieta, a leader of the conservative anti-Machado opposition, as a replacement for Grau.[32]

This activity convinced Welles that he had successfully detached Batista from the government and that it could not last more than a few days. While Welles's optimistic reports calmed the growing uneasiness in Washington, the assessment of the situation which they contained was incorrect. Batista was not as yet sufficiently sure of his control over the army to use it decisively. Many of the newly appointed officers feared that a more conservative regime would bring back the old officers, while others wished to make the military an arm of the revolution. Batista's purpose at this time was thus the modest one of assuring his continued rule of the military regardless of whether nationalists or moderates held power at the palace. In early October, Batista moved to protect his position within the "revolution" which had brought him to power (and which, despite Welles's description, was still a popular if not potent force) and with those of his officers who opposed dealing with the opposition. Batista took up again, in his public statements, the themes of the sacredness of the cause of the Revolution of September 4 and insistence upon nonintervention by the United States in Cuban affairs.[33]

This setback to hopes for a more moderate regime caused Welles to set out his thinking on the relative merits of nonrecognition. He admitted that recognizing Grau (who had now unexpectedly survived five weeks) would quiet anti-Yankeeism and perhaps afford the United States the opportunity to gain some influence over the regime's economic nationalism. However, he argued that recognition of a dictatorship (Welles alternately accused Grau's regime of being dictatorial and ineffectual) supported by a small anti-U.S. minority would be only a temporary expedient and that such an unpopular regime could not stabilize Cuba and would sooner or later be overthrown. Emphasizing the importance of Cuban stability to the long-run interests of the United States, Welles concluded that "our own commercial and export interests in Cuba cannot be revived under this government."[34]

Though pressures for the United States to recognize the Cuban government continued to flow into the State Department from nations such as the United Kingdom, Panama, Argentina, and Mexico, and from liberal journals such as the *Nation*, the *New Republic*, *Christian Century*, and *World Tomorrow*, the influence of Welles's judgment and his undaunted expectations of imminent success for the nonrecognition policy once again quieted doubts in Washington.[35]

With Batista unable to act decisively, Welles now pressed for a compromise formula that would retain Grau as a figurehead and create a council of state composed of government and opposition members to control key areas of legislation. Partly owing to his underestimation of the influence of Cuban (that is, anti-U.S.) nationalism on the students, workers, and portions of the army, Welles once again was surprised by the failure of a formula to which all, in private, had agreed. By late October, new factions (pro- and anti-Batista) arose in the army, while the Directorio divided between those who wanted compromise and those who refused it, and the ABC discussed the alternatives of alliance with or assault upon Batista. All of this occurred against a background of continued strikes, Communist-led demonstrations, and the bleakest economic conditions. By the beginning of November, Welles had still been unable to wed the political opposition to the new army under Batista. Indeed, by this time, the ABC and other opposition elements decided on one last revolt in an effort both to break Batista's hold on the army and to topple the Grau government.[36]

The Atares Revolt and the Ascendancy of Batista

Since mid-September Welles had been opposed to an uprising by the opposition. Despite his constant references to the broad support for the moderate anti-Machadistas, he was pessimistic about their chances of success against the army, and he feared anarchy and the possibility of social revolution if Batista's forces were split or less than decisively defeated. Nevertheless, on November 9, armed supporters of the ABC, with small units of the army and ex-officers, attempted to stage a military uprising in Havana. Fighting raged for a day, but the majority of the army remained loyal to Batista, who isolated the rebels in the Atares fortress and forced their submission.[37]

Once again, Batista had dominated the opposition in a confrontation and, once again, as in the aftermath of the defeat of the old officer corps, his confidence rose, as did doubts in Washington concerning the continuation of nonrecognition. By this time, criticism of Welles's actions had surfaced even within the Department of State. Charles Taussig, an unofficial advisor to FDR on Cuban affairs, had long called for recognizing Grau and, with the suppression of the Atares revolt, reiterated his position to the president. Laurence Duggan, of the Latin American Division, sympathized with the aims of the Grau regime, while the head of the Pan American Union and a former State Department official, Leo Rowe, supported recognition. Even Under Secretary of State William Phillips had his doubts, confiding to his diary that "in my opinion, Welles is doing no good in Habana, he has become so involved with the various political parties and is being so violently attacked in the local press and otherwise that his presence there has no longer any healing effect."[38]

To counter the trend of thinking in Washington, Welles played his trump card—his personal relationship with FDR. On November 13 he asked permission to return to see the president. Roosevelt agreed to meet with Welles at Warm Springs and, to forestall any rumor of a recall, the president had Acting Secretary of State Phillips announce to the press that the ambassador would return to Havana after the meeting. The two met on November 19 and, though there is no record of their conversation, an agreement was apparently reached which upheld the nonrecognition policy but also provided for the replacement of Welles by Caffery, though in a manner which would not be interpreted as a recall.[39]

Welles then traveled to Washington to hammer out the wording of the latest statement of the nonrecognition policy. For three days he dueled with

State Department officials, particularly Caffery and Phillips, concerning its content and manner of promulgation. Welles wanted a strong statement which would make it clear to the contending Cuban factions that Grau would not be recognized. He also wished it to be made public as a presidential statement, to maximize its force. Caffery seems not to have objected to the tone of the statement but, for fear of offending other Latin American states, preferred that it be conveyed through diplomatic channels rather than publicly. Welles, realizing the importance of its pyschological impact within Cuba, insisted on a public presidential declaration. Phillips was also opposed to a public statement, fearing especially that it would be seen as an attack on the Cuban government by the United States and thus poison the atmosphere of the approaching Montevideo Conference. He also objected to certain passages in the statement, and when Roosevelt asked that it be shortened, Phillips was able to excise a paragraph which constituted a defense of the Céspedes regime and which described Grau's government as one opposed by political organizations, the business community, and the people in general. However, the final draft did state:

> We have not believed that it would be a policy of friendship and justice to the Cuban people as a whole to accord recognition to any provisional government in Cuba unless such government clearly possessed the support and the approval of the people of that Republic.

The statement then went on to hold out the economic plum once again by asserting that the United States wished to revise its trade relations with the island but that this was not possible until a popular and stable regime was in power.

Welles did succeed in having Roosevelt issue the statement as a presidential announcement and in adding that the ambassador would return to Washington "upon termination of his mission"—though Phillips was able to append "which will be in the near future." Thus, the statement was something of a compromise, though its general effect was to increase pressure upon the Grau government.[40] Once again, while there was resistance to Welles's hard line on recognition, no viable alternative policy was proposed. There would be no experiment with Grau as a new basis for hegemony as long as the more limited shift from the Machadistas to the moderate anti-Machadistas held the prospect of being sufficient.

The Montevideo Interlude

Despite the reiteration of the nonrecognition principle, those states restless under the traditional policy of withholding their recognition of a Latin American government until the United States had done so continued to press for a change of U.S. policy. With the forum of an Inter-American Conference at hand, Cordell Hull became apprehensive lest larger designs be thwarted by pro-Cuban speeches and demonstrations at Montevideo.[41]

Good Neighbor rhetoric notwithstanding, few Washington policy makers expected or indeed desired that much be accomplished at Montevideo beyond general expressions of inter-American fraternity. Under Secretary of State Phillips actually wished to postpone the conference, and Hull had many doubts as to its success. Roosevelt feared that the Latin American states would demand trade commitments which might undermine domestic recovery. In fact, he had his personal secretary, Louis Howe, draft a long directive to Hull warning him to avoid "like the plague" any discussion of questions such as tariffs, currency stabilization, or the situations in Leticia, the Chaco, or Cuba. The directive urged the secretary of state to emphasize such pedestrian matters as international law, peace, "the political and civil rights of women," intellectual cooperation, improved navigation, air travel, and the Pan American Highway. It suggested that Hull confine himself to "the usual words about good neighbors, band of brothers, etc."[42]

To deal with the possibility of an embarrassing discussion of the Cuban question at Montevideo, Hull prepared himself in several ways. While he urged no revision of nonrecognition policy, he nevertheless expressed the hope that compromise between Grau and the opposition—which Welles, as always, thought imminent—would be achieved in time for him to announce U.S. recognition at the conference. Barring this, Hull requested a complete defense of nonrecognition as background material. At the secretary's urging, Roosevelt informed several of the Latin American representatives in Washington that he hoped they would "take no precipitate action at Montevideo in regard to recognition" of Cuba.

At the start of the conference, Hull was agitated that the Mexicans and Cubans seemed bent upon forcing the issue of Cuban recognition. Holding, with Welles, that the Grau regime was unpopular and irresponsible, he privately threatened to leave the conference if such a question arose. A member of the U.S. delegation records him as saying: "I know we must have patience with backward peoples, but there is a limit."

As it turned out, Hull showed no public petulance, choosing instead to flatter the Cuban delegates (and others as well). He met privately with them and implied that the United States was willing to revoke the Platt Amendment, that his own position was one of strict noninterference in Cuban affairs, and that he favored U.S. support for the economic rehabilitation of the island. Hull even went so far as to find words of praise for the speech of Angel Giraudy, Grau's secretary of labor and a delegate to the conference. Giraudy's speech, while rather less strident than Hull had feared, nevertheless condemned U.S. interference in Cuban affairs. Roosevelt also relented somewhat and advised Hull that he should not try to block other states if they were strongly disposed to grant recognition to Grau.

Hull's gracious and sympathetic attitude toward the other delegates, combined with the end of Welles's stint as ambassador to Cuba (which occurred during the conference), caused most of them to be hopeful regarding a possible softening of U.S. attitudes toward Grau. In this atmosphere, none chose to press the issue of nonrecognition. Thus, the question of Cuba did not turn out to be more than a minor embarrassment to the United States at Montevideo.[43]

The Failure of Negotiations and the Arrival of Jefferson Caffery

Welles had returned to Havana from his meeting with Roosevelt on November 19 and immediately resumed contacts with all political factions. In his absence, the Uruguayan minister, Benjamín Fernández Medina, had gained nominal support for a compromise formula which allowed for the temporary retention of Grau until a new cabinet of nationalists and moderates, supplemented by a fifty-member council of state representing all factions, could choose a successor as provisional president. Though suspicious of Fernández Medina's motives, Welles was more disconcerted by Batista's indecision. He wanted to "solve" the Cuban crisis in the few weeks remaining before his announced return to Washington and therefore lent his general support to the formula. Nevertheless, because the proposal failed to deal with the status of the army, negotiations bogged down once again.[44]

Grau was generally amenable to a shortening of his tenure, but by this time fears that either Batista or U.S. intervention would cause the revocation of the nationalist decree legislation led to the formation of a left wing within the cabinet, centered around the radical nationalist secretary of the interior, Antonio Guiteras.[45] This group hoped either to create an armed force independent of Batista or to cause his removal by more nationalist officers. It also called for the development of a mass base for the government and the nationalization of certain U.S. interests.

This development of a leftist position, and Grau's ambivalent attitude toward it, once again convinced Welles that Grau's removal was a precondition of the return of stability. Welles now backed a new formula, also prepared by the Uruguayan minister, which called for Grau's immediate removal and replacement by Mendieta and included guarantees of Batista's position. In several secret midnight meetings, Welles obtained the agreement of the Cuban president (who had by now alienated both the moderates and radicals within his administration) to these conditions. With just two days left before his return to Washington, Welles once again reported the imminent success of his mission.[46]

Alas, negotiations broke off yet again. Batista was still not ready to trust his fate to the opposition and was unsure whether the ending of Welles's tenure signaled a relenting of U.S. opposition to Grau. Moreover, the opposition, especially the ABC, was not happy with Mendieta as a replacement for Grau, while the left wing of the government threatened to lead a real revolution if Grau were removed. Another unsettling factor was the periodic surfacing of plans for U.S. military intervention, proposals for which had percolated through the U.S. Department of the Navy ever since Céspedes had been overthrown. The fact that U.S. intervention continued to be seen as a possibility within the island (statements to the contrary from Washington notwithstanding) greatly destabilized negotiations, especially as the time for Welles's expected return to Washington approached.[47]

Jefferson Caffery arrived in Havana on December 18, and despite the hopes and fears on all sides that U.S. policy might change, he set about to reinforce both of Welles's central policies—nonrecognition of Grau and encouragement of Batista to ally with the opposition.

Caffery was more disturbed than Welles about communism in Cuba and was under growing pressure from U.S. sugar interests, who were telling him that the sugar harvest, which usually began in early January, would not take place if the present government remained in power. He drew the same conclusions as Welles had about the regime, describing it as being opposed by "all the better classes" and "supported only by the army and ignorant masses." Nevertheless, Caffery concluded that Grau would not fall until Batista was secure enough in his position vis-à-vis the new officer corps to bring the army over to the opposition. With his less aloof and more candid manner, Caffery was able to gain Batista's confidence and to make it clear to him that the United States would never deal with Grau and that Batista's future would be assured under a new regime.[48]

With his doubts resolved, Batista prepared to make an arrangement with the opposition. These groups, however, were still uneasy about casting their lot with the "Revolutionary Army." They were particularly agitated at this point about the question of their relative shares in a new cabinet and the question of which of them would see its chief become provisional president. Carlos Mendieta, the leader of the Unión Nacionalista, was the one whom Batista preferred and whom Welles had supported. However, Mendieta, like most opposition leaders, did not favor being named as a lame-duck provisional president, preferring instead to run for the full presidential term in elections set for the spring of 1934. As the possibility of ousting Grau increased, the divisions within the opposition came to play a greater role.

The left nationalists in the cabinet, realizing now that Batista was ready to desert the government and that Caffery's role was to be no different from that of Welles, attempted feebly to force Grau into a radical stance which would gain him the popular support necessary to withstand the defection of the army. Secretary of the Interior Guiteras now took a strong prolabor position, going so far as to intervene the Cuban Electric Company and two of the largest U.S. sugar mills.[49]

With the left nationalists splitting the government and threatening to make Grau their political captive, Batista on January 14 finally asked Grau to resign. He still hedged his bets, however. Inasmuch as Mendieta would not take the provisional presidency unless assured in advance of U.S. recognition, and in view of the fact that he was unacceptable to many of the moderate and all of the radical Grauistas, Batista now supported the compromise candidacy of Grau's secretary of agriculture, Carlos Hevia. Hevia had made himself acceptable to the United States by mediating between the embassy and the radical nationalists concerning the application of the nationalization-of-labor law (the 50 percent law) to the vast properties of the United Fruit Company. As a supporter of Grau, he was generally acceptable to the moderate nationalists.[50]

Hevia became provisional president of Cuba on January 15 and was immediately faced by a strike wave which included the electric utilities industry and the government agencies. These actions were in part the culmination of long-standing grievances and in part a response of labor to Batista's ousting of Grau. Faced now with the threat of a formidable labor–left nationalist coalition, Batista decided that only U.S. recognition could forestall a situation which he could not control. By January 18 Batista had become convinced that only Mendieta could bring stability and U.S. recognition. For his part, Hevia, under pressure from left nationalists to oust Batista, did not wish to precipitate civil war. That evening the opposition, with Batista's backing, named Carlos Mendieta as provisional president in place of Hevia.[51]

Once Mendieta was in place, the United States moved with unseemly haste to grant him the recognition it had withheld from Grau. While Roosevelt would not promise recognition in advance, almost all members of the State Department were convinced that Mendieta could create the kind of government in Havana needed to complement U.S. policy designs. Less than one hour after Mendieta's inauguration, Hull (still at sea en route from Montevideo) cabled to Caffery asking his estimation of the new situation. Caffery answered that he was sure the hours-old government would be popular (opposed only by the "communistic element"), would deal firmly with the wave of strikes, and "will be capable of maintaining law and order."[52]

Hull's ship docked at Key West the next day, and Caffery flew there to meet him. After the meeting Caffery spoke by phone to FDR, conveying his suggestion for immediate recognition. Roosevelt was impressed, but felt that he should wait a few days before acting, at least until a Cuban cabinet had been named. An acceptable cabinet was named on January 21, and two days later the United States recognized the Mendieta government.[53]

The overthrow of the first nationalist government in the island's history was clearly the result of work by two activist U.S. ambassadors supported by Washington. Yet despite the power arrayed against it, the Grau regime appeared condemned to self-destruction. Like so many of the movements which flowered in response to the crisis in Cuban society brought on by the sugar and industrial depressions, it suffered not only from disunity but from a lack of vitality. Absent was the confidence associated with crisis movements certain of their direction and historical inevitability. The government seemed benumbed by the knowledge that just over the horizon lay an ineluctable force which might descend upon it at any time and render naught all that had been achieved or planned. Also, at times, it seemed fatally lured toward that very same force as a possible solution to its problems.

The necessity of acting within the constricted possibilities defined by the U.S. presence in the island was accepted with ease by those moderate forces which had from the start defined their purpose in apposition to that presence. Every major turning point would find them gathering their bearings at the U.S. embassy. For those forces struggling to elaborate the contours of their antihegemonic designs, the fear of the colossus and the hope that it could be appeased created a like necessity, leading them to blunt the edge of their dissent. As a result, U.S. policy makers, just beginning to emancipate themselves from narrower visions of the national interest, and thus as yet unable to strike easy system-preserving bargains with rising nationalist forces, were afforded the time necessary to adjust to changes in Cuban society, and eventually to master them.

CHAPTER TEN

The Restoration of Hegemonic Stability

THE OVERTHROW OF THE REGIME of Grau San Martín had an economic as well as a political dimension. U.S. hegemony enabled Sumner Welles to withhold not only diplomatic, but vital economic support as well. Whereas the U.S. ambassador had moved swiftly to initiate debt renegotiation, emergency relief, and a new trade treaty and sugar quotas in order to sustain the government of Carlos Manuel de Céspedes, he halted or reversed these actions once the latter had been replaced by a less cooperative, nationalist regime.

Before the fall of the Machado government, Welles had proposed that the United States support a plan allowing a partial default of Cuban government debts to U.S. banks. Machado was to use delayed interest payments to pay government salaries, thereby sustaining one of the last groups supporting his government. However, when Machado threatened a general moratorium and became uncooperative about his succession, Welles asked the State Department to withhold any debt relief until the Cuban president agreed to some plan for the orderly termination of his mandate.[1]

Once Céspedes was in place, Welles again proposed a partial debt moratorium and went so far as to predict that the regime could not remain in power unless a new loan to pay back salaries was quickly negotiated. Because the New York banks refused to lend additional sums to the bankrupt Cuban Treasury, Welles proposed various schemes by which U.S. government agencies could act in their place. To formulate a specific program of financial relief for Céspedes, a mission headed by Adolf Berle, Jr., was sent to Cuba at the beginning of September. The report of this mission proposed arranging the Cuban debt according to repayment priorities which would allow the diversion of certain interest and sinking-fund payments in order to meet internal obligations. While the U.S. banks and some members of the State and Treasury Departments were upset by the unorthodox concept of putting Cuban stability ahead of bondholders' interests, the proposed program clearly indicated a developing policy of employing debt relief as a way of sustaining Céspedes.[2] This policy was shelved, however, once Céspedes fell

171

from power. Indeed, all forms of economic aid were stopped and were replaced by a program of economic denial.

Economic Pressure

Emergency Relief and Silver Loans

The day before Céspedes was overthrown, a severe hurricane hit central Cuba. Welles immediately cabled Washington asking for a Red Cross relief mission. A disaster relief ship was ready to sail on September 5, but, on that day, citing the previous night's coup, Welles recommended that the shipment be delayed. It was not until a week later, after Welles had gained assurance that supporters of Céspedes would be in charge of the relief supplies and funds, that the ambassador gave permission for the mission to proceed.[3]

The placing of political conditions on disaster relief was a portent of things to come. Welles's position, after the advent of Grau, became one of consistently withholding economic relief. His criteria were purely political for, as he told Assistant Secretary of State Caffery, "if a stable government is installed here which we can recognize we must start assisting it within twenty-four hours' time thereafter."[4]

The ambassador's change of heart extended to the larger question of debt renegotiation as well. One of the many proposals for saving Céspedes had been a plan to "lend" Cuba silver with which to make coinage to pay its internal debts. While there was no time to work out such a soft loan before September 4, the Treasury Department did expedite the minting of an issue of Cuban coinage which Machado had previously arranged with the Chase National Bank. In late August, the U.S. Mint in Philadelphia was ordered to run overtime to have the coinage ready as soon as possible. After September 4, Welles urged that this expediting process be suspended and tried to have shipment of the already completed coinage held up. The Treasury Department gained the cooperation of the Chase Bank, and in September the minting was halted.[5] Moreover, when Grau desired to acquire additional silver for coinage later in the year, Welles, who had previously advised a pragmatic interpretation of article 2 of the Platt Amendment (which gave the United States a veto over the issuance of unfunded Cuban government debts), urged that the treaty be invoked.[6]

Welles's desire to prevent Grau from raising funds was reinforced by his knowledge that the Cuban government was almost totally out of money. The ambassador, through secret contacts in the Cuban Treasury Department, kept track of government balances and hoped to use Grau's inability to meet the government payroll as a means of forcing his resignation or removal. Indeed, U.S. embassy access to unpublished Cuban government statistics gave it great leverage in its efforts to unseat the president.[7]

Trade Treaty and Sugar Quota

Long-range programs of economic relief were also withheld from Grau. Revision of the trade treaty and negotiation of a new sugar tariff or import quota (along with revocation of the Platt Amendment) were held out as rewards to be granted only to a more cooperative regime.

Welles had moved to initiate talks on a new trade treaty from his first week in Havana and, despite the failure of the U.S. Congress to pass trade legislation, had pursued negotiations through the summer aimed at reviving Cuban-U.S. trade. These negotiations were forced into suspension at the fall of Machado, but shortly after the installation of Céspedes, Welles urged that they be renewed. Céspedes' regime, however, was too short-lived to engage in anything but initial discussions. After Grau's accession, and despite indications of the new president's willingness to pursue the negotiations, Welles reversed his position. He wished to use the Cuban government's need for increased trade—most government revenue was derived from customs receipts—as a lever to weaken Grau and to bring about a regime less desirous of tariff autonomy. The "reward" of a new treaty (with its expectation of an assured market for Cuban sugar) would be withheld until the arrival of a regime acceptable to the United States. As President Roosevelt stated U.S. policy later in the year: "No progress along these lines [of revising the trade treaty] can be made until there exists in Cuba a provisional government which through the popular support which it obtains and which through the general cooperation which it enjoys shows evidence of genuine stability."[8]

The most important sources of economic sustenance to Cuba were a higher price (that is, lower tariff) on the sugar that it sold in the U.S. market and an assured share of that market. Despite opposition from domestic beet and insular sugar interests, the State Department strongly advocated both a lowering of the sugar duty and a 2 million ton quota for Cuban cane. This position was supported by the U.S. sugar companies on the island, by the major New York banks which held the bonds of these companies, and by most U.S.-based sugar refiners. Roosevelt also advocated a 2 million ton quota for Cuba. Welles continually expressed his belief that a favorable market share for Cuban sugar would do much to restore economic stability in the island and that such an arrangement would rally political support to the Cuban regime on which it was bestowed. It would take some clever timing by the State Department and a certain amount of luck to ensure that this economic reward was not bestowed upon the wrong regime.[9]

Pursuant to the marketing agreement provisions of the Agricultural Adjustment Act, continental and territorial sugar producers had been meeting in Washington in the summer of 1933 to determine quota shares of the U.S. market. Owing to disagreements within this group, final quota allocations were still undetermined on September 4. At that point, Welles began to convey to Washington his fear that a determination of Cuba's quota would ease political opposition to the Grau government. He requested that the State Department work to delay publication of any "favorable sugar quota suggested for Cuba [as it] will at once be misconstrued here as a demonstration of friendship by the United States toward the present regime here." News of the quota levels under discussion leaked out of the industry meetings nonetheless. Believing that a definitive producers' agreement was at hand, Welles attempted to devise some manner in which Cuban ratification could be negotiated with representatives of the Cuban sugar industry rather than with the Cuban government. The issue became moot, however, when the secretary of agriculture rejected the producers' recommendations.[10]

Welles's efforts to weaken and supplant the nationalist government of Cuba derived from the belief, shared by most State Department officials, that the anti-U.S. posture of the regime, the economic chaos which it fostered, and the radicalism which it condoned were the principal obstacles to the creation of a new economic relationship with the island. The goal of that relationship was to salvage the fortune of U.S. investors by means of an economic recovery on the island based upon political stability and the restoration of U.S.-Cuban trade. That goal, in turn, derived in great measure from the larger New Deal program to reverse the sharp decline in domestic commodity prices (including sugar) and to restore the pre-1929 volume of U.S. foreign trade. Because of executive and congressional preoccupation with this larger program, it was necessary to coordinate the effort to achieve Cuban stability with the pace of that program. The need for such coordination greatly complicated stabilization policy, but it also ensured its success.

Cuba and the Rationalization of the U.S. Sugar Market

To recapitulate the previous discussion, the effort to stabilize the U.S. sugar industry had been hampered by strong disagreement among producers as to their respective shares of a closed U.S. market. In August 1933, the industry finally had hammered out a series of production quotas which favored continental beet growers and left Cuba with an allotment of 1.7 million tons—less than half the level of Cuban imports during the late twenties. The State Department, supported by the president, had advocated a 2 million ton quota to alleviate the depressed economic conditions on the island and enable Cuba to become a major purchaser of U.S. goods once again. The Cubans themselves had requested a quota of 2.5 million tons.[11]

Despite the low Cuban quota, however, the State Department was generally inclined to accept the industry proposal because the domestic producers were now willing to drop their opposition to congressional lowering of the sugar tariff, another basic element of U.S. Cuban policy. Moreover, intervention by Roosevelt brought forth industry agreement to a proposal that the Reconstruction Finance Corporation purchase and hold as a reserve 300,000 tons of Cuban sugar, thus giving the island an effective quota of 2 million tons for 1934.[12]

Nevertheless, as noted earlier, the whole matter became moot when, on October 9, Secretary of Agriculture Henry Wallace declared the quota agreement in violation of AAA guidelines and rejected the industry proposal. Wallace held that the various production quotas totaled more than projected demand and would thus not raise prices. He also felt that the economic benefits of the industry plan accrued mostly to refiners and processors, not farmers. Furthermore, the low quota for Cuba would force a large amount of its sugar onto the world market, depressing the world price and further undercutting the attempt to raise domestic sugar prices.[13]

Wallace wanted to resolve the issue by having the AAA set quotas rather than the industry. This, however, was not possible, because sugar had not been designated as a "basic agricultural commodity" in the original legislation. The secretary wished to have Congress so designate sugar at its next session. Once this was done, the secretary would have broad powers to control production, including the setting of quotas and the levying of a processing tax, the proceeds of which could be used to compensate domestic growers for their reduced production levels.[14]

While thankful that Wallace's actions had afforded it the opportunity to lobby once again for a higher Cuban quota, the State Department, in view of the unexpected survival of the Grau regime, began to exhibit concern that the quota question might proceed to resolution before trade negotiations could be initiated with a cooperative Cuban regime. The department renewed its proposal for a 2 million ton quota but worked to ensure that any decision on quotas be used as a bargaining tool for gaining access to Cuban markets rather than being taken as a unilateral measure.

State Department policy makers were also fearful of untimely congressional action on the question of the sugar tariff. Such action could remove the other principal bargaining weapon for obtaining greater access to the Cuban market. The U.S. Tariff Commission had already recommended a 25 percent reduction in the sugar tariff, but the Latin American Division of the State Department urged withholding such action, because "except for an enlarged sugar market, the United States has very little to offer Cuba in exchange for concessions on American products." However, despite these fears and the difficult timing requirements, the State Department pressed forward in its efforts to obtain quota and tariff levels sufficient to form a basis for Cuban stability.[15]

Though beet sugar interests continued to press Wallace to accept the original quota division drawn up by the producers (which favored their industry), the State Department was finally able to obtain formulation of a new quota allocation. In this effort, the hope for a restored Cuban market as well as the marginal nature of much beet production convinced Wallace and

FDR that protecting the Cuban sugar industry (albeit at a reduced capacity) would be the most effective way of stemming the decline of sugar prices and expanding U.S. exports.

Fortunately for Cuban policy, the position of the Agriculture Department was not formulated until after State Department pressure had forced Grau from the presidential palace in January 1934. In February, Roosevelt asked Congress to designate sugar as a basic agricultural commodity and to authorize the secretary of agriculture to establish production quotas. The president recommended a formula which reduced the quotas of all non-Cuban producing sectors from the levels provided for in the industry proposal of the previous summer. The greatest reduction was made in the continental beet quota, while Cuba was to be granted 1,940,000 tons.[16]

The resultant legislation, the Jones-Costigan Act, did not, however, fully reflect the president's pro-Cuban position. Beet sugar forces used their greater influence with Congress to restore a portion of their quota, while Cuba's share was reduced to 1,902,000 tons. Refining interests were able to reduce severely the amount of finished sugar imported from the island. Finally, Cuba did not participate in the compensation payments provided in return for reduction in plantings. Nevertheless, the Jones-Costigan Act did halt the decline of Cuban sugar imports and set them at a level which allowed for a modest economic recovery in the island. Perhaps most important of all, the act tied the Cuban economy more closely to political decisions made by the U.S. Congress and executive, thus exposing the island to a more direct expression of hegemony than that formerly exercised by the U.S. sugar companies and banks.[17]

Once a moderate Cuban economic recovery was provided for by means of the sugar quota, Roosevelt moved to raise Cuban income by reducing the sugar tariff. The domestic forces which had perennially fought against lowering the tariff no longer had to fear a flood of Cuban sugar, and so in May 1934, Roosevelt, employing the little-used flexible provisions of the Tariff Act of 1930, reduced the duty on Cuban sugar from two cents to one and one-half cents per pound. A further reduction of the duty was held in abeyance to be used as a bargaining tool in the final negotiation of a new trade treaty. This lowering of the duty enabled Cuban producers to recover a larger portion of their sale price in the U.S. market and once again made profitable operations of many of the island's sugar companies which had been operating in the red for several years. Nevertheless, because of the enforced low volume, these companies never returned to the high production and profit levels they had known in the 1920s.[18]

With a friendly regime in place in Havana, and with a further reduction of the sugar duty available whenever the U.S. president so chose, the way was now clear to conclude trade negotiations with Cuba.

Cuba and the Export Expansion Program

While the Cubans, as we have seen, hardly needed to be consulted regarding the determination of a sugar quota, the United States had to negotiate with someone in authority in the island to produce a new trade treaty. Thus, the unwillingness of the U.S. government to deal with Grau, as well as domestic conflicts of interest, delayed progress in trade matters.[19]

As noted earlier, the general purpose of revising the treaty was to stem the decline in the U.S. share of the Cuban market by altering those Cuban trade regulations which inhibited increased U.S. imports. Both the State Department negotiators and the major U.S. exporters to Cuba had concluded that to recapture U.S. domination of the Cuban market it was necessary to isolate the particular barrier to increased exports of each product. Where U.S. goods faced foreign competition, the goal was to increase the U.S. preference. If such increase was not enough to make U.S. products competitive, the effort was to gain both a larger preference and an *increase* in the Cuban tariff. When the major competitor was a native Cuban product, the key to export expansion was to lower the Cuban tariff. In case the Cuban government should attempt to compensate for lessened tariff protection by internal taxes against U.S. goods, the State Department negotiators also planned to request treaty controls in this area. It was expected that because of Cuba's dire need for economic relief and her extreme dependence on the U.S. market for her sugar exports, she would be amenable to making these extraordinary concessions.[20]

Negotiations for a new commercial treaty had begun while Machado was still in office. By June 1933, Sumner Welles had the staff of the commercial attaché in Havana hard at work detailing the specific needs of a wide range of U.S. products. In order to gain economic relief, Machado showed signs of willingness to compromise the protective aspects of the tariff changes which he had inaugurated in 1927 and which had led, in a few lines, to impressive import substitution achievements.[21]

As trade negotiations proceeded, the State and Commerce Departments received innumerable requests from harried exporters desiring better access to the Cuban market. By the time of Machado's overthrow, these requests had been supplemented by detailed studies of U.S. trade needs by the Havana embassy and a group of the largest U.S. exporters (the Jessup Study). This information was funneled into a new bureau established to coordinate the U.S. position in the negotiation of a series of reciprocal trade treaties projected under the Reciprocal Trade Agreements Act soon to be placed before Congress. This bureau, the Interdepartmental Advisory Board on Reciprocity Treaties, had been formed in July and was studying communications from Welles which described the items on which the Cuban government had offered to grant better treatment. Despite the demise of the Céspedes government in early September, the Subcommittee on Cuba of the Interdepartmental Advisory Board worked on codification of the concessions already granted and the specification of others which would be requested once negotiations with the Cuban government were resumed. This committee met regularly in October, November, and December 1933, and by January 1934 it had worked out a detailed presentation of U.S. export needs in the Cuban trade.[22]

The New U.S.-Cuban Trade Agreement

Once a cooperative Cuban regime was in place, official trade negotiations were resumed. Because of Cuba's monoculture and traditional dependence on U.S. goods, the island had been a heavy importer of both agricultural and industrial products from the United States. This dependence placed the United States in the favorable position of being able to demand concessions which would expand commodity as well as manufactured exports. Relief for domestic agricultural interests, who would bear the brunt of expected concessions to Cuban sugar and tobacco, would ensure broad political support for the Cuban settlement within the United States. Of particular concern to the farm bloc was the Cuban tariff on pork products, especially lard. This protective duty had caused a severe decline in what had been a major U.S. export and led to the growth of a significant native industry. To restore the competitiveness of the U.S. product, negotiators requested an 80 percent reduction in the Cuban tariff.

Protection of U.S. manufacturers was not neglected either, especially those facing the recent surge of Japanese competition. This Asian threat occasioned demands for an increase in the Cuban tariff on certain manufactures, combined with a larger preference on U.S. products. Only in this manner could the island be sealed off from a flood of low-priced Japanese goods. The negotiators, however, were careful not to request tariff levels high enough to encourage native production.[23]

Nevertheless, some economic sectors in the United States were unhappy with the proposed treaty. The banks which held Cuban government bonds feared that a general increase in U.S. preferences would reduce Cuban government revenues and lead to a general default. The bankers, however, also held the debts of the major U.S. sugar companies in Cuba, and State Department planners contended that a revival of the island's sugar industry would secure sugar company bonds and that a general revival of the Cuban economy would eventually increase the Cuban government's tax revenues.

The suggestion that Cuba tax sugar exports to recapture lost tariff revenues was opposed by U.S. negotiators, who preferred that the full tariff benefit accrue to the sugar sector, and who feared that the Cuban government might use the money to carry out programs of income equalization which would work against U.S. interests. Though some of the most liberal New Dealers hoped to use the treaty negotiations to ensure that the Cuban sugar worker received a share of increased sugar revenues, the general position among the negotiators was to let such benefits trickle down as a result of restored profit levels.[24]

Proponents of liberalized trade like Cordell Hull and Francis Sayre were disturbed by the protectionism (quotas) and bilateralism (most-favored-nation treatment was not a part of the treaty) which formed the basis of U.S.-Cuban trade. Nevertheless, the prospect that a new trade treaty would aid U.S. exports by restoring Cuban "prosperity," while necessitating only minor sacrifices from domestic producers (beet sugar farmers and processors) created a certain agreement among both autarkists and internationalists and allowed the Cuban treaty negotiations to proceed smoothly. This general unanimity also allowed the United States to face Cuba with a concerted set of demands.[25]

As a result, the United States was able to gain agreement from Cuba to preferences of 50 percent and more in some cases, and to "bind" (that is, freeze for the term of the treaty) certain Cuban tariff rates and even internal taxes when they affected U.S. goods. A reciprocal binding of U.S. rates was not possible, and was not seriously proposed. Moreover, Cuban preferences on U.S. goods were set for at least the three-year life of the treaty, while the major U.S. "concessions"—the sugar quota and tariff—could be altered by Congress or the executive and were tied to the political and judicial fate of the Jones-Costigan Act.[26]

In August 1934, the new U.S.-Cuban trade treaty was signed. It extended increased preferences to a large group of U.S. exports and contained provision for quotas on the importation of Cuban sugar and tobacco. The treaty also entailed a reduction in Cuban consular fees and prevented "unfavorable changes in . . . the determination of dutiable value and conversion of currencies." Controlled also were the internal taxes affecting most imports, changes in duty resulting from currency devaluation, and such exchange controls "as would tend to nullify the value of the concessions." As part of this settlement the sugar tariff was further reduced from 1.5 cents per pound to 0.9 cents.[27]

The Effects of the Trade Agreement

Dissonant voices within Cuba objected to the removal of protection for many of those industries which had grown up in the island as a result of the tariff reform of 1927. Despite the fact that New Deal rhetoric spoke of the need to diversify Cuban agriculture and get the Cuban agricultural worker "back to the land," the results of the treaty were to intensify sugar monoculture. By the late 1930s, sugar and its derivatives again represented some 80 percent of the value of exports, returning to the dominant position they had held in the twenties. Cuban dependence on U.S. goods also increased. Whereas the United States supplied 54 percent of Cuban imports during the depression year of 1932, by 1938 U.S. goods represented 71 percent of all imports. Thus, the U.S. exporters' goal of reversing their declining share of the Cuban market was achieved.[28]

While trade benefits to the United States were significant, Cuban rewards were meager at best. The Cuban share of the U.S. sugar market, which had reached over 50 percent in the early and mid-twenties, failed to recover much from the low of 25 percent to which it had fallen in the early thirties. By 1940 it was still below 30 percent. Indeed, the sugar quota system initiated in 1934 ensured that Cuba could never regain its dominant position in the U.S. market. Nor did the volume of Cuban exports show anything like the increase registered for U.S. goods. By the end of the decade, U.S. trade with the island had expanded by more than 70 percent over 1933 levels, while it more than tripled in value. Cuban trade rose only about 10 to 20 percent and did not quite double in value over the same period.[29]

Most of the increased value of Cuban exports was the result of slightly improved sugar prices, the major benefit of which accrued to an island industry owned predominantly by U.S. companies. Because world sugar surpluses and restricted access to the U.S. market forced a drop in cane production in the island (predepression levels were not restored until after World War II), the duration of the harvesting season or *zafra* was reduced by about 50 percent, thus causing a reduction in the yearly income of field and mill workers. Indeed, consular reports from the countryside in the mid- and late thirties noted the continuation of depressed economic conditions among the agricultural proletariat.[30]

In the years after the new trade treaty, Cuba suffered a relative decline in its trade with countries other than the United States. Whereas the decline in Cuban-U.S. trade had been greater than that of the island with other states in the early thirties, the recovery of the former outstripped that of the latter in the late thirties. This growing dependence on the U.S. market was a function of the enhanced preferences provided U.S. goods in the 1934 trade agreement. While much of Latin America was entering a period of enforced separation from traditional markets due to world depression and then world war, to which they responded with varying degrees of economic autarky and industrialization, Cuba was moving in the opposite direction.[31]

Stabilizing the Mendieta Regime

The conclusion of a sugar quota, lower tariff, and new trade treaty under the Mendieta government set in place the major elements of U.S. policy toward Cuba. Continental sugar producers had been protected from a flood of low-cost Cuban sugar (and subsidized for any loss in production), U.S. sugar companies in Cuba had been saved from disaster, and U.S. goods were provided with easier access to the Cuban market. Nevertheless, all of these economic programs were long-range solutions. There was still a pressing need to ensure long life for the new cooperative regime in Cuba so that there would be enough time to work them out.

In order to provide such a tenure for Mendieta's government, the United States had moved with alacrity to recognize his regime. The State Department then pressed forward with economic relief measures. Three days after recognizing the new Cuban government, in a measure indicative of the dual need to raise agricultural prices in the United States and to ensure Cuban stability, Roosevelt offered a $2 million credit with which Cuba could purchase "food relief" from the surplus stocks of the Agriculture Department.[32]

Ever since the late twenties, when a new tariff cut off most U.S. lard and pork product exports to Cuba, agricultural interests had been pressing for an attack on Cuban protectionism. In the fall of 1933, they had hoped to force a reduction in lard and pork duties as part of a triangular credit which contemplated sending these products to Cuba in exchange for sugar to be sold to the Soviet Union on credit from the Reconstruction Finance Corporation.[33] This particular deal did not go through, but throughout the winter of 1933–1934, the AAA (sitting on growing surplus agricultural stocks) and the pork farmers (with their eye on the Cuban tariff) continued to press for "humanitarian" relief to impoverished Cuba. It was in this context, and with the added purpose of supporting Mendieta, that in January 1934 Welles (now assistant secretary of state) cabled to Caffery a list of the surplus lard and pork products which "Agriculture would like to see the sales [of] to Cuba." This aspect of the Cuban program was eventually accomplished as part of the new commercial treaty, which provided for a revival of the trade the pork farmers had sought.[34]

To rationalize the economic relief program and to provide for the revival of U.S.-Cuban trade, the Roosevelt administration created an Export-Import Bank in March 1934. The purpose of this institution was to provide trade credit for commerce with the island. The bank was immediately pressed into service in stabilizing Mendieta. Whereas the State Department had blocked efforts by the Grau government to obtain silver for coinage, it now quickly obtained a $3.8 million Eximbank loan so that Mendieta could obtain coinage needed to pay back salaries. A corollary aspect of the deal was that it satisfied the demands of western silver-producing states for relief for their "surplus" commodity. Many silver states were also beet-producing states, and this transaction helped ease congressional resistance to a lowered sugar tariff.[35]

Loan relief for Mendieta went further than the provision of silver coinage. Just as the State Department had sympathized with Céspedes' need for a debt moratorium, it acquiesced—despite the complaints of the bankers—

when Mendieta ceased interest payments in April. The State Department even swallowed a moratorium on debt principal decreed by Mendieta in August. Though the question of debt payments was to become an unpleasant issue in the late thirties, the funds made available to Mendieta by means of silver loans and debt moratoriums eased some of the internal pressure against the Cuban government.[36]

As a further gesture of support for Mendieta, the U.S. government granted him, almost without struggle, the prize that Cuban nationalists had sought since the very beginning of the republic—the abrogation of the hated Platt Amendment. Having concluded that the right of intervention was a dubious asset at best, and having set in motion the engines of economic and political stability that were to replace it, on May 29, 1934, the United States signed a new Treaty of Relations between the two states. This instrument preserved U.S. rights regarding the naval base at Guantanamo Bay and reasserted the validity of the acts of the 1899–1902 occupation government. In all other respects, the original treaty, including the intervention clause, was abrogated. With Cuba integrated more fully than ever before into the U.S. economic orbit, the island was granted the full measure of legal sovereignty.[37]

With an irony worthy of the gods, the United States pronounced the final independence of Cuba and the end to its right to intervene in the island's affairs. It would be twenty-five years before Washington would again feel the need to bring down a Cuban government. In the interim, the new weapons which the centralization of economic decision-making had placed in the hands of the U.S. president would be sufficient to ensure the necessary level of Cuban stability.

CHAPTER ELEVEN

Hegemony and Stalemate

THE ABILITY OF THE UNITED STATES to maintain its hegemony over Cuban society, despite the rise of nationalist and anticapitalist doctrines and movements on the island in the 1930s, resulted from the ties of structural dependency which had been woven into the fabric of the Cuban economy and into the mind-sets of the island's elite during more than three decades of political tutelage and massive economic presence. This state of dependency led native leaders to accept U.S. social values and models of economic development, and caused a realignment of their economic pursuits so as to conform to the needs of the U.S. economy. Given their new beliefs and life-style and the new economic role which necessarily complemented them, the traditional Cuban elite had become by the late twenties closely associated in appearance and fact with both the U.S. economic presence and the foreign policy which supported it. Their dependent position stripped them of any autonomous economic base or social philosophy and rendered them incapable of mounting an effective material or ideological challenge to the power of the United States in the island. Consequently, this traditional elite could not assume command of (or alternatively, effectively compete with) the anti-Yankee movement created by the frustration of Cuban independence and the autonomist and anticapitalist developments flowing from the economic depression.[1]

To ride out the storm which threatened its interests in the early thirties, U.S. policy gradually shifted away from support for this integrated Cuban bourgeoisie. It moved instead toward an alliance with the moderate wing of the nationalist movement, offering as inducement a new U.S. policy which eschewed overt political interference and supported the antidictatorial consensus within the island. The fundamental expressions of this new policy were the ending of support for Machado in 1933 and the abrogation of the Platt Amendment in 1934. In return, the new moderate allies were to accept a tightening of the U.S. economic presence and the necessity of adjusting the Cuban economy to the new condition of sugar depression, as the old elite had adjusted it to serve the sugar boom. While the United States would now

183

tolerate a slightly altered division of wealth within the island to accommodate its new allies, this new Cuban elite in turn would accept the continued
determination in Washington and New York of the portion of sugar income
which would be passed into the Cuban economy.[2]

This change in the relationship between the United States and Cuba was
necessitated by the sugar depression of the late 1920s. That epochal event
signaled the end of the traditional elite's legitimacy within the island and
thereby their ability to continue serving as the partners of U.S. hegemony.
The cement which had bound that partnership was the sugar boom of the
first two decades of the twentieth century. The bonanza in sugar profits had
elicited a massive U.S. investment in land, mills, banking, and internal
transportation and commerce, creating an economic presence which served
as the basis for U.S. domination. This new investment also supplanted or
rendered dependent the original land-owning base of the traditional elite, at
the same time providing the economic developments that created the new
roles which that group and the aspiring middle class were to play. Interstices
within the new Cuban economy not filled by U.S. firms provided an economic base for these groups. They moved into urban real estate, the professions, and secondary service operations for the economic interchange between the island and the United States, and generally acted as middlemen
between U.S. capital and the Cuban factors of production. It was in these
positions that the Cuban bourgeoisie established a life-style influenced by
Yankee values and almost wholly dependent upon the Yankee dollar.[3]

With the end of the sugar boom, the Cuban elite which served the U.S.
presence lost both its economic strength and its social role. The rationale of
the structure of domination was called into question, and the U.S. economic
presence and political influence were now seen to be an intolerable burden,
especially to the postindependence generation of Cuban youth who defined
sovereignty in other than purely formal terms. The decline of the sugar
latifundium ended the flow of sugar income to U.S. milling companies and
banks. Within the island, this decline removed the amenities of middle-class
life and all sense of economic security from the working class, casting a large
portion of it into extreme privation. Sugar decline and the subsequent loss of
purchasing power also dried up the channel of trade between the United
States and Cuba. In this manner, it extended the sugar depression through
the entire island by undermining the earnings of much of the remainder of
the population which serviced or sold the sugar and tobacco moving north or
the large range of agricultural and finished goods moving south. Most devas-
tating of all, sugar was entering a long period of overproduction and low
prices which would render superfluous much of that portion of the Cuban
population which had become dependent upon it during the period of its
expansion.[4]

It was this new economic and political situation to which both U.S. policy makers and Cuban nationalists began to respond. To sustain its hegemony, the United States had to learn how to manage sugar decline as effectively as it had managed sugar growth. A new basis of domination had to be created.

Working against the flexibility needed to shift the basis of U.S. hegemony, however, were the constants of U.S. policy. During the 1930s, the basic goals of policy remained essentially what they had been in 1902. These goals were: (1) to substitute U.S. economic and military presence for that of other powerful states, (2) to protect and enhance U.S. trade and investment in the island, and (3) to ensure Cuban political stability, lack of which might threaten the U.S. economic stake or cause the United States or other powerful nations to intervene. This was a conservative and protective policy which, in the new context of depression, denied Cuba the possibility of finding a way out of the sugar collapse other than by depressing living standards (especially those of the agricultural proletariat), submerging nationalist aspirations, and enduring lean years until a return of sugar profits restored the old dispensation. While U.S. policy makers were learning to be more pragmatic in implementing policy, especially on the issues of intervention and support of incumbent regimes, the protection of U.S. interests implicit at the base of policy precluded meaningful cooperation with movements of economic nationalism in the island. Thus, despite progressive Good Neighbor and New Deal rhetoric, and the necessity of finding credible native allies, some form of confrontation with Cuban nationalism could not be avoided.

Throughout the sugar and general economic depression, U.S. representatives resisted direct assaults against the U.S. economic presence, thereby blocking this means of relieving the pressure of economic decline within the island. For their part, native nationalist elements argued that capitalist depression justified and necessitated the uncoupling of the Cuban and U.S. economies. U.S. spokesmen branded these elements as radicals, charging that their actions undermined stability and thereby blocked the restoration of profitable economic interchange between Cuba and the United States. Naturally, U.S. resistance to nationalist demands reinforced that movement's anti-Yankee bias. At the same time, the demonstrative failure of capitalism in Cuba was leading to the expression of national and international socialist alternatives. All of this foreshadowed a tense period in U.S.-Cuban relations and held out the possibility of the first concerted attack on U.S. hegemony since the turn of the century.

Fortunately for U.S. interests, the oncoming struggle between nationalism and hegemony was confused and in part dissipated by the rise of the brutal dictatorship of Gerardo Machado. Inserting itself into the growing anti-Yankee consciousness, the question of dictatorship and the response to it of the Cuban nationalists, on the one hand, and that of the State Department, on the other, blunted confrontation with U.S. interests.

In the initial phase of the movement against the Machado dictatorship (1927–1932), the United States was regarded (more or less correctly) as a major prop of the Havana administration. Consequently, during these years the antidictatorial and anti-imperialist aspects of the nationalist movement were compatible. However, when Machado himself became a destabilizing factor, owing to his repression of the legitimate opposition in the early thirties, U.S. policy turned first neutral, then hostile.

U.S. hostility toward the dictator, coupled with Machado's alienation of the moderate political opposition, led to the dual result of weakening the compatibility of the antidictatorial and anti-Yankee strains within the original nationalist movement, while at the same time diluting the radical thrust of that movement by joining to it the now outcast conservative-moderate political opposition. The actions of the U.S. government during this period complemented this disorientation of nationalist ideology. Washington once again took a stand in favor of political reform in Cuba and held forth the progressive goals of the early New Deal as indicative of its new Cuban program.

Inasmuch as dictatorship in the island was not a necessary element of U.S. policy, the hegemonic power, in 1933, took a careful but effective stand against the Machado tyranny, using its power to ensure—and, in part, preempt—the success of the antidictatorial movement. This seemingly benevolent use of U.S. power divided the diluted and schizophrenic nationalist movement into two groups: moderates, who wished to cooperate with an apparently friendly government in Washington to find a way out of the profound economic depression; and radicals, distrustful of any U.S. interference in Cuban affairs, who sought to ease Cuban poverty by altering the exchange relationship between U.S. capital and Cuban land and labor. Some of the radicals also wished to establish the basis for an autonomous or socialist economic structure.[5]

It was this division of the nationalist movement that laid the basis for an alliance between the United States and a new native elite. The moderate nationalists eventually gained the support of Washington, thus replacing the old conservative supporters of the pre-Machado era. With these new native allies, and with the power to nourish them and to deprive the noncooperative nationalists, the United States acquired maneuvering room in which to arrange an even closer economic relationship with the island, one which precluded nonhegemonic forms of economic development. Aiding U.S. diplomacy in this process was a State Department policy which sought a place for a modest Cuban economic recovery within the larger U.S. recovery program. Also facilitating this outcome was Cuba's prior integration into the U.S. economic sphere, which made dual recovery both possible and, in the case of sugar, necessary.[6] Within the United States, this same integration offered internationalists a politically safe step toward the goal of multilateral trade expansion and gave nationalists a secure opportunity in controlled bilateral commerce.

In this manner, and despite the temporary rise to power of radical nationalism in the fall of 1933, U.S. hegemony was retained. The United States was able to contain the forces of social revolution, mitigate the effects of nationalist reforms upon its interests, and actually tighten its control over Cuban developments. In the final analysis, however, its actions gave to moderate forces a substance which they no longer intrinsically possessed. When radical revolt once again broke through the dike of presidential power in 1959, the weakness of truly conservative social forces was finally revealed.

The Stalemated Society

In the years after 1934, and as a direct consequence of the revolutionary upsurge of the early thirties, populism became the dominant theme of Cuban politics. U.S. hegemony was brought into question, and its functioning became fraught with tensions and compromises which had been unknown in the pre-Machado period. The continuation of U.S. domination in the period after the rise of populist nationalism, despite the mobilization of the Cuban proletariat during the insurgency of the early thirties, created a stalemate in Cuban society between status-quo and radical forces. While U.S. power blocked autonomous or noncapitalist development, the radicalized proletariat and newly organized middle sectors gained sufficient political leverage to prevent the consolidation of trickle-down programs and force Cuban governments into experiments with interventionist economics, which continually exacerbated relations with the United States. Moreover, these same forces acquired the economic leverage to alter the rate of profit on doing business in Cuba. The result was a modest proletarian recovery from the subsistence levels of the thirties, but one which took place within an overall economy that was not achieving significant growth, in part because proletarian gains discouraged further investment.[7]

In the post–World War II period, Cuba became not a haven for U.S. investment, but rather a place where businessmen complained that unionized employees were immune from dismissal and where hundreds of petty nationalist regulations and bureaucrats exacted their toll of red tape and graft. As sugar no longer constituted the bonanza it had in the twenties, all but the most efficient of the large U.S. mills were eventually sold to Cuban interests. Nevertheless, the claim of the Cuban bourgeoisie that it had recaptured the heights of the island's economy was belied by the fact that a large percentage of the Cuban crop was still ground at the remaining U.S. mills (40 percent in 1955), and by the continued domination of the U.S. market for the island's sugar.[8]

The partial move away from sugar investment coincided (not incidentally) with the increased presence of U.S. capital and brands in the internal market. This move from investment in competitive, low-growth, and low-profit areas of the Cuban economy into those where oligopoly position or rising demand provided higher profits extended the influence and visibility of U.S. goods throughout the entire economy and ensured that any subsequent movement for radical autonomy would come up against U.S. firms and their protectors in the U.S. embassy.

The failure of any class in Cuba to achieve social hegemony in the post-Machado period was in many ways the result of the frustration of the revolution of 1933. The ideological flowering which produced the nationalist renaissance of the late twenties and early thirties—with its newly articulated neoliberal, socialist, and corporatist social visions—produced no viable working model for Cuban society. The result, rather, was a superficial populism and state capitalism, combined with a bureaucratized army and cartelized labor unions and middle-sector organizations. This structure, from which any truly conservative forces had long been eliminated and into which the reformist and revolutionary organizations of the thirties had been successfully integrated, attracted scant allegiance from the Cuban people.

The lack of legitimacy which characterized the regimes of the 1940s and 1950s created an ideological vacuum that served as an important precondition for the decisive victory of a new generation of radical nationalists in the 1960s and for their subsequent intellectual alliance with socialism.

NOTES

BIBLIOGRAPHY

INDEX

Notes

Chapter 1. The Origins of Hegemony, 1880–1902

1. Julio Le Riverend, *Economic History of Cuba* (Havana: Inst. del Libro, 1966), pp. 132–38. Until the nineteenth century, Spanish commercial regulations effectively isolated Cuba from the economic forces which spread slavery and sugar agriculture through other areas of the Caribbean. By the time the sugar plantation system expanded to the island, a white class of small tobacco and coffee farmers had developed. In no other Caribbean territory did the slave plantation system encounter such a large body of self-sufficient farmers. Ramiro Guerra y Sánchez, *Sugar and Society in the Caribbean* (New Haven: Yale University Press, 1964), pp. xxii, 42–43. In the nineteenth century, this coffee and tobacco middle class was greatly weakened by the expanding sugar latifundium, with much of its membership being forced onto marginal land or into dependence on sugar. Thereafter, no powerful rural middle class existed outside the sugar economy. The small sugar planter was in turn to undergo pressure from the industrialization of the sugar latifundium in the late nineteenth and early twentieth centuries. However, because a multiclass rural structure had existed in Cuba, there was resistance to the latifundium. This resistance enabled the planter class to cushion their growing dependence upon the mills by obtaining governmental protection during the twentieth century. Their demands upon Havana often clashed with the needs of the large U.S. milling interests and made them a component of the anti-U.S. nationalism of the twenties and thirties.

2. Le Riverend, *Economic History*, pp. 138–40; Guerra y Sánchez, *Sugar and Society*, pp. 66–67. Because tobacco was grown on privately owned small plots without slave labor, liberals championed its economic and political influence and decried its subservience to the absentee-owned, enslaving, and later proletarianizing sugar industry. In the twentieth century these agricultural romanticists were joined by more modern economic theorists who favored agricultural diversification. For the classic statement of this position see Fernando Ortiz y Fernández, *Cuban Counterpoint: Tobacco and Sugar* (New York: Random House, 1970).

3. Important events in this regard were Spanish trade liberalization, U.S. independence, and the Haitian Revolution. See Guerra y Sánchez, *Sugar and Society*, p. 45.

4. On the beet sugar industry in nineteenth-century Europe see Leland Jenks, *Our Cuban Colony: A Study in Sugar* (New York: Vanguard Press, 1928), pp. 27–28; and Hugh Thomas, *Cuba: The Pursuit of Freedom* (New York: Harper and Row, 1971), p. 125. On the U.S. beet sugar industry see Irwin Bettman, "The Beet Sugar Industry: A Study in Tariff Protection," *Harvard Business Review*, 11, no. 3 (April 1933):369.

5. Jenks, *Our Cuban Colony*, pp. 26–27; Sidney Mintz, foreword to Guerra y Sánchez, *Sugar and Society*, p. xxviii.

6. Thomas, *Cuba*, pp. 275–76. The *colono*, as the planter was called, rarely had his own capital and was usually financed by the *central*. This nonmilling planter began to appear in the 1870s, selling his cane at the nearest mill. The *central's* great milling capacity created the need

for a large and steady cane supply. This led to very strict contracts between it and the *colonos* who furnished the sugar. The *central*'s need for cane control also led in the twentieth century to cane-raising directly by the *central* on its own lands (known as administration cane), in many cases eliminating the *colono* entirely. With the end of slavery in the 1880s, labor costs became an important factor in the industry. The *colono* system shifted responsibility for labor from the miller to the planter. Thus the *colono*, the new agricultural middle class, was squeezed not only by his dependence on the cane price paid by the *central*, but by the demands of his cane workers as well. The *colono* often had to compensate for his complete lack of freedom in the market for his goods by exploiting his position as employer of labor. This meant that when the market pressure on his profits became unbearable in the 1920s and 1930s, he would find no ally against the *central* among labor. See Guerra y Sánchez, *Sugar and Society*, p. 148.

7. Le Riverend, *Economic History*, pp. 178–79.

8. Ibid., pp. 179–80, 186–87.

9. Thomas, *Cuba*, chap. 11. U.S.-owned mills date back to 1818. The first large U.S. acquisition was by E. F. Atkins in 1882. Though sugar consolidation had begun in the 1870s, it was not until the arrival of large-scale U.S. capital that consolidation spread throughout all the sugar-growing areas of Cuba and the great expansion of production took place. See Guerra y Sánchez, *Sugar and Society*, p. xxix. The stream of land consolidations and mill expansions became a torrent between 1900 and 1925, setting the stage for the political and social unrest of the late twenties and early thirties.

10. Thomas, *Cuba*, p. 419; Charles E. Chapman, *A History of the Cuban Republic* (New York: Macmillan Co., 1927), p. 589. The sugar latifundium, as it undermined the land-owning aristocracy, also displaced the independent small farmer. That is, its pressure was felt by both the upper and middle classes of the countryside, making the former economically dependent, and forcing the latter in many cases into proletarian status. The upper class, with the exception of some of the intellectuals among them, made their peace with their changed condition. But the formerly independent small farmer, in his landless dependency, formed a new class consciousness that was to be a source of great unrest during the post-1925 sugar depression. On the displacement of the independent farmer see Guerra y Sánchez, *Sugar and Society*, pp. xxxvi–xxxviii. On the dependent nature of the Cuban upper class see Robin Blackburn, "Prologue to the Cuban Revolution," *New Left Review*, October 1963, pp. 57–61.

11. David M. Pletcher, *The Awkward Years* (Columbia: University of Missouri Press, 1952), pp. 288–92. By 1894 the United States was taking 87 percent of Cuban exports, with only 6 percent going to Spain (Thomas, *Cuba*, p. 289).

12. Jenks, *Our Cuban Colony*, pp. 29–31.

13. Mira Wilkins, *The Emergence of Multinational Enterprise* (Cambridge, Mass.: Harvard University Press, 1970), p. 151; Carleton Beals, *The Crime of Cuba* (Philadelphia: J. P. Lippincott Co., 1933), p. 404; and Jenks, *Our Cuban Colony*, pp. 34–35. As noted, the Atkins acquisition was in 1882. Other U.S. sugar investors of this period were the Cuban-American Rionda family based in New York, Spreckels & Co., Mapos Co., Hugh Kelley, and Perkins and Welsh (see Thomas, *Cuba*, p. 290). The Boston Fruit Co., soon to be the United Fruit Co., bought its first sugar plantation in 1898 (Wilkins, *Multinational Enterprise*, p. 155). Atkins was influential regarding Cuban policy during this period (see Edward F. Atkins, *Sixty Years in Cuba* [Cambridge, Mass.: Riverside Press, 1926], pp. 235–36; David F. Healy, *The United States in Cuba, 1898–1902* [Madison: University of Wisconsin Press, 1963], p. 11; and Thomas, *Cuba*, pp. 288, 332).

14. Jenks, *Our Cuban Colony*, pp. 36–37; Thomas, *Cuba*, p. 290; and Wilkins, *Multinational Enterprise*, pp. 150, 153.

15. Philip S. Foner, *The Spanish-Cuban-American War*, vol. 2 (New York: Monthly Review Press, 1972), passim.

16. For a discussion of the differing goals of the agrarian businessmen and the banker-industrialists regarding Cuba, see William Appleman Williams, *The Roots of the Modern*

American Empire (New York: Vintage Books, 1970), esp. pp. 388–89, 408–10, 425–27, 435. As the expansion of the home market lessened the need for agricultural exports between 1900 and 1914, absorbing the efforts of the agrarians at home, the banker-industrialists and their connections in the State Department were able to chart economic relations with Cuba relatively unhindered. However, World War I and its immense opportunities for agricultural exports brought rural interests back into the policy-making arena. When, after 1920, the European export market ended, and the domestic market could not absorb the now expanded productive capacity of U.S. farms, the agricultural businessmen again fought effectively for control of foreign economic policy. They succeeded by means of the sugar tariff in partially undermining the vast sugar and infrastructure investments which the banker-industrialists had amassed in the first two decades of the century.

17. The major effort to avoid this polarization was Ramiro Guerra y Sánchez, *Azúcar y población en las Antillas*, 2d ed. (Madrid: Cultural S.A., 1935). This became the classic statement of opposition to the sugar latifundium during the 1920s and 1930s. Based upon an agricultural fundamentalism resembling that of Thomas Jefferson, it decried the destruction of the rural small-property-owning class and its proletarianization. However, Guerra attacked the latifundium, not as an expression of "Yankee imperialism," but as a heartless and disembodied creation for which particular countries or policies were not responsible. This allowed dependent Cuban political leaders to support the thesis while separating themselves from those who attacked the United States. Guerra called for government controls over the sugar industry to distribute its benefits more fairly and oversee its growth. The goal was to curb the latifundium and rebuild the rural middle class. Guerra wanted to ensure the prosperity of the sugar companies upon which he acknowledged Cuban well-being to depend. At the same time, however, he hoped to modify their growth pattern to protect the *colono* and resurrect the small farmer. Guerra y Sánchez, *Sugar and Society*, pp. 101, 136.

Ironically this work appeared in 1927, just at the end of the long sugar boom. Stagnation of the sugar industry between 1925 and the 1940s changed the nature of the problem from one of controlling sugar expansion to one of rationalizing sugar contraction. Cuban governments after 1927 adopted many forms of control over sugar in order to cushion the impact of this retraction, but these controls had only minor restructuring effects.

18. Healy, *United States in Cuba*, p. 129; Foner, *Spanish-Cuban-American War*, vol. 2, pp. 456, 462.

19. Healy, *United States in Cuba*, pp. 162–63, 169–70, 178; Foner, *Spanish-Cuban-American War*, vol. 2, chaps. 27, 28.

20. Healy, *United States in Cuba*, pp. 143, 174–75.

21. Louis A. Pérez, Jr., *Army Politics in Cuba, 1898–1958* (Pittsburgh: University of Pittsburgh Press, 1976), pp. 4–14.

22. Healy, *United States in Cuba*, p. 215.

23. For occupation officials who became leaders in the Cuban government, see Healy, *United States in Cuba*, p. 56; and Thomas, *Cuba*, pp. 422, 464, 467–68, 542.

24. Healy, *United States in Cuba*, chap. 7.

25. The Cuba Company issued only 160 shares, which were closely held by large investment and railroad interests in the United States. Major stockholders of this period included Thomas Ryan, Levi Morton, Henry Whitney, Peter Widener, William Elkins, Jacob Schiff, August Belmont, E. H. Harriman, Grenville Dodge, Henry M. Flagler, and J. J. Hill—a veritable Who's Who of U.S. millionaires. See Thomas, *Cuba*, p. 465n. Ryan and Widener were also principals of the American Tobacco Company, which controlled Cuban cigar production and trade at this time.

26. Jenks, *Our Cuban Colony*, pp. 130–32; Thomas, *Cuba*, chap. 38; Wilkins, *Multinational Enterprise*, p. 155; and Beals, *Crime of Cuba*, pp. 404–05. For the background of Mario Menocal see Thomas, *Cuba*, pp. 467–68.

27. Thomas, *Cuba*, p. 466; Beals, *Crime of Cuba*, p. 401.

28. Heinrich E. Friedlaender, *Historia económica de Cuba* (Havana: Jesús Montero, 1944), p. 471; Lowry Nelson, *Rural Cuba* (Minneapolis: University of Minnesota Press, 1950), p. 96.

29. Le Riverend, *Economic History*, p. 219; Wilkins, *Multinational Enterprise*, pp. 92, 156; Thomas, *Cuba*, p. 466; Jenks, *Our Cuban Colony*, pp. 155–56; and Beals, *Crime of Cuba*, p. 401.

30. Jenks, *Our Cuban Colony*, pp. 208–09.

31. Rural congressional representatives were concerned that eastern banking and industrial interests would not be satisfied with the mere expansion of trade opportunities and would attempt to establish tighter economic and political controls over foreign nations. Their particular fear in the case of Cuba was that this effort would end in annexation, thereby jumping the tariff barrier which was the only protection this group possessed. The Teller and Foraker amendments can be seen in this light rather than as pure expressions of anti-imperialism. Teller represented a beet sugar state. Foner, *Spanish-Cuban-American War*, vol. 1, p. 271.

32. Healy, *United States in Cuba*, pp. 82–84; Thomas, *Cuba*, pp. 438–39.

33. Healy, *United States in Cuba*, pp. 191–93; Thomas, *Cuba*, p. 466; Foner, *Spanish-Cuban-American War*, vol. 2, pp. 472–73.

34. Healy, *United States in Cuba*, pp. 191–93; Thomas, *Cuba*, p. 466.

35. Foner, *Spanish-Cuban-American War*, vol. 2, pp. 474–75; José R. Alvarez Díaz, *A Study on Cuba* (Coral Gables, Fla.: University of Miami Press, 1965), p. 185.

Between 1536 and 1729, the *cabildos* had granted most of the lands of the island in the form of *mercedes*. These were usually circular grants and were devoted to livestock production. In later years additional claimants were given grazing rights within the area of the original grants. In this manner, the original *mercedes* were transformed into what were known as *haciendas comuneras*.

By the early nineteenth century, when crop agriculture (sugar, tobacco, coffee) had created great pressure for the breakup of the cattle *mercedes*, title, usage rights, and boundaries within the original grants had become vague and complex. Though most of the *haciendas comuneras* were eventually broken down and parceled out as cane or other crop lands, the process was slowed by legal impediments arising from the complex nature of the rights of the old land-owning class. Governor Wood's Military Order 62 did much to facilitate the transfer process. See Nelson, *Rural Cuba*, pp. 84 ff.

36. Thomas, *Cuba*, p. 466; Wilkins, *Multinational Enterprise*, p. 156.

37. Alvarez Díaz, *A Study*, p. 184.

38. Healy, *United States in Cuba*, pp. 194–96; Foner, *Spanish-Cuban-American War*, vol. 2, p. 633.

39. Healy, *United States in Cuba*, pp. 195–97.

40. Ibid., pp. 197–98. The beet industry owed its very existence to government assistance in the form of tariffs, bounties, irrigation, education, and research. See John E. Dalton, *Sugar: A Case Study of Government Control* (New York: Macmillan Co., 1937), pp. 146–47.

41. Healy, *United States in Cuba*, p. 198.

42. Ibid., pp. 198–99; Foner, *Spanish-Cuban-American War*, vol. 2, pp. 641–45.

43. Healy, *United States in Cuba*, pp. 200–01; Foner, *Spanish-Cuban-American War*, vol. 2, pp. 646–51.

44. Healy, *United States in Cuba*, pp. 203–04.

45. Ibid., pp. 204–06.

Chapter 2. U.S. Economic and Political Presence, 1902–1924

1. For some of the literature concerning the relations between the stages of capitalist development and the nature of their economic expression abroad, see Andre G. Frank, *Capitalism and Underdevelopment in Latin America* (New York: Monthly Review Press, 1969); Paul Baran,

The Political Economy of Growth (New York: Monthly Review Press, 1957); Keith Griffin, *Underdevelopment in Spanish America* (London: George Allen and Unwin Ltd., 1969); Michael Barratt Brown, *Economics of Imperialism* (Harmondsworth, Eng.: Penguin, 1974); and Fernando Henrique Cardoso, *Dependencia y desarrollo en América Latina* (Mexico, D.F.: Siglo XXI, 1969).

2. Cleona Lewis, *America's Stake in International Investment* (Washington, D.C.: Brookings Institution, 1938), pp. 590–91. In 1924 the U.S. sugar investment in Cuba represented 63 percent of *all* U.S. agricultural investments worldwide. The eight largest U.S. sugar companies with Cuban holdings had an *average* investment of $45 million.

3. Article 2 of the Platt Amendment gave the United States the right to intervene in Cuba for the "preservation of Cuban independence, the maintenance of a government adequate for the protection of life, property and individual liberty" (*United States Statutes at Large*, vol. 21, p. 897).

4. Lewis, *America's Stake*, p. 275; Max Winkler, *Investments of the United States in Latin America* (Boston: World Peace Foundation, 1929), pp. 184 ff.

5. Lewis, *America's Stake*, pp. 267, 590. For background on the Rionda interests see n. 7 below.

6. Atkins's interests had become associated with the American Sugar Refining Company before the war, and Atkins served a term as chairman of the board of ASRC (Thomas, *Cuba*, p. 537). The West India Finance Company was connected to Howell & Son, the sugar broker, which later had connections with ASRC (see n. 7 below). The connection of refining interests to those of the sugar companies complicated the interest structure of the industry. Because cane was for them a raw material, they had a certain interest in keeping the price at moderate levels. *Centrales* in Cuba without strong refiner connections were more sensitive to low prices for cane than were those which had such connections.

7. Jenks, *Our Cuban Colony*, pp. 179–80. The Rionda interests were extensive. Spanish-born Manuel Rionda was managing partner of Czarnikow Rionda Co., a worldwide sugar merchant firm based in New York and London (in London it was the leading dealer in European beet and cane sugar sales). Rionda's refining connection was with the W. J. McCahan Sugar Refining Co. of Philadelphia. Czarnikow Rionda controlled important shipping contracts and coal docks in Havana. (Jenks, *Our Cuban Colony*, pp. 179–80.)

The Cuba Cane Sugar Company formed a syndicate at this time which raised $50 million to buy up Cuban sugar mills. Unlike other U.S. interests, Cuba Cane did not build mills; it bought and managed existing ones. In 1918, Cuba Cane was the largest sugar enterprise in the world. It was managed by Czarnikow Rionda, but its directors were a broad range of New York–based capitalists (Thomas, *Cuba*, p. 538). During the war period many Cuban-owned mills were sold, not because of a credit squeeze or a poor market outlook, but because of the high prices offered by U.S. companies (Jenks, *Our Cuban Colony*, p. 221). Cuba Cane in many cases paid twice the pre-1914 value of the mills it bought. This meant of course that after 1920, when sugar prices dropped sharply, companies like Cuba Cane were saddled with a heavy load of debt (Le Riverend, *Economic History*, p. 223).

By this time U.S. houses also dominated the sugar brokerage business. The major U.S. firms of this period were: (1) Cuba Trading Company, which managed those of the Rionda interests which were marketed by Czarnikow Rionda, including the Cuba Cane Sugar Company. The banking connections of Cuba Trading Company were with Chase National Bank, Guaranty Trust Company, Hayden Stone & Company, and J. & W. Seligman; (2) Lowry & Company, which managed the Atkins interests, including Punta Alegre. Horace Havemeyer, founder of ASRC, was a partner in Lowry & Co.; (3) B. H. Howell & Son, which managed certain of the sugar interests of the ASRC and of the National City Bank of New York. Its senior partner, James H. Post, was chairman of the board of the Cuban American Sugar Company. (Jenks, *Our Cuban Colony*, pp. 287–88.)

The National City Bank controlled its wholly owned mills through the General Sugar Corporation via the National City Company. It marketed its sugar with that of the Cuban Dominican Corporation, a syndicate headed by National City Bank directors. National City had ties to the ASRC through one of its directors, Earl D. Babst, who was president of the refining firm. National City also had interests in the Cuba Company and the Atlantic Fruit and Sugar Company. (Jenks, *Our Cuban Colony*, pp. 287–88.)

The Royal Bank of Canada controlled most of the British-owned mills. A summary of these interlocks can be found in Oscar Pino-Santos, *El asalto a Cuba por la oligarchia financiera yanqui* (Havana: Casa de la Americas, 1973), pp. 92–135.

8. Lewis, *America's Stake*, pp. 267–70; Jenks, *Our Cuban Colony*, pp. 178–81.

9. Raymond Leslie Buell, *Problems of the New Cuba* (New York: Foreign Policy Association, 1935), p. 221. U.S. Tariff Commission, *The Effects of the Cuban Reciprocity Treaty of 1902* (Washington, D.C.: Government Printing Office, 1929), p. 13.

10. U.S., National Archives, Washington, D.C., Record Group 59, General Records of the Department of State—Central Files 1930–1939, 611.373Sugar/194, Report of May 29, 1933, by H. S. Tewell, American Consul, Havana, pp. 1–2. (Hereafter, all citations to the U.S. National Archives will be preceded only by the appropriate Record Group [R.G.] number or, in the case of documents from R.G. 59 [Department of State—Central Files], by no designation other than the document number itself.)

11. Coca Cola had built its bottling plant in Havana in 1906 (Wilkins, *Multinational Enterprise*, p. 156). In addition to its milling properties, the Hershey Company also built a refinery and bought the Havana-Matanzas Railroad (Thomas, *Cuba*, p. 541).

12. Le Riverend, *Economic History*, pp. 220–25; Jenks, *Our Cuban Colony*, pp. 209–13. Other U.S. banks present at this time were First National Bank of Boston and agencies of the Federal Reserve banks of Atlanta and Boston (Robert W. Dunn, *American Foreign Investments* [New York: B. W. Huebsch and Viking, 1926], p. 132; Winkler, *Investments of the United States*, p. 192; Henry C. Wallich, *Monetary Problems of an Export Economy: The Cuban Experience, 1914–1947* [Cambridge, Mass.: Harvard University Press, 1950], pp. 69–72).

The presence of the Federal Reserve Banks resulted in part from the fact that the U.S. dollar made up a great portion of the circulating medium in Cuba (Alvarez Díaz, *A Study*, p. 231). The U.S. dollar was legal tender and drove the Cuban peso out of circulation. Until about 1932 Cuba's currency was in effect the U.S. dollar. As a result, Cuba was not able to establish an independent monetary or exchange policy. (See chap. 14, by Henry C. Wallich, in *Economic Problems in Latin America*, ed. Seymour Harris [New York: McGraw-Hill, 1944], p. 350.)

13. Alvarez Díaz, *A Study*, p. 232. Concerning the role of the United States in the banking crisis, see Wallich, *Monetary Problems*, pp. 58–72; and Léon Primelles, *Crónica cubana*, vol. 2 (Havana: Ed. Lex, 1958), pp. 375–79.

14. Le Riverend, *Economic History*, pp. 228–32.

15. Even some of the U.S. banking houses came under heavy pressure during the crisis, which prompted the Federal Reserve Board to consider setting up a branch in Cuba to stabilize the banking industry (see U.S. Federal Reserve Board, *Annual Report*, 1923; and Carl Parrini, *Heir to Empire: United States Economic Diplomacy, 1916–1923* [Pittsburgh: University of Pittsburgh Press, 1969], p. 117). For a discussion of the functions of the Federal Reserve Board in Cuba during the years 1923–1938, see Wallich, *Monetary Problems*, pp. 69–72.

16. Thomas, *Cuba*, chap. 46; Jenks, *Our Cuban Colony*, pp. 282–83, 244–45. Other firms coming into sugar properties in the crisis were Lowry & Co., Chase National Bank, Cuba Trading Co., and the Bank of Montreal (Lewis, *America's Stake*, p. 272). In many cases the proceeds from the sale of stock in the consolidation firms which were created from the defaulted properties were used by the managing banks to pay the debts owed them by the bankrupt sugar companies. These banks thus were able to pass some of their debts on to the public. (See Lewis, *America's Stake*, p. 272.)

The conquest of the banking industry by U.S. firms did not increase the flow of U.S. capital to Cuba. Rather than appropriating a part of their U.S.-generated capital for use in their Cuban operations, the banks often took their Cuban-generated deposits and sent them to New York for investment. (Jenks, *Our Cuban Colony*, p. 295.)

17. Beals, *Crime of Cuba*, p. 406; Jenks, *Our Cuban Colony*, pp. 282–84.

18. Lewis, *America's Stake*, pp. 272–73.

19. Ibid., p. 273. Bank-controlled groups expanded production by 700,000 tons in the 1920s (Jenks, *Our Cuban Colony*, p. 283).

20. Dunn, *American Foreign Investments*, p. 129; Wilkins, *Multinational Enterprise*, pp. 47, 156; and Thomas, *Cuba*, pp. 475–76, 485–86.

21. Buell, *Problems*, pp. 398–99; Jenks, *Our Cuban Colony*, p. 289.

22. Phillip C. Newman, *Joint International Business Ventures—Cuba* (New York: Columbia University Press, 1958), p. 95; Dunn, *American Foreign Investments*, p. 129; and Buell, *Problems*, pp. 416–19.

23. Jenks, *Our Cuban Colony*, pp. 289–90; Dunn, *American Foreign Investments*, p. 131.

24. Thomas, *Cuba*, p. 557; Jenks, *Our Cuban Colony*, pp. 290–91; Dunn, *American Foreign Investments*, pp. 127–28; and Buell, *Problems*, pp. 433–36. The United Railways was connected with J. H. Schreoder of London. It controlled the Havana Central Railway and the Havana Terminal Railroad Company. As of 1931 it represented 45 percent of the public track mileage. For the history of United see Newman, *Joint International Business Ventures*, pp. 39–40. The Consolidated represented 35 percent of the mileage. For the directors of the Consolidated and of the Cuba Company see Dunn, *American Foreign Investments*, p. 127, and Jenks, *Our Cuban Colony*, p. 290. The only other public railroad of significance was the much smaller Guantanamo and Western, which had a Cuban board of directors, but U.S. stockholders. This road was eventually absorbed by the Consolidated as well. For U.S. involvement in the consolidation of the Cuba Northern see Beals, *Crime of Cuba*, pp. 362–63; Buell, *Problems*, pp. 433–36.

25. Jenks, *Our Cuban Colony*, pp. 291–94; Winkler, *Investments of the United States*, p. 188; Dunn, *American Foreign Investments*, p. 126; Le Riverend, *Economic History*, p. 220; Brooks Emeny, *The Strategy of Raw Materials* (New York: Macmillan Co., 1934), pp. 59, 73; and Beals, *Crime of Cuba*, pp. 402–03. For Bethlehem interlocks with Cuba Company, National City, E. B. & S. Co., American and Foreign Power Corp., and others see Beals, *Crime of Cuba*, p. 402. The mining industry illustrates the ultimate in economic dependence. The ore deposits, worse than being exploited for the benefit of the U.S. economy without regard to the needs of the Cuban economy, were in many cases not exploited at all. They were held as reserves by the large U.S. steel companies. A similar situation existed in sugar, where hundreds of thousands of acres were left unplanted by the large sugar companies. See Thomas, *Cuba*, p. 1171, on ore reserves. For sugar land reserves see Farr and Company, *Manual of Sugar Companies*, 12th ed. (New York: Farr and Company, 1933), passim.

26. The major economic motives behind such moves are set out in Lewis, *America's Stake*, chap. 14.

27. Jenks, *Our Cuban Colony*, pp. 144, 295–97; Winkler, *Investments of the United States*, pp. 156, 190–92; Dunn, *American Foreign Investments*, pp. 130–31; Newman, *Joint International Business Ventures*, p. 39; and R. G. 59, D. R. A. Conference Book File, "Latin American Handbook 1932," passim. The American Chamber of Commerce of Cuba had 260 member firms. Pan American Airways controlled air travel. See Matthew Josephson, *Empire of the Air* (New York: Harcourt, Brace and Co., 1944); and A. M. Burden, *The Struggle for Airways in Latin America* (New York: Council on Foreign Relations, 1943), p. 27.

28. Jenks, *Our Cuban Colony*, p. 296; Dunn, *American Foreign Investments*, p. 131. Note that there are two *English*-language dailies in Havana. The Govins also owned the New York-based *Journal of Commerce*. (Dunn, *American Foreign Investments*, p. 121.)

29. Robert Freeman Smith, *The United States and Cuba: Business and Diplomacy, 1917–*

1960 (New York: Bookman Associates, 1960), p. 29; Jenks, *Our Cuban Colony*, p. 281; and U.S. Department of Commerce, Bureau of Foreign and Domestic Commerce, *A New Estimate of American Investments Abroad*, Foreign Trade Bulletin no. 767 (Washington, D.C.: Government Printing Office, 1931), p. 16.

30. Beals, *Crime of Cuba*, p. 375, has a higher figure. For a lower estimate (18 percent) see Dudley Seers, *Cuba: The Economic and Social Revolution* (Chapel Hill: University of North Carolina Press, 1964), pp. 75–76. Guerra y Sánchez, *Sugar and Society*, p. 73, put the figure at 20 percent or about 50 percent of all arable land. Buell, *Problems*, p. 268, perhaps the most reliable source, says that 30 percent of all land was held or controlled by all sugar mills, with about four-fifths of this area held by U.S. companies. Paul G. Minniman, *The Agriculture of Cuba*, Foreign Agriculture Bulletin no. 2 (Washington, D.C.: Government Printing Office, 1942), p. 26, says that this figure was 28 percent as of 1940 and that only one-quarter to one-half of this amount was ever planted with cane, the rest being held in reserve or used for ancillary purposes. This massive capital base gave the United States great leverage in the Cuban economy, but did not represent a large flow of dollars from the United States to Cuba. U.S. banks in Cuba worked with large amounts of Cuban capital. Much of the value of the large sugar investment represented reinvested earnings and increased real-estate values. Moreover, U.S. companies purchased most of their supplies in the United States. In addition, of course, capital in the form of interest, profits, copyrights, and so on flowed out of Cuba. The effect of U.S. dollars, when they were invested, was to consume Cuban resources for production which met a foreign need, while making such economic structure as it created dependent upon the nature and level of that need. (Griffin, *Underdevelopment in Spanish America*, pp. 271–73; James O'Connor, *The Origins of Socialism in Cuba* [Ithaca: Cornell University Press, 1970], pp. 34, 141.)

31. Of course the State Department had to balance the needs of diplomacy (alliance responsibilities, international law, world "public opinion," regional stability, disarmament, and larger trade and payments patterns) with the needs of the export and foreign investing sector of the nation. Therefore, high-level representatives of the State Department (though themselves often businessmen or more typically lawyers with corporate clients) often disagreed with representatives of business concerning the priorities of a given situation, and the proper relation of political to economic interests.

The State Department had also to take into consideration the perspectives of other executive agencies, Congress, public opinion (the editorial stands of the major newspapers), and of course the president. The most sophisticated representatives of the State Department worked to mesh all these forces in a way which most effectively utilized U.S. power in the world. However, many of them—like some of their counterparts in business—took narrow bureaucratic and even personal stands on some issues. When this happened, policy became unclear in purpose and often resulted in a serious compromise of intentions.

One can focus on the differences within the policy establishment and conclude that the resulting compromises constitute the reality to be apprehended. I have chosen to view such compromises when they occur as deflections in the course of consistent underlying tendencies of policy which were thereby rarely altered.

32. See Dudley Seers, "The Stages of Economic Growth of a Primary Producer in the Middle of the Twentieth Century," in *Imperialism and Underdevelopment*, ed. Robert Rhodes (New York: Monthly Review Press, 1970), pp. 163–80. On twentieth-century U.S. foreign policy, see William Appleman Williams, *The Tragedy of American Diplomacy* (New York: Delta Books, 1962), chaps. 3–6, and his "Latin America: Laboratory of American Foreign Policy in the 1920's," *Inter-American Economic Affairs*, 11, no. 2 (Autumn 1957):3–30. Also William Domhoff, *The Higher Circles* (New York: Random House, 1970), chap. 5; Lloyd C. Gardner, *Economic Aspects of New Deal Diplomacy* (Madison: University of Wisconsin Press, 1964); and Gabriel Kolko, *The Roots of American Foreign Policy* (Boston: Beacon Press, 1969).

33. On the threat of nationalism to U.S. policies in Latin America, see David Green, *The Containment of Latin America* (Chicago: Quadrangle Books, 1971), chap. 1. On accessibility see Celso Furtado, "United States Hegemony and the Future of Latin America," in *Latin American Radicalism,* ed. Irving L. Horowitz (New York: Vintage, 1969), pp. 61–75.

34. Estrada Palma was the first of a line of Cuban presidents elected less for their popularity with Cubans than for their responsiveness to and understanding of U.S. preferences. Estrada had lived in the United States in the 1880s and 1890s, teaching at a private school in upstate New York. He was a naturalized U.S. citizen. As president of the Revolutionary Junta in New York City during the Independence War he became familiar with U.S. politics and politicians. (See Thomas, *Cuba,* pp. 314, 453, 459, 516.) Estrada hoped for eventual annexation (Healy, *United States in Cuba,* p. 175).

35. Allen Reed Millett, *The Politics of Intervention: The Military Occupation of Cuba, 1906–1909* (Columbus: Ohio State University Press, 1968), p. 249.

36. Crowder had served in the Philippines and was Magoon's secretary of justice. He was provost marshal of the U.S. Army in 1917–1919 and presidential representative to Cuba in 1919 and 1921–1923. He was the first U.S. ambassador to Cuba and served in that post from 1923 until 1927. In his later years he became connected to Cuban sugar interests. See David H. Lockmiller, *Enoch H. Crowder* (Columbia: University of Missouri Press, 1955), and chap. 3 below.

37. Thomas, *Cuba,* chap. 40; Lester D. Langley, *The Cuban Policy of the United States: A Brief History* (New York: John Wiley and Sons, Inc., 1968), pp. 128–29.

38. Millett, *Politics of Intervention,* pp. 260–61.

39. Thomas, *Cuba,* p. 485.

40. Ibid., p. 490; Pérez, *Army Politics,* chap. 2.

41. Taft described this policy as "doing all within [our] power to induce Cuba to avoid every reason that would make intervention possible at any time" (Jenks, *Our Cuban Colony,* p. 325; Thomas, *Cuba,* p. 509).

42. Thomas, *Cuba,* pp. 508–09; 837.00/541.

43. Lockmiller, *Crowder,* p. 177; Thomas, *Cuba,* pp. 510, 523. The effects of the repression were felt throughout the entire republican period. Except within the Cuban Communist party, no significant black leader was to emerge before 1959. For a contemporary analysis of the effects of U.S. racism on race relations in Cuba see Arnold Roller, "Black Ivory and White Gold in Cuba," *Revista Bimestre Cubana,* 25 (1930):281. Concerning the possibility that the black revolt was manipulated by Cuban annexationists to precipitate a new U.S. occupation see Rafael Fermoselle, *Politica y color en Cuba: la guerrita de 1912* (Montevideo: Ed. Geminis, 1974).

44. 711.37/148, p. 7. For a summary of U.S. policy toward the black uprising see R.G. 59, "Studies on Latin America (1906–1939)," D.R.A. Confidential Book File; Box 5, "Political Relations between the United States and Cuba 1900–1925," pp. 254–64.

45. 837.00/1106a, Feb. 18, 1917; 837.00/1254, March 23, 1917.

46. Smith, *United States and Cuba,* pp. 18–19; Langley, *Cuban Policy of the United States,* p. 131.

Menocal's "reelection" in 1916 was an outright fraud—with about 160 percent of those eligible casting votes (Thomas, *Cuba,* pp. 527–31; John Edwin Fagg, *Cuba, Haiti and the Dominican Republic* [Englewood Cliffs, N.J.: Prentice-Hall, Inc., 1965], pp. 63–64). Menocal, even more than other Cuban presidents, was connected to U.S. capital. He was descended from a wealthy Cuban family whose fortunes had declined. Menocal spent most of his early years in the United States and graduated from Cornell University. He worked as an engineer for a U.S. firm in Nicaragua. After service in the Liberation Army he was appointed Havana police chief and inspector of public works under the first U.S. occupation. He helped the Hawley interests in the organization of the Cuban-American Sugar Company and was made manager of its largest *central*—Chaparra. After his election in 1912, he remained a director of Cuban-American. While president, he received help from the West Indies Sugar Finance Corporation (a New York–based sugar investment and management firm set up by Thomas Howell, the large sugar broker) in purchasing *central* Palma. After several years in office, the president was able to buy out much of the West Indies' interest. Menocal was personally close to several directors of both the Cuban-American Sugar Co., whose property he had managed, and to his backers in the West Indies Sugar Finance Corporation. (Fagg, *Cuba, Haiti and the Dominican Republic*, p. 64; Hubert Edson, *Sugar: From Scarcity to Surplus* [New York: Chemical Publishing Co., 1958], pp. 125–26; Jenks, *Our Cuban Colony*, pp. 130–31; and Thomas, *Cuba*, pp. 467–68, 542.) His $1 million fortune expanded fortyfold while he was in office (Thomas, *Cuba*, p. 525).

47. Benjamin Harrison Williams, *Economic Foreign Policy of the United States* (New York: McGraw Hill, 1929), pp. 200–03; Thomas, *Cuba*, p. 510.

48. B. H. Williams, *Economic Foreign Policy*, pp. 200–03; idem, *American Diplomacy* (New York: McGraw Hill, 1936), p. 200.

World War I ended British investment influence in most areas of the Cuban economy. Until 1914 United Kingdom investments had been larger than those of the United States. However, the war forced the sale of most of the United Kingdom holdings. Much of the bonded indebtedness of the big sugar companies had been held in England and Europe. By war's end most of these bondholders were U.S. citizens. (Lewis, *America's Stake*, p. 276n.; Jenks, *Our Cuban Colony*, pp. 163–64; and J. Fred Rippy, *Caribbean Danger Zone* [New York: G. P. Putnam and Sons, 1940], pp. 109–10.)

49. Herbert Feis, *The Diplomacy of the Dollar, 1919–1932* (New York: W. W. Norton and Co., 1966), pp. 6–7, 11, 19. For the special Caribbean interests of the State Department see ibid., pp. 25–29. For the differing loan policies of the United States toward strong and weak debtor states see B. H. Williams, *American Diplomacy*, pp. 188–89. For a general discussion of loan policy in the 1920s see Joan Hoff Wilson, *American Business and Foreign Policy, 1920–1933* (Boston: Beacon Press, 1971), chap. 4.

50. 711.37/148, p. 1. This is a State Department study entitled "Summary of the Procedures in Approving Loans under Article II [of the Platt Amendment]."

51. Thomas, *Cuba*, p. 533; Smith, *United States and Cuba*, p. 98.

52. Smith, *United States and Cuba*, pp. 88–94; 711.37/148, p. 15; Peter F. Krogh, "The United States, Cuba and Sumner Welles: 1933" (Ph.D. dissertation, Fletcher School of Law and Diplomacy, 1966), p. 87; U.S. Department of State, *Foreign Relations of the U.S.*, 1922, vol. I (Washington, D.C.: Government Printing Office), pp. 1004–52.

53. The Latin American Division of the State Department fought against the lessening of U.S. government controls over loans. In the early twenties Sumner Welles recommended that the State Department have a special loan policy for Latin America so that it could continue to "exert as much influence as may be possible and proper" over such loans to Latin American governments. See Joseph S. Tulchin, *The Aftermath of War: World War I and United States Policy Toward Latin America* (New York: New York University Press, 1971), p. 180; 811.51/2981, Oct. 6, 1921, from Welles to Dearing. Larger currents, however, were working in a different direction. Easier credit conditions in the United States and the postwar completion of U.S. economic domination of much of Latin America removed the immediate need for political support for U.S. lenders, or banker support for U.S. policy (Tulchin, *Aftermath of War*, pp. 242–43).

54. The State Department's "Summary of Loan Policy" states that "as a practical matter, so long as the bankers consult the Department, an effective check on Cuban financing is retained" (711.37/148, p. 5). The bankers consulted the State Department concerning the 1926 public works financing, the 1927 Morgan loan, and the loans of 1928 and 1930 (ibid., p. 3).

55. Smith, *United States and Cuba*, p. 32; 637.113/61, p. 1. In 1920, the peak year, Cuba was actually the fourth largest export market for U.S. goods and until the late twenties was consistently the largest Latin American market for U.S. goods. See M. Carlisle Minor, "Cuba and Congress," *Barrons*, 10, no. 3 (January 20, 1930):5.

56. Smith, *United States and Cuba*, pp. 42–43.

57. Beet production expanded from 45,000 tons in 1897 to 1.1 million tons in 1920. The chairmen of the Senate Finance Committee (Reed Smoot) and the House Ways and Means Committee (Joseph W. Fordney) favored beet interests (see Bettman, "Beet Sugar Industry," p. 370).

58. U.S. Senate, Subcommittee of the Committee on the Judiciary, *Lobby Investigation, Hearings*, 71st Cong., 1st sess., 1929–1930, pts. 1, 2, and 3, passim.

59. Smith, *United States and Cuba*, pp. 44–48; Jenks, *Our Cuban Colony*, p. 256. Banker opposition to the tariff was assuaged after a series of meetings among Dwight Morrow, Herbert Hoover (secretary of commerce), and Senator Smoot which provided for the sale in Europe of half a million tons of sugar that the banks were holding (Jenks, *Our Cuban Colony*, pp. 256–57).

60. An attempt was made to intervene in the 1920 election by persuading the major contenders—Alfredo Zayas and Miguel Mariano Gomez—to retire from the race in favor of a more desirable candidate. Sumner Welles, chief of the Latin American Division of the State Department, supported the candidacy of Carlos Manuel de Céspedes as a person disposed to accept U.S. advice. (Primelles, *Crónica cubana*, vol. 2, pp. 179, 314 ff.; 837.00/2216, March 1, 1921, memo by Welles.) Nevertheless, the Cuban candidates refused to retire and the matter was not pressed. Céspedes would eventually become Cuban president for a brief period in 1933, during Welles's ambassadorship (see chap. 8).

61. Smith, *United States and Cuba*, pp. 137–38. Crowder was authorized to use the loan negotiations then in progress to gain compliance (*Foreign Relations of the U.S.*, 1920, vol. 2, p. 42).

62. Jenks, *Our Cuban Colony*, pp. 258–59.

63. Primelles, *Crónica cubana*, vol. 2, p. 483, quoting from Zayas Papers, National Archives, Havana. Also see 837.00/2087, April 21, 1921; *Foreign Relations of the U.S.*, 1922, vol. 1, pp. 1032–33.

64. Carlos Manuel de Céspedes (chosen as secretary of state) was born and educated in the United States and had been Cuban minister in Washington for eight years. The secretary of war was a West Point graduate and was close to Crowder. Another cabinet member (Aristides Agramonte) had been educated in the United States and had fought in the U.S. Army in the Spanish-Cuban-American War. The secretary of the treasury (Manuel Despaigne) was known to the U.S. government as head of the Cuban economic mission in Washington during World War I. Crowder considered these four men very able and the other three members of the cabinet, acceptable. (Primelles, *Crónica cubana*, vol. 2, p. 487.)

65. Primelles, *Crónica cubana*, vol. 2, pp. 494–98.

66. *Foreign Relations of the U.S.*, 1923, vol. 1, pp. 837–53.

67. Despite the necessity of congressional action to enable Crowder as an army officer to become a regular diplomatic representative of the United States, business and banking support for him was so great that by 1923 Congress had passed the enabling legislation and Crowder became the first U.S. ambassador to Cuba. He remained in that post until 1927. (Smith, *United States and Cuba*, pp. 94–96.)

68. Ibid., pp. 98–102.

69. Concerning the *decadencia* school see Jorge Mañach, *Indagación del choteo* (Havana: Ed. Lex, 1936). Evidence of the favorable attitude toward U.S. intervention of one of Cuba's best-known *pensadores*, Fernando Ortiz, can be found in Primelles, *Crónica cubana*, vol. 2, p. 28; 711.37/102, April 29, 1927, conversation between Ortiz and Stokley Morgan of the Latin American Division; 710F/146; 837.00/3450; Fernando Ortiz, "Las responsabilidades de los E. E. U. U. en los males de Cuba," *Revista Bimestre Cubana*, 33, no. 2 (March–April 1934): 250 ff.

70. See such works as Raúl Maestri, *El latifundismo en la economía cubana* (Havana: Ed. Rev. de Avance, 1929); and Emilio Roig de Leuchsenring, *Los problemas sociales de Cuba* (Havana, 1927).

Chapter 3. Hegemony and Depression: The U.S. Economic Presence, 1925–1932

1. Concerning the operations of U.S. sugar companies in Cuba, see Le Riverend, *Economic History*, p. 234; Jenks, *Our Cuban Colony*, pp. 284, 299; Lewis, *America's Stake*, p. 275; Gregorio Selser, *Diplomacia garrote y dolares en América Latina* (Buenos Aires: Ed. Palestra, 1962), p. 123; and Farr and Company, *Manual*, passim.

In 1924, for example, the twelve largest U.S. sugar companies accounted for about 55 percent of the Cuban crop. The Cuba Cane Sugar Corporation (which became the Cuba Cane Products Company in 1930) alone milled 13 percent of Cuban sugar production (see Cuba Cane Sugar Corporation, *Annual Report (1924)*, p. 22). The mills of the large U.S. companies hired the majority of all the Cubans working in the sugar industry. During the grinding season these huge *centrales* hired over five thousand persons each, with giant mills like Vertientes, Delicias, Manati, and Preston having more than ten thousand each (Eric Williams, *From Columbus to Castro: The History of the Caribbean, 1492–1969* [Kent, G.B.: Andre Deutsch, 1970], p. 437).

2. Alberto Arredondo, *Cuba: tierra indefensa* (Havana: Ed. Lex, 1945), p. 333; Primelles, *Crónica cubana*, vol. 2, pp. 76, 241. By 1932 only 9 percent of the cane land was still owned by Cuban *colonos* (Minniman, *Agriculture of Cuba*, p. 26).

Immigration represented 33 percent of the population increase and 50 percent of the increase in the labor force in the first quarter of the century (Julián Alienes y Urosa, "Tesis sobre el desarrollo económico de Cuba," *Revista Bimestre Cubana* [July–December 1951], p. 237). At the height of the *Danza* in 1919 and 1920, over 100,000 West Indian laborers were brought to Cuba. When after 1925 the sugar depression rendered most of these people superfluous, they formed part of the large army of unemployed and semiemployed who swelled the social disturbances of the thirties.

3. Le Riverend, *Economic History*, pp. 233–35; Alvarez Díaz, *A Study*, p. 351. Unemployment among those over fourteen ran about 40 percent in the "good" years of the first two decades of the twentieth century (ibid., p. 206). Total wages in the sugar industry fell 60 percent between 1929 and 1931. The census of 1931 showed a lowering of the life expectancy compared with that of 1919. (José A. Duarte Oropesa, *Historiología cubana*, vol. 5 [Hollywood, Calif.: privately printed, 1969], pp. 341, 354.)

4. Farr and Company, *Manual*, pp. 19, 22.

5. For the causes of the collapse of the world sugar market see Seers, *Cuba: Economic and Social Revolution*, pp. 9–11; and Farr, *Manual*, pp. 22, 38, 54.

6. Per capita income was not much different in the 1950s than it had been in the early twenties. See International Bank for Reconstruction and Development, Economic and Technical Mission to Cuba, *Report on Cuba* (Baltimore: Johns Hopkins Press, 1951), p. 65.

7. For indications that the big mills were making money in this period see Clifford L. James, "International Control of Raw Sugar," *American Economic Review*, 21 (September 1931): 482.

8. Guerra y Sánchez, *Sugar and Society*, p. 161; James, "International Control," pp. 482–83.

9. Guerra y Sánchez, *Sugar and Society*, p. 159.

10. For statistics on the level of U.S. bank credit see Alvarez Díaz, *A Study*, p. 231 and table 151.

11. Boris Swerling, *International Control of Sugar, 1918–1941* (Palo Alto: Stanford University Press, 1949), pp. 33–34.

A theme of control mechanisms even in this early period was protection for the Cuban cane grower. The independence and economic status of the *colono* had slowly been eroded by technological change. By the twentieth century, the *colono*, who had previously been able to sell his cane to the highest bidder, was forced to sell his crop to the *central* whose lands and railways now controlled all sugar movements and land rents throughout its area of operations. The only way of getting his crop to market was by using the private tracks of the *central* which dominated that sugar zone. (Guerra y Sánchez, *Sugar and Society*, pp. 67, 78, 88.) Once the sugar zones of the respective *centrales* became stabilized there was only one buyer for sugar, and it was in the interest of that buyer to pay the grower only the price necessary to induce him to grow cane rather than to leave his land fallow.

The economic laws operating in such a situation could only be circumvented by political action: that is, attempting to use the leverage, however small, possessed by the Cuban government through its legal "independence" in order to legislate relief for the remaining native elements of sugar production. (Alvarez Díaz, *A Study*, pp. 240–41.)

Ultimately, these and other laws protected the *colono* from extinction and were complemented by the creation in the thirties of a *colono* organization which wielded considerable political power, especially as the monopolistic position of the big U.S. mills came under increasing attack by nationalists. Under the more nationalistic governments following 1933, there was some redistribution of sugar profits in favor of the planter class. This "irrational" encumbrance on the technological consolidation of the industry discouraged innovative investment by the sugar companies and was a major component of the economic stagnation that plagued the Cuban economy in the later republic. For a study of this later period see O'Connor, *Origins of Socialism.*

12. Primelles, *Crónica cubana*, vol. 2, pp. 395–96.

13. In order to recover the cost of their bad debts, the banks not only increased production at their mills, but also sold stock in their newly created sugar companies at inflated values (see n. 16, chap. 2). When the market crash of 1929 made much of this stock worthless, there was great resentment in the United States against the banks and their sugar companies (see U.S. Senate, Subcommittee of the Committee on the Judiciary, *Lobby Investigation, Hearings*, 71st Cong., 1st sess. pts. 1, 2, and 3.) This climate of hostility hurt Cuban-based sugar interests in their struggle to control the sugar tariff and U.S. policy toward Cuba in the early thirties.

The price decline after 1925 was due to overproduction, to which the large Cuban mills were great contributors. World production in 1924–1925 jumped over 3.5 million tons (the largest one-year increase in the century), and over half of this increase came from expanded Cuban production. (Farr, *Manual*, pp. 54–55.)

14. Anger over the alienation of Cuban land, though slow to develop, began to be registered by Cuban intellectuals and in the Cuban Congress as the latifundium approached its height (Primelles, *Crónica cubana*, vol. 1, pp. 65, 183). See also Manuel Sanguily, *Defensa de Cuba* (Havana: Oficina del Historiador de la Ciudad, 1948).

The attitude of Cuban intellectuals toward land alienation was nevertheless muted until the late twenties, with the main thrust of social criticism reserved for internal Cuban "decadence" and "cultural decline." The U.S. economic presence was not necessarily seen as an inherent component of these issues. See, for example, Jorge Mañach, *La crisis de la alta cultura en Cuba* (Havana: Imprenta La Universal, 1925); and Fernando Ortiz y Fernández, *La decadencia cubana* (Havana: Imprenta La Universal, 1924). Nevertheless, social criticism until the mid-twenties (when social changes began to derive from economic decline rather than expansion) rarely challenged the generally understood benevolence of the U.S. presence. For an analysis of such criticism see José F. Normano, *The Struggle for South America* (Boston: Houghton Mifflin, 1931), pp. 178–203. For a discussion of some explicitly pro-U.S. positions from this period see Miguel Jorrin and John Martz, *Latin American Political Thought and Ideology* (Chapel Hill: University of North Carolina Press, 1970), pp. 395–97.

15. Swerling, *International Control of Sugar*, pp. 35–36; Alvarez Díaz, *A Study*, p. 241. The act also provided that no new cane land was to be cleared.

Despite its origins in the complaints of Cuban millers, the final form of the Verdeja Act was altered to conform to the interests of the large U.S. mills. A central feature was the delay of the beginning of cane-grinding until January 1. Despite its appearance as an attempt to curtail output, it was in fact a concession to U.S. interests. Since Cuban cane achieves full maturity in February, a later grinding season meant higher yields (that is, the cane was ground when its sugar content was highest), which favored the high-capacity mills. Despite being held to quotas, such mills could reach their limits in an intense and brief period of grinding, thus reducing overhead. On the other hand, a shortened *zafra* was of no benefit to *colonos* and a hardship for the workers. (Buell, *Problems*, p. 241.) The non-mill-owning segment of the sugar industry was almost wholly Cuban. It included planters, cane cutters, cane haulers, mill workers, railroad workers, and the myriad labor, service, and commercial functions attendant upon the sugar economy. In rural and small-town Cuba this segment included the vast majority of the population. The well-being of these people was dependent not only upon the *price* they received for their cane, or labor, or goods, but on the *volume* of cane cut, hauled, milled, and shipped in their particular area. Their economic status was totally dependent on the amount of wealth distributed by the *central* which dominated the sugar zone in which they lived. When a mill paid less for cane or labor, or when it ground less cane in a shorter period of time, the surrounding communities shriveled, and if the mill ceased to grind, these communities died. The grinding season, which had previously averaged 136 days, was now only 87 days (ibid., p. 242). The shortened period of employment for cane and mill workers coincided with a drop in their wages as well. For a survey of wages in Cuba at this time see Lee R. Blohm, "General Survey of Wages in Cuba, 1931 and 1932," *Monthly Labor Review*, 35 (December 1932): 1403–11. This period also witnessed the return in some areas to the now illegal system of payment by tokens instead of cash. These tokens were redeemable only at the stores run by the *central*. There was at this time a general decline in standards throughout the sugar industry and a return in many cases to conditions similar to those during slavery. (Arredondo, *Cuba: tierra indefensa*, pp. 330–36.) Economic depression and the return to slavelike employment conditions had their counterpart in labor strikes and mill seizures in the early thirties.

16. Swerling, *International Control of Sugar*, pp. 36–37. In an attempt to keep the cane grower from being rendered economically superfluous as a result of crop reductions, the act required that the *centrales* not increase the percentage of their milling which came from their own fields. This was meant to ensure that the *colono* did not suffer any greater a decrease in cuttings than did the cane grown by the mill itself (see Alvarez Díaz, *A Study*, p. 241). Indeed, the entire *public* rationale of the Verdeja program was the protection of the small Cuban miller and cane grower (Arredondo, *Cuba: tierra indefensa*, p. 308).

17. Alvarez Díaz, *A Study*, p. 242; Swerling, *International Control of Sugar*, pp. 36–37; and Buell, *Problems*, p. 234.

18. Farr, *Manual*, pp. 22, 54–55. The other major sugar-growing areas were: beet—Germany, Czechoslovakia, USSR, France, and the United States; cane—Australia, Java, India, Brazil, Hawaii, Puerto Rico, and the Philippines. The last three states, because they sold their cane duty-free in the artificially high U.S. market, were more immune to price drops and took advantage of Cuban controls to capture a larger share of that market. The Cuban share of the U.S. market fell from 57 percent in 1922 to 44 percent in 1930 and to 28 percent in 1932. The three U.S. insular possessions raised their market shares from 19 percent in 1922 to 36 percent in 1930 and to 48 percent in 1932. (Farr, *Manual*, p. 30.)

19. National City Bank, *Monthly Bank Letter*, September 1928, pp. 145–48; James, "International Control," pp. 483–85.

20. Swerling, *International Control of Sugar*, pp. 37–38; Alvarez Díaz, *A Study*, p. 327; and Farr, *Manual*, p. 19.

21. By the late 1920s there no longer existed a true world sugar market. European and North American states had built up domestic beet sugar industries behind a system of bounties and tariffs. This beet sugar was sold almost wholly within the protected markets of these high-consumption countries. The largest internal markets were in the United States and Great Britain. Most of the import segment of the sugar consumption in these two countries was provided by their colonial possessions. Thus, the majority of world sugar was either consumed in the states where it was grown (about 60 percent) or sold in a protected market (about 10 percent). The amount of sugar on the "free" market, then, was less than one-third of world

production. In effect, there was no truly free market for sugar by this time, and therefore market forces could not work freely to favor efficient producers like Cuba. (See Farr, *Manual*, pp. 54–55, 102.)

22. Swerling, *International Control of Sugar*, p. 42. For the amount of debt held by U.S. banks, see 837.51/1576½. On the profitability of Cuban mills, see Frank W. Taussig, *Some Aspects of the Tariff Question* (Cambridge, Mass.: Harvard University Press, 1931), p. 376. For the economic difficulties of the U.S. sugar companies in Cuba, see Farr, *Manual*, passim. For statistics indicating that the market price for sugar was actually *below* the normal costs of production for Cuban sugar, see U.S. Tariff Commission, *Report to the President on Sugar*, report no. 73 (Washington, D.C., 1934), pp. 15, 21; and Taussig, *Aspects of the Tariff Question*, p. 381.

Concerning the unhappiness of the bankers as sugar businessmen, see the statements of Floyd Blair of the National City Bank to Under Secretary of State William Phillips contained in 837.51/1562 of May 3, 1933.

23. A proposal to nationalize the sugar industry actually appeared before the Cuban House of Representatives at this time (Buell, *Problems*, p. 243n.).

24. Buell, *Problems*, pp. 243–44. In 1930, average world prices dropped below two cents per pound for the first time in the century (Farr, *Manual*, p. 19).

25. Ibid., pp. 38, 41; Buell, *Problems*, pp. 246–48; Swerling, *International Control of Sugar*, pp. 42, 43. Sugar stabilization might also protect the loans made to the Cuban government (see n. 56 below).

26. Buell, *Problems*, pp. 246–47; Swerling, *International Control of Sugar*, pp. 42–43. Chadbourne reputedly had invested over $2 million in the Cuban sugar industry during the 1920–1921 crisis. See Thomas, *Cuba*, p. 561.

27. Buell, *Problems*, pp. 247–48; Swerling, *International Control of Sugar*, pp. 43–44; and Alvarez Díaz, *A Study*, pp. 326–28. Cuba's dependent position is illustrated by her having to make prior and specific commitments in order to evoke a response from domestic U.S. interests. In fact, Buell states that the Sugar Stabilization Act was itself drawn up in New York. Cuba's status was similarly dependent concerning trade agreements with the United States. (See chap. 7.)

28. Alvarez Díaz, *A Study*, p. 327; Buell, *Problems*, p. 247. Because U.S. banks financed most of the sugar crop, they were able to obtain a central role in the control program in Cuba. Not only were they represented on the Sugar Export Corporation, but the Chase National Bank was appointed by President Machado to be the trustee for the government bonds issued against surplus sugar. The National City Bank was made fiscal agent to receive the proceeds from the sugar tax and from the sale of sugar by the Export Corporation. (James, "International Control," p. 488.)

29. Buell, *Problems*, p. 248; Swerling, *International Control of Sugar*, pp. 44–46; Alvarez Díaz, *A Study*, pp. 329–30. For a discussion of the interest alliances formed for and against the Chadbourne Plan see Harry F. Guggenheim, *The United States and Cuba: A Study in International Relations* (New York: Macmillan, 1934), p. 142.

30. Swerling, *International Control of Sugar*, pp. 45–47; Alvarez Díaz, *A Study*, p. 329. The nine agreement countries were: Belgium, Czechoslovakia, Germany, Hungary, Poland, and Yugoslavia (beet exporters); and Cuba, Java, and Peru (cane exporters).

31. Alvarez Díaz, *A Study*, p. 329; Farr, *Manual*, pp. 22, 30.

32. Swerling, *International Control of Sugar*, pp. 48–50; Buell, *Problems*, p. 258. For an attack on the actions of U.S. banks see Cuba, Secretaría de Hacienda, *Comisión especial de investigación de los obligaciones contraídas con el Chase National Bank* (Havana, 1935).

33. Since many of the members of the Machado administration had backgrounds as sugar investors or had business relations with U.S. firms, they saw the interests of Cuba as derivative of the interests of U.S. businesses. For the business interests of Machado and his aides, see

Primelles, *Crónica cubana*, vol. 1, p. 365; Buell, *Problems*, p. 403n.; Thomas, *Cuba*, p. 548; and Beals, *Crime of Cuba*, pp. 325, 408. When the economic decline of the U.S. companies in Cuba rendered impossible trickle-down programs of economic recovery for the masses, the politicians most closely connected with these companies were discredited. The closeness of Machado to U.S. business interests was a major component of the movement against his government in the early thirties.

34. These two were from the wealthiest of about a dozen Cuban families with large sugar investments. Viriato Gutiérrez was the heir of Laureano Falla Gutiérrez, the largest of the old Spanish mill owners, and held the powerful position of secretary to the presidency in the Machado cabinet. His family controlled seven mills. José Tarafa was a large investor in the Consolidated Railroads of Cuba and controlled about six sugar mills. (Buell, *Problems*, p. 226.)

35. The other major suppliers of the U.S. market, the so-called insular areas, were supplying about 20 percent of that market by the early twenties (Farr, *Manual*, p. 30). These were the U.S. dependencies—Hawaii, Puerto Rico, and the Philippines—whose sugar came into the United States duty-free and was thus immune to the use of the tariff weapon. In fact, the experience of the twenties was that the high tariffs obtained by the beet sugar interests, instead of allowing them to gain more of the U.S. market for themselves, merely allowed insular cane to substitute for Cuban cane. The major beneficiary of the changing situation was the Philippines, which moved from 4.2 percent of the U.S. market in 1922 to 16.7 percent of the market ten years later. Opponents of Philippine cane eventually hit upon the device of Philippine independence as a way of removing its sugar from within the tariff wall. On Philippine sugar and independence see 811B.01/130-183A and Shirley Jenkins, *American Economic Policy Toward the Philippines* (Palo Alto: Stanford University Press, 1954), pp. 34–37.

36. For a discussion of conditions among Cuban sugar workers see 837.61351/623 of April 11, 1932, and 837.504/382 of Dec. 27, 1931. For the condition of beet sugar workers in the United States, the largest portion of whom were Mexicans, see 611.003/2862, Report of J. R. Ruberson to the Industrial Commission of Colorado, May 12, 1933.

37. The discussion here generally follows Smith, *United States and Cuba*, chap. 4.

38. Ibid., p. 62.

39. *Foreign Relations of the U.S.*, 1929, vol. 1, p. 998; Smith, *United States and Cuba*, p. 63.

40. Smith, *United States and Cuba*, p. 66. Concerning the "sugar defense fund" see U.S. Senate, Subcommittee of the Committee on the Judiciary, *Lobby Investigation, Hearings*, 71st Cong., 1st sess., pts. 1–3.

Implicated in the activities of the Cuban sugar lobby were former Cuban Ambassador Enoch H. Crowder, the president of the Cuba Company, Herbert Lakin, the chairman of the Senate Finance Committee, Reed Smoot, and House Ways and Means Committee member Cordell Hull (ibid., pp. 1510 ff., 1553 ff., 1583, 1607, 1797 ff., 1978 ff.). Concerning the dependent position of the Cubans in the tariff negotiations see ibid., pp. 1578–83, 1695, 1749.

41. Smith, *United States and Cuba*, pp. 67–71.

42. Oscar Pino-Santos, *El imperialismo norteamericano en la economía de Cuba* (Havana: Ed. Lex, 1960), pp. 32–33; James O'Connor, "The Political Economy of Pre-Revolutionary Cuba" (Ph.D. dissertation, Columbia University, 1964), p. 15; Arredondo, *Cuba: tierra indefensa*, pp. 289–300; and Antonio Barro y Segura, *The Truth About Sugar in Cuba* (Havana: Ucar, Garcia y Cia, 1943).

43. There was, nevertheless, a minor nationalist theme to the Machado administration, and his was the first to entertain antihegemonic ideas. Ramiro Guerra y Sánchez held an important cabinet post under Machado, and his proposals for controlling the growth (but not the ownership) of the latifundium were partially implemented during this period.

44. Great Britain, Department of Overseas Trade, *Economic Conditions in Cuba—April 1932*, report 518 (London: Her Majesty's Stationery Office, 1932), p. 30; Buell, *Problems*, p. 352. The contraction of Cuban imports was perhaps greater than that of any other country in the

world during the Great Depression (U.S. Tariff Commission, *Report to the President on Sugar*, no. 73, p. 18).

45. Alvarez Díaz, *A Study*, p. 222; idem, *Cuba: geopolitica y pensamiento economico* (Miami: Coleción de Economía de Cuba en el Exilio, 1964), pp. 276–79. There were also indications that the new tariff was initially a way of putting pressure upon the United States to renegotiate the 1903 trade treaty (see Smith, *United States and Cuba*, pp. 49–50; and Pino-Santos, *El asalto a Cuba*, p. 170).

46. U.S. Department of Commerce, Bureau of Foreign and Domestic Commerce, *Cuban Readjustment to Current Economic Forces*, Trade Information Bulletin no. 725 (Washington, D.C.: Government Printing Office, 1930), passim; Minniman, *Agriculture of Cuba*, passim; Great Britain, Department of Overseas Trade, *Economic Conditions in Cuba—1932*, pp. 11–13.

U.S. economic hegemony and the resultant sugar monoculture were such that despite the basis for a well-rounded agricultural economy in Cuba, during the twenties agricultural products made up about 33 percent of all Cuban imports. The growth of domestic agriculture, though impressive in some areas, had reduced this percentage only slightly by the late thirties. (Minniman, *Agriculture of Cuba*, p. 126.)

47. Great Britain, Department of Overseas Trade, *Economic Conditions in Cuba—April 1932*, p. 15; Buell, *Problems*, pp. 58, 63, 65; George Wythe, *Industry in Latin America*, 2d ed. (New York: Columbia University Press, 1949), pp. 347–49; Alvarez Díaz, *A Study*, p. 372; and U.S. Department of Commerce, BFDC, *Cuban Readjustment*, pp. 18–20. See also Joseph C. Rocca, "Agricultural Policies in Cuba," *Pan American Union Bulletin*, 67 (February 1933): 109; and U.S. Department of Commerce, BFDC, *The Market for Oils and Fats in Cuba and the Cuban Vegetable Oil Industry* (Washington, D.C.: Government Printing Office, 1931).

On the greater import propensities of U.S. firms in Cuba see O'Connor, *Origins of Socialism*, p. 141n. For the role of U.S. firms producing finished goods in Cuba see 637.113/41 of May 12, 1933, and 637.113/73 of Sept. 8, 1933.

48. Buell, *Problems*, pp. 354–55; Alvarez Díaz, *A Study*, p. 316.

49. For the contemporary reaction of the State Department to Cuban import taxes and duties see 611.0031/377½ of Nov. 15, 1931, pp. 100–01.

50. The so-called sugar mentality was the psychological response to the structural reality of Cuba's sugar dependence. The "mentality" consisted of the belief, usually self-fulfilling, that any economic risk-taking depended ultimately on the movement of the sugar market and therefore on forces beyond one's control. A slight rise in sugar created for the investor more wealth than years of work, savings, or nonsugar investment. This situation undermined private development strategies and even those of public bodies, which generally accepted the loss of control over economic planning which sugar dependence implied. Moreover, because no sector of the economy other than sugar stood on its own capital or market base, there was no significant potential for a countercyclical shift of productive factors away from sugar in time of crisis in that product. So thorough had been the penetration of the latifundia into rural landholdings that there was no longer even much of a subsistence sector of the rural economy into which the unemployed population could be absorbed in time of depression. Finally, the structure of the banking and currency system rendered almost impossible the carrying out of monetary and exchange policies by the Cuban government. (Wallich, *Monetary Problems*, pp. 11–18.)

The structural reality on which the sugar mentality rested was so firm that even the consciousness-wrenching depression of the late twenties and thirties did not bring forth viable proposals for controlling sugar dependence—although it did produce a mild redistribution of sugar rewards. Indeed, elements of sugar dependence have survived even the profound social revolution of the 1960s.

51. Russell H. Fitzgibbon, *Cuba and the United States, 1900–1935* (New York: Russell and Russell, Inc., 1964), pp. 236–37.

52. Charles Kindleberger, *International Economics*, 3d ed. (Homewood, Ill.: Richard D.

Irwin, 1963), p. 387; Parrini, *Heir to Empire*, pp. 273–74; Smith, *United States and Cuba*, pp. 122–23.

53. Smith, *United States and Cuba*, pp. 123–25. For the relations between the members of the Machado administration and the Chase National Bank see Buell, *Problems*, p. 390; Smith, *United States and Cuba*, p. 128.

54. Smith, *United States and Cuba*, p. 124; Fitzgibbon, *Cuba and the United States*, pp. 238–39. Article 2 of the Platt Amendment stated: "That said [Cuban] government shall not assume or contract any public debt, to pay the interests upon which, and to make reasonable sinking fund provision for the ultimate discharge of which, the ordinary revenues of the island, after defraying the current expenses of government shall be inadequate." See *United States Statutes at Large*, vol. 21 (Washington, D.C.: Government Printing Office, 1902), p. 897. The "ordinary revenues" were indeed insufficient for the public works program, but it was not these regular budget revenues but rather the legally separate "special public works revenues" which were pledged in this case; or so the argument ran.

55. Lewis, *America's Stake*, pp. 384–85; Smith, *United States and Cuba*, p. 125; Beals, *Crime of Cuba*, p. 370; Buell, *Problems*, pp. 383–85; *Foreign Relations of the U.S.*, 1928, vol. 2, pp. 642–54. By 1932, debt service on the pre-1927 "external" debt was some $8 million, while service on the "public works" debt was $7 million ($6 million for service on certificates and $1 million for amortization of the credit). See 837.51/1576½, pp. 3, 6.

The attempt to generate revenues by raising internal and import taxes had the secondary effect of keeping the price level of goods sold in Cuba much higher than otherwise. In view of the large decline in spendable income, this high cost of living increased the hardships of the depression period and was another factor in the rising opposition to Machado.

56. Smith, *United States and Cuba*, p. 126; Buell, *Problems*, pp. 385–86; Beals, *Crime of Cuba*, p. 371; and Thomas, *Cuba*, p. 581.

57. Smith, *United States and Cuba*, pp. 126–27; Fitzgibbon, *Cuba and the United States*, p. 240; Buell, *Problems*, pp. 385–86; and Beals, *Crime of Cuba*, p. 371. The various Chase Bank loans also brought handsome commissions to Machado's advisors (Buell, *Problems*, p. 391; U.S. Senate, Committee on Banking and Currency, "Stock Exchange Practices," *Hearings*, 73d Cong., 1st and 2d sess. [1933 and 1934], pt. 5). Concerning the history of the profitability of Cuban loans to the bankers see U.S. Senate, Committee on Finance, *Sale of Foreign Bonds or Securities in the United States*, *Hearings*, 72d Cong., 1st sess., 1931–1932, pp. 1944–2043. For a summary account see Rippy, *Caribbean Danger Zone*, pp. 229–31.

58. 837.51/1576½, August 1933, p. 5.

59. Smith, *United States and Cuba*, pp. 127–29; Alvarez Díaz, *A Study*, p. 410; *Foreign Relations of the U.S.*, 1930, vol. 2, pp. 672–78; *Foreign Relations of the U.S.*, 1931, vol. 2, pp. 56–59.

60. Alvarez Díaz, *A Study*, pp. 313–14. These consumption taxes "fall principally on articles of general consumption, and their immediate incidence has been largely on the working people" (Buell, *Problems*, p. 358).

61. As of 1933, the Cuban public debt was about $200 million. The servicing of the external debt alone, exclusive of the public works debt, took about 20 percent of the rapidly diminishing government revenues. The public works debt absorbed 90 percent of those taxes gathered in the public works budget. No attempt was being made to reduce the internal debt of some $42 to $50 million, which was itself greater than the total of government revenues, which stood at some $40 million. Even at the depth of the depression, the Cuban government was paying out some $15 million a year in interest and amortization. (See Alvarez Díaz, *A Study*, pp. 315–16; 837.51/1576½, pp. 1–3, 6.) Machado had reduced the expenditures of government departments drastically, with the exception of the Department of National Defense (Buell, *Problems*, p. 370).

62. See E. Curtis Wilgus, *The Caribbean Area* (Washington, D.C.: George Washington

University Press, 1934), p. 171. For a discussion of the movement against Machado see chap. 4 below.

63. Smith, *United States and Cuba*, pp. 129–31.

64. See 837.51/1576½, p. 5; *Foreign Relations of the U.S.*, 1933, vol. 5, pp. 546–50.

65. Smith, *United States and Cuba*, pp. 129–31.

66. *Foreign Relations of the U.S.*, 1933, vol. 5, pp. 558–62.

67. The central program of the publicists in this group was tariff union with the United States. They accepted the inevitability of U.S. economic hegemony and proposed a form of economic annexation to enable Cuba to derive as much market security and access to capital as possible. They wanted to perfect hegemony and not weaken it. See, for example, J. Clemente Zamora, "La unión aduanera entre Cuba y los EEUU," *Universidad de la Habana* (December 1929); Orestes Ferrara, *El panamericanismo y la opinión européa* (Paris: Edit. Le Livre Libre, 1930); idem, "Economic Loss from the High Tariff on Sugar," *Annals*, 144 (July 1929): 63–69; and Alberto Lamar-Schweyer, *La crisis del patriotismo* (Havana: Ed. Marti, 1929).

68. In return for the granting of a 20 percent preference for Cuban sugar, Cuba had granted preferences of 20 to 40 percent on many categories of U.S. goods entering the island. The cost of Cuban sugar was less than one-half that of U.S. beet sugar and about 30 percent less than that of insular cane sugar (see 837.61351/624, p. 13; U.S. Tariff Commission, *Report to the President on Sugar*, p. 14). For an analysis of the lack of benefit to Cuba under the treaty see Dalton, *Sugar: A Case Study*, p. 247.

69. The tying of Cuban sugar to the fate of economic decisions made in the United States was complemented by the granting of the Cuban domestic market to U.S. goods by means of the tariff perferences contained in the 1903 trade treaty. The flow of preferential U.S. imports isolated Cuba from trade with other states and was another fundamental feature of U.S. hegemony. On the U.S. share of the Cuban trade see Alvarez Díaz, *A Study*, pp. 286–87, and 611.373 Sugar/194. For Cuban trade with Europe and Latin America see Alvarez Díaz, *A Study*, pp. 285–86, 404.

70. *Foreign Relations of the U.S.*, 1926, vol. 2, pp. 10–14; Alvarez Díaz, *A Study*, pp. 283–84.

71. Since the preferential rate was a percentage of the full tariff rate, an increased preference represented a decrease in the tariff on Cuban sugar.

72. *Foreign Relations of the U.S.*, 1927, vol. 2, pp. 503–06; Alvarez Díaz, *A Study*, p. 284. While the balance of trade between Cuba and the United States was almost always in Cuba's favor, this says little or nothing about the transfer of wealth between the two societies. Such statistics do not take into consideration the fact that the majority of goods sold to the United States by Cuba were the property of U.S. companies, and that on the service and capital accounts Cuba's balance was decidedly negative. (Alvarez Díaz, *A Study*, pp. 285–87.)

73. R. G. 151, BFDC, 046 Cuba, Hoover to Kellogg, Feb. 7, 1928, Memorandum by Henry Chalmers (Chief, Division of Foreign Tariffs), Feb. 20, 1928, and Hoover to Kellogg, March 16, 1928; 611.3731/250, Kellogg to Hoover, Jan. 24, 1928; 611.3731/285, Kellogg to Hoover, July 6, 1928; *Foreign Relations of the U.S.*, 1928, vol. 2, pp. 640–42.

74. See National Foreign Trade Council, *Fifteenth Convention—April 25–27, 1928* (New York: National Foreign Trade Council, 1928), pp. 170–72. Ferrara repeatedly called for a customs union with the United States based upon his belief that the natural and inevitable position of Cuba was as a mercantile and agricultural provider to the U.S. market (Ferrara, "Economic Loss," pp. 63–69; 611.3731/358 and 837.61351/657). For Ferrara's connections with U.S. capital see Thomas, *Cuba*, p. 506; Beals, *Crime of Cuba*, p. 408; and Jenks, *Our Cuban Colony*, p. 122.

75. Smith, *United States and Cuba*, p. 50; *Foreign Relations of the U.S.*, 1929, vol. 2, pp. 887–93; 611.3731/358, Jan. 30, 1930. The State Department's inaction was based upon the findings of the U.S. Tariff Commission study, *The Effects of the Cuban Reciprocity Treaty of*

1902. This study concluded that the treaty was initially more favorable to Cuba than to the United States, and that the advantages granted to U.S. goods were not decisive to the dominant position gained by U.S. products in the island. The study did, nevertheless, acknowledge a major point of the Cuban case—that since Cuban sugar made up nearly all of the duty-paying sugar entering the United States, the effective tariff rate was not the full rate but the Cuban preferential rate (80 percent of the full rate) and that Cuba no longer benefited from her "preference." However, the main conclusion of the commission was that the Cuban preference for U.S. goods was of little importance and (by implication) that increased preferences by Cuba would not constitute a quid pro quo for further U.S. concessions. This attitude left the Cubans with very little leverage.

76. Had it not come to be in the interest of larger economic forces that at least a portion of the Cuban sugar-producing capacity be rationalized as part of a broad solution to the world sugar depression, integrationist ideas might have been entirely eliminated as a competing ideology during the political revolution of 1933. See chap. 10.

77. The value of U.S. trade with Cuba had averaged $170 million from 1921 to 1929. In 1930 it fell to $92 million, and in 1931 was only $46 million (see 611.373 Sugar/194).

78. 611.3731/386, June 10, 1931; 837.61351/657.

79. Memorandum by H[erbert] F[eis] to Assistant Secretary of State Francis White, Jan. 4, 1932, "The Suggested Customs Union with Cuba," in 837.61351/657.

80. 611.373 Sugar/161; 837.61351/624.

81. At this time Bertron was the head of an organization of industrialists pressing for government support of expanded U.S.-Soviet trade. See Robert Paul Browder, *The Origins of Soviet-American Diplomacy* (Princeton, N.J.: Princeton University Press, 1953), p. 40.

Bertron's proposal to Stimson, which was in effect a plan to remove the sugar industry totally from market forces, is contained in 837.61351/657.

82. Sullivan and Cromwell is a prestigious New York law firm then specializing in international affairs, many of whose members (like John and Allen Dulles) moved on to high foreign policy–making positions in Washington (Kolko, *Roots of American Foreign Policy*, pp. 17–19). The firm was counsel to the Sugar Institute (the trade association of the U.S. cane sugar refining industry) and also represented many of the U.S. sugar companies in Cuba (Smith, *United States and Cuba*, p. 226; Farr, *Manual*, p. 95).

Chapter 4. Hegemony and Nationalism, 1925–1932

1. W. A. Williams, "Latin America," p. 10; Joseph S. Tulchin, *The Aftermath of War*, pp. 241–42; Krogh, "U.S., Cuba and Sumner Welles," p. 35; Bryce Wood, *The Making of the Good Neighbor Policy* (New York: Columbia University Press, 1961), p. 3; Burton Kaufman, "United States Trade and Latin America: The Wilson Years," *Journal of American History*, 58 (1972): 342–63.

2. W. A. Williams, *Tragedy of American Diplomacy*, pp. 148–55; Wood, *Making of the Good Neighbor Policy*, chap. 1; and Arthur Link, *Woodrow Wilson and the Progressive Era, 1910–1917* (New York: Harper Torchbooks, 1954), chap. 5.

3. Thomas, *Cuba*, p. 569; Buell, *Problems*, p. 403; Beals, *Crime of Cuba*, p. 242; Primelles, *Crónica cubana*, vol. 1, p. 365; and Leland Jenks, "La influencia de los intereses americanos," *Revista Bimestre Cubana*, 35 (March–April 1935): 242–43. Machado was also associated with domestic enterprises, and thus his investments spanned those typical of both the national and the dependent bourgeoisie.

4. Thomas, *Cuba*, p. 572; Gonzalo de Quesada y Miranda, *En Cuba libre*, vol. 1 (Havana: Seoane Fernández, 1938), p. 63; Smith, *United States and Cuba*, pp. 114, 216. The State Department interview is recorded in 033.3711/32a, April 23, 1925.

5. Thomas, *Cuba*, pp. 447–48, 472–75, 489–90; Le Riverend, *Economic History*, pp. 207–08;

American University, Foreign Area Studies Division, *Special Warfare Area Handbook for Cuba* (Washington, D.C.: Government Printing Office, 1971), pp. 38–39; Philip W. Bonsal, *Cuba, Castro and the United States* (Pittsburgh: University of Pittsburgh Press, 1971), pp. 250–55. For a discussion of Machado's "business nationalism" see Smith, *United States and Cuba*, chap. 8.

6. R. B. Merrifield, "The Magazine Press and Cuba, 1906–1933," *Mid America*, 34 (October 1952): 248–50. An early defense of Machado's regime by the American Chamber of Commerce of Cuba appears in R.G. 151, 640(Cuba), June 26, 1926.

7. Gerardo Machado, *Declarations of General Gerardo Machado y Morales Regarding His Electoral Platform* (Havana: National Press Bureau, 1928), pp. 14–15.

8. Smith, *United States and Cuba*, pp. 115–16; Quesada y Miranda, *En Cuba libre*, vol. 1, p. 100.

9. Thomas, *Cuba*, p. 580; Smith, *United States and Cuba*, p. 116; and Fitzgibbon, *Cuba and the United States*, pp. 187–88.

10. Smith, *United States and Cuba*, p. 116. Crowder's request for "informal assurances" to Machado is in 837.00/2627, Feb. 14, 1927. Though the United States continued to recognize Machado's government, the Legal Department of the State Department concluded that the actions of the constitutional convention were unlawful and that therefore the constitutional amendments which formed the legal basis of Machado's second term were unconstitutional. See Francis V. Jackman, "America's Cuban Policy During the Period of the Machado Regime" (Ph.D. dissertation, Catholic University, 1964), p. 82.

11. See 033.3711/73, April 23, 1927, quoted in *Foreign Relations of the U.S.*, 1927, vol. 2, p. 525.

12. For a discussion of the distortions caused by the domination of the internal economic development of one state by the hegemonic position of the capital, goods, technology, and personnel of another, more highly developed state, see: Baran, *Political Economy of Growth;* Frank, *Capitalism and Underdevelopment;* Dale Johnson, *The Sociology of Change and Reaction in Latin America* (New York: Bobbs-Merrill, 1973); Rhodes, *Imperialism and Underdevelopment;* and Gail Omvedt, "Towards a Theory of Colonialism," *The Insurgent Sociologist*, Spring 1973, pp. 1–24.

For non-Marxist approaches to this subject see Celso Furtado, *Development and Underdevelopment* (Berkeley: University of California Press, 1964); Griffin, *Underdevelopment in Spanish America;* Cardoso, *Dependencia y desarrollo;* Stanley Stein and Barbara Stein, *The Colonial Heritage of Latin America* (New York: Oxford University Press, 1970); and Ivar Oxaal, Tony Barnett, and David Booth, eds., *Beyond the Sociology of Development* (London: Routledge and Kegan Paul, 1975).

13. Charles Page, "The Development of Organized Labor in Cuba" (Ph.D. dissertation, University of California, Berkeley, 1952), pp. 13–14, 18–23; Foner, *The Spanish-Cuban-American War*, vol. 2, chap. 22.

14. Page, "Development of Organized Labor," p. 40. For the relevant provisions of the Penal Code see "Social Legislation of Cuba," *Monthly Labor Review*, September 1929, p. 508.

15. Page, "Development of Organized Labor," p. 40; Alvarez Díaz, *A Study*, pp. 180, 275; Victor Alba, *Politics and the Labor Movement in Latin America* (Palo Alto: Stanford University Press, 1968), p. 289. A general strike occurred as early as 1902. One of the major demands of the native segment of Cuban labor even at this early date was for legislation to increase the percentage of native labor employed in the work force. See Calixto Masó y Vasquez, "El movimiento obrero cubano," *Panoramas*, 9 (May–June 1964): 71.

16. For descriptions of labor repression and collaboration under the presidency of Mario Menocal see Page, "Development of Organized Labor," p. 54; Primelles, *Crónica cubana*, vol. 1, p. 388; Mario Riera Hernández, *Historial obrero cubano, 1574–1965* (Miami: Rema Press, 1965), p. 44. For Cuban socialism during this period see Ramón Eduardo Ruiz, *Cuba: The Making of a Revolution* (Amherst: University of Massachusetts Press, 1968), p. 121; and Luis E.

Aguilar, *Cuba 1933: Prelude to Revolution* (Ithaca: Cornell University Press, 1972), p. 85.

17. "Social Legislation of Cuba," pp. 508–09; Buell, *Problems*, pp. 208–09.

18. Riera Hernández, *Historial obrero cubano*, p. 50; Page, "Development of Organized Labor," pp. 55–58; Masó y Vasquez, "El movimiento obrero cubano," p. 74; and Chapman, *History of the Cuban Republic*, pp. 628–29.

19. Buell, *Problems*, pp. 186–87; Moisés Poblete Troncoso, *El movimiento obrero latino americano* (Mexico, D. F.: Fondo de Cultura Economica, 1946), pp. 193–95; Riera Hernández, *Historial obrero cubano*, pp. 60–63; Page, "Development of Organized Labor," pp. 60–63. For a discussion of the progovernment unions see 837.504/331, June 18, 1931. For the role of the AFL and the PAFL in Cuban labor affairs during the early republic see PAFL, *Report of Proceedings of the Fifth Congress, July 18–23, 1927* (Washington, D.C., 1927), pp. 43–52, 120–21.

20. 837.504/325, April 11, 1930; 837.504/331, June 18, 1931.

21. Page, "Development of Organized Labor," pp. 64–65. The Chilean and Argentine labor federations were the only comparable ones.

22. Jaime Suchlicki, *University Students and Revolution in Cuba, 1920–1968* (Coral Gables, Fla.: University of Miami Press, 1969), pp. 18–19; Aguilar, *Cuba 1933*, p. 68. For statistics on matriculation at the University of Havana see Buell, *Problems*, pp. 154–55. During the late twenties, about 86 percent of all graduates obtained degrees in medicine or law.

23. Raúl Roa, *Retorno a la alborada* (Universidad Central de las Villas, 1964), vol. 1, pp. 234–51; Suchlicki, *University Students*, pp. 20–21; and Thomas, *Cuba*, p. 565. For more detail on the student movement in this period see Eduardo Suárez Rivas, *Un pueblo crucificado* (Miami: Service Offset Printers, 1964), pp. 10–21; Riera Hernández, *Historial obrero cubano*, pp. 71–73; and Aguilar, *Cuba 1933*, pp. 72–75.

24. Roa, *Retorno a la alborada*, vol. 1, pp. 251–55; Suárez Rivas, *Un pueblo crucificado*, p. 21; Suchlicki, *University Students*, pp. 22–24; and Aguilar, *Cuba 1933*, pp. 76–77.

25. Suchlicki, *University Students*, pp. 102–03; Aguilar, *Cuba 1933*, pp. 102–03.

26. Suchlicki, *University Students*, pp. 27–28; Aguilar, *Cuba 1933*, pp. 104–06. The text of the DEU "Manifiesto Programa" of October 23, 1930, can be found in Duarte Oropesa, *Historiología cubana*, pp. 332–35.

27. Aguilar, *Cuba 1933*, pp. 116–17; Suchlicki, *University Students*, p. 28. The program of the Ala Izquierda Estudiantil can be found in *Pensamiento Crítico*, April 1970, pp. 123–29.

28. Aguilar, *Cuba 1933*, pp. 44–47; Bonsal, *Cuba, Castro and the U.S.*, p. 256.

29. A theoretical framework for this treatment of the Cuban bourgeoisie can be found in Cardoso, *Dependencia y desarrollo*. Since much of the Cuban bourgeoisie was actually Spanish in origin or North American in identification, and since most were integrated with or dependent upon U.S. capital, its "national" segment was extremely weak.

30. Arthur Whitaker, *The Western Hemisphere Idea: Its Rise and Decline* (Ithaca: Cornell University Press, 1954), pp. 128–29; Wyatt Macgaffey and Clifford R. Barnett, *Twentieth Century Cuba* (Garden City, N. Y.: Anchor Books, 1965), pp. 259–65; and Aguilar, *Cuba 1933*, pp. 68–69.

31. Aguilar, *Cuba 1933*, pp. 70–71; José Antonio Portuondo, *El contenido social de la literatura cubana* (Mexico: Ed. Colegio de Mexico, 1944), pp. 64–65. For intellectual ferment prior to 1920 see ibid., pp. 56–64. The revisionist writers later concentrated around the journal *Revista de Avance*. See Carlos Ripoll, *La generacion del 23 en Cuba* (New York: Las Americas Publishing Co., 1968), pp. 49–50. For the text and signers of the "Protesta," see Riera Hernandez, *Historial obrero cubano*, p. 276.

32. Portuondo, *El contenido social*, p. 65; Emilio Roig de Leuchsenring, ed., *Curso de introducción a la historia de Cuba*, vol. 1 (Havana: Oficina del Historiador de la Ciudad, 1938), pp. 420–22; and Ripoll, *La generación del 23*, p. 50. For the members of the Grupo Minorista

see Riera Hernández, *Historial obrero cubano*, p. 278. For their 1927 statement see Duarte Oropesa, *Historiología cubana*, pp. 319–22. The 1927 statement had certain antiliberal elements that were fascist in tone. Also in keeping with fascist expression during this period was the theme of anti-imperialism. Nevertheless, many of the leaders of Minorismo moved to the left and became members of the Cuban Communist party. See Riera Hernández, *Historial obrero cubano*, pp. 276, 278.

33. Portuondo, *El contenido social*, p. 70; Roig de Leuchsenring, *Curso de introducción*, pp. 421–25. For the intellectual production of the left Minoristas see Portuondo, *El contenido social*, pp. 71 ff.

Two of the major supporters of Machado were the authors Ramiro Guerra y Sánchez and Alberto Lamar-Schweyer, both of whom served in the cabinet. See Alberto Lamar-Schweyer, *How President Machado Fell* (Havana: La Casa Montalvo Cardenas, 1938), passim.

34. Thomas, *Cuba*, p. 567; Fitzgibbon, *Cuba and the United States*, pp. 184–85; Smith, *United States and Cuba*, pp. 97–98; and Jenks, *Our Cuban Colony*, p. 269.

35. The amalgamation of the traditional parties into the Machadato led to the destruction of most of their strength after the fall of the regime. See Mario Riera Hernández, *Cuba política, 1899–1955* (Havana: Imp. Modelo, 1955).

36. Fitzgibbon, *Cuba and the United States*, pp. 187, 191; Aguilar, *Cuba 1933*, pp. 92–93. For the efforts of the Unión Nacionalista (UN) to obtain the invocation of the Platt Amendment or at least the removal of U.S. recognition, see *Foreign Relations of the U.S.*, 1930, vol. 2, pp. 649–80. Also see Cosme de la Torriente y Peraza, *Cuarenta años de mi vida* (Havana: El Siglo XX, 1939), pp. 225–31.

37. Presidential proclamation to the Cuban people reported in the *Havana Post* of February 3, 1931, contained in Enclosure 2 to 837.00/2971.

38. Aguilar, *Cuba 1933*, pp. 107–08 and 111–15; Torriente, *Cuarenta años*, pp. 245–47.

39. Alvarez Díaz, *Cuba, geopolítica y pensamiento economico*, p. 403; Page, "Development of Organized Labor," p. 67; Samuel Farber, "Revolution and Social Structure in Cuba, 1933–1959" (Ph.D. dissertation, University of California, Berkeley, 1969), pp. 84–92; Aguilar, *Cuba 1933*, pp. 118–21.

For the text of the *Manifiesto Programa* see Partido ABC, *Doctrina del ABC: manifiesto programa* [*del 1932*] (Havana: Ed. Cenit, 1942).

40. Farber, "Revolution and Social Structure," pp. 87–90; Arredondo, *Cuba: tierra indefensa*, pp. 472–73.

41. Beals, *Crime of Cuba*, p. 347, and Cuban Information Bureau, *Ambassador Guggenheim and the Cuban Revolt* (Washington, D.C.: Cuban Information Bureau, 1931), p. 14.

42. See chapter 5.

43. Ruiz, *Cuba: Making of a Revolution*, p. 121; Thomas, *Cuba*, p. 576.

44. Ruiz, *Cuba: Making of a Revolution*, p. 122; Thomas, *Cuba*, p. 576; and Suchlicki, *University Students*, p. 21. Mella entered the University of Havana in 1921. As early as 1923 he moved his political activities outside the university. He established the Universidad Popular José Martí, which was inspired by the ideas concerning workers' education of Haya de la Torre. (Riera Hernández, *Historial obrero cubano*, p. 68.)

In the four years between his becoming a member of the PCC and his assassination, the indefatigable Mella organized the Cuban Anti-Imperialist League, the Anti-Clerical Federation, and the Association of Cuban Revolutionary Emigres (Jaime Suchlicki, "Stirrings of Cuban Nationalism: The Student Generation of 1930," *Journal of Inter-American Studies*, 10, no. 3 [July 1968]: 353; Riera Hernández, *Historial obrero cubano*, p. 281).

For the story of Mella's short and stormy career in international Communist affairs and of his exile and assassination in Mexico, see Eudocio Ravines, *The Yenan Way* (New York: Scribner's, 1951), pp. 57–58; Suárez Rivas, *Un pueblo crucificado*, pp. 22–23; Victor Alba, *Esquemo his-*

tórico del comunismo en Ibero-America, 3d ed. (Mexico: Ed. Occidentales, 1954), pp. 60–61, 96–97; Alberto Baeza Flores, *Las cadenas vienen de lejos* (Mexico: Ed. Letras, 1960), pp. 81–85; and Riera Hernández, *Historial obrero cubano*, pp. 73–77.

For Mella's own writings see his *La lucha revolucionaria contra el imperialismo* (Havana: Ed. Sociales, 1940), and *Documentos para su vida* (Havana, 1964).

45. Thomas, *Cuba*, pp. 577–78; 837.00B/180.

46. Aguilar, *Cuba 1933*, pp. 85–86; Thomas, *Cuba*, pp. 580–81; Robert J. Alexander, *Communism in Latin America* (New Brunswick, N.J.: Rutgers University Press, 1957), p. 271; and Buell, *Problems*, pp. 195–96.

47. Aguilar, *Cuba 1933*, p. 93, relates a division between the "intellectuals" and the "workers" in the party over the question of "bolshevization" and "proletarianization." An actual split did occur in the early thirties as a result of which a small faction, led by Sandalio Junco, left the party. This group opposed the belief of the majority of the leadership that a socialist revolution was possible in Cuba without a prior or simultaneous revolution in the United States. (See 837.00B/180, June 6, 1934, p. 16.) Junco's group later formed a Trotskyist party (Partido Bolshevique Leninista) and eventually formed the labor leadership of the Auténtico party of Ramón Grau San Martín. (See Alexander, *Communism in Latin America*, p. 280n.)

48. Thomas, *Cuba*, p. 596; 837.504/331, June 18, 1931, pp. 9–10; 837.00B/28, Feb. 13, 1930; and 837.00B/29, May 28, 1930.

49. 837.504/325, April 11, 1930; 837.504/329, Oct. 4, 1930; 837.504/331, June 18, 1931, pp. 8–11; 837.00B/180, dated June 6, 1934, pp. 22–23. Concerning the 1930 general strike see Jorge García Montes and Antonio Alonso Avila, *Historia del Partido Comunista de Cuba* (Miami: Editorial Universal [Rema], 1970), pp. 106–08.

50. 837.00B/44; 810.00B/73; 837.00B/38.

51. Aguilar, *Cuba 1933*, pp. 94, 122–24; García Montes, *Historia del Partido Comunista*, pp. 111, 114–17. García Montes states that after the failure of the 1930 general strike, the faction of the party which called for greater cooperation with the bourgeois opposition to Machado was able to introduce a united-front policy. Efforts were made to come to agreements with the ABC, the UN, and the DEU, but were rejected by these organizations. Some success, however, was made concerning cooperation with the noncommunist labor organizations. Nevertheless, the majority of the party leadership judged the united front a failure and brought about a return to a more "sectarian" position, and the expulsion of the minority who favored the united front. This minority was accused of "Trotskyism." The definitive account of this period, from the point of view of the party majority, can be found in the 1933 pamphlet of the Partido Comunista de Cuba, *El Partido Comunista y los problemas de la revolución cubano* (Havana: Comité Central del Partido Comunista de Cuba, 1933).

52. PCC, *Partido Comunista y los problemas*, pp. 10–11. For a statement of the majority within the party in early 1933 written by one of the most influential members of the leadership see Rubén Martínez Villena, "The Rise of the Revolutionary Movement in Cuba," *Communist*, 12, no. 6 (June 1933):559–69.

53. Buell, *Problems*, p. 196; 837.00B/180, pp. 18–22. Concerning the shaky status of party discipline at this time see PCC, *Partido Comunista y los problemas*, pp. 43–48. On the ideology of the Ala Izquierda see ibid., p. 45.

54. This section follows the discussion in Pérez, *Army Politics in Cuba*, chap. 5.

55. Merrifield, "Magazine Press and Cuba," pp. 248–51; Minor, "Cuba and Congress," p. 5; "Cuba in Revolt," *Commerce and Finance*, August 19, 1931, p. 1201; and Rupert Bentham, "Cuba Maintains Her Credit," *Barron's*, 12, no. 51 (December 19, 1932): 11.

56. For Latin American policy under Stimson see Robert H. Ferrell, *American Diplomacy in the Great Depression* (New York: W. W. Norton, 1957), chap. 13; Henry L. Stimson and McGeorge Bundy, *On Active Service in Peace and War* (New York: Harper, 1948), pp. 174–87.

57. Stimson and Bundy, *On Active Service*, pp. 182–83.

58. Joseph Brandes, *Herbert Hoover and Economic Diplomacy* (Pittsburgh: University of Pittsburgh Press, 1962), pp. 197–202. The quotation from Stimson is in his *American Policy in Nicaragua* (New York: Scribners, 1927), pp. 122–23.

For a discussion of the difficulties of combining increased economic presence and lessened political intervention see W. A. Williams, "Latin America," pp. 3–30, and idem, *Tragedy of American Diplomacy*, pp. 148–55.

59. For the text of the Root interpretation of the Platt Amendment see Robert Smith, *What Happened in Cuba?* (New York: Twayne Publishers, 1963), p. 127. For Stimson's defense of the Root interpretation see Stimson Diary, Sept. 18, 1930, Henry L. Stimson Papers; Stimson's letter to Representative Hamilton Fish, Jr., Jan. 25, 1933, in 837.00/3431; Stimson's letter to Postmaster General Walter F. Brown, July 5, 1932, in 837.00/3454. Also see "Memorandum on Article III of the Platt Amendment," April 10, 1931, in 711.37/153.

60. For Ambassador Judah's reports to the State Department see Jackman, "America's Cuban Policy," pp. 21 ff.; "Relations Between the United States and Cuba," Feb. 28, 1933, memorandum by H. Freeman Mathews, p. 2, Stimson Papers; and Aguilar, *Cuba 1933*, p. 92. For background on Harry Guggenheim and his family's financial interests see Beals, *Crime of Cuba*, chap. 20.

61. Guggenheim, *U.S. and Cuba*, pp. iii, 192; Harvey O'Connor, *The Guggenheims* (New York: Covici-Friede, 1937), p. 441; and Beals, *Crime of Cuba*, pp. 332–36.

Grosvenor Jones was the chief of the Finance and Investment Division of the Commerce Department but while in Cuba served Guggenheim in a personal capacity. Jones worked on a study of Cuba's debt structure. (See Carleton Beals, *The Coming Struggle for South America* [Philadelphia: J. P. Lippincott, 1938], p. 199; Cuban Information Bureau, *Guggenheim and the Cuban Revolt*, p. 15.)

The study of the Platt Amendment was carried out by Phillip Jessup, then a professor of international law at Columbia University.

62. *Foreign Relations of the U.S.*, 1930, vol. 2, pp. 649–78.

63. 711.37/174, Jan. 20, 1933, pp. 1–4.

For Stimson's rejection of U.S. interference in the Cuban political crisis see his telegram to Guggenheim, Nov. 15, 1930, in 837.00/2887. Also see his press conference of October 2, 1930, quoted in *Foreign Relations of the U.S.*, 1930, vol. 2, pp. 663–65, in which the secretary indicated that the United States would not intervene except in the case of anarchy. Nevertheless, for fear that a policy of total nonintervention might actually encourage revolt, Stimson purposely left unclear the exact conditions under which the United States would consider intervening.

64. *Foreign Relations of the U.S.*, 1931, vol. 2, pp. 48–51, 55–59.

65. Ibid., pp. 51–54; R.G. 84, Post Records, American Embassy, Havana, pt. 10, 800, 1931, C8.11; Krogh, "U.S., Cuba and Sumner Welles," pp. 55–56. For Stimson's fears concerning revolution see *Foreign Relations of the U.S.*, 1931, vol. 2, p. 54.

66. For U.S. policy toward the revolt see *Foreign Relations of the U.S.*, 1931, vol. 2, pp. 67–71. For Guggenheim's response to the revolt see ibid., pp. 71–74. For Machado's reaction to Guggenheim's proposal to step down see 711.37/162, Oct. 23, 1931, p. 4.

67. *Foreign Relations of the U.S.*, 1931, vol. 2, pp. 75–82; ibid., 1932, vol. 5, p. 533 ff. For Stimson's position see ibid., pp. 543–47; Krogh, "U.S., Cuba and Sumner Welles," pp. 57–58.

68. For a general discussion of pressures for intervention addressed to the State Department see Jackman, "America's Cuban Policy," chap. 4. Also see 710.11/1544; 837.00/3458 and 3459.

Chapter 5. The New Deal Prepares for Power

1. *Current Biography, 1940* (New York: H. W. Wilson Co.), p. 850; Thomas Millington, "The Latin American Diplomacy of Sumner Welles" (Ph.D. dissertation, Johns Hopkins University,

School of Advanced International Studies, 1966), p. 109; Daniel M. Smith, *Aftermath of War* (Philadelphia: American Philosophical Society, 1970), pp. 118–19; *New York Times Magazine,* August 3, 1941, p. 9. Also see Frank Graff, "The Strategy of Involvement: A Diplomatic Biography of Sumner Welles, 1933–1943" (Ph.D. dissertation, University of Michigan, 1971), pp. 4–5.

2. Krogh, "U.S., Cuba and Sumner Welles," pp. 84–85. The quotation is from a memorandum by Welles, March 1, 1921, in 837.00/2216.

3. Krogh, "U.S., Cuba and Sumner Welles," pp. 86–87; Graff, "Strategy of Involvement," p. 9n.

4. Krogh, "U.S., Cuba and Sumner Welles," p. 103n. Also see letters from Welles to Davis, Aug. 6, 1921, and April 29, 1926, Norman Davis Papers.

5. Welles to Davis, April 29, 1926, pp. 1–4, Norman Davis Papers. Another version has it that Coolidge did not support Welles because of a personal matter. See *New York Times Magazine,* August 3, 1941, p. 9.

6. Welles to Davis, Sept. 2, 1925, and April 29, 1926, p. 5, Norman Davis Papers.

7. For Welles's Wilsonianism in regard to the Haitian occupation, see his instruction to the special representative of the president in Haiti, General John H. Russell, in 123R914/1a, Feb. 11, 1922, quoted in Krogh, "U.S., Cuba and Sumner Welles," pp. 90–94. For his support of the Crowder moralization program see Primelles, *Crónica cubana,* vol. 2, pp. 179, 314 ff. For an example of Welles's paternalism see his handling of the 1923 Washington Conference of Central American states as described in Krogh, "U.S., Cuba and Sumner Welles," p. 125. The quotations regarding intervention are from Welles's "Is America Imperialistic?", *Atlantic Monthly,* 134 (September 1924): 413–14, 421–22. For Welles's aggressive use of U.S. "friendly mediation," see his handling of the 1924 civil war in Honduras in *Foreign Relations of the U.S.,* 1924, vol. 2, pp. 300–21. Though on his mission to Honduras Welles stated a preference for joint action by the Central American states rather than unilateral U.S. involvement (see 815.00/3089, April 11, 1924), in practice he found it expedient to act otherwise (see 815/00/3105, April 19, 1924). Welles's swift and satisfactory settlement of the armed political dispute between the Honduran parties may have led him to believe that his mission to Cuba in 1933 would not be difficult. The procedure employed by Welles in Honduras was that of obtaining the support of the warring factions for the appointment of a neutral provisional president who would oversee honest elections and the return to constitutional processes. This same procedure was at the heart of Welles's proposals for Cuba during the crisis of the late Machadato in 1933. See chapter 6 below.

8. Samuel F. Bemis, *The Latin American Policy of the United States* (New York: W. W. Norton, 1967), p. 220; Sumner Welles, *Naboth's Vineyard,* vol. 2 (New York: Payson and Clark, Ltd., 1928), pp. 924–31. Other Good Neighbor–type positions taken were opposition to the high tariff on Latin American imports (ibid., p. 930) and an acceptance of legislation by Latin American states whose purpose was to assure greater control over their basic resources (ibid., pp. 910–11). The work defends Wilsonian idealism but acknowledges that it was often not "preventive" enough and thus became embroiled in reactive interventions. Hughes's preventive policy gains praise.

9. On the Roosevelt family's tradition of noblesse oblige see Daniel Fusfeld, *The Economic Thought of F.D.R. and the Origins of the New Deal,* Columbia Studies in the Social Sciences, no. 586 (New York: AMS Press, 1970), pp. 251–52. Concerning FDR's Caribbean trip in 1917 see Frank B. Freidel, *F.D.R.,* vol. 1 (Boston: Little, Brown and Company, 1952), pp. 275–84; Hans Schmidt, *The United States Occupation of Haiti, 1915–1934* (New Brunswick: Rutgers University Press, 1971), pp. 106–11.

10. The quotations are cited in Freidel, *F.D.R.,* vol. 1, pp. 277–78, from Roosevelt's diary, January 24, 1917.

11. Freidel, *F.D.R.,* vol. 1, pp. 280–84; Schmidt, *U.S. Occupation of Haiti,* pp. 86, 110–12.

12. James MacGregor Burns, *Roosevelt: The Lion and the Fox* (New York: Harcourt, Brace, 1956), chap. 5.

13. Elliot Roosevelt, ed., *F.D.R.: His Personal Letters, 1928–1945*, vol. 1 (New York: Duell, Sloan and Pierce, 1950), pp. 12–13, 177, 221, 263, 271.

14. Group 14, FDR Correspondence 1928–1929, Box 13, Welles to FDR, January 20, 1928, FDR Papers.

15. For the documents of the Central American Conference see *Foreign Relations of the U.S.*, 1923, vol. 1, pp. 297–327.

16. 815.00/3105, Welles to Hughes, April 19, 1924, in *Foreign Relations of the U.S.*, vol. 2, p. 309; also see n. 7 above.

17. The Clark memorandum was published in 1930. See U.S. Department of State, *Memorandum on the Monroe Doctrine* (Washington, D.C.: Government Printing Office, 1930).

18. Millington, "Latin American Diplomacy of Sumner Welles," pp. 110–11, 197.

19. Krogh, "U.S., Cuba and Sumner Welles," p. 162; Franklin D. Roosevelt, "Our Foreign Policy: A Democratic View," *Foreign Affairs*, 6, no. 4 (July 9, 1928): 573–86. The quoted passage is from pp. 584–85.

20. Krogh, "U.S., Cuba and Sumner Welles," pp. 169–74; letters between Welles and Davis during February and March 1931, Norman Davis Papers; Group 12, FDR Private Correspondence, 1928–1932, Box 77, letter of Feb. 17, 1931, Welles to FDR, and letter of Feb. 25, 1931, Davis to FDR, FDR Papers.

21. Norman Davis, "Wanted: A Consistent Latin American Policy," *Foreign Affairs*, 9, no. 4 (July 1931): 547–67. For the secretary of state's speech to the Council on Foreign Relations see Henry L. Stimson, "The United States and the Other American Republics," *Foreign Affairs*, 9, no. 3 (April 1931), supp.

22. B. H. Williams, *Economic Foreign Policy*, pp. 257–58, 285–86.

23. Ibid., p. 265.

24. The body of work on this theme, centering upon the studies of William Appleman Williams, is quite large. See, for example, Williams's *Tragedy of American Diplomacy*, and Walter LaFeber, *The New Empire* (Ithaca: Cornell University Press, 1963). For works that treat the expansionist "impulse" as structural rather than psychological see the works cited in chap. 4, n. 12; Gabriel Kolko, *The Politics of War* (New York: Random House, 1968); and Gabriel and Joyce Kolko, *The Limits of Power* (New York: Random House, 1970).

25. Tulchin, *Aftermath of War*, p. 241; Smith, *U.S. and Cuba*, pp. 26–27; and Burton Kaufman, "United States Trade and Latin America," pp. 342–63.

26. Parrini, *Heir to Empire*, p. 228. The Versailles settlement had actually increased the area under European tariff control.

27. 611.3731/387, June 11, 1931.

28. Changing patterns of capital investment in the United States had increased the relative strength of the large industrial and banking units. These forces, because of their strong competitive position, generally favored lowered tariffs. Their political leverage was much greater with the executive branch of government than with the Congress, with its popular-based bias against concentrated wealth. The attempt to move tariff decisions from an arena where popular constituencies were dominant to one in which economic "laws" would be more influential was a reflection of the struggle between the needs of the large economic units to rationalize the structure of the national economy and those of small-scale enterprise, which depended upon retaining a space for their economic operations free from the oligopolizing tendencies of the capital-rich firms.

29. Richard N. Gardner, *Sterling-Dollar Diplomacy* (New York: McGraw-Hill Book Co., 1969), p. 18.
The attack upon the European preferential tariff systems was implicit in the "flexible" provisions of the Fordney-McCumber Act of 1922, which allowed the president to alter tariff rates by as much as 50 percent. See William S. Culbertson, *Reciprocity: A National Policy for Foreign*

Trade (New York: McGraw-Hill, 1937), p. 8; J. M. Letiche, *Reciprocal Trade Agreements in the World Economy* (New York: Columbia University Press, 1948), p. 10. This same purpose was reflected in the adoption of the unrestricted form of the most-favored-nation clause. Paradoxically, the unrestricted clause (a long-time goal of free-trade forces) was not a step toward freer trade. Unconditional treatment, while more equitable in theory, did not necessarily imply any lowering of rates, as all it demanded was that rates, whatever their levels, be applied equally to all states (Letiche, *Reciprocal Trade Agreements*, pp. 9–12). Even if a particular rate *were* lowered, the class of goods to which the lower rate applied could be so narrowly defined as to include only the goods of a particular state, and thus the extension of such a benefit to all states would be without effect (See Kindleberger, *International Economics*, p. 239.)

While accepting the Fordney-McCumber Act and its flexible tariff as the best compromise available, low-tariff forces like the National Foreign Trade Council and bankers such as Thomas Lamont and Paul M. Warburg were unsatisfied with the bill. Protectionist forces like the American Protective League, representing small and medium manufacturing, were, for their part, wary of the implications of a "rational" tariff. (Parrini, *Heir to Empire*, pp. 233–35.)

The protectionists seemed to have won a round when they were able to define the criteria to be used by the Tariff Commission in determining the proper level of rates as that which would "equalize money costs of production at home and abroad," which directly negated the "law" of comparative advantage upon which international trade rested (see Letiche, *Reciprocal Trade Agreements*, p. 11). This protectionist's dream became something of a nightmare when the Tariff Commission's cost studies later revealed great differences in the foreign and domestic costs of many products. One of the most glaring of these discrepancies was in sugar.

30. Parrini, *Heir to Empire*, pp. 246–47; John D. Hicks, *Republican Ascendancy* (New York: Harper and Row, 1960), pp. 57–58. Herbert Hoover believed that private foreign lending and investment could support increased U.S. exports without the need for lowering tariffs. Indeed, Hoover favored both trade and overseas capital expansion *and* a protected domestic market. See Wilson, *American Business and Foreign Policy*, pp. 87–91.

31. Rexford G. Tugwell, *The Brains Trust* (New York: Viking Press, 1968), pp. 194–95.

32. Elliot Rosen, "Roosevelt and the Brains Trust," *Political Science Quarterly*, 87, no. 4 (December 1972): 531–57, and "Intranationalism versus Internationalism: The Interregnum Struggle for the Sanctity of the New Deal," *Political Science Quarterly*, 81, no. 2 (June 1966): 274. Rosen takes the position that Frankfurter was willing to accept a greater level of economic nationalism than most writers have indicated. He claims that the strongest "internationalist" influence came from outside Roosevelt's political circle, particularly from Secretary of State Stimson.

33. Howard Jablon, "Cordell Hull, the State Department and the Foreign Policy of the First Roosevelt Administration, 1933–1936" (Ph.D. dissertation, Rutgers University, 1967), pp. 2–7.

34. Ernest K. Lindley, *The Roosevelt Revolution: The First Phase* (New York: Viking Press, 1933), pp. 30–31, 310–11; Tugwell, *Brains Trust*, p. 201; and Joseph Alsop and Robert Kintner, *Men Around the President* (New York: Doubleday, 1939), pp. 22–23.

35. Tugwell, *Brains Trust*, pp. 475–79; Raymond Moley, *The First New Deal* (New York: Harcourt, Brace, 1966), p. 90; and Freidel, *F.D.R.*, vol. 3, p. 356.

36. Graff, "Strategy of Involvement," pp. 25–28; E. Roosevelt, *F.D.R.: His Personal Letters*, p. 263; OF 470 (Welles), Welles to FDR, Dec. 17, 1932, FDR Papers; PPF 2961 (Welles), Welles to FDR, Jan. 23, 1933, FDR Papers; Edgar B. Nixon, ed., *F.D.R. and Foreign Affairs* (Cambridge, Mass.: Harvard University Press, 1968), "Draft by Sumner Welles of a Statement on Pan-American Policy," pp. 18–19.

37. The quoted material is from Group 14, General Correspondence, Box 13 (Welles), Welles to FDR, Jan. 20, 1928, FDR Papers.

38. Davis to Welles, Jan. 17, 1933, Norman Davis Papers.

39. Ferrell, *American Diplomacy*, pp. 231–38.

40. Ibid., pp. 239–42; Stimson Diary, vol. 25, Jan. 9, 1933, and vol. 26, Oct. 26, 1933, Henry L. Stimson Papers. Stimson felt that the loyalty of the Cuban Army was a function of their training by U.S. officers who had taught them to stay out of politics. He attributed Cuba's problems to the reduction in the number of small farms, the dependence upon sugar exports, and the importation of black labor. Stimson Diary, vol. 25, Jan. 9, 1933, p. 1.

41. Stimson Diary, vol. 25, Jan. 10, 1933, pp. 1–3, Henry L. Stimson Papers. For information as to Taussig's role as Cuban advisor see Box 38 (Cuba), Charles Taussig Papers.

42. Box 31 (Tariff), "Memorandum for A. A. Berle Jr.," Jan. 11, 1933, and Box 37 (State Department), "Memorandum for Secretary Hull," March 14, 1933, p. 4, Charles Taussig Papers.

43. Krogh, "U.S., Cuba and Sumner Welles," pp. 71–73; Box 37 (State Department), "Memorandum for Secretary Hull," March 14, 1933, pp. 4–5, Charles Taussig Papers; Stimson Diary, vol. 25, Jan. 16, 1933, Henry L. Stimson Papers; Mario Lazo to Jessup, Feb. 13, 1933, Phillip Jessup Papers.

44. Box 37 (State Department), "Memo for Secretary Hull," March 14, 1933, Charles Taussig Papers.

Taussig's description of the opposition was somewhat confused. He ignored organized labor and the Cuban Communist party as major opponents of the dictatorship. On the other hand, he considered the ABC to be extremist and to contain some Communists (ibid., p. 1). Taussig did not have a high opinion of the bankers, feeling that they had encouraged loans by the Cuban government, loans which were now being repaid by means of "cruel" taxation (ibid., pp. 2–3).

Certain of Taussig's ideas reflect those of the director of the Foreign Policy Association, Raymond Leslie Buell. See Box 33 (Buell), Buell to Taussig, March 10, 1933, Charles Taussig Papers.

45. Box 37 (Barrett), Barrett to Taussig, dated Feb. 23, 1933, and April 27, 1933, Charles Taussig Papers; Lindley, *Roosevelt Revolution*, pp. 221–22; *New York Herald Tribune*, April 16, 1933, p. 12; Box 37 (State Department), "Memorandum for Secretary Hull," March 14, 1933, p. 5, Charles Taussig Papers; Carleton Beals, "Young Cuba Rises," *Scribner's Magazine*, 94 (November 1933): 271.

Chapter 6. The New Deal and the Search for Cuban Stability—Part 1

1. For requests to the State Department and the U.S. embassy in Havana for some type of intervention see 837.00/3415–3460 and R.G. 84, F800Cuba/1933, vol. 15/Misc. Correspondence. For Stimson's response see, for example, 837.00/3431 and 837.00/3432. For the position of the banks, see Mario Lazo to Jessup, Feb. 10, 1933, Phillip Jessup Papers.

The strongest pressure in the U.S. Congress for a more active Cuban policy came from Congressman Hamilton Fish and Senator William Borah. See Krogh, "U.S., Cuba and Sumner Welles," pp. 73–74.

2. Davis to Welles, Jan. 17, 1933, Norman Davis Papers; Mario Lazo to Jessup, Feb. 13, 1933, Phillip Jessup Papers. See also Rosen, "Roosevelt and the Brains Trust," pp. 562; Jablon, "Hull, the State Department and Foreign Policy," pp. 7–18; Lloyd Gardner, "From New Deal to New Frontiers: 1937–1941," *Studies on the Left* (Fall 1959): 29–43; and Gardner, *Economic Aspects of New Deal Diplomacy*, pp. 12–16.

3. Charles W. Taussig, *Some Notes on Sugar and Molasses* (New York: privately printed, 1940), pp. 23–24; Lindley, *Roosevelt Revolution*, pp. 30, 311; Alsop and Kintner, *Men Around the President*, p. 23; Beals, *Crime of Cuba*, pp. 355–67; Thomas Mathews, *Puerto Rican Politics and the New Deal* (Gainesville: University of Florida Press, 1960), p. 131; Max Freedman, *Roosevelt and Frankfurter: Their Correspondence, 1928–1945* (London: Bodley Head, 1968), p. 103; Stimson Diary, vol. 25, Jan. 19, 1933, p. 5, Henry L. Stimson Papers; and Thomas, *Cuba*, p. 560.

4. 711.37/178a, printed in *Foreign Relations of the U.S.*, 1933, vol. 5, pp. 279–86. On the likelihood of Welles's authorship of his own instructions see Krogh, "U.S., Cuba and Sumner Welles," p. 180n., and Wood, *Making of the Good Neighbor Policy*, p. 59. In Cordell Hull and A. Berding, *Memoirs* (New York, 1948), p. 313, Hull states, however, that the instructions were his own. While the addition of the final paragraph concerning Cuban sovereignty and U.S. desire not to intervene reflect language more common to Hull than Welles, the remainder of the eight-page memorandum very closely reflects Welles's thinking as it had developed over the previous decade. Moreover, Hull's background indicates no great familiarity with Latin American or Cuban affairs, and neither his personal papers nor those of the Department of State indicate any involvement on his part in the formulation of Cuban policy during this period. (Krogh, "U.S., Cuba and Sumner Welles," pp. 76–77.)

5. *Foreign Relations of the U.S.*, 1933, vol. 5, pp. 287–89.

6. Ibid., pp. 289–90. It is perhaps too strong to characterize Welles's mission as one designed to "save" Machado as is done by Robert Smith, *United States and Cuba*, p. 144. However, the goals of political compromise and economic revival were more consonant with support for the incumbent Cuban president than with his removal from office. There is no hard evidence, despite the hostility to the dictator expressed in Taussig's memos, that Welles went to Cuba with the intention of forcing Machado from office. Indeed, his early dispatches from Havana indicate quite the reverse. For support of this position see Krogh, "U.S., Cuba and Sumner Welles," pp. 186–87, and Torriente y Peraza, *Cuarenta años*, p. 406.

7. *Foreign Relations of the U.S.*, 1933, vol. 5, pp. 290–92.

8. Ibid., p. 295; Lamar-Schweyer, *How President Machado Fell*, pp. 78–79.

9. For the concern of the opposition with the trade negotiations see OF470 (Welles), Memorandum from Taussig to FDR, April 18, 1933, FDR Papers.

Another element of the compromise was Welles's demand that the opposition stop their campaign of terrorism against the dictatorship. In addition, Welles made a strong effort to galvanize U.S. authorities to suppress the activities of U.S.-based exile organizations. See R.G. 84, F800Cuba/1933, vol. 15/Acts of Cuban Revolutionaries in the United States, cable, Welles to Hull, April 20, 1933.

10. For Welles's thinking at this stage see OF470 (Welles), Welles to FDR, April 18, 1933, FDR Papers.

11. Hull's only public statement on Cuba had come at his press conference on April 4, 1933, wherein he stated that Cuban relations would be handled the same as those of the United States with any other state (Krogh, "U.S., Cuba and Sumner Welles," p. 77). This statement was not well received by the opposition in Cuba (see 711.37/177, Chargé Edward L. Reed to Hull, April 18, 1933).

Welles made a practice of requesting that his important cables to the State Department be sent to Roosevelt, and on several occasions he wrote directly to the president. Roosevelt on occasion answered Welles directly. His communications were friendly and laudatory, but FDR usually dodged the attempts by the ambassador to obtain personal presidential endorsement of specific acts. However, Roosevelt took no action designed to thwart Welles's general policy. See E. Roosevelt, *F.D.R. His Personal Letters*, pp. 350, 354; Box 5-Cuba, Samuel Rosenman Papers.

In his public press conferences, the president generally claimed ignorance of Welles's activities in Cuba (PPF 1-P, Box 201, Press Conferences, 1:373 of June 9, 1933, FDR Papers).

12. E. Roosevelt, *F.D.R. His Personal Letters*, p. 350; R.G. 84, F800Cuba/1933, vol. 18, no. 851, Welles to Secretary of State, May 25, 1933; *Foreign Relations of the U.S.*, 1933, vol. 5, p. 296.

13. *Foreign Relations of the U.S.*, 1933, vol. 5, pp. 299–301.

14. Ibid., pp. 302–05. Welles was gratified that Machado's statement covered "precisely" the points he had made to the Cuban president and noted that he was "afforded the opportunity of

revising the text." While U.S. hegemony in Cuba had always made its ambassador one of the most powerful men on the island, Welles's actions during this period went beyond previous practice. Though some in the State Department were later to voice reservations, at this time there was no questioning of Welles's behavior, least of all by Roosevelt, who wrote to the ambassador that he was pleased that he "seemed to be getting the situation under control and to have the confidence of the people who count" (OF470 [Welles], FDR to Welles, June 24, 1933, FDR Papers).

15. Aguilar, *Cuba 1933*, pp. 130–33: 837.00/3552, p. 3.

Menocal's refusal to join the mediation caused Welles to recommend that his activities in the United States be kept under close surveillance (*Foreign Relations of the U.S.*, 1933, vol. 5, pp. 304, 307; 837.00/3577).

Two small offshoots of the ABC, the ABC Radical and the OCRR (Organización Celular Radical Revolucionaria) differed with the main party over its acceptance of the mediation. OCRR emphasized the early ABC goals of land reform and nationalization of natural resources. It rejected the mediation at first but later, after undergoing a split, joined the talks. ABC Radical emphasized the anti-Yankee nationalism of the early ABC. It never joined the mediation, and later, after the coup of September 4, 1933, joined the nationalist government of Ramón Grau San Martín. For the attitudes of the various opposition groups toward the mediation see R.G. 84, F800Cuba/1933, vol. 14/Mediation Acceptances. Also see 837.00/3581 and 837.00/3619. For contemporary statements by the leaders of the ABC whose position combined nationalism with essentially a pro-U.S. position see Juan Andres Lliteras, "Relations Between the United States and Cuba," *International Conciliation*, 296 (January 1934): 5; and Jorge Mañach, "Revolution in Cuba," *Foreign Affairs*, 12 (October 1933): 46–56.

16. Aguilar, *Cuba 1933*, p. 133; R.G. 84, F800Cuba/1933, vol. 14/Mediation Acceptances, letter to Welles from the Directorio Estudiantil del Instituto de Habana, no date.

17. *Foreign Relations of the U.S.*, 1933, vol. 5, pp. 307–10; 837.00/3458, statement by the Cuban American Friendship Council, Jan. 22, 1933. The quoted material is from OF470(Welles), Welles to FDR, May 18, 1933, FDR Papers. Because of opposition to the mediation from elements of the New York Junta, Welles desired its dissolution. See *Foreign Relations of the U.S.*, 1933, vol. 5, pp. 308–09. One of the leaders of the dissident group within the Junta was Ramón Grau San Martín, whose relationship to Welles is discussed in chapters 8 and 9 below. The New York Junta did dissolve in June 1933. See Charles W. Hackett, "Cuban Peace Prospects," *Current History*, 38 (August 1933): 594.

18. OF470 (Welles), Welles to FDR, May 18, 1933, FDR Papers; *Foreign Relations of the U.S.*, 1933, vol. 5, pp. 310–11.

19. *Foreign Relations of the U.S.*, 1933, vol. 5, p. 314; R.G. 84, F800Cuba/1933, vol. 14/ Mediation Acceptances.

20. *Foreign Relations of the U.S.*, 1933, vol. 5, p. 317; 837.00/3569, Enclosure 2, "Statement by Ambassador Welles." Roosevelt's statement, which was written by Phillips, is in *Foreign Relations of the U.S.*, 1933, vol. 5, p. 310.

21. *Foreign Relations of the U.S.*, 1933, vol. 5, pp. 317, 321, 323. Despite its militant nationalist rhetoric and terrorist tactics, Welles eventually came to see the ABC as the only popular, mass-based, nonleftist political movement. He later worked to enable it to secure the center of the political spectrum and to become a moderate alternative to left-wing nationalism. The ABC did play this role briefly in August 1933 under the Céspedes regime (see chapter 8) and later, in the early months of 1934, under the government of Carlos Mendieta. Ultimately, because they developed technocratic and even fascist leanings, they lost their popularity, and their role was preempted in the later thirties by the more electorally viable populist caudillo, Fulgencio Batista. For the rise of Batista see chapter 9.

22. R.G. 84, F800Cuba/1933, vol. 14/Mediation-General, "Summary of Meeting with Opposition" of July 3, 5, 7, and 10, 1933; Lamar-Schweyer, *How President Machado Fell*, pp. 104–05.

23. Aguilar, *Cuba 1933*, pp. 134–35; Lamar-Schweyer, *How President Machado Fell*, p. 76. An important indicator of U.S. support for Machado up to this point was the absence of any effort to restrict or halt the sale of arms to his government (see 837.24/234).

24. *Foreign Relations of the U.S.*, 1933, vol. 5, pp. 324–25. There is no indication of a reply from Roosevelt.

As before, Welles was still "keeping the negotiation of a commercial treaty as leverage until I know definitely where I stand on the political solution" (ibid., p. 325).

Beginning in June, Welles had made several requests to Acting Secretary of State Phillips that he make public statements denying reports that the former was acting without the support of the State Department. See Irwin Gellman, "Good Neighbor Diplomacy and the Rise of Batista" (Ph.D. dissertation, Indiana University, 1970), p. 37.

25. *Foreign Relations of the U.S.*, 1933, vol. 5, pp. 326–29.

The opposition objected to anything which would recognize the legality of the second Machado term. This position was, of course, in direct conflict with Welles's program of achieving a constitutional succession to the Machadato. See R.G. 84, F800Cuba/1933, vol. 14/Mediation-General, "Summary minutes of meeting of July 19, 1933," p. 8.

In effect, Welles did acknowledge the de facto nature of Machado's second term (see *Foreign Relations of the U.S.*, 1933, vol. 5, pp. 280, 316, 324). The actions of the 1928 Constituent Assembly which extended Machado's term were described as "apparently illegal" by the State Department even before Welles went to Cuba (H. Freeman Matthews, Memorandum on "Relations between the United States and Cuba," dated Feb. 28, 1933, Henry L. Stimson Papers).

Taussig also considered Machado's second term to be illegal (see Box 37 [State Department], Memorandum for Hull, March 13, 1933, Charles Taussig Papers). Welles's instructions (to himself) indicated the likelihood that the Constituent Assembly of 1928 had acted "ultra vires" (*Foreign Relations of the U.S.*, 1933, vol. 5, p. 280). Therefore, the determination of the U.S. ambassador to treat the late Machadato as de jure was not based upon any misconception as to its legal status, but rather upon his desire to use the power of conservation implicit in the procedures of the Cuban constitution to control and emotionally defuse the process of determining a successor regime.

26. Aguilar, *Cuba 1933*, p. 128.

The hegemonic position of the United States in Cuba, combined with the active interventionist role played by Sumner Welles in 1933, caused the dependent nature of Cuban politics to be revealed in an unusual degree. In the course of his Cuban mission, practically every conservative and moderate (and on occasion even radical) Cuban political and social group sought audience or corresponded with the U.S. ambassador. The entire range of offers and appeals was made: requests for intervention; suggestions for appointments to office—from Havana police chief to the president of the republic; pleas for legal redress; requests for political support; solicited and unsolicited statements of support; offers of cooperation; leaks of confidential information—including police and military intelligence; and a vast array of suggestions for political and economic programs.

The Havana embassy files thus reveal not only the usual ambassadorial contacts with local U.S. officials, foreign diplomats, U.S. businessmen, and Cuban government officials, but extensive communication (though much of it one-way) with every major element of Cuban society. Comparison of Welles's position with that of a governor general is not inappropriate. For this correspondence see R.G. 84, F800Cuba/1933, vols. 10 and 11/Confidential File, vol. 14/Mediation, and vol. 15/Miscellaneous Correspondence.

However, because most of the correspondence and verbal communication in which Welles engaged on his own initiative are in his personal papers and are not open as of this writing, the full extent of his involvement in Cuban politics during this period cannot be determined.

27. Lamar-Schweyer, *How President Machado Fell*, p. 116; 837.00/3582½, "Memorandum of

Conversation with the Cuban Ambassador," July 25, 1933. Cintas also made charges against Welles in an interview with Phillips on August 2. Cintas said that Welles was using the prospective commercial treaty to pressure Machado. Phillips, knowing that he was not speaking the truth, denied this. (*Foreign Relations of the U.S.*, 1933, vol. 5, pp. 331–32.)

28. *Foreign Relations of the U.S.*, 1933, vol. 5, p. 330; Aguilar, *Cuba 1933*, p. 140; R.G. 84, F800Cuba/1933, vol. 10, no. 118, Welles to Jefferson Caffery, July 27, 1933.

29. Krogh, "U.S., Cuba and Sumner Welles," p. 218; 837.00/3597; 837.00/3592.

30. Buell, *Problems*, p. 287; Blohm, "General Survey of Wages in Cuba," pp. 1403–05. For a survey of wages in the sugar industry in 1929 see Carlos Loveira, "Labour in the Cuban Sugar Industry," *International Labor Review*, September 1929, pp. 424–29. General wage levels actually stood at or below those recorded in 1909–1910 (Buell, *Problems*, p. 86). Buell's study estimates that 60 percent of the Cuban population was not able to maintain a "physically satisfactory living" in 1933 (p. 87). It should be kept in mind that agricultural wages were paid in most cases only during the harvest period. The length of the sugar harvest (*zafra*), in which the large majority of agricultural workers were engaged, had declined from about 130 days in the middle twenties to only 80 days in 1932–1933. For much of the remainder of the year (the "dead season" or *tiempo muerto*) there was little if any work available. About 50 percent of the working population was totally unemployed in 1933. Many sugar mills ground no cane at all that year, and in many sections of rural Cuba the market economy all but disappeared. (U.S. Department of Commerce, BFDC, *Cuban Readjustment to Current Economic Forces*.)

31. Page, "Development of Organized Labor in Cuba," p. 65; R.G. 84, F800Cuba/1933, vol. 18/Economic Conditions—Textile workers strike call at Cayo de la Rosa, July 14, 1933; Fabio Grobart, "La caída de Machado, símbola de la unidad del pueblo," *Bohemia*, February 2, 1973, p. 101.

32. R.G. 84, F800Cuba/1933, vol. 18/850.4(Labor Unions), letter, June 18, 1933, from Luis Fabregat, of the Federación Cubano de Trabajo, to Welles.

33. Charles A. Thomson, "The Cuban Revolution: Fall of Machado," *Foreign Policy Reports*, 11, no. 21 (December 18, 1935):254; Joaquín Ordoqui, *Elementos para la historia del movimiento obrero en Cuba* (Havana: Imprenta Nacional de Cuba, 1961), p. 28; and Gellman, "Good Neighbor Diplomacy," pp. 44–45.

Welles in his 837.00/3653, and García Montes, *Historia del partido comunista*, pp. 120–22, give a more complex and perhaps more accurate account of the origins of the strike, which includes the involvement of the owners of the various bus lines and the electric railway as parties to the strike. From such an explanation, the strike can be seen not so much as a grievance by workers as a joint effort by both workers and employers to force Machado out of office. See also R.G. 151, BFDC, Reports of Commercial Attaché—Havana, Box 1451, Economic and Trade Notes, no. 34, Oct. 11, 1933.

34. 837.00/3653; *Foreign Relations of the U.S.*, 1933, vol. 5, p. 334.

35. Ibid., pp. 336–37.

36. The figures on the July 16, 1933, elections are taken from R.G. 84, F800Cuba/1933, vol. 10, no. 81.

37. *Foreign Relations of the U.S.*, 1933, vol. 5, p. 338.

38. Aguilar, *Cuba 1933*, p. 145.

39. Of the sources which treat the Partido Comunista de Cuba and which were available to this author, none contains a definitive or even consistent interpretation of the motives and decisions of the party during this period. The interpretation herein has been constructed from many sources, the principal ones being: Partido Comunista de Cuba, *El partido comunista y los problemas de la revolución cubano*, pp. 4–20; García Montes, *Historia del partido comunista*, pp. 111–24; Aguilar, *Cuba 1933*, pp. 145–47; Alexander, *Communism in Latin America*, p. 272; Grobart, "La caída de Machado," pp. 104–05; D. R. D., "The Revolutionary Battles in Cuba," *Communist International*, 11, no. 2 (January 15, 1934): 59; Bijowsky, "Weakness and Mistakes

of the Communist Press in Cuba," *Communist International*, 11, no. 7 (April 5, 1934): 260; and "The Present Situation, Perspectives, and Tasks in Cuba," *The Communist*, 13, no. 9 (September 1934): 884–85.

40. Alexander, *Communism in Latin America*, pp. 272–73; García Montes, *Historia del partido comunista*, pp. 124–25; Aguilar, *Cuba 1933*, pp. 145–46; Ordoqui, *Elementos para la historia del movimiento*, pp. 28–29; Duarte Oropesa, *Historiología cubana*, pp. 384–85; *Hoy*, January 20, 1965, p. 2; and Grobart, "La caída de Machado," pp. 104–05. Concerning the career of Martínez Villena, a respected poet, see Roa, *Retorno a la alborada*, pp. 100–39.

41. Aguilar, *Cuba 1933*, p. 146; Riera Hernández, *Historial obrero cubano*, p. 83; and Thomson, "Cuban Revolution: Fall of Machado," p. 256.

42. Quesada y Miranda, *En Cuba libre*, p. 222.

The ABC request that Welles ask Machado to take a leave of absence is contained in a letter to the ambassador from the directors of the ABC dated August 5, 1933. Welles did make such a request of the Cuban president on the following day, and it may be that the ABC was the source of this idea. Such a suggestion was probably made without the knowledge of the ABC membership because it was pressing the leadership to leave the mediation and return to direct action against the dictator. (R.G. 84, F800Cuba/1933, vol. 14/Mediation Acceptances.)

43. Thomson, "Cuban Revolution: Fall of Machado," p. 255.

44. *Foreign Relations of the U.S.*, 1933, vol. 5, pp. 338–40.

45. Thomson, "Cuban Revolution: Fall of Machado," p. 255; *Foreign Relations of the U.S.*, 1933, vol. 5, p. 341. This was Welles's last interview with Machado. The president's supporters claim that Welles gave Machado forty-eight hours to respond. (Lamar-Schweyer, *How President Machado Fell*, p. 171.)

Welles's effort to separate Machado from his congressional supporters was an attempt not only to weaken the president but to save the Cuban Congress from the same fate, so that it would remain to serve as the source of constitutional continuity.

46. *Foreign Relations of the U.S.*, 1933, vol. 5, pp. 342–44. In his dispatches requesting withdrawal of recognition, Welles hinted that he was already contemplating the question of a successor for Machado. He also brought up the possibility that fighting would break out upon the fall of Machado and that U.S. warships should be on hand in such an event (ibid., p. 344).

47. Gellman, "Good Neighbor Diplomacy," p. 47; Lamar-Schweyer, *How President Machado Fell*, pp. 164–65; Royal Institute of International Affairs, *Survey of International Affairs—1933* (London, 1934), pp. 379–80.

48. Thomson, "Cuban Revolution: Fall of Machado," p. 257; Horacio Ferrer, *Con el rifle al hombro* (Havana: El Siglo XX, 1950), pp. 297–99; 837.00/3222. The U.S. military attaché reported on November 28, 1932, that "the better element within the Army very much resents the retaliatory killings of members of the Opposition by the Government's agents and its subsequent failure to prosecute those who have committed them" (R.G. 165, Cuba, 2012-133/2).

49. *Foreign Relations of the U.S.*, 1933, vol. 5, p. 351; Ferrer, *Con el rifle al hombro*, pp. 317–21; Pérez, *Army Politics in Cuba*, pp. 72–75.

Though Welles did use the army revolt to force the removal of Machado on terms which he had laid down, there is no evidence among the U.S. government records examined that he involved himself in the officers' insurgency. He did, however, through his military attaché, Colonel T. N. Gimperling, maintain regular contact with the Cuban armed forces. For example, Welles sent Gimperling to assure the officer corps that the mediation was not considering a reduction in the armed forces. Such a proposal had been a part of the original ABC program. (R. G. 165, 2012-133/7.) Some sources charge however that Gimperling knew of and encouraged the army revolt (Quesada y Miranda, *En Cuba libre*, p. 227; Ruby Hart Phillips, *Cuba, Isle of Paradox* [New York: McDowell-Obelensky, 1959], p. 35; Lamar-Schweyer, *How President Machado Fell*, p. 184; Aguilar, *Cuba 1933*, p. 148n.; and Riera Hernández, *Historial obrero cubano*, p. 83). The opposite contention is made in Ricardo Adam y Silva, *La gran mentira: 4 de*

Septiembre 1933 (Havana: Ed. Lex, 1947), pp. 42–49; and in Torriente y Peraza, *Cuarenta años*, pp. 317–18. Gimperling's G-2 reports indicate no specific knowledge of the revolt until it surfaced, but he does acknowledge that he was often asked for his advice on the attitude the army should take toward the president. He states that he gave none. (R.G. 165, 2012-133/7.)

50. Box 5—Cuba, "Confidential Memorandum for the President," Aug. 9, 1933, from Phillips, Samuel Rosenman Papers; PPF, 1-P, Box 201, Press Conferences 2:149-54, Aug. 9, 1933, FDR Papers. For the reaction of Latin American states to the pressure on Machado see *Foreign Relations of the U.S.*, 1933, vol. 5, pp. 350–51.

51. Ibid., pp. 347–48; Samuel Rosenman, *Public Papers and Addresses of F.D.R.* (New York: Random House, 1938), p. 319.

52. *Foreign Relations of the U.S.*, 1933, vol. 5, pp. 351–52; R.G. 84, F800Cuba/1933, vol. 10/C.F., statement of Aug. 10, 1933, by the Conservative party; *Foreign Relations of the U.S.*, 1933, vol. 5, pp. 349–50; Thomson, "Cuban Revolution: Fall of Machado," p. 256.

For accounts of Welles's interview with Ferrara, see Lamar-Schweyer, *How President Machado Fell*, pp. 172–74, and Alfred Fábre-Luce, *Révolution à Cuba* (Paris: Editions de Pamphlet, 1934), pp. 42–43. Fábre-Luce (p. 45) says that when Ferrara asked for economic aid, Welles indicated that a new trade treaty and the revocation of the Platt Amendment would be negotiated with the *next* government.

53. *Foreign Relations of the U.S.*, 1933, vol. 5, pp. 352–53; Krogh, "U.S., Cuba and Sumner Welles," pp. 242–43. Krogh feels that this statement by Roosevelt to Cintas on August 10 was the final stroke in breaking Machado's resistance (pp. 255–56).

Because Cintas, in his interview on August 9, had asked for a day's time in which Machado could put forward his own basis for stepping down, and because Phillips feared that Welles was embarrassing the United States by leaning too hard on the Cuban government, he and Roosevelt cabled Welles that "some misapprehension has arisen as to what you are doing and there has been some adverse comment." They urged him to act in a mediatory capacity only. (*Foreign Relations of the U.S.*, 1933, vol. 5, p. 354.) Nevertheless, all public statements from the U.S. government contained full support for Welles. See Krogh, "U.S., Cuba and Sumner Welles," p. 243.

54. *Foreign Relations of the U.S.*, 1933, vol. 5, pp. 296, 355–56; R.G. 84, F800Cuba/1933, vol. 14/Mediation General, July 11, 1933. The need for a cabinet member to succeed the president (there was no office of vice-president at this time) was set out in a constitutional amendment of 1928. The first in line of succession was the secretary of state, but Welles's plan involved the resignation of the entire cabinet except for Herrera, so that he would be next in line. (Gellman, "Good Neighbor Diplomacy," p. 51.)

55. *Foreign Relations of the U.S.*, 1933, vol. 5, p. 355.

56. Ferrer, *Con el rifle al hombro*, pp. 321–23.

57. Ibid., pp. 323–27; Thompson, "Cuban Revolution: Fall of Machado," p. 257; Adam y Silva, *La gran mentira*, pp. 44–45.

58. Ferrer, *Con el rifle al hombro*, pp. 328, 332–33; Duarte Oropesa, *Historiología cubana*, p. 393; Thomson, "Cuban Revolution: Fall of Machado," p. 257; and *Foreign Relations of the U.S.*, 1933, vol. 5, pp. 356–57.

Machado's final proposal for the terms of his resignation called for U.S. concessions regarding a new trade treaty and the end of the Platt Amendment (see R.G. 84, F800Cuba/1933, vol. 10, Machado to Welles, Aug. 11, 1933). For Machado's version of his overthrow see OF159Cuba (Box 2), Machado to FDR, Sept. 5, 1933, FDR Papers.

59. Ferrer, *Con el rifle al hombro*, p. 334; *Foreign Relations of the U.S.*, 1933, vol. 5, pp. 358–59.

60. Ferrer, *Con el rifle al hombro*, p. 334; *Foreign Relations of the U.S.*, 1933, vol. 5, pp. 358–59.

Sensitivity in Cuba regarding U.S. hegemony was so intense between 1933 and 1960 that a major historical debate arose over whether the choice of Céspedes as provisional president was made by Cuban parties (the opposition, political parties, army) or by the U.S. ambassador. It is known that Welles was seeking a suitable replacement for Machado during the mediation and that several names were suggested by the opposition. It is possible that Welles was the first to put forward the name of Céspedes, but more likely it was offered by some opposition members and then seconded by Welles. Céspedes' success over other candidates might very well have been due to strong support from Welles, whose high opinion of Céspedes is on record long before this period.

Both Céspedes himself and Cosme de la Torriente y Peraza, who often spoke for the conservative opposition, deny that Welles made the initial choice of a provisional president (see Torriente y Peraza, *Cuarenta años*, p. 318, and Adam y Silva, *La gran mentira*, pp. 50–51). Welles has also denied paternity in regard to Céspedes. In a letter to Samuel Guy Inman, October 30, 1933, Welles stated that Céspedes' name was first raised in June and that by late July he had been accepted by most opposition groups. He denied taking any part in the decision. (Samuel G. Inman Papers.) While Welles's intimate involvement in every phase of the mediation and his evident willingness to put forth proposals on his own behalf indicate that he would have actively participated in this major decision, the records of the State Department and of the Havana embassy give no indication that he did so. Indeed, the name of Céspedes does not appear in Welles's dispatches to the State Department until August 12 (*Foreign Relations of the U.S.*, 1933, vol. 5, p. 358). On the other hand, Welles is reported to have met with Céspedes before that date (see Ferrer, *Con el rifle al hombro*, p. 335), and the ambassador did not always report the full extent of his involvement in domestic Cuban politics to the department.

The embassy records do show that several names, including that of Céspedes, were put forward by the opposition prior to August 12 (R.G. 84, F800Cuba/1933, vol. 14/Mediation Acceptances, letter to Welles from OCRR, Aug. 11, 1933). Welles's reaction to these suggestions does not appear in the records. Indeed, the Post Records for the period of Welles's ambassadorship contain very little correspondence *from* the ambassador, and his telephonic and verbal communications are almost never recorded. As Welles's papers are not yet open, this question cannot be answered definitively.

61. Thomson, "Cuban Revolution: Fall of Machado," pp. 257–58; R.G. 84, F800Cuba/1933, vol. 10, no. 153; Lamar-Schweyer, *How President Machado Fell*, pp. 212–20; *Foreign Relations of the U.S.*, 1933, vol. 5, pp. 358–59; Phillips, *Cuba, Isle of Paradox*, p. 38.

The tortured "legal" proceedings were actually much more complex. Because the constitution provided that elections had to be held within sixty days of the resignation of the president, and because the opposition, whose political organizations were still illegal, felt unprepared to contest the old political parties at the polls on such short notice, it was necessary to formulate a plan whereby Machado would merely ask for a leave of absence. An interim president could serve indefinitely. Thus, Machado's statement to the Congress requested only a leave which at some later date would become a resignation. This still left as a stumbling block the law that a cabinet minister could not rise to the presidency until after thirty days in office. This law was revoked by that last ephemeral "meeting" of the Congress on August 12. See Enrique Hernández Corujo, *Historia constitucional de Cuba* (Havana: Cia Editora de Libros y Folletos, 1960), pp. 154–58.

Another debate concerns, not the choice of Machado's successor (see note 60), but the devising of the various plans for ending the Machadato. While Welles rigorously enforced his demand that such plans provide for constitutional stability, the general content of the various plans may have come to him in proposals from the opposition. For several of these proposals see 837.00/3458; Cuban American Friendship Council, Press Release, Jan. 22, 1933 (Washington, D.C., 1933); Torriente y Peraza, *Cuarenta años*, p. 253; R.G. 84, F800Cuba/1933, vol. 14/ Mediation Acceptances, letters from ABC, June 15 and Aug. 5, 1933, and from OCRR, Aug. 11, 1933; Duarte Oropesa, *Historiología cubana*, p. 378; and Krogh, "U.S., Cuba and Sumner Welles," p. 189.

Chapter 7: The New Deal and the Search for Cuban Stability—Part 2

1. Arthur D. Gayer and Carl T. Schmidt, *American Economic Foreign Policy* (New York: American Coordinating Committee for International Studies, 1939), chap. 2; B. H. Williams, *American Diplomacy*, chap. 10; Letiche, *Reciprocal Trade Agreements*, pp. 8–12; and Raymond Leslie Buell, *A New Commercial Policy for the United States* (New York: Foreign Policy Association, 1932), pp. 3–7.

The U.S. investment in Cuban sugar was around $600 million in the twenties. Only copper and petroleum investments rivaled those of sugar, and these were spread among several countries. See Gayer and Schmidt, *American Economic Foreign Policy*, pp. 19–21; Jenks, *Our Cuban Colony*, p. 284.

2. James M. McHale, "The New Deal and the Origins of Public Lending for Foreign Economic Development, 1933–1945" (Ph.D. dissertation, University of Wisconsin, 1970).

3. Rosen, "Roosevelt and the Brains Trust," pp. 531–57; Rexford G. Tugwell, *The Battle for Democracy* (New York: Columbia University Press, 1935), pp. 164–70.

4. Gardner, *Economic Aspects of New Deal Diplomacy*, pp. 13–17; Charles A. Beard, *The Idea of National Interest* (New York: Macmillan Co., 1934), pp. 545–48; and Herbert Feis, *1933: Characters in Crisis* (Boston: Little, Brown and Co., 1966), pp. 77, 102.

5. Though initiated by the more internationally minded, the new Cuban policy, as we shall see, contained opportunities for protectionists as well, especially quota agreements and the dumping of agricultural surpluses. The new policy also appealed to isolationists who favored a closed-door sphere of influence in the hemisphere as a complement to abstinence from European involvement. The effectively bilateral nature of the proposed trade arrangements was decidedly illiberal. Perhaps the new Cuban policy is best described as an act of imperial market control similar in design to the British Imperial Preference system and similar in effect to the Roca-Runciman treaty between Britain and Argentina, the latter nation's economic relationship to Britain being similar to that of Cuba with the United States. See Ronald Chilcote and Joel Edelstein, eds., *Latin America: The Struggle with Dependency and Beyond* (Cambridge, Mass.: Schenkman Publishing Co., 1974), pp. 344–45.

6. For the ideological underpinnings of the NRA and AAA see: William E. Leuchtenburg, *Franklin D. Roosevelt and the New Deal* (New York: Harper Torchbooks, 1963), chap. 3; Barton Bernstein, ed., *Towards a New Past* (New York: Random House, 1968), pp. 264–80; Paul K. Conkin, *F.D.R. and the Origins of the Welfare State* (New York: Thomas Y. Crowell Co., 1967), pp. 34–44; and Ellis W. Hawley, *The New Deal and the Problem of Monopoly* (Princeton: Princeton University Press, 1966), chaps. 1–4.

7. National Foreign Trade Council, *Twentieth Convention—April 26–28, 1933* (New York, 1933), Final Declaration, pp. vii–xv. Also see Smith, *United States and Cuba*, p. 158. Concerning the Jessup study for the Pan American group see OF 159 Cuba, Box 1, "An Analysis of the United States Export Trade with Cuba," pp. i–ii, FDR Papers; and R. G. 84, F800Cuba/1933, vol. 9/631.00, letter, May 24, 1933, from Juan Trippe to Welles. The companies in the group were: Chrysler, DuPont, General Electric, Libby McNeill and Libby, National Cash Register, Pan American, Procter and Gamble, Remington Rand, Swift, and United States Steel.

For exporters' complaints to the State Department see 637.113/3-80; 611.3731/394 and 395; 611.0031/519; 637.113 Silk Hosiery/1; OF159 Cuba, Box 2, Garcia, Cuban Chamber of Commerce in the United States, to Roosevelt, April 4, 1933, FDR Papers. The letter from the Cuban Chamber of Commerce in the United States is dated April 4, 1933, and is in 611.3731/398. Also see R. G. 151, BFDC, 253 Cuba, letter from Florsheim Shoe Company, June 22, 1933. On the larger question of Latin American trade see 610.1131/51; 873.00/3481½; 710.11/1518.

8. The value of U.S. exports to Cuba had fallen from $200 million in 1925 to only $27 million in 1932 (see 611.3731/503½).

228 de Pages 116–120

9. *Foreign Relations of the U.S.*, 1933, vol. 1, pp. 921–22; Henry J. Taska, *Reciprocal Trade Policy* (Philadelphia: University of Pennsylvania, 1938), pp. 22–23.

10. *Foreign Relations of the U.S.*, 1933, vol. 5, pp. 278, 285; R.G. 151, BFDC, Report of Commercial Attaché, Havana, Weekly Report for Feb. 7, 14, 21, 1933, and April 11, 25, 1933. Also see 611.3731/390, "Changes in the Reciprocity Treaty which would Probably Benefit the United States Export Trade with Cuba," March 30, 1933, and 637.113/29-67, "The Effect of Increased Cuban Tariffs upon Imports from the United States," April–August 1933.

Ambassador Guggenheim had suggested a renegotiation of the trade treaty to counteract the slow inroads that foreign competition was making into the once dominant position of U.S. goods in Cuba. However, his plan for Cuban economic recovery was not as far-sighted as that of the Roosevelt administration. See 611.3731/390.

11. *Foreign Relations of the U.S.*, 1933, vol. 5, pp. 278, 285, 289–91, 293, 294; R.G. 151, BFDC, Report of Commercial Attaché, Havana, Weekly Reports of May 29, 1933, and June 12, 1933; 611.3731/416½, telephone conversation, Hull and Welles, May 18, 1933; 550.S1 Washington/415, "Memorandum of Conversation between Under Secretary Phillips and Cuban Ambassador Cintas," May 4, 1933.

12. Box 37 (State Department), "Question of Increasing the Cuban Differential," Charles Taussig Papers; OF159 Cuba, Box 2, Wayne Johnson memorandum to the Secretary of State, May 22, 1933; Box 37 (State Department) Duggan to Taussig, May 25, 1933, Charles Taussig Papers; OF66, Box 1, letter, Phillips to FDR, June 5, 1933. Also see Nixon, *F.D.R. and Foreign Affairs*, pp. 180–82.

13. *Foreign Relations of the U.S.*, 1933, vol. 1, p. 294; vol. 5, p. 304; 611.0031/501; R. G. 151, BFDC, Report of Commercial Attaché, Havana, Weekly Report for June 12, 1933.

14. U.S. Tariff Commission, *Foreign Trade of Latin America*, pt. 2, vol. 2, Report no. 146 (Washington, D.C.: Government Printing Office, 1942), p. 249; Smith, *United States and Cuba*, p. 29.

15. Dick H. Steward, "In Search of Markets: The New Deal, Latin America and Reciprocal Trade" (Ph.D. dissertation, University of Missouri, 1969), pp. 15–16, 29–30; Francis B. Sayre, *Glad Adventure* (New York: Macmillan Co., 1957), pp. 170, 173; Benjamin B. Wallace, "Tariff Bargaining," *Foreign Affairs*, 11, no. 4 (July 1933): 624; OF66, Box 1, Phillips to FDR, June 5, 1933, "Draft Message Concerning Tariff Reciprocity Bill," p. 3, FDR Papers.

16. The non-Cuban suppliers were: continental beet sugar growers and refiners, continental cane growers in Louisiana and Florida, and insular cane sugar growers and millers in the Philippines, Hawaii, and Puerto Rico.

For a discussion of the U.S. beet sugar industry see Dalton, *Sugar: A Case Study*, pp. 146–50. For the U.S. cane industry see ibid., pp. 166–71. For the insular cane industry see ibid., pp. 188–205.

17. Farr and Co., *Manual*, p. 30; U.S. Tariff Commission, *Report to the President on Sugar*, pp. 87, 197.

18. Lindley, *The Roosevelt Revolution*, pp. 222–23.

19. Murray Benedict and Oscar Stine, *The Agricultural Commodity Programs* (New York: Twentieth Century Fund, 1956), p. 285; 611.373 Sugar/180, letter from Robert L. O'Brien to FDR, April 11, 1933; records of the U.S. Tariff Commission, Box 21 (Sugar Schedule), O'Brien to FDR, April 11, 1933; 611.0031/478, Thomas Walker Page, vice-chairman, U.S. Tariff Commission, to Hull, April 20, 1933.

The Tariff Commission found that the cost of production of the large mills in Cuba was cut in half between 1929 and 1932 and that a major part of this reduction was achieved by a sharp drop in wage expenditures (see *Report to the President on Sugar*, pp. 66–67). Furthermore, the price paid by the mills for *colono*-grown cane was less than the cost of production to the grower (ibid., p. 68). Cuban production costs were found to be 40 to 60 percent lower than those in other areas supplying the U.S. market (ibid., p. 83). These facts explain the frustration of the continental beet interests as well as the revolutionary potential of the situation in the Cuban countryside.

20. 611.373 Sugar/182, Memorandum by Frederick Livezey (Office of the Economic Advisor), April 19, 1933, "Cuban Sugar Quota Project."

There was strong farm-state opposition to any program which would aid Cuban sugar because it was controlled by "a small group of financial interests, principally in New York," and because it threatened beet farmers. See U.S. Congress, *Congressional Record*, 73d Cong., 2d sess., vol. 78, pt. 3, pp. 3225–33, and pt. 4, p. 3633. These sentiments indicate one form of agrarian protectionist opposition to the internationalist proposals for restoring Cuban stability. For other examples of populist-based opposition to Cuban policy during this period see ibid., pt. 9, p. 9944 (remarks by Huey Long), and pt. 11, pp. 11552, 11556–57 (remarks by Everett Dirksen).

21. Allen Rau, *Agricultural Policy and Trade Liberalization in the United States, 1934–1956* (Geneva: Librairie E. Droz, 1957), pp. 55–58; Dalton, *Sugar: A Case Study*, p. 75; and Conkin, *F.D.R. and the Origins of the Welfare State*, pp. 42–43.

22. Dalton, *Sugar: A Case Study*, pp. 77–83; Lindley, *Roosevelt Revolution*, pp. 310–11; Bernard Sternsher, *Rexford Tugwell and the New Deal* (New Brunswick: Rutgers University Press, 1963), p. 211; 837.61351/637, Hull [Duggan] to Welles, May 12, 1933; Correspondence 1931–1935, Forbes to Sergio Osmena, July 18, 1933, W. Cameron Forbes Papers; 811.6135/40½; Harold L. Ickes, *The Secret Diary of Harold L. Ickes: The First Thousand Days, 1933–1936*, vol. 1 (New York: Simon and Schuster, 1953–1954), p. 147; Henry Agard Wallace, *America Must Choose* (Boston: World Peace Foundation, 1934), pp. 1–3, 18–19; and Gardner, *Economic Aspects of New Deal Diplomacy*, p. 39.

23. 611.373 Sugar/194; Dalton, *Sugar: A Case Study*, pp. 80–81.

For the attitudes of the various producing groups see 611.373Sugar/174, 175, 185, 187; 611.0031/519; 811.6135/6½, 7½, 23, 27B, 35, 40; 837.00/3582½; F800Cuba/1933, vol. 20/861.35; R.G. 16, Correspondence File of the Secretary—Farm Relief (Sugar), Memorandum to Coulter from "Cuban Delegation" to the sugar conference, July 3 and July 7, 1933. Also see Lippert S. Ellis, *The Tariff on Sugar* (Freeport, Ill.: The Rawleigh Foundation, 1933), pp. 13–20, 71–73; and Mathews, *Puerto Rican Politics and the New Deal*, pp. 131–35.

24. 550.S1 Economic Commission/6, 8, 10, 13, 19, 25, 26, 27, 30, 35, 44, 48, 49, 53; Box 37 (State Department), Memorandum, May 17, 1933, Charles Taussig Papers; Nixon, *F.D.R. and Foreign Affairs*, p. 262.

25. Dalton, *Sugar: A Case Study*, p. 81; OF241, Box 1, Phillips to FDR, July 28, 1933, FDR Papers; 811.6135/40.

26. *Foreign Relations of the U.S.*, 1933, vol. 5, p. 546.

27. Ibid., pp. 563–68.

28. Smith, *United States and Cuba*, p. 225; 837.51/1562; Quesada y Miranda, *En Cuba libre*, p. 151.

29. *Foreign Relations of the U.S.*, 1933, vol. 5, pp. 568–77; 387.51/1566, 1567–68, 1572, 1576.

30. These early plans for Cuba, as we shall see, involved expanding the role of governmental agencies, particularly Hoover's Reconstruction Finance Corporation, not only into the field of export financing, but into government-to-government loans as well. Here, in the midst of the most autarkic period of the New Deal, can be found the origins of the Export-Import Bank and clear expression of the need to create federal institutional arrangements which would support foreign trade and foreign policy.

31. *Foreign Relations of the U.S.*, 1933, vol. 5, pp. 578–80.

32. Ibid.; Box 37 (State Department), "Possible Plan for Emergency Financing in Cuba," Charles Taussig Papers; 837.51/1579½, 1582½, 1588, 1611; R.G. 84, F800Cuba/1933, vol. 18/851.0, Nufer to Welles, Aug. 19, 1933.

An even more exotic arrangement to grant Cuba some economic relief was suggested by the Agriculture Department. The matter went as follows: the AAA had an offer from the USSR to buy sugar. The packing-house industry was pressing AAA to find an outlet for its huge stocks of lard. The Cubans were in need of lard. The trouble was that neither the Soviets nor the Cubans could afford to buy. J. A. Marcus of the AAA suggested a triangular deal. The AAA would swap

Cuba lard for sugar and then finance the sale of the sugar to the Soviet Union. The packers added the suggestion that in return for the United States' taking Cuba's surplus sugar, Cuba might be induced to lower its duties on pork and pork products. This is an example of the ingenuity required to arrange government financing of foreign trade before a specific vehicle was created for the purpose. It is noteworthy that the two foreign states in this suggested deal were the first to be covered by Eximbank loan authority. See 611.3731/480½, 481½, 482½, 483½.

33. *Foreign Relations of the U.S.*, 1933, vol. 5, pp. 581–88; 837.51/1612½, "Schedule A" and "Supplement."

The New York banks had less influence over Cuban policy at this point than they had had for decades. See Box 37 (State Department), "Memorandum for Ambassador Welles," Charles Taussig Papers; Nixon, *F.D.R. and Foreign Affairs*, p. 354; FDR, Press Conference of Aug. 11, 1933; 837.51/1586½. Thomas Chadbourne, the unofficial representative of the banks to the Cuban sugar industry, was cut out of the sugar conference delegations at both Washington and London by the State Department. See 811.6135/6, 7, 9, 14; 611.3731/407.

34. Matthews, *Puerto Rican Politics and the New Deal*, pp. 134–35; Benedict and Stine, *Agricultural Commodity Programs*, pp. 292–93; and Dalton, *Sugar: A Case Study*, pp. 84–91.

35. R.G. 151, BFDC, Report of Commercial Attaché, Havana, Sept. 31, 1933, "Cuba's Foreign Trade during the First Five Months of 1933"; OF159 Cuba, Box 1, "An Analysis of the United States Export Trade with Cuba," by Phillip Jessup, presented to the Honorable Franklin D. Roosevelt, July 10, 1933, FDR Papers; 637.113/28-73, "The Effects of Increased Cuban Tariffs Upon Imports from the United States"; Mario Lazo to Jessup, Aug. 24, 1933, and Jessup, "An Analysis of the United States Export Trade with Cuba," pp. 30, 101, Phillip Jessup Papers; R.G. 151, BFDC, 046Cuba, W. L. Thorp (director, BFDC), to Juan Trippe, Nov. 1, 1933.

For a discussion of Japanese competition, which was particularly acute in 1933–1935, see Beals, *Crime of Cuba*, p. 379; C. Harvey Gardiner, "The Japanese and Cuba," *Caribbean Studies*, 12, no. 2 (July 1972): 57–59; 610/9417/4, 7, 11; R.G. 151, BFDC, Reports of the Commercial Attaché, Havana, Special Report no. 4, Sept. 28, 1933. Japanese exports to Cuba were valued at 641,000 yen in 1931 and by 1933 had jumped to 3,300,000 yen (see 610.9417/7). Also see 600.9417/27; 611.3731/490; 810.5151/28.

Chapter 8. The Cuban Revolution of September 1933

1. Aguilar, *Cuba 1933*, pp. 153–54; Thomson, "Cuban Revolution: Fall of Machado," p. 259; Duarte Oropesa, *Historiología cubana*, p. 404.

Céspedes had served briefly as secretary of state early in the first Machado term, but since 1926 had lived outside Cuba as ambassador to Great Britain, France, and Mexico. He had retired from diplomatic service in 1932. For Welles's relationship to Céspedes in the early twenties see chapter 2.

2. Thomson, "Cuban Revolution: Fall of Machado," p. 259; Gellman, "Good Neighbor Diplomacy," p. 59; Phillips, *Cuba, Isle of Paradox*, pp. 40–50. Many Machadista office holders remained in or returned to their jobs during Céspedes' rule.

3. Thomson, "Cuban Revolution: Fall of Machado," p. 260; Hernández Corujo, *Historia constitucional*, pp. 159–63; Buell, *Problems*, p. 12; and Aguilar, *Cuba 1933*, p. 159.

4. *Foreign Relations of the U.S.*, 1933, vol. 5, pp. 360–62; Hull, *Memoirs*, p. 314.

5. Rosenman, *Public Papers and Addresses of F.D.R.*, vol. 2, pp. 322–23; PSF Cuba 1933–35, Box 5, handwritten memorandum by Hull, Aug. 13, 1933, FDR Papers; *Foreign Relations of the U.S.*, 1933, vol. 5, p. 363.

The purpose and effect of the U.S. warships was to inhibit extralegal actions by radical groups and not merely to protect U.S. citizens. Thus, their presence served a political as well as a humanitarian function. The ships arrived August 14 and remained until August 18. See Krogh, "U.S., Cuba and Sumner Welles," pp. 275–76; 837.00/3675.

6. Aguilar, *Cuba 1933*, pp. 154–55; *Foreign Relations of the U.S.*, 1933, vol. 5, p. 364. For statements of the ABC leadership during the Céspedes regime see Mañach, "Revolution in Cuba," p. 46 ff.; 837.00/3749.

7. *Foreign Relations of the U.S.*, 1933, vol. 5, pp. 365–66. The secretary of war also asked that marine reinforcements be sent to Key West and Guantanamo.

8. Ibid., pp. 367–69. As early as July 7, Welles noted his desire to prepare for the Montevideo Conference and suggested he be replaced by Caffery "not later than the end of September." See *Foreign Relations of the U.S.*, 1933, vol. 5, pp. 317, 319; OF470 (Sumner Welles), Stephen Early to Hull, Aug. 28, 1933, FDR Papers; diary entry of Aug. 28, 1933, Wilbur Carr Papers.

9. *Foreign Relations of the U.S.*, 1933, vol. 5, pp. 369–76; 837.00/3745.

Because many of the Supreme Court justices were themselves Machado appointees, a quorum of the high court could not be obtained, so Céspedes himself decreed the illegality of the Machado constitution. The Céspedes government thus lost whatever de jure status the United States still preferred to think it had.

10. *Foreign Relations of the U.S.*, 1933, vol. 5, pp. 376–78. Welles generally discounted the influence of Cuban communism up to this point. His military attaché, Colonel Gimperling, however, took a decidedly different attitude; see R.G. 165, 1657-Q-330/199, 200.

11. Page, "Development of Organized Labor," pp. 66, 67–70; Thomson, "Cuban Revolution: Fall of Machado," pp. 259–60; 837.00/3669, 3791; 837.5041/55; R.G. 84, F800Cuba/1933, vol. 13, "Political Reports from Consuls," Dickinson at Antilla, Aug. 10, 1933, Knox at Cienfuegos, Aug. 10, 1933, Schoenrich at Santiago, Aug. 16, 1933, Sept. 3, 4, 1933; R.G. 84, F800Cuba/1933, vol. 18/850.4, Dickinson at Antilla to Havana Embassy, Aug. 30, 1933; R.G. 151, BFDC, Reports of the Commercial Attaché, Havana, Aug. 25 and Oct. 26, 1933; R.G. 165, 2012-133/6; 2657-Q-330/199, 200.

12. Suchlicki, *University Students*, pp. 31–34; Boris Kozolchyk, *The Political Biographies of Three Castro Officials* (Santa Monica: Rand Corp., 1966), pp. 29–34.

13. Aguilar, *Cuba 1933*, pp. 157–59; Phillips, *Cuba, Isle of Paradox*, p. 59; Duarte Oropesa, *Historiología cubana*, p. 408.

14. R.G. 165, 2012-100/45, "Strength and Composition of Cuban Army"; Aguilar, *Cuba 1933*, p. 156; Adam y Silva, *La gran mentira*, pp. 60–88; Pérez, *Army Politics*, pp. 78–81.

15. Gellman, "Good Neighbor Diplomacy," p. 67; Phillips, *Cuba, Isle of Paradox*, pp. 62–63.

16. Adam y Silva, *La gran mentira*, pp. 98–106.

Batista had joined the army in 1921. He learned shorthand and typing while in service and left the army in 1923 to go into business or journalism. The depressed condition of the economy, however, forced him back into the army. In 1928 he became a sergeant and served as a stenographer at many of the military tribunals of the late Machadato, thus becoming familiar with the politics of the anti-Machado defendants. It is likely that he became a member of the ABC, but no specific opposition activities are attributed to him. See Edmund A Chester, *A Sergeant Named Batista* (New York: Henry Holt and Co., 1954), pp. 15–33; Adam y Silva, *La gran mentira*, pp. 99–101.

17. Adam y Silva, *La gran mentira*, p. 107; Aguilar, *Cuba 1933*, p. 156. The early plotters are also referred to as the Unión Militar Revolucionaria and the Junta de los Ocho.

18. Adam y Silva, *La gran mentira*, pp. 483–84; Ferrer, *Con el rifle al hombro*, p. 346.

19. For indications that Batista initiated contacts with political groups at this time see Adam y Silva, *La gran mentira*, pp. 120–22; Aguilar, *Cuba 1933*, p. 160.

20. Chester, *A Sergeant Named Batista*, pp. 38–40; Adam y Silva, *La gran mentira*, pp. 125–30.

21. Chester, *A Sergeant Named Batista*, pp. 40–47; Adam y Silva, *La gran mentira*, pp. 130–40; and Fulgencio Batista y Zaldívar, *Cuba Betrayed* (New York: Vantage Press, 1962), pp. 194–99.

22. For discussions of these events see Adam y Silva, *La gran mentira*, pp. 140–64; Rafael García Bárcena, "Razón y sinrazón del 4 de septiembre," *Bohemia*, September 7, 1952, pp.

60–61; Chester, *A Sergeant Named Batista*, pp. 60–67; Rubén de León, "La verdad de lo occurido desde el cuatro de septiembre," *Bohemia*, February 4, 1934, pp. 28–30; and Aguilar, *Cuba 1933*, pp. 160–61.

23. Phillips, *Cuba, Isle of Paradox*, pp. 53, 57; R.G. 84, F800Cuba/1933, vol. 12, "Reports from the Secretary of War"; R.G. 165, 2012-133/6, 7; 2657-Q-330/199, 200; 837.48 Cyclone of 1933/2, 3, 4, 7, 8; *El Pais*, September 5, 1933, 1st ed., p. 1, col. 4; *Foreign Relations of the U.S.*, 1933, vol. 5, p. 379.

Though the two warships sent at the time of Machado's overthrow were removed on August 18, Coast Guard archives show that on August 24, as trouble began to build for Céspedes, Roosevelt called the commandant of the Coast Guard to Hyde Park to discuss plans for the possible deployment of a much larger force of ships in Cuban waters. (R.G. 26, Box 1804, 601 File "Cuban Revolt.")

On September 3, Welles asked the State Department to rush Red Cross relief to the Céspedes government (837.48, Cyclone of 1933/2, 3, 4, 7, 8). For his attitude toward such relief under the "revolutionary" government see chapter 10.

24. *Foreign Relations of the U.S.*, 1933, vol. 5, p. 30.

25. *El Pais*, September 5, 1933, 1st ed., p. 1, col. 5, and final ed., p. 1, col. 1.

26. "Proclama de la Agrupación Revolucionaria de Cuba," in Adam y Silva, *La gran mentira*, pp. 484–85. The themes of the proclamation were essentially restorative. It referred to its goals not as new attainments, but as "recoveries" (*"reivindicaciones"*). It called for economic "reconstruction" and the punishment of those responsible for the Machadato, "without which it is impossible to reestablish true order and justice." The "Proclama" seems closest to the attitude of the nonmediationist opposition to Machado, bearing the stamp of earlier statements by the New York Junta (see Duarte Oropesa, *Historiología cubana*, pp. 372–78) and the Directorio Estudiantil (see Directorio Estudiantil Universitario, statement of August 24). Indeed, the "Proclama" refers to the DEU as the leading element of the Agrupación Revolucionaria. The "Proclama," however, contained no references to workers' rights, agrarian reform, or nationalization of foreign property, and was not even as radical a document as the ABC Manifiesto Programa of 1932.

27. Gellman, "Good Neighbor Diplomacy," pp. 71–72; *Foreign Relations of the U.S.*, 1933, vol. 5, pp. 382–84. Welles called the ideas of Irizarri, Portela, and Grau San Martín "frankly communistic"; Carbó he labeled a "communist"; and Franca, "supposedly conservative." Franca's role in the Pentarchy turned out to be minimal.

28. "Proclama de la Comision Ejecutiva," in Adam y Silva, *La gran mentira*, pp. 485–86. For a discussion of the background of the Pentarchy members see Box 5 (Cuba), "Memorandum for the Chief," Samuel Rosenman Papers.

29. Adam y Silva, *La gran mentira*, pp. 178–84, 210–13; Riera Hernández, *Historial obrero cubano*, pp. 89–90; Thomson, "Cuban Revolution: Reform and Reaction," p. 163; and Chester, *A Sergeant Named Batista*, p. 70.

The first statement issued by the Junta Militar, in the name of the "Alistados de la Marina y Guerra," displayed *dependencia* doctrine and called for public order so as not to provoke intervention. See *El Pais*, September 5, 1933, final ed., p. 4, col. 3.

30. *Foreign Relations of the U.S.*, 1933, vol. 5, p. 383; Adam y Silva, *La gran mentira*, pp. 487–92. Cuban politics was so sensitive to U.S. power that in his first proclamation to the Cuban people as "Chief of the Revolutionary Forces" Batista emphatically (and dishonestly) asserted that Welles accepted the new government and that there was no possibility of U.S. intervention. He also stated that the movement was neither communist, socialist, nor fascist. He did not say what it *was*. (See Adam y Silva, *La gran mentira*, pp. 490–91.) Welles, in his report to the State Department on his meeting with Batista, felt it appropriate to note that he "appears to be a mulatto with an admixture of Chinese blood." This sentence was omitted from the published version of the cable but appears in 837.00/3750.

31. Adam y Silva, *La gran mentira*, pp. 487–88; PSF Cuba, Box 5, "Memorandum of Conversation, Sterling-Duggan," Sept. 7, 1933, FDR Papers; Krogh, "U.S., Cuba and Sumner Welles," pp. 338–40, 358.

32. *Foreign Relations of the U.S.*, 1933, vol. 5, pp. 379–83. Other examples are: "There is absolutely no semblance of order of any kind" (ibid., p. 385); the presence of U.S. warships has "prevented untrammeled disorder" (ibid., p. 391); "where quiet prevails it is the quiet of panic" (ibid., p. 406).

33. *El Pais*, September 5, 1933, final ed., p. 1, col. 3, and p. 2, col. 5; *Foreign Relations of the U.S.*, 1933, vol. 5, pp. 383–84.

The Cuban leaders with whom Welles conferred included: Carlos Mendieta, Méndez Peñate, Mario Menocal, Miguel Mariano Gómez, and the top leaders of the ABC, Martínez Sáenz and Carlos Saladrigas.

34. *El Pais*, September 5, 1933, final ed., p. 4, col. 1, p. 4, col. 8; *Foreign Relations of the U.S.*, 1933, vol. 5, p. 384.

Welles's part in the meeting at the palace is not known to this writer. The ambassador never even reported his presence to the State Department. *El Pais*, in two separate reports, states that he was present, however.

35. *Foreign Relations of the U.S.*, 1933, vol. 5, pp. 380, 385–88.

Most observers conclude that Roosevelt and Hull opposed any form of intervention from the very first. Up to this point, however (the night of September 5), no firm decision had been reached. One can only speculate as to what action might have been taken had sufficient forces been on hand at this time.

Despite Welles's references to angry crowds and armed paramilitary groups roaming the streets, there was no shooting or fighting of any kind in Havana that night (see R.G. 84, F800Cuba/1933, vol. 10/CE, no. 200). Nevertheless, Colonel Gimperling, the military attaché, expected violence, said the new government was "leaning toward communism," and called for U.S. intervention (R.G. 165, 2627-Q-201). There was serious unrest in eastern Cuba, especially at Santiago (see 837.00/3759, 3761).

36. *Foreign Relations of the U.S.*, 1933, vol. 5, pp. 389–90. Krogh, "U.S., Cuba and Sumner Welles," p. 308, draws a similar conclusion, speculating further that Welles may have purposely worded later dispatches (specifically his 837.00/3767) with a view to making his policy appear in agreement with that of the secretary of state.

37. Nixon, *F.D.R. and Foreign Affairs*, pp. 385–88. The chief of the Latin American Division met with the other Latin American ambassadors the same day and conveyed a similar statement (see *Foreign Relations of the U.S.*, 1933, vol. 5, pp. 392–93). Several Caribbean states actually *favored* a U.S. landing. The Trujillo government of the Dominican Republic offered the use of its territory to U.S. forces, and the Ubico government of Guatemala, citing "communistic tendencies" in Havana, called intervention "essential" (ibid., pp. 393–94, 404–05). The principal opposition to U.S. intervention at this time came from Mexico. That government informed the U.S. government that the members of the Pentarchy were not radicals but respectable Cuban professional men with high social standing. The Mexican minister of foreign affairs politely informed the U.S. State Department that intervention would impair inter-American relations and cloud the hopes of all regarding the upcoming conference at Montevideo. In less direct language, the Argentine government told the U.S. secretary of state of its confidence that, notwithstanding the Platt Amendment, the United States would adhere to the lofty principles espoused by the Good Neighbor policy. (Ibid., pp. 394–95, 409, 416, 428–31.)

Another opponent of intervention was the U.S. ambassador to Mexico, Josephus Daniels. Next to Welles, Daniels was the most frequent telephone caller to Hull during this period, and he wrote to the secretary of state regularly. See Desk Diary, 1933, Cordell Hull Papers. Daniels favored the involvement of other Latin American states in easing tensions in Cuba and multilateral action if intervention became unavoidable. Not only was Daniels a sincere rather than rhetorical multilateralist, but his liberal New Dealism allowed him to accept the reformist nationalism of the Pentarchy and the subsequent Grau San Martín government. (See *Foreign Relations of the U.S.*, 1933, vol. 5, pp. 394, 401, 412–15; 837.00/4177; letters to Hull, Sept. 25, Oct. 3, and Oct. 4, 1933, Josephus Daniels Papers. Also see E. David Cronon, *Josephus Daniels in Mexico* [Madison: University of Wisconsin Press, 1960], pp. 67–76.)

38. *Foreign Relations of the U.S.*, 1933, vol. 5, pp. 396–98; Krogh, "U.S., Cuba and Sumner Welles," pp. 310–12.

39. *Foreign Relations of the U.S.*, 1933, vol. 5, p. 402.

40. Ibid., pp. 403–04, 405–07; 837.00/3769; R.G. 84, F800Cuba/1933, vol. 10/CF, no. 210.

Welles was aware of the opposition of the CCP to the Pentarchy and was either using the term "Communist" very loosely or was hoping to frighten Hull into some action (see 837.00/3759). The secretary of state was sensitive to the "dangers" of communism in Cuba as indicated by his suggestion to Welles that he gain access to the cable traffic into the island to ascertain whether foreign Communist directives were being received (837.00/3824, p. 2, and 837.00/3839, p. 3).

41. Krogh, "U.S., Cuba and Sumner Welles," p. 317; Wood, *Making of the Good Neighbor Policy*, p. 75.

Opposition to intervention was quite general in the United States. Roosevelt tightened the operating orders of the flotilla stationed around the island. Ship captains were ordered to land only for the purpose of removing endangered U.S. citizens, to limit any such landings to coastal areas, and not to fire unless fired upon. (See R.G. 26, Box 1804, 601 File "Cuban Revolt," Operation Order no. 8-33 [revised], of Sept. 10, 1933.) Roosevelt's personal attitude toward the Pentarchy was noncommittal (see Nixon, *F.D.R. and Foreign Affairs*, p. 392).

The U.S. cabinet discussed the question of intervention on September 8 and again on September 15, with most if not all members expressing opposition to such a move except as a last resort (see Ickes, *Secret Diary*, pp. 87, 92–93). For reference to newspaper editorial opinion on the subject, see Gellman, "Good Neighbor Diplomacy," p. 78. For further expressions of opposition see Daniels to FDR, OF237, Box 1, Sept. 5, 1933, FDR Papers; Samuel G. Inman to Jefferson Caffery, in 710.11/1834, Sept. 9, 1933.

There were, of course, demands *for* intervention as well. These came mainly from conservative Cuban and U.S. business interests in the island. See 837.00/3755, 3765, 3766, 3768, 3770, 3773, 3774, 3785, 3792, 3795.

42. Riera Hernández, *Historial obrero cubano*, pp. 89–90; Duarte Oropesa, *Historiología cubana*, p. 430; Chester, *A Sergeant Named Batista*, p. 70; and Adam y Silva, *La gran mentira*, pp. 492–94.

43. *Foreign Relations of the U.S.*, 1933, vol. 5, p. 399; PSF Cuba, Box 5, Memorandum of Conversation—Sterling-Duggan, Sept. 7, 1933, FDR Papers.

44. *Foreign Relations of the U.S.*, 1933, vol. 5, pp. 400–03.

45. As noted above, Porfirio Franca never played an active role in the Pentarchy and was not present.

46. Adam y Silva, *La gran mentira*, pp. 272–77. This is essentially the account given by Chibás (see article by Eduardo Chibás in *Prensa Libre*, May 24, 1944).

Chapter 9. The New Deal and the Collapse of Cuban Stability

1. Julius W. Pratt, *American Secretaries of State—Cordell Hull*, vol. 12 (New York: Cooper Square Publishers, 1964), p. 148; Dexter Perkins, *The United States and the Caribbean* (Cambridge, Mass.: Harvard University Press, 1947), pp. 120–21; Sumner Welles, *The Time for Decision* (New York: Harper and Bros., 1944), pp. 196–99; and Aguilar, *Cuba 1933*, p. 200.

2. For Roosevelt's attitude toward Welles's activities see 837.00/4539. For Hull's attitude see Memorandum of Nov. 26, 1933, Samuel G. Inman Papers. For Hull's solution to Cuban economic and political problems see letter to Josephus Daniels, Sept. 14, 1933, Cordell Hull Papers.

3. *Foreign Relations of the U.S.*, 1933, vol. 5, p. 390.

4. Ibid., p. 410.

5. William L. Neumann, *Recognition of Governments in the Americas* (Washington, D.C.: Foundation for Foreign Affairs, 1947), pp. 8–12.

6. Memorandum of Legal Division, Department of State, for Secretary of State Stimson, undated, "Policy of Recognition," pp. 1–3, Henry L. Stimson Papers, Latin American File. See also Wilson to Hull, Sept. 7, 1933, in 810.01/49. This principle was illustrated by the refusal of the United States to recognize the Chilean government of Carlos Dávila because it failed, in the department's opinion, to afford "adequate protection to foreign rights" (see "Policy of Recognition," p. 3). The proclamation of a Chilean Socialist Republic in June 1932 had much to do with determining the unrecognizability of this particular de facto regime.

7. *Foreign Relations of the U.S.*, 1933, vol. 5, p. 422.

8. Ibid., pp. 423–24.

9. Ibid., p. 424.

10. 837.00/3803, Sept. 10, 1933, pp. 1–2; Memorandum of Telephone Conversation, Hull and Welles, 9:45 A.M., Sept. 11, 1933, in 837.00/3839, p. 1. Welles's first dispatch after the inauguration of Grau (837.00/3803, of Sept. 10, 1933) was the only one in which he seriously considered recognition. By the next day, however, when the political forces which had composed the Céspedes regime could make no satisfactory arrangement with the new government, the ambassador's momentary ambivalence ended. This change illustrates the fact that Welles's true criterion of recognition was the social and political composition of the groups composing the government rather than the question of stability or popularity. See also Welles to FDR, Sept. 25, 1933, in 837.00/4007, pp. 2–3.

11. *Foreign Relations of the U.S.*, 1933, vol. 5, p. 440. For U.S. embassy contacts with government and opposition figures during September see ibid., pp. 438–45, 451–53, 460–62.

12. For Hull's cautious position see letters to Josephus Daniels, Sept. 12 and 14, 1933, Cordell Hull Papers.

Not only Latin American but Japanese reaction was a factor. Ambassador to Japan Joseph Grew noted in his diary that the Japanese might use U.S. intervention in Cuba to defend their incursions into China. See diary, vol. 69, Sept. 20, 1933, p. 706, Joseph C. Grew Papers.

For the Mexican position see *Foreign Relations of the U.S.*, 1933, vol. 5, pp. 428–30.

For the reports of the U.S. military attaché in Havana see R.G. 165, 2657-Q-330/202, Sept. 12, 1933.

For reports of ship captains favorable to Grau see R.G. 84, F800Cuba/1933, vol. 12, "Reports from Ships: U.S.S. Dupont," Station Ship File, Oct. 4, 1933; Memorandum by Commanding Officer, U.S.S. Dupont to Commander Special Service Squadron, Oct. 8, 1933; Station Log, U.S.S. Ellis, Dec. 1, 1933.

For the position of Josephus Daniels see Cronon, *Josephus Daniels in Mexico*, pp. 67–76, and 837.00/4177.

Because Sumner Welles enjoyed the confidence of Roosevelt and because he controlled the flow of the largest stream of information on conditions in Cuba, he was able to establish a negative image of the Grau regime in Washington. See 837.00/4008½, "Policy Followed in Not Recognizing to Date Government of Dr. Grau San Martín," Sept. 18, 1933. Welles filled the diplomatic pouch with all manner of denunciations of the regime—some of them outrageous and even ludicrous—in an effort to show the extent of its unpopularity. See 837.00/3755, 3993, 4009, 4102, 4108, 4155, 4176, 4192, 4207, 4241, 4246, 4344, 4371, 4385, 4386, 4459, 4539. Concerning Welles's exaggeration of the level of disorder under Grau see Krogh, "U.S., Cuba and Sumner Welles," pp. 345–51.

13. 837.00/3839, phone conversation, Hull-Welles, Sept. 11, 1933, p. 3.

14. See below; pp. 155–58.

15. The situation became complicated in the late thirties, when Batista made an informal alliance with the Cuban Communist party. By that time, of course, the CCP no longer followed

a revolutionary line. See K. S. Karol, *Guerrillas in Power* (New York: Hill and Wang, 1970), pp. 81–94. The United States was uneasy about the alliance, but by that time the needs of Cuban populism were better understood in Washington and there was no disruption of cooperative relations with Batista. (Diplomatic Papers, Box II, 1940, Folder C, Messersmith to Welles, letters, July 12 and Oct. 22, 1940, George S. Messersmith Papers.)

16. Browder, *Origins of Soviet-American Diplomacy*, pp. 37–38, 49–54, 68.

17. Donald G. Bishop, *The Roosevelt-Litvinov Agreements* (Syracuse: Syracuse University Press, 1965), pp. 7, 10.

18. Robert Bowers, "Hull, Russian Subversion in Cuba and the Recognition of the Union of Soviet Socialist Republics," *Journal of American History*, 53 (December 1966): 543–46.

19. 837.00/3986.

20. *Foreign Relations of the U.S.*, 1933, vol. 5, pp. 409, 413; 837.00/3839, 3986, 3988; vol. 8, Confidential Cable from Joseph Baird to Robert Bender, Raymond Clapper Papers; Diary, Oct. 20, 1933, Raymond Clapper Papers; Bowers, "Hull, Russian Subversion in Cuba," pp. 547–48.

21. Bowers, "Hull, Russian Subversion in Cuba," pp. 549–53. For Caffery's concern regarding communism in Cuba see *Foreign Relations of the U.S.*, 1933, vol. 5, p. 408.

22. 837.044/39–47.

23. 837.00/3759, 3765, 3785, 3795, 3829, 3850, 3863, 3893, 3896, 3913, 3918, 3960, 4009, 4071, 4238. R.G. 151, BFDC, Reports of Commercial Attaché, Havana, Sept. 22, 1933.

24. For the decrees of the Grau government see 837.044/39–47. For the complaints to the State Department from U.S. interests in the island see 837.00/3755, 3784, 3873, 3891, 3896, 3944, 3974, 4012, 4024, 4026, 4065. For the position of the American Chamber of Commerce of Cuba see 837.00/4192, 4246, 4539. The chamber spoke for almost all of the major U.S. corporations doing business in Cuba.

25. OF259Cuba, Box 2, telegram, Early to Phillips, Nov. 22, 1933, FDR Papers; 837.00/4432, 4568.

26. *Foreign Relations of the U.S.*, 1933, vol. 5, pp. 441–45.

27. For discussions of internal Cuban politics during this period see Enrique Lumen, *La revolución cubana: crónica de nuestra tiempo, 1902–1934* (Mexico: Ed. Botas, 1934), pp. 147 ff.; Phillips, *Cuba, Isle of Paradox*, pp. 80–153; Buell, *Problems*, chap. 9; Adam y Silva, *La gran mentira*, chap. 23; Aguilar, *Cuba 1933*, chaps. 14–16. For State Department documents describing Cuban politics of the period see 837.00/3829, 3850, 3865, 3879, 3919, 3935, 3998, 4011, 4020–21, 4060, 4101, 4110, 4164, 4192, 4238–41, 4328, 4371, 4477, 4522, 4550, 4582, 4599, 4651, 4672.

28. *Foreign Relations of the U.S.*, 1933, vol. 5, pp. 451–52.

29. Ibid., pp. 469–71.

30. Ibid., p. 472; 837.00/4135, 4162.

31. *Foreign Relations of the U.S.*, 1933, vol. 5, p. 474.

32. Ibid., pp. 475–79.

33. R.G. 84, F800Cuba/1933, vol. 15/Miscellaneous Correspondence, Memorandum from Agustín Castellano, Oct. 13, 1933, 837.00/4258. Batista's inability to create a role for himself independent of either U.S. hegemony or Cuban nationalism reflected the almost total domination of the political arena by these two forces.

34. *Foreign Relations of the U.S.*, 1933, vol. 5, pp. 489–90.

35. For the Mexican position see ibid., pp. 394–95, 401, 413. For the Argentine position see ibid., pp. 409, 491. For the Panamanian position see ibid., p. 475. For the position of the United Kingdom on Grau see Great Britain, Public Records Office, Foreign Office Correspondence, File 371/17515, document numbers 29/29/14, 171/29/14, 410/29/14, 733/29/14, 658/29/14, 322/29/14, 348/29/14, 479/29/14, 1387/29/14, 680/29/14, 755/29/14, and 1127/29/14.

For the position of the liberal periodical press see *Christian Century*, editorials, "What Do We Want in Cuba?" (September 20, 1933), "Cuban Crisis Continues" (September 27, 1933),

"Why Not Recognize the Cuban Government?" (October 4, 1933), "Yes We Have No Imperialism" (November 15, 1933), "What Will Be the Next Move in Cuba?" (December 27, 1933); *Nation*, editorials, untitled, September 20, 1933; "Shall Our Sugar Refiners Ruin Cuba?" (October 11, 1933); untitled, November 8, 1933; *New Republic*, editorials, "Cuban Hurricane" (September 20, 1933); "Situation Intolerable" (September 27, 1933); "Anarchy" (November 22, 1933); "Yanqui Imperialism" (December 6, 1933); *World Tomorrow*, editorials, "Radicals Climb Into Cuban Saddle" (September 14, 1933); "Hands Off Cuba" (September 28, 1933); "Less Imperialistic?" (October 12, 1933); "Imperialism in Action" (November 19, 1933); "Will Roosevelt Wreck Cuba?" (December 7, 1933).

36. *Foreign Relations of the U.S.*, 1933, vol. 5, pp. 492–96, 500–02, 504, 509–10.

37. Ibid., p. 514. There is evidence that the ABC made an approach to Batista several days before the revolt, but that nothing came of it (see R.G. 84, F800Cuba/1933, vol. 11/C.F., Memorandum of Conversation between Batista and "Mr. Acosta," Nov. 5, 1933). For Welles's dispatches concerning the revolt see 837.00/4352, 4379, 4380.

38. Taussig's statement is in Box 37 (Banking), letter to FDR, Nov. 16, 1933, Charles Taussig Papers. For Duggan's position see R.G. 59, DRA Studies, Box 20, "Political Resume for the Use of Delegates to the Seventh International Conference of American States—Montevideo, 1933," pp. 19–23. For Rowe's position see 710.G Personnel/102. Also see diary, vol. 3, Nov. 6, 1933, William Phillips Papers.

39. *Foreign Relations of the U.S.*, 1933, vol. 5, pp. 520–21, 523; diary, vol. 3, Nov. 14, 16, 19, 1933, William Phillips Papers.

40. Diary, vol. 3, Nov. 20–23, 1933, pp. 49–51, William Phillips Papers; OF159 Cuba, Box 2, telegram, Phillips to FDR; Nov. 22, 1933, FDR Papers; Krogh, "U.S., Cuba and Sumner Welles," pp. 368–71. For the text of the final statement see Rosenman, *Public Papers and Addresses of F.D.R.*, pp. 499–501.

41. Mexico, Spain, Uruguay, Panama, Peru, Belgium, and Sweden recognized the Cuban government. Hull was informed by the Brazilian foreign minister that Argentina and Chile desired that Brazil join them in announcing recognition of Grau. There were also reports that the Cuban delegates at the Montevideo Conference would make a vigorous attack on U.S. policy. See 710.G/367; diary, vol. 3, Nov. 25, 1933, pp. 59–60, William Phillips Papers. In addition, the British were hinting that they might recognize Grau. See diary, vol. 3, Nov. 23, 1933, pp. 53–54, William Phillips Papers.

42. Diary, vol. 3, Oct. 30, 1933, William Phillips Papers; Alfred B. Rollins, *Roosevelt and Howe* (New York: Knopf, 1962), pp. 399–401; PSF, Box 32 (State, 1933–35), Nov. 4, 1933, Phillips to FDR, FDR Papers.

43. *Foreign Relations of the U.S.*, 1933, vol. 5, pp. 527–28, 533; 837.00/4449; Box 13, handwritten note by Inman, Nov. 26, 1933, Samuel G. Inman Papers; Herminio Portell Vilá, *Cuba y la conferencia de Montevideo* (Havana: Imp. Heraldo Cristiano, 1934), pp. 7–29.

Under Secretary of State Phillips felt at this time that both Roosevelt and Hull were seeking ways to enable them to recognize Grau. See 837.00/4449; diary, vol. 3, Nov. 25, 1933, pp. 59–60, William Phillips Papers; Krogh, "U.S., Cuba and Sumner Welles," pp. 375–80. Krogh contends that U.S. policy actually was changed after Welles's return to Washington in December. While Roosevelt and Hull desired to be rid of the difficulties resulting from nonrecognition of the Cuban government, neither put forward an alternative policy. Moreover, I find no evidence to indicate that policy changed after Welles was replaced by Caffery.

44. *Foreign Relations of the U.S.*, 1933, vol. 5, pp. 529–36. For the draft of the agreement see 837.00/4494.

45. For Guiteras's background and philosophy see Rafael Masferrer Landa, *El pensamiento politico del Dr. Guiteras* (Manzanilla: Ed. El Arte, 1944).

46. *Foreign Relations of the U.S.*, 1933, vol. 5, pp. 537–39. For the draft of the second agreement see 837.00/4651.

47. *Foreign Relations of the U.S.*, 1933, vol. 5, pp. 540–41; Adam y Silva, *La gran mentira*, pp. 354–55. For the events of Welles's last days in Havana see *Alma Mater*, vol. 6, nos. 62–66, December 9–14, 1933. At the last moment, Welles requested a few more days in which to settle the crisis, but was overruled by Roosevelt. See diary, Dec. 9, 1933, p. 80, and Dec. 12, 1933, p. 86, William Phillips Papers.

The intervention plans of the Navy Department, which went well beyond mere contingency, are detailed in a letter from the secretary of the navy, H. L. Roosevelt, to FDR, Dec. 30, 1933, in OF159A, Box 4, FDR Papers. Anti-Grau plotting by U.S. naval intelligence officers in Cuba is discussed in Phillips, *Cuba, Isle of Paradox*, p. 77; 837.00/4249; and esp. R.G. 84, F800Cuba/1933, vol. 12, reports from Ships, Memorandum from Major P. A. del Valle to the Commander of the Special Service Squadron, Sept. 27, 1933. Also see Adam y Silva, *La gran mentira*, p. 374.

Apparently the Chemical Warfare Division of the War Department also drew up intervention plans, in their case calling for the airborne use of chemical warfare agents to capture the major military installations of the island. See 837.24/257.

For efforts by the opposition and U.S. business interests to overthrow Grau see 837.24/257 and Box 37 (Banking), letter, Taussig to FDR, Nov. 16, 1933, Charles Taussig Papers; and 837.113/523.

48. *Foreign Relations of the U.S.*, 1933, vol. 5, p. 544; 1934, vol. 4, pp. 95–98. There are indications that some Cuban sugar interests were contemplating support for Grau as the only way to ensure a sugar harvest. See Aguilar, *Cuba 1933*, pp. 215–16.

49. *Foreign Relations of the U.S.*, 1934, vol. 4, pp. 98–101; Aguilar, *Cuba 1933*, pp. 215–16.

50. Aguilar, *Cuba 1933*, pp. 224–27, 837.00/4560, 4562; R.G. 151, BFDC, File 121, Havana, letter from Commercial Attaché, Havana, to Assistant Director, BFDC, Jan. 16, 1934.

51. Thomas, *Cuba*, pp. 675–77; 837.00/4623, 4629; R.G. 165, 2657-Q-300/250; and Rubén de Leon, *El origen del mal* (Miami: Service Offset Printers, Inc., 1964), pp. 305–06.

52. Diary, vol. 3, Jan. 14, 17, 18, 1934, pp. 27, 33–35, William Phillips Papers; 837.00/4609; telegram, Hull to Caffery, telegram, Caffery to Hull, Jan. 18, 1934, Cordell Hull Papers.

53. Diary, vol. 3, Jan. 19, 20, 21, 22, 23, 1934, pp. 38, 41–45, William Phillips Papers; 837.00/4645; R.G. 84, F800Cuba/1934, vol. 16, "Mendieta," Jan. 19, 1934.

Chapter 10. The Restoration of Hegemonic Stability

1. *Foreign Relations of the U.S.*, 1933, vol. 5, pp. 568–77.

2. Ibid., pp. 578–88; 837.51/1547½, 1576½, 1612½.

3. 837.48 Cyclone of 1933/1–6, 10, 30.

4. 837.50 Economic Commission Personnel/9.

5. *Foreign Relations of the U.S.*, 1933, vol. 5, p. 575; 837.515/91–92.

6. *Foreign Relations of the U.S.*, 1933, vol. 5, pp. 568–69; 711.37/200.

7. R.G. 84, F800Cuba/1933, vol. 18/Economic Conditions—Financial/851.0. This series includes the weekly reports on Cuban government finances which were conveyed to the ambassador.

Welles's attempt to keep Grau from obtaining funds even extended to withholding the U.S. contribution to the Havana-based Inter-American Trademark Office, whose director was a Grau appointee. See 710.D4/492–504. U.S. support for this international body resumed after Grau's removal.

8. 611.3731/416½; R.G. 151, BFDC, 121 Havana, "Communication from the Ambassador to Cuba," June 15, 1933, and Nufer (Commercial Attaché, Havana) to H. Russel Amory (Assistant Director, BFDC), Aug. 21, 1933; *Foreign Relations of the U.S.*, 1933, vol. 5, pp. 373, 377–78, 525.

Grau's nationalistic decrees did work against certain U.S. firms doing business in Cuba, especially the utilities, banks, and low-wage employers. Though he hoped to lessen Cuban dependence on the U.S. market, however, he did not raise the tariff and indicated his willingness to negotiate a new trade treaty. See 837.044/39–47 for summaries of his decrees affecting U.S. economic interests.

9. 611.3731/502; 837.51/1586; 837.00/4104; 811.6135/46A.

10. 811.6135/47, 50; R.G. 84, F800Cuba/1933, vol. 20/861.36, U.S. Quota on Cuban Sugar. *United States Statutes at Large*, vol. 48, chap. 25, pp. 31–36.

11. Dalton, *Sugar: A Case Study*, chap. 6; Murray Benedict and Oscar Stine, *The Agricultural Commodity Programs* (New York: Twentieth Century Fund, 1956), p. 293; 811.6135/67, 77.

12. 811.6135/67, 77; 611.3731/503½.

13. 611.3731/503½; R.G. 16, Correspondence File of the Secretary—Farm Relief (Sugar), letter, Wallace to FDR, Sept. 28, 1933, and letter, Mordecai Ezekial to Wallace, Sept. 5, 1933.

14. 811.6135/91; Dalton, *Sugar: A Case Study*, pp. 92–95.

15. 811.6135/91; R.G. 84, F800Cuba/1933, vol. 20/861.35 Sugar Quota, memorandum by Latin American Division, Nov. 27, 1933; 611.3731/503½.

16. Mathews, *Puerto Rican Politics*, p. 134; Rosenman, *Public Papers and Addresses of F.D.R.*, pp. 86–87; Dalton, *Sugar: A Case Study*, pp. 96–98; and Buell, *Problems*, pp. 258–60.

17. Mathews, *Puerto Rican Politics*, p. 144; Dalton, *Sugar: A Case Study*, pp. 102–06.

18. Rosenman, *Public Papers and Addresses of F.D.R.*, pp. 219–20; Buell, *Problems*, pp. 260–63; Dalton, *Sugar: A Case Study*, pp. 252–55.

19. The Grau government on several occasions communicated its willingness to participate in trade negotiations. See 611.3731/515; 611.373 Sugar/217.

20. For details concerning proposals to increase the U.S. market share of Cuban imports see pp. 125–27.

21. 611.3731/466; R.G. 151, BFDC, 041.2Cuba, W. J. Donnelly (Acting Chief, Division of Foreign Tariffs) to Nufer (Commercial Attaché, Havana), June 20, 1933. Also see U.S. Department of Commerce, BFDC, *Cuban Readjustment to Current Economic Forces*.

22. R.G. 151, BFDC, 041.2Cuba, Correspondence from Export Firms; R.G. 353, Records of the Inter Departmental Committee on Reciprocal Treaties, 1933, Box 1, Minutes of the Meeting of the Committee for South America, Sept. 25, 1933; R.G. 16, Correspondence File of the Secretary—Executive Council, 1933, Reports from the Secretary of State, October–December 1933; 611.3531/232.

23. 611.3731/559, 577, 587, 925; *Foreign Relations of the U.S.*, 1934, vol. 5, pp. 129–34. For the demands of U.S. exporters for protection from Japanese competition see 610.9417/10 and chap. 7, n. 35 above.

24. 837.51/1695, 1704, 1706, 1707; 611.3731/576, 800; R.G. 151, BFDC, 334Cuba, Nufer to Caffery, June 21, 1934.

25. 611.3731/581A, 583. For evidence of the ambivalent attitude of the Open Doorsmen at the State Department see, for example, R.G. 151, 041.2Cuba, 1934, "General Principles for the Negotiation of the Revision of the Reciprocity Treaty with Cuba," March 29, 1934.

The prime advocate of bilateral trade expansion and principal opponent of Hull's liberal trade ideas, George N. Peek, was pleased with the Cuban treaty. In 1933, Peek was administrator of the AAA. For the details of the Hull-Peek controversy see Gilbert C. Fite, *George N. Peek and the Fight for Farm Parity* (Norman: University of Oklahoma Press, 1954), pp. 244–66; George Peek and Samuel Crowther, *Why Quit Our Own?* (New York: Van Nostrand, 1936), pp. 107–19; and Dick Steward, *Trade and Hemisphere* (Columbia: University of Missouri Press, 1975), chap. 2.

26. 611.3731/609A, 612A, 684, 732A, 733, 803, 879; 611.373 Sugar/257. Indeed, the Agricultural Adjustment Act, the parent legislation of Jones Costigan, was declared unconstitutional by the Supreme Court in 1936. It took a Joint Resolution by Congress to revive the sugar quota system.

240 • *Notes to Pages 179–182*

27. R.G. 40, General Records of the Department of Commerce, Office of the Secretary, General Correspondence, Box 798, no. 95112, "Trade Agreement Between the United States of America and the Republic of Cuba." The passages quoted are from U.S. Department of State, *Press Releases*, Aug. 24, 1934, "Trade Agreement Signed by the United States and Cuba."

28. 611.3731/842A, 2038; Alvarez Díaz, *A Study*, p. 358; U.S. Tariff Commission, *Foreign Trade of Latin America*, pp. 239, 241, 246. For the effect of growing native production on U.S. imports in the twenties see U.S. Department of Commerce, BFDC, *Cuban Readjustment to Current Economic Forces*, pp. 12–13.

Throughout the thirties, reformist policy makers in the United States continued to call for agricultural diversification in Cuba. However, they did not abandon the policies aimed at the integration of the island's economy which made such an outcome unlikely. See, for example, Box II, 1940 B, letter of March 9, 1940, Henry Wallace (Secretary of Agriculture) to George S. Messersmith (Ambassador to Cuba), and Box II, 1940 C, letter of Dec. 18, 1940, Messersmith to Welles, George S. Messersmith Papers.

29. U.S. Tariff Commission, *Foreign Trade of Latin America*, pp. 249–53; 611.3731/1391½.

30. 611.3731/1217, 1570; Alvarez Díaz, *A Study*, p. 347; Minniman, *Agriculture of Cuba*, pp. 27–28; R.G. 20, Country File—Cuba, Report from the American Vice Consul (Vogenitz), Cienfuegos, Jan. 12, 1935.

31. Minniman, *Agriculture of Cuba*, p. 128. For a discussion of the effect of the new treaty on the Cuban economy see Alvarez Díaz, *A Study*, pp. 317, 406–07; Buell, *Problems*, pp. 62–64; Celso Furtado, *Economic Development of Latin America* (Cambridge: Cambridge University Press, 1971), p. 237; Seers, *Cuba: Economic and Social Revolution*, pp. 15, 278; James O'Connor, "The Foundations of Cuban Socialism," *Studies on the Left*, Fall 1964, pp. 104–05. Because of this increased dependency during the thirties, Cuba never developed the industrial base established in comparable Latin American countries.

32. 837.48 Relief Measures/1.

33. See chap. 7, n. 32.

34. 611.3731/482½; 837.48 Relief Measures, 1, 1½, 1A, 2. Also see Charles Kindleberger, *The World in Depression, 1929–1939* (Berkeley: University of California Press, 1973), p. 96.

35. Smith, *United States and Cuba*, p. 163; and Nixon, *F.D.R. and Foreign Affairs*, pp. 663–64. Another loan, for the same purpose, was granted to Cuba in the amount of $4.4 million in December 1934.

The early New Deal witnessed the beginnings of a program which was to make the federal government a major source of credit for export expansion. With private lenders hesitant to take risks abroad, the Eximbank can now be seen to have been a forerunner of the massive federal foreign lending institutions of the 1940s and later. Eventually the use of national tax revenues to underwrite exports was elaborated into broad programs of foreign "aid" and loan and investment guarantees. The use, projected or actual, of such early federal financial institutions as the Reconstruction Finance Corporation (including its Commodity Credit Corporation) and the Export Import Bank to protect U.S. interests in Cuba by "saving" the island's economy, marks Cuban policy in 1933–1934 as one of the earliest expressions of this development. For discussions of New Deal lending for export expansion see H. W. Arndt, *The Economic Lessons of the Nineteen-Thirties* (London: Frank Cass and Co., 1963), pp. 89–92; Riverend, *Economic History*, p. 251; and Smith, *United States and Cuba*, p. 170.

36. Fitzgibbon, *Cuba and the United States*, p. 243; 837.51/1643, 1772, 1782, 1889½, 1909½. For the efforts of the bankers to recover their debts see 800.51/650–750. For a later discussion of the debt issue (which was not resolved until World War II) see 711.37/289, 299, 306.

Despite strong U.S. support for Mendieta, 1934 and 1935 were years of continuing revolutionary activity by the Cuban Communist party and by the radicalized followers of Grau and Antonio Guiteras. Labor insurgency continued unabated until the middle of 1935. Effective stability was not restored until Batista used the army to break the general strike of March 1935.

For a discussion of these events see Thomas, *Cuba*, pp. 695–700; Suchlicki, *University Students*, pp. 41–45; and Wood, *Making of the Good Neighbor Policy*, pp. 106–08.

37. "Treaty of Relations with Cuba Abrogating the Platt Amendment," May 29, 1934, *United States Statutes at Large*, vol. 48, 1682. While the abrogation of the Platt Amendment is often treated as an expression of the anti-imperialism of the Good Neighbor policy, it is dealt with here as symbolic of the changed nature of the expression of U.S. hegemony.

✓Chapter 11. Hegemony and Stalemate

1. For a discussion of Cuban class structure see Elias José Entralgo, *Perioca sociográfica de la cubanidad* (Havana: J. Montero, 1947), pp. 62–65; Ruiz, *Cuba: Making of a Revolution*, pp. 142–48; Anthony P. Maingot, "Social Life of the Caribbean," in *The United States and the Caribbean*, ed. Tad Szulc (Englewood Cliffs, N.J.: Prentice-Hall, Inc., 1971), pp. 42–46.

Concerning the dependency of the Cuban elite and its effects on ruling-class ideology in Cuba see O'Connor, "Political Economy of Pre-Revolutionary Cuba," pp. 175–80, 184; O'Connor, "Foundations of Cuban Socialism," pp. 102, 106–09, 111. Also see Samuel Farber, "Revolution and Social Structure in Cuba, 1933–1959" (Ph.D. dissertation, University of California, Berkeley, 1969), pp. 3–6.

2. By accepting this situation the new Cuban elite cut itself off from the possibility of becoming an indigenous capitalist class replacing the old land-owning class. Whereas the depression and its attendant protective tariffs, exchange controls, and so on saw the continuation of a moderate entrepreneurial development in such states as Argentina, Chile, and Mexico, Cuba in these years opened her economy to greater U.S. penetration. For the failure of industrial development in Cuba see Furtado, *Economic Development of Latin America*, pp. 236–37; Seers, *Cuba: Economic and Social Revolution*, pp. 15, 294; and O'Connor, "Political Economy of Pre-Revolutionary Cuba," pp. 170–75.

3. While it is true that certain Cuban, Cuban-American, and Cuban-Spanish residents of the island became or remained wealthy land owners or merchants, this group was extremely small and generally integrated at high levels with U.S. families and enterprises. For the background of some of these individuals see Thomas, *Cuba*, pp. 1496–1507.

4. The superfluousness of the agricultural proletariat, especially that portion which had been brought to the island as contract labor during the sugar boom, caused it to be very receptive to the organizing effort of the Cuban Communist party. For these workers, capitalism had been a poor provider at best and now seemed to hold no promise at all for the future. Concerning the chronic underutilization of rural land and labor in Cuba due to the structural demands of the latifundium see Seers, *Cuba: Economic and Social Revolution*, pp. 80 ff., and O'Connor, "Political Economy of Pre-Revolutionary Cuba," chaps. 2, 4.

5. The ambivalent attitude of the nationalist movement toward the United States was exhibited even within the government of Grau San Martín. Grau at times castigated and at times attempted to pacify the United States. His moves against U.S. economic interests were cautious and never extralegal. Moreover, he tried to retain the support of those Cubans who were willing to follow the U.S. prescription for dealing with the sugar depression. In fact, Grau endeavored at times to conciliate *all* domestic groups. As a result, his policies were inconsistent and often self-defeating. To most Cubans he was always doing either too much or too little. Hence his regime fell into a middle ground where it held the passive sympathy but not the active support of most Cubans. This in turn allowed the United States the room in which to maneuver him out of office. On the divisions within Cuban political forces during this period see Farber, "Revolution and Social Structure in Cuba," pp. 74–81. Concerning the division between the bourgeois nationalist and Communist movements see Karol, *Guerrillas in Power*, pp. 60–81.

6. Concerning the retrospective aspects of dependency and its structural effects on Latin American society see Dale Johnson, *Sociology of Change and Reaction*, pp. 5–12, 26–32; Celso

Furtado, *Development and Underdevelopment*, pp. 127–40; Darcy Ribeiro, *The Americas and Civilization* (New York: E. P. Dutton, 1971), pp. 19–45; and Helio Jaguaribe, *Economic and Political Development* (Cambridge, Mass.: Harvard University Press, 1968), pp. 3–12. Also see recent works by James Petras, Andre Gunder Frank, Pablo Gonzalez Casanova, Fernando Enrique Cardoso, and Theotonio dos Santos.

7. The collectivization and cartelization of the middle sectors was a fundamental aspect of the stalemated Cuban society. Sugar and tobacco planters, whose numbers had been reduced after 1925, resisted their growing tenantization by forming associations which pressed for government protection. Eventually, the planting segment of the sugar industry took on a structure similar to that of the oligopolized millers. For the organizing of the *colonos* see Aguilar, *Cuba 1933*, pp. 233–34; Alvarez Díaz, *A Study*, pp. 336–39, Seers, *Cuba: Economic and Social Revolution*, pp. 79–80; and O'Connor, "Political Economy of Pre-Revolutionary Cuba," pp. 45–46, 64–65. For the decline of the tobacco growers see Ortiz, *Cuban Counterpoint*, pp. 51–57, 69, 79.

8. The pattern of the transfer of sugar mills into Cuban hands after 1933 indicates that the gain in the number controlled by Cubans (based upon the apparent nationality of the reputed ownership of stock in the milling company) occurred first at the expense of the non-U.S. mill owners. That is, the Cubans bought mills formerly belonging to Spanish, English, Canadian, Dutch, or French nationals.

While about fifty mills passed over to Cuban "ownership" (disregarding the extent to which U.S. banks may have held claims against them) between 1935 and 1950, only twenty of these had been U.S.-owned. Moreover, the sell-off of the U.S. mills did not take place during the depression, but rather in two stages; first, during and just after World War II, and second, during the Korean War. The fact that these sales took place during periods of war, when prices for sugar and hence sugar properties were relatively high, indicates that many U.S. companies had been waiting for a rise in sugar values to sell their properties at a profit. Many of the companies owning the weaker mills felt there would never again be a true sugar boom and had merely been waiting throughout the thirties for the chance to unload their properties at a reasonable price. In any event, the owners of the largest and most efficient mills held on to their properties. Of the seventy U.S.-owned mills held in the 1930s, about forty were still in U.S. hands at the time of the Cuban Revolution.

By retaining the most effective producing units, the U.S.-controlled share of the island's sugar crop declined much more slowly than its percentage of mill ownership. U.S. mills had ground about 60 percent of the total crop during the thirties and still controlled about 40 percent at the time of the revolution. Thus, while there was a partial Cubanization of the sugar industry after 1933, it continued to represent an important element of U.S. economic domination.

For statistics on mill ownership and production see Newman, *Joint International Business Ventures*, pp. 29–30; Cuba, Económica y Financiera, *Anuario azucarero de Cuba* (Havana: Ed. Mercantil, 1936–). Concerning the diversification of U.S. investments in Cuba see Don Villarejo, "American Investments in Cuba," *New University Thought*, 1, no. 1 (Spring 1960):79–88; Smith, *United States and Cuba*, pp. 166–68; Roland Ely, "Cuba and Sugar—Four Centuries of Evolution," *Caribbean Studies*, 7, no. 3 (October 1967):67–69; and U.S. Department of Commerce, BFDC, *Investment in Cuba* (Washington, D.C.: Government Printing Office, 1956), pp. 3–12.

Bibliography

Unpublished Government Documents

Great Britain–Public Records Office

Foreign Office Correspondence, (F.O. 371) 17515–17519, Files 29 and 2003

United States—National Archives, Washington, D. C.

Record Group 16, Records of the Office of the Secretary of Agriculture, Correspondence File

Record Group 20, Records of the Office of Special Advisor to the President on Foreign Trade

Record Group 26, Records of the United States Coast Guard

Record Group 39, Treasury Department Records—Country File (Cuba)

Record Group 40, General Records of the Department of Commerce

Record Group 43, Records of United States Participation in International Conferences

Record Group 59, General Records of the Department of State—Central Files 1930–1939

Record Group 84, Records of the Foreign Service Posts of the Department of State. Correspondence of the American Embassy, Havana, 1933–1934 (F800Cuba)

Record Group 151, General Records of the Bureau of Foreign and Domestic Commerce

Record Group 165, Records of the War Department General Staff—Reports of Military Attachés

Record Group 353, Records of Interdepartmental and Intradepartmental Committees—Interdepartmental Advisory Board on Reciprocity Treaties, 1933–1934

Manuscript Collections

Wilbur Carr Papers. Library of Congress, Manuscript Division, Washington, D.C.

Raymond Clapper Papers. Library of Congress, Manuscript Division, Washington, D.C.

Josephus Daniels Papers. Library of Congress, Manuscript Division, Washington, D.C.

Norman Davis Papers. Library of Congress, Manuscript Division, Washington, D.C.

W. Cameron Forbes Papers. Houghton Library, Harvard University, Cambridge, Massachusetts.

Joseph C. Grew Papers. Houghton Library, Harvard University, Cambridge, Massachusetts.

Harry F. Guggenheim Papers. Library of Congress, Manuscript Division, Washington, D.C.

Cordell Hull Papers. Library of Congress, Manuscript Division, Washington, D.C.

Samuel G. Inman Papers. Library of Congress, Manuscript Division, Washington, D.C.

Phillip Jessup Papers. Library of Congress, Manuscript Division, Washington, D.C.

George S. Messersmith Papers. University of Delaware Library, Special Collections, Newark, Delaware.

John Bassett Moore Papers. Library of Congress, Manuscript Division, Washington, D.C.
William Phillips Papers. Houghton Library, Harvard University, Cambridge, Massachusetts.
Franklin D. Roosevelt Papers. Franklin Delano Roosevelt Library, Hyde Park, New York.
Samuel Rosenman Papers. Franklin Delano Roosevelt Library, Hyde Park, New York.
Henry L. Stimson Papers. Yale University, Sterling Library, New Haven, Connecticut.
Charles Taussig Papers. Franklin Delano Roosevelt Library, Hyde Park, New York.

Books, Pamphlets, and Government Publications

[Partido] ABC. *Doctrina del ABC: manifiesto programa [del 1932]*. Havana: Ed. Cenit, 1942.
———. *Hacia la Cuba nueva*. Havana, 1934.
Adam y Silva, Ricardo. *La gran mentira: 4 de Septiembre 1933*. Havana: Ed. Lex, 1947.
Aguilar, Luis E. *Cuba 1933: Prelude to Revolution*. Ithaca: Cornell University Press, 1972.
Alba, Victor. *Esquemo histórico del comunismo en Ibero-América*. 3d ed. Mexico: Ed. Occidentales, 1954.
———. *Politics and the Labor Movement in Latin America*. Palo Alto: Stanford University Press, 1968.
Alexander, Robert J. *Communism in Latin America*. New Brunswick, N.J.: Rutgers University Press, 1957.
———. *Organized Labor in Latin America*. New York: Free Press, 1965.
Alienes y Urosa, Julian. *Caracteristicas fundamentales de la economía cubana*. Havana: Banco Nacional de Cuba, 1950.
Alvarez Acevedo, Julio M. *La colonia española en la economía cubana, 1902–1936: un balance historico*. Havana: Ed. Ucar Garcia y Cia, 1936.
Alvarez Díaz, José R. *Cuba, geopolitica y pensamiento económico*. Miami: Coleción de Economía de Cuba en el Exilio, 1964.
———. *Las sociedades anónimas en Cuba*. Havana: Imp. Sanchez Fernández y Cia, 1943.
———. *A Study on Cuba*. Coral Gables, Fla.: University of Miami Press, 1965.
Alvarez Tabío, Fernando. *Evolución constitucional de Cuba, 1928–1940*. Havana: Tall. Grafica, 1953.
American Political Science Association. *Papers Presented at Annual Meeting of 1968*. "Cuban Political Development: A Historical Analysis." Washington, D.C.: American Political Science Association, September 1968.
American University, Foreign Area Studies Division. *Special Warfare Area Handbook for Cuba*. Washington, D.C.: Government Printing Office, 1971.
Araquistaín, Luis. *La agonía antillana*. Madrid: Espasa-Calpe, S.A., 1928.
Arndt, H. W. *The Economic Lessons of the Nineteen-Thirties*. London: Frank Cass and Co., 1963.
Arredondo, Alberto. *Cuba: tierra indefensa*. Havana: Ed. Lex, 1945.
Asociación Nacional de Hacendados de Cuba. *El tratado de reciprocidad de 1934*. Havana: Asociación Nacional de Hacendados de Cuba, 1939.
Atkins, Edward F. *Sixty Years in Cuba*. Cambridge, Mass.: Riverside Press, 1926.
Baeza Flores, Alberto. *Las cadenas vienen de lejos*. Mexico City: Ed. Letras, 1960.
Baran, Paul. *The Political Economy of Growth*. New York: Monthly Review Press, 1957.
Barratt Brown, Michael. *The Economics of Imperialism*. New York: Penguin Books, 1974.
Barro y Segura, Antonio. *The Truth About Sugar in Cuba*. Havana: Ucar, Garcia y Cía, 1943.
Batista y Zaldívar, Fulgencio. *Cuba Betrayed*. New York: Vantage Press, 1962.
———. *The Growth and Decline of the Cuban Republic*. New York: Devin Adair Co., 1964.
———. *Revolución social o politica reformista*. Havana: Prensa Indoamericana, 1944.
Beals, Carleton. *America South*. Philadelphia: J. P. Lippincott Co., 1937.

————. *The Coming Struggle for South America.* Philadelphia: J. P. Lippincott Co., 1938.

————. *The Crime of Cuba.* Philadelphia: J. P. Lippincott Co., 1933.

Beard, Charles A. *American Foreign Policy in the Making, 1932–1940.* New Haven: Yale University Press, 1946.

————. *The Idea of National Interest.* New York: Macmillan Co., 1934.

Benedict, Murray, and Stine, Oscar. *The Agricultural Commodity Programs.* New York: Twentieth Century Fund, 1956.

Bernhardt, Joshua. *The Sugar Industry and the Federal Government: A Thirty Year Record, 1917–1947.* Washington, D.C.: Sugar Statistics Service, 1948.

Bishop, Donald G. *The Roosevelt-Litvinov Agreements.* Syracuse: Syracuse University Press, 1965.

Bonsal, Philip. *Cuba, Castro and the United States.* Pittsburgh: University of Pittsburgh Press, 1971.

Braden, Spruille. *Diplomats and Demagogues.* New Rochelle, N. Y.: Arlington House, 1971.

Brandes, Joseph. *Herbert Hoover and Economic Diplomacy.* Pittsburgh: University of Pittsburgh Press, 1962.

Browder, Robert Paul. *The Origins of Soviet-American Diplomacy.* Princeton: Princeton University Press, 1953.

Buell, Raymond Leslie. *A New Commercial Policy for the United States.* New York: Foreign Policy Association, 1932.

————. *Problems of the New Cuba.* New York: Foreign Policy Association, 1935.

Burden, A. M. *The Struggle for Airways in Latin America.* New York: Council on Foreign Relations, 1943.

Bustamante, José Angel. *Raíces psicológicas del cubano.* Havana: Ed. Librerías Unidas, 1960.

Calderio, Francisco [Blas Roca]. *Los fundamentos de socialismo en Cuba.* Havana: Ed. Popular, 1960.

Cardoso, Fernando Henrique. *Dependencia y desarrollo en America latina.* Mexico: Siglo XXI, 1969.

Carter, John Franklin ["Unofficial Observer"]. *The New Dealers.* New York: Simon and Schuster, 1934.

Casanova y Diviño, José Manuel. *Presupuestos de la nación.* Havana: Molina y Cía, 1939.

Casuso, Teresa. *Cuba and Castro.* New York: Random House, 1961.

Chapman, Charles E. *A History of the Cuban Republic.* New York: Macmillan Co., 1927.

Chase National Bank of New York. *Cuban Public Works Financing: Reply to the Report of Special Committee Created by Decree Law 140 of April 16, 1934.* New York: Chase National Bank, 1934, 1935.

Chester, Edmund A. *A Sergeant Named Batista.* New York: Henry Holt and Co., 1954.

Chilcote, Ronald, and Edelstein, Joseph, eds. *Latin America: The Struggle with Dependency and Beyond.* Cambridge, Mass.: Schenkman Publishing Co., 1974.

Clavijo Aguilera, Fausto. *Los sindicatos en Cuba.* Havana: Ed. Lex, 1954.

Comité Central del Sindicato General de Empleados del Comercio de Cuba. *El Sindicato General de Empleados del Comercio de Cuba: frente al IV congreso obrero nacional, Federación Obrero de Cuba.* Havana, 1934.

Comité de Jóvenes Revolucionarios Cubanos. *El terror en Cuba.* Madrid: Imp. Editorial Castro, 1933.

Concheso, Aurelio Fernández. *Cuba en la vida internacional.* Jena and Leipzig: Wilhelm Gronau, 1935.

Confederación Nacional Obrera de Cuba. *IV congreso nacional de Unión Sindicalista— resoluciones y acuerdos.* Havana, 1934.

Conkin, Paul K. *F.D.R. and the Origins of the Welfare State.* New York: Thomas Y. Crowell Co., 1967.

Connell-Smith, Gordon. *The Inter-American System*. New York: Oxford University Press, 1966.

Cotoño, Manuel. *Primera conferencia nacional de Ala Izquierda Estudiantil: tesis politica*. Havana: Imp. Molina y Cia, 1934.

Crawford, W. Rex. *A Century of Latin American Thought*. New York: Praeger, 1966.

Crevenna, Theodore R. *Materiales para el estudio de la clase media en la America Latina*. Washington, D.C.: Pan American Union, 1950–1951.

Cronon, E. David. *The Cabinet Diaries of Josephus Daniels, 1913–1921*. Lincoln: University of Nebraska Press, 1963.

———. *Josephus Daniels in Mexico*. Madison: University of Wisconsin Press, 1960.

Cuba. Comisión Nacional de Estadísticas y Reformas Económicas. *Estadisticas, 1933*. Havana, 1935.

Cuba. Dirección General del Censo. *Censo de 1931*. Havana: Carasa y Cia, 1932.

Cuba. Económica y Financiera. *Anuario azucarero de Cuba*. Havana: Ed. Mercantil, 1936–.

Cuba. Ministerio de Relaciones Exteriores. *The Position of Sugar in the United States*. Havana, 1960.

Cuba. Secretaria de Hacienda. *Comisión especial de investigación de los obligaciones contraídas con el Chase National Bank*. Havana, 1935.

Cuban Information Bureau. *Ambassador Guggenheim and the Cuban Revolt*. Washington, D.C., 1931.

Cuban Planters Association. *Proclamation to the People of Cuba and General Program*. Havana: Díaz y Peredes, 1934.

Culbertson, William S. *Reciprocity: A National Policy for Foreign Trade*. New York: McGraw-Hill, 1937.

Dalton, John E. *Sugar: A Case Study of Government Control*. New York: Macmillan Co., 1937.

Daniels, Josephus. *Shirt Sleeve Diplomat*. Chapel Hill: University of North Carolina Press, 1947.

Davis, Kenneth S. *F.D.R.: The Beckoning Years, 1882–1928*. New York: Putnam, 1971.

DeConde, Alexander. *Herbert Hoover's Latin American Policy*. Palo Alto: Stanford University Press, 1951.

Deerr, Noel, *The History of Sugar*. London: Chapman Hall, 1949–1950.

Dewart, Leslie. *Christianity and Revolution: The Lesson of Cuba*. New York: Herder and Herder, 1963.

Diebold, William, Jr. *New Directions in Our Trade Policy*. New York: Council on Foreign Relations, 1941.

Duarte Oropesa, José A. *Historiologia cubana*. Vol. 5. Hollywood, Calif.: privately printed, 1969.

Dunn, Robert W. *American Foreign Investments*. New York: B. W. Huebsch and Viking, 1926.

Eichner, Alfred S. *The Emergence of Oligopoly: Sugar Refining as a Case Study*. Baltimore: Johns Hopkins Press, 1969.

Ellis, Lippert S. *The Tariff on Sugar*. Freeport, Ill.: The Rawleigh Foundation, 1933.

Emeny, Brooks. *The Strategy of Raw Materials*. New York: Macmillan Co., 1934.

Entralgo, Elias José. *Perioca sociográfica de la cubanidad*. Havana: J. Montero, 1947.

Fábre-Luce, Alfred. *Révolution à Cuba*. Paris: Editions de Pamphlet, 1934.

Farr and Company. *Manual of Sugar Companies, 1933*. 12th ed. New York: Farr and Company, 1933.

Feis, Herbert. *The Diplomacy of the Dollar, 1919–1932*. New York: W. W. Norton and Co., Inc., 1966.

———. *1933: Characters in Crisis*. Boston: Little, Brown and Co., 1966.

Fermoselle, Rafael. *Politica y color en Cuba*. Montevideo: Ed. Geminis, 1974.

Fernández, Julio César. *En defensa de la revolución*. Havana: Editorial Juventud, 1936.

Ferrara, Orestes. *El panamericanismo y la opinión europea*. Paris: Edit. Le Livre Libre, 1930.

Ferrell, Robert H. *American Diplomacy in the Great Depression*. New York: W. W. Norton, 1957.

Ferrer, Horacio. *Con el rifle al hombro*. Havana: El Siglo XX, 1950.

Fite, Gilbert C. *George N. Peek and the Fight for Farm Parity*. Norman: University of Oklahoma Press, 1954.

Fitzgibbon, Russell H. *Cuba and the United States, 1900–1935*. New York: Russell and Russell, Inc., 1964.

Foner, Philip S. *The Spanish-Cuban-American War*. 2 vols. New York: Monthly Review Press, 1972.

Frank, Andre Gunder. *Capitalism and Underdevelopment in Latin America*. New York: Monthly Review Press, 1969.

Freedman, Max. *Roosevelt and Frankfurter: Their Correspondence, 1928–1945*. London: Bodley Head, 1968.

Freidel, Frank B. *F.D.R.* 3 vols. Boston: Little, Brown and Co., 1952.

Friedlaender, Heinrich E. *Historia económica de Cuba*. Havana: Jesús Montero, 1944.

Furtado, Celso. *Development and Underdevelopment*. Berkeley: University of California Press, 1964.

———. *Economic Development of Latin America*. Cambridge: Cambridge University Press, 1971.

Fusfeld, Daniel. *The Economic Thought of F.D.R. and the Origins of the New Deal*. Columbia Studies in the Social Sciences, no. 586. New York: AMS Press, 1970.

García Montes, Jorge, and Avila, Antonio Alonso. *Historia del Partido Comunista de Cuba*. Miami: Editorial Universal (Rema), 1970.

Gardner, Lloyd. *Economic Aspects of New Deal Diplomacy*. Madison: University of Wisconsin Press, 1964.

Gardner, Richard N. *Sterling-Dollar Diplomacy*. New York: McGraw-Hill Book Co., 1969.

Gayer, Arthur D., and Schmidt, Carl T. *American Economic Foreign Policy*. A Report to the Twelfth International Studies Conference, Bergen, August–September 1939, by the American Coordinating Committee for International Studies, New York. (U.S. Memorandum no. 6.) New York: American Coordinating Committee for International Studies, 1939.

Goldenberg, Boris. *The Cuban Revolution and Latin America*. New York: Praeger, 1965.

González Carbajal, Ladislao. *Julio Antonio Mella*. Havana: Editorial Berea, 1941.

Grau San Martín, Ramón. *Le Revolución Cubana ante America*. Mexico: Ediciones del Partido Revolucionario Cubano, 1936.

Great Britain. Department of Overseas Trade (Consulate, Habana). *Economic Conditions in Cuba—November 1929*. London: Her Majesty's Stationery Office, 1930.

———. *Economic Conditions in Cuba—April 1932*. (Report 518.) London: Her Majesty's Stationery Office, 1932.

———. *Economic Conditions in Cuba—April 1935*. (Report 614.) London: Her Majesty's Stationery Office, 1935.

Green, David. *The Containment of Latin America*. Chicago: Quadrangle Books, 1971.

Griffin, Keith. *Underdevelopment in Spanish America*. London: George Allen and Unwin Ltd., 1969.

Guerra y Sánchez, Ramiro. *Azúcar y población en las Antillas*. 2d ed. Madrid: Cultural S.A., 1935.

———. *Historia de la nación cubana*. Havana: Editorial Historia de la Nación Cubana, S.A., 1952.

———. *La industria azucarera de Cuba*. Havana: Cultural, 1940.

———. *Sugar and Society in the Caribbean*. New Haven: Yale University Press, 1964.

Guggenheim, Harry F. *The United States and Cuba: A Study in International Relations*. New York: Macmillan Co., 1934.

Gutiérrez y Sánchez, Gustavo. *El desarrollo económico de Cuba.* Havana: Junta Nacional de Economía, 1952.

Hawley, Ellis W. *The New Deal and the Problem of Monopoly.* Princeton: Princeton University Press, 1966.

Healy, David F. *The United States in Cuba, 1898–1902.* Madison: University of Wisconsin Press, 1963.

Henríquez Ureña, Max. *Panorama historica de la literatura cubana.* New York: Las Americas Publishing Co., 1963.

Hernández Corujo, Enrique. *Historia constitucional de Cuba.* Havana: Cia Editora de Libros y Folletos, 1960.

Horowitz, Irving L., ed. *Latin American Radicalism.* New York: Vintage, 1969.

―――. *Masses in Latin America.* New York: Oxford University Press, 1970.

Hull, Cordell, and Berding, A. *Memoirs.* New York, 1948.

Ickes, Harold L. *The Secret Diary of Harold L. Ickes: The First Thousand Days, 1933–1936.* Vol. 1. New York: Simon and Schuster, 1953–1954.

International Bank for Reconstruction and Development, *Economic and Technical Mission to Cuba. Report on Cuba.* Baltimore: Johns Hopkins Press, 1951.

International Missionary Council. *The Cuban Church in a Sugar Economy.* London and New York: Department of Social and Economic Research and Counsel, 1942.

International Sugar Council. *The World Sugar Economy and Politics.* Vol. 7. London: J. P. Lippincott, 1963.

Jaguaribe, Helio. *Economic and Political Development.* Cambridge, Mass.: Harvard University Press, 1968.

Jenkins, Shirley. *American Economic Policy Toward the Philippines.* Palo Alto: Stanford University Press, 1954.

Jenks, Leland. *Our Cuban Colony: A Study in Sugar.* New York: Vanguard Press, 1928.

Johnson, Dale. *The Sociology of Change and Reaction in Latin America.* New York: Bobbs-Merrill, 1973.

Johnson, Walter. *The History of Cuba.* B. F. Buck and Co., 1920.

Jones, Chester Lloyd. *Caribbean Backgrounds and Prospects.* New York: Appleton, 1931.

Jorrin, Miguel, and Martz, John. *Latin American Political Thought and Ideology.* Chapel Hill: University of North Carolina Press, 1970.

Josephson, Matthew. *Empire of the Air.* New York: Harcourt, Brace, 1944.

Joven Cuba. *Programa.* Havana: Ed. Siglo XX, 1934.

Karol, K. S. *Guerrillas in Power.* New York: Hill and Wang, 1970.

Kaye, Martin, and Perry, Louise. *Who Fights for a Free Cuba?* New York: Workers Library Publishers, September 1933.

Kindleberger, Charles. *The World in Depression, 1929–1939.* Berkeley: University of California Press, 1973.

―――. *International Economics.* 3d ed. Homewood, Ill.: Richard D. Irwin, Inc., 1963.

Kolko, Gabriel. *The Politics of War.* New York: Random House, 1968.

―――. *The Roots of American Foreign Policy.* Boston: Beacon Press, 1969.

―――, and Kolko, Joyce. *The Limits of Power.* New York: Random House, 1970.

Kozolchyk, Boris. *The Political Biographies of Three Castro Officials.* Memorandum RM-4994-RC. Santa Monica: Rand Corp., 1966.

LaFeber, Walter. *The New Empire.* Ithaca: Cornell University Press, 1963.

Lamar-Schweyer, Alberto. *La crisis del patriotismo.* Havana: Ed. Martí, 1929.

―――. *How President Machado Fell.* Havana: La Casa Montalvo Cardenas, 1938.

Langley, Lester D. *The Cuban Policy of the United States: A Brief History.* New York: John Wiley and Sons, Inc., 1968.

Laurent, Emlio O. *De oficial a revolucionario.* Havana: Imp. Ucar Garcia y Cia, 1941.

León, Rubén de. *El origen del mal.* Miami: Service Offset Printers, Inc., 1964.

Letiche, J. M. *Reciprocal Trade Agreements in the World Economy.* New York: Columbia University Press, 1948.

Leuchtenburg, William E. *Franklin D. Roosevelt and the New Deal.* New York: Harper Torchbooks, 1963.

Lewis, Cleona. *America's Stake in International Investment.* Washington, D.C.: Brookings Institution, 1938.

Lichtheim, George. *Imperialism.* New York: Praeger, 1971.

Lindley, Ernest K. *The Roosevelt Revolution: The First Phase.* New York: Viking Press, 1933.

Lizaso, Félix. *Panorama de la cultura cubana.* Mexico: Fondo de Cultura Economica, 1949.

Lobo, Julio. *El plan Chadbourne: nuestra cancer social.* Havana: Maza, Caso y Cia, 1933.

Lockmiller, David H. *Enoch H. Crowder.* Columbia: University of Missouri Press, 1955.

————. *Magoon in Cuba.* Westport, Conn.: Greenwood Press, 1969.

Lopez Segrera, Francisco. *Cuba: capitalismo dependiente y subdesarrollo (1510–1959).* Havana: Casa de las Americas, 1972.

Ludwig, Emil. *Biografía de una isla.* Mexico: Ed. Centauro, 1948.

Lumen, Enrique. *La revolución cubana: crónica de nuestra tiempo, 1902–1934.* Mexico: Ed. Botas, 1934.

Lynsky, Myer. *Sugar Economics, Statistics and Documents.* New York: United States Cane Sugar Refiners Association, 1938.

Macgaffey, Wyatt, and Barnett, Clifford R. *Twentieth Century Cuba.* New York: Anchor Books, 1965.

Machado, Gerardo. *Declarations of General Gerardo Machado y Morales Regarding His Electoral Platform.* Havana: National Press Bureau, 1928.

Maestri, Raúl. *Capitalismo y anticapitalismo.* Havana: Ed. Atalaya, 1939.

————. *El latifundismo en la economía cubana.* Havana: Ed. Rev. de Avance, 1929.

Magill, Roswell, and Shoup, Carl. *The Cuban Fiscal System, 1939.* New York, 1939.

Mañach, Jorge. *La crisis de la alta cultura en Cuba.* Havana: Imprenta La Universal, 1925.

————. *Doctrina de ABC.* Havana: Pubs. de Partido ABC, Ed. Cenit, 1942.

————. *Indagación del choteo.* Havana: Ed. Lex, 1936.

Marinello, Juan. *Sobre la inquietud cubana.* Havana: Rev. de Avance, 1930.

Márquez Sterling, Manuel [and Carlos]. *Las conferencias del Shoreham: el ceasarismo en Cuba.* Mexico: Ed. Botas, 1933.

————. *Proceso histórico de la enmienda Platt.* Havana: Imp. Siglo XX, 1941.

Martínez Sáenz, Joaquín. *La revolución de Roosevelt.* Havana: Centro de Estudio Politico y Social de Cuba, 1947.

Masferrer Landa, Rafael. *El pensamiento político del Dr. Guiteras.* Manzanilla: Ed. El Arte, 1944.

Mathews, Thomas. *Puerto Rican Politics and the New Deal.* Gainesville: University of Florida Press, 1960.

McKenzie, Kermit. *Comintern and World Revolution, 1928–1943.* New York: Columbia University Press, 1964.

Mella, Julio Antonio. *Documentos para su vida.* Havana, 1964.

————. *La lucha revolucionaria contra el imperialismo.* Havana: Ed. Sociales, 1940.

Menocal y Cueto, Raimundo. *Origen y desarrollo de pensamiento cubano.* Havana: Ed. Lex, 1945–1947.

Millett, Allen Reed. *The Politics of Intervention: The Military Occupation of Cuba, 1908–1909.* Columbus: Ohio State University Press, 1968.

Minniman, Paul G. *The Agriculture of Cuba.* Foreign Agriculture Bulletin no. 2. Washington, D.C.: Government Printing Office, 1942.

Moley, Raymond. *After Seven Years.* New York: Harper, 1939.

———. *The First New Deal.* New York: Harcourt, Brace, 1966.

Monopolios norteamericanos en Cuba. Havana: Ed. de Ciencias Sociales, 1973.

Munro, Dana Gardner. *The United States and the Caribbean Area.* Boston: World Peace Foundation, 1934.

National Foreign Trade Council. *Twentieth Convention—April 26–28, 1933.* New York, 1933.

———. *Twenty-First Convention—1934.* New York, 1934.

Nearing, Scott, and Freeman, Joseph. *Dollar Diplomacy: A Study in American Imperialism.* New York: Monthly Review Press, 1969.

Nelson, Lowry. *Rural Cuba.* Minneapolis: University of Minnesota Press, 1950.

Neumann, William L. *Recognition of Governments in the Americas.* Washington, D.C.: Foundation for Foreign Affairs, 1947.

Newman, Phillip C. *Cuba Before Castro: An Economic Appraisal.* Ridgewood, N.J.: Foreign Studies Institute, 1965.

———. *Joint International Business Ventures—Cuba.* New York: Columbia University Press, 1958.

Nixon, Edgar B., ed. *F.D.R. and Foreign Affairs.* Vol. 1. Cambridge, Mass., Harvard University Press, 1968.

Normano, José F. *The Struggle for South America.* Boston: Houghton Mifflin, 1931.

Nourse, Edward G.; Davis, Joseph S.; and Black, John D. *Three Years of the A.A.A.* Brookings Institution of Economics Publication no. 73. Washington, D.C.: Brookings Institution, 1937.

O'Connor, James. *The Origins of Socialism in Cuba.* Ithaca: Cornell University Press, 1970.

Ordoqui, Joaquín. *Elementos para la historia del movimiento obrero en Cuba.* Havana: Imprenta Nacional de Cuba, 1961.

Ortiz y Fernández, Fernando. *Cuban Counterpoint: Tobacco and Sugar.* New York: Random House, 1970.

———. *La decadencia cubana.* Havana: Imprenta La Universal, 1924.

———. *Las responsabilidades de los EEUU en los males de Cuba.* Washington, D.C., 1932.

Oxaal, Ivar; Barnett, Tony; and Booth, David, eds. *Beyond the Sociology of Development.* London: Routledge and Kegan Paul, 1975.

Pan American Federation of Labor. *Report of the Proceedings of the Fifth Congress of the Pan American Federation of Labor.* July 18–23, 1927. Washington, D.C., 1927.

Pan American Union. *Fourth Pan American Commercial Conference.* "United States Trade with Latin America in 1930." Washington, D.C., 1931.

———. *Proceedings of the First Pan American Reciprocal Trade Conference.* Sacramento, Calif., 1930.

Pardeiro, Francisco A. *Historia de la economía de Cuba.* Havana: Ed. Universidad de la Havana, 1966.

Parrini, Carl. *Heir to Empire: United States Economic Diplomacy, 1916–1923.* Pittsburgh: University of Pittsburgh Press, 1969.

Partido Aprista Cubano. *El aprismo ante la realidad cubana.* Havana: Ed. Apra, 1934.

Partido Comunista de Cuba. *El Partido Comunista y los problemas de la revolución cubano.* Havana, 1933.

———. *Segundo congreso del Partido Comunista de Cuba: resoluciones.* Havana, 1934.

Partido Revolucionario Cubano. *Al pueblo de Cuba.* Havana, 1935.

———. *Programa constitucional de gobierno.* Havana, 1934.

Pearson, James C. *The Reciprocal Trade Agreement Program.* Washington, D.C.: Catholic University, 1942.

Peek, George, and Crowther, Samuel. *Why Quit Our Own?* New York: Van Nostrand, 1936.

Pérez, Louis A., Jr. *Army Politics in Cuba, 1898–1958.* Pittsburgh: University of Pittsburgh Press, 1976.

Pérez Cubillas, José. *Roosevelt el New Deal y Cuba.* Havana: Jesús Montero, 1937.

Phillips, Ruby Hart. *Cuba, Isle of Paradox*. New York: McDowel-Obelensky, 1959.
——. *The Cuban Dilemma*. New York: Ivan Obelensky, 1962.
——. *Cuban Sideshow*. Havana: Cuban Press, 1935.
Phillips, William. *Ventures in Diplomacy*. Boston: Beacon Press, 1952.
Pincus, Arthur. *Terror in Cuba*. New York: Workers Defense League, 1936.
Pino-Santos, Oscar. *El asalto a Cuba por la oligarquía financiera yanqui*. Havana: Casa de las Americas, 1973.
——. *Historia de Cuba—aspectos fundamentales*. Havana: Editora del Consejo Nacional de Universidades, 1964.
——. *El imperialismo norteamericano en la economía de Cuba*. Havana: Ed. Lex, 1960.
Pletcher, David M. *The Awkward Years*. Columbia: University of Missouri Press, 1952.
Poblete Troncoso, Moisés. *El movimiento obrero latino americano*. Mexico: Fondo de Cultura Económica, 1946.
——. *The Rise of the Latin American Labor Movement*. New York: Bookman Associates, 1960.
Portell Vilá, Herminio. *Cuba y la conferencia de Montevideo*. Havana: Imp. Heraldo Cristiano, 1934.
——. *The Nonintervention Pact of Montevideo and American Interests in Cuba*. Havana: Molina y Cia, 1935.
——. *The Sugar Industry and Its Future*. Havana: Ucar Garcia, 1943.
Portuondo, José Antonio. *El contenido social de la literatura cubana*. Jornadas no. 21. Mexico: Ed. Colegio de Mexico, 1944.
Pratt, Julius W. *American Secretaries of State—Cordell Hull*. Vol. 12. New York: Cooper Square Publishers, 1964.
Primelles, León. *Crónica cubana*. 2 vols. Havana: Ed. Lex, 1958.
Quesada y Miranda, Gonzalo de. *En Cuba libre!* 2 vols. Havana: Seoane Fernández, 1938.
Radosh, Ronald. *American Labor and United States Foreign Policy*. New York: Random House, 1969.
Rau, Allen. *Agricultural Policy and Trade Liberalization in the United States, 1934–1956*. Geneva: Librairie E. Droz, 1957.
Rhodes, Robert, ed. *Imperialism and Underdevelopment*. New York: Monthly Review Press, 1970.
Ribeiro, Darcy. *The Americas and Civilization*. New York: E. P. Dutton, 1971.
Riera Hernández, Mario. *Cuba política, 1899–1955*. Havana: Imp. Modelo, 1955.
——. *Historial obrero cubano, 1574–1965*. Miami: Rema Press, 1965.
Ripoll, Carlos. *La generación del 23 en Cuba*. New York: Las Americas Publishing Co., 1968.
Rippy, J. Fred. *Caribbean Danger Zone*. New York: G. P. Putnam and Sons, 1940.
——. *Globe and Hemisphere*. Chicago: H. Regnery, 1958.
Riverend, Julio Le. *Economic History of Cuba*. Havana: Inst. del Libro, 1967.
——. *La republica: dependencia y evolución*. Havana: Ed. Universidad, 1966.
——. *Reseña histórica de la economía cubana y sus problemas*. Mexico, D.F.: Litografía Machado, 1956.
Roa, Raul. *Retorno a la alborada*. Vol. 1. Havana: Universidad Central de las Villas, 1964.
Roig de Leuchsenring, Emilio, ed. *Curso de introducción a la historia de Cuba*. Vol. 1. Havana: Oficina del Historiador de la Ciudad, 1938.
——. *Historia de la enmienda Platt: una interpretación de la realidad cubana*. Vol. 1. Havana, 1935.
——. *Los problemas sociales de Cuba*. Havana, 1927.
——. *Revaloración de la historia de Cuba por los congresos nacionales de historia*. Havana: Oficina del Historiador de la Ciudad de la Habana, 1959.
Rollins, Alfred B. *Roosevelt and Howe*. New York: Knopf, 1962.

Roosevelt, Elliot, ed. *F.D.R. His Personal Letters: 1928–1945.* Vol. 1. New York: Duell, Sloan and Pierce, 1950.

Rosell, Mirta, comp. and ed. *Luchas obreras contra Machado.* Havana: Insto. Cubano del Libro, 1973.

Rosenman, Samuel. *Public Papers and Addresses of F.D.R.* 3 vols. New York: Random House, 1938.

Rowe, J. W. F. *Markets and Men: A Study of Artificial Control Schemes in Some Primary Industries.* New York: Macmillan Co., 1936.

Royal Institute of International Affairs. *Survey of International Affairs—1933.* London, 1934.

Ruiz, Ramón Eduardo. *Cuba: The Making of a Revolution.* Amherst: University of Massachusetts Press, 1968.

Sanguily, Manuel. *Defensa de Cuba.* Havana: Oficina del Historiador de la Ciudad, 1948.

Santovenia y Echaide, Emeterio Santiago. *El ABC ante la mediación.* Havana: Mazo, Caso y Cia, 1934.

Sapir, Boris. *The Jewish Community in Cuba.* New York: Jewish Teachers' Seminar and Peoples' University, 1948.

Sayre, Francis B. *Glad Adventure.* New York: Macmillan Co., 1957.

Seers, Dudley, ed. *Cuba: The Economic and Social Revolution.* Chapel Hill: University of North Carolina Press, 1964.

Selser, Gregorio. *Diplomacia garrote y dolares en América Latina.* Buenos Aires: Ed. Palestra, 1962.

Simons, William. *Hands Off Cuba.* New York: Workers Library Publishers, October 1933.

Smith, Daniel M. *Aftermath of War.* Philadelphia: American Philosophical Society, 1970.

Smith, Robert Freeman. *Background to Revolution: The Development of Modern Cuba.* New York: Knopf, 1966.

——. *The United States and Cuba: Business and Diplomacy, 1917–1960.* New York: Bookman Associates, 1960.

——. *What Happened in Cuba?* New York: Twayne Publishers Inc., 1963.

Snow, Sinclair. *The Pan American Federation of Labor.* Durham, N.C.: Duke University Press, 1964.

Spaulding, E. Wilder. *Ambassadors Ordinary and Extraordinary.* Washington, D.C.: Public Affairs Press, 1961.

Stein, Stanley, and Stein, Barbara. *The Colonial Heritage of Latin America.* New York: Oxford University Press, 1970.

Sternsher, Bernard. *Rexford Tugwell and the New Deal.* New Brunswick: Rutgers University Press, 1963.

Steward, Dick. *Trade and Hemisphere: The Good Neighbor Policy and Reciprocal Trade.* Columbia: University of Missouri Press, 1975.

Stimson, Henry L. *American Policy in Nicaragua.* New York: Scribners, 1927.

——, and Bundy, McGeorge. *On Active Service in Peace and War.* New York: Harper, 1948.

Strode, Hudson. *The Pageant of Cuba.* New York: Harrison Smith and Robert Haas, 1934.

Suárez Rivas, Eduardo. *Un pueblo crucificado.* Miami: Service Offset Printers, 1964.

Suchlicki, Jaime. *University Students and Revolution in Cuba, 1920–1968.* Coral Gables, Fla.: University of Miami Press, 1969.

Swerling, Boris. *International Control of Sugar, 1918–1941.* Palo Alto: Stanford University Press, 1949.

Tabares del Real, José A. *La revolución del 33: sus dos últimos anos.* Havana, 1971.

Taska, Henry J. *Reciprocal Trade Policy.* Philadelphia: University of Pennsylvania, 1938.

Taussig, Charles W. *Some Notes on Sugar and Molasses.* New York: privately printed, 1940.

Taussig, Frank W. *Some Aspects of the Tariff Question.* Cambridge, Mass.: Harvard University Press, 1931.

Taylor, Alonzo Englebert. *The New Deal and Foreign Trade.* New York: Macmillan Co., 1935.

Thomas, Hugh. *Cuba: The Pursuit of Freedom, 1762–1969.* New York: Harper and Row, 1971.

Thomas, Norman. *The New Deal: A Socialist Analysis.* New York: Socialist Party of America, Committee on Education and Research, December 1933.

Torriente y Peraza, Cosme de la. *Cuarenta años de mi vida.* Havana: El Siglo XX, 1939.

Tugwell, Rexford G. *The Battle for Democracy.* New York: Columbia University Press, 1935.

———. *The Brains Trust.* New York: Viking Press, 1968.

Tulchin, Joseph S. *The Aftermath of War: World War I and United States Policy Toward Latin America.* New York: New York University Press, 1971.

Unión Nacionalista. *Nuestra propósito.* Havana, 1929.

Unión Social Económica de Cuba. *Commercial Relations Between Cuba and the United States.* Havana, 1936.

United States. Congress. *Congressional Record.* 73d Cong., 1st sess., vol. 77, and 2d sess., vol. 78. Washington, D.C.: Government Printing Office, 1933–1934.

United States. Department of Agriculture. Bureau of Agricultural Economics. *Agricultural Adjustment: May 1933–February 1934.* Washington, D.C.: Government Printing Office, 1934.

———. *World Trade Barriers in Relation to American Agriculture.* Letter from the Secretary of Agriculture. Washington, D.C.: Government Printing Office, 1933.

United States. Department of Commerce. Bureau of Foreign and Domestic Commerce. *American Direct Investment in Foreign Countries—1936.* Washington, D.C.: Government Printing Office, 1938.

———. *Cuban Imports of Trade Agreement Commodities from the United States, 1935–1938.* Washington, D.C.: Government Printing Office, 1940.

———. *Cuban Readjustment to Current Economic Forces.* Trade Information Bulletin no. 725. Washington, D.C.: Government Printing Office, 1930.

———. *Investment in Cuba.* Washington, D.C.: Government Printing Office, 1956.

———. *The Market for Oils and Fats in Cuba and the Cuban Vegetable Oil Industry.* Washington, D.C.: Government Printing Office, 1931.

———. *A New Estimate of American Investments Abroad.* Foreign Trade Bulletin no. 767. Washington, D.C.: Government Printing Office, 1931.

———. Division of Foreign Trade Statistics. *Trade of the United States with Cuba, 1901–1937.* Washington, D.C.: Government Printing Office, 1938.

United States. Department of State. *Foreign Relations of the United States,* 1920, vol. 2; 1921, vol. 1; 1922, vol. 1; 1923, vol. 1; 1924, vol. 2; 1926, vol. 2; 1927, vol. 2; 1928, vol. 2; 1929, vols. 1, 2; 1930, vol. 2; 1931, vol. 2; 1932, vol. 5; 1933, vols. 1, 5; 1934, vol. 5; 1946, vol. 11. Washington, D.C.: Government Printing Office.

———. *Memorandum on the Monroe Doctrine.* Washington, D.C.: Government Printing Office, 1930.

United States. Senate. Committee on Banking and Currency. *Stock Exchange Practices. Hearings.* 73d Cong., 1st and 2d sess., pt. 5, 1933–1934.

United States. Senate. Committee on Finance. *Sale of Foreign Bonds or Securities in the United States. Hearings.* 72d Cong., 1st sess., 1931–1932. ("Johnson Investigations.")

United States. Senate. Subcommittee of the Committee on the Judiciary. *Lobby Investigation. Hearings.* 71st Cong., 1st sess., pts. 1, 2, 3, 1929–1930.

United States Statutes at Large. Vols. 21, 48. Washington, D.C.: Government Printing Office.

United States. Tariff Commission. *Economic Controls and Commercial Policy in Cuba.* Washington, D.C.: Government Printing Office, 1946.

———. *The Effects of the Cuban Reciprocity Treaty of 1902.* Washington, D.C.: Government Printing Office, 1929.

————. *Foreign Trade of Latin America.* Part 2, vol. 2, report no. 146, 2d ser. Washington, D.C.: Government Printing Office, 1942.

————. *Mining and Manufacturing in Cuba.* Washington, D.C.: Government Printing Office, 1947.

————. *Report to the President on Sugar.* Report no. 73. Washington, D.C.: Government Printing Office, 1934.

United States. War Department. *Census of Cuba—1899.* Washington, D.C.

Vega Cobiellas, Ulpiano. *Los Doctores Ramón Grau San Martín y Carlos Saladrigas Zayas.* Havana: Ed. Lex, 1944.

————. *Interpretación—Juan Marinello Vidaurreta.* Havana: Cultural, n.d.

Vogt, Paul L. *The Sugar Refining Industry in the United States.* Philadelphia: University of Pennsylvania, 1908.

Wallace, Henry Agard. *America Must Choose.* Boston: World Peace Foundation, 1934.

Wallich, Henry C. *Monetary Problems of an Export Economy: The Cuban Experience, 1914–1947.* Cambridge, Mass.: Harvard University Press, 1950.

Welles, Sumner. *Naboth's Vineyard.* Vol. 2. New York: Payson and Clark, Ltd., 1928.

————. *The Time for Decision.* New York: Harper and Bros., 1944.

Whitaker, Arthur F. *The Western Hemisphere Idea: Its Rise and Decline.* Ithaca: Cornell University Press, 1954.

Wilgus, E. Curtis. *The Caribbean Area.* Washington, D.C.: George Washington University Press, 1934.

Wilkins, Mira. *The Emergence of Multinational Enterprise.* Cambridge, Mass.: Harvard University Press, 1970.

Williams, Benjamin Harrison. *American Diplomacy.* New York: McGraw Hill, 1936.

————. *Economic Foreign Policy of the United States.* New York: McGraw Hill, 1929.

————. *Foreign Loan Policy of the United States Since 1933.* New York: Council on Foreign Relations, 1939.

Williams, Eric. *From Columbus to Castro: The History of the Caribbean, 1492–1969.* Kent, G.B.: Andre Deutsch, 1970.

Williams, William Appleman. *The Contours of American History.* New York: World Publishing Co., 1961.

————. *The Roots of the Modern American Empire.* New York: Vintage Books, 1970.

————. *The Tragedy of American Diplomacy.* New York: Delta Books, 1962.

Wilson, Joan Hoff. *American Business and Foreign Policy, 1920–1933.* Boston: Beacon Press, 1971.

Winkler, Max. *Investments of the United States in Latin America.* Boston: World Peace Foundation, 1929.

Wood, Bryce. *The Making of the Good Neighbor Policy.* New York: Columbia University Press, 1961.

Wright, Philip G. *The Cuban Situation and Our Treaty Relations.* Institute of Economics, Brookings Institution, Publication no. 42. New York: Macmillan Co., 1934.

————. *Sugar in Relation to the Tariff.* New York: McGraw Hill, 1924.

Zeitlin, Maurice. *Revolutionary Politics and the Cuban Working Class.* New York: Harper and Row, 1970.

Articles

Alienes y Urosa, Julian. "Tesis sobre el desarrollo económico de Cuba." *Revista Bimestre Cubana,* July–December 1951, pp. 237–45.

Beàls, Carleton. "Young Cuba Rises." *Scribner's Magazine,* 94 (November 1933):267–71.

Bentham, Rupert, "Cuba Maintains Her Credit." *Barron's,* 12, no. 51 (December 19, 1932):11.

Bettman, Irwin, Jr. "The Beet Sugar Industry: A Study in Tariff Protection." *Harvard Business Review*, 11, no. 3 (April 1933):369–75.

Blackburn, Robin. "Prologue to the Cuban Revolution." *New Left Review*, October 1963, pp. 53–91.

Blohm, Lee R. "General Survey of Wages in Cuba, 1931 and 1932." *Monthly Labor Review*, 35 (December 1932):1403–11.

Bowers, Robert. "Hull, Russian Subversion in Cuba and the Recognition of the Union of Soviet Socialist Republics." *Journal of American History*, 53 (December 1966):542–55.

Buell, Raymond L. "The Caribbean Situation: Cuba and Haiti." *Foreign Policy Reports*, 9, no. 8 (June 21, 1933):81–87.

Corbitt, Duvon C. "Cuban Revisionist Interpretations of Cuba's Struggle for Independence." *Hispanic American Historical Review*, 43 (August 1963):395–403.

———. "Immigration in Cuba." *Hispanic American Historical Review*, 22 (May 1942):280.

"Cuba and Sugar." *Business Week*, May 3, 1933, p. 24.

"Cuba in Revolt." *Commerce and Finance*, August 19, 1931, p. 1201.

Cuban American Friendship Council. "Press Release, January 22, 1933." Washington, D.C., 1933.

D.R.D. "The Revolutionary Battles in Cuba." *Communist International*, 11, no. 2 (January 15, 1934):54–60.

Davis, Norman. "Wanted: A Consistent Latin American Policy." *Foreign Affairs*, July 1931, pp. 547–67.

DeWilde, John C. "Sugar: An International Problem." *Foreign Policy Reports*, 9, no. 15 (September 27, 1933):162–72.

Ely, Roland T. "Cuba and Sugar—Four Centuries of Evolution." *Caribbean Studies*, 7, no. 3 (October 1967):65–76.

Ferrara, Orestes. "Economic Loss from the High Tariff on Sugar." *Annals*, 144 (July 1929):63–69.

———, and Walling, William E. "President Machado's Administration of Cuba." *Current History*, 32 (May 1930):257–67.

Gallagher, John, and Robinson, Ronald. "The Imperialism of Free Trade." *Economic History Review*, 6, no. 1 (1953):1–15.

Garcia Barcena, Rafael. "Razón y sinrazón del 4 de septiembre." *Bohemia*, 4 (September 7, 1952):60–61.

Gardiner, C. Harvey. "The Japanese and Cuba." *Caribbean Studies*, 12, no. 2 (July 1972):52–73.

Gardner, Lloyd. "From New Deal to New Frontiers: 1937–1941." *Studies on the Left*, Fall 1959, pp. 29–43.

Grobart, Fabio. "La caída de Machado, símbolo de la unidad del pueblo." *Bohemia*, February 2, 1973, pp. 101–06.

Gruening, Ernest. "Cuba Under the Machado Regime." *Current History*, 34 (May 1931):214–19.

Guggenheim, Harry F. "Amending the Platt Amendment." *Foreign Affairs*, 12 (April 1934):448–57.

Hackett, Charles W. "American Mediation in Cuba." *Current History*, 38 (September 1933):724–26.

———. "Cuba Lives Through Another Revolt." *Current History*, 39 (January 1934):462–64.

———. "Cuban Peace Prospects." *Current History*, 38 (August 1933):594–95.

———. "Guerrilla Warfare in Cuba." *Current History*, 38 (July 1933):469–71.

Herring, Hubert. "Another Chance for Cuba." *Current History*, 39 (March 1934):656–60.

———. "Can Cuba Save Herself?" *Current History*, 39 (November 1933):151–58.

———. "The Downfall of Machado." *Current History*, 39 (October 1933):14–24.

Hitchman, J. H. "The Platt Amendment Revisited." *Americas*, 23 (April 1967):343–69.

Hunter, John M. "Investment as a Factor in the Economic Development of Cuba, 1899–1935." *Inter-American Economic Affairs*, 5, no. 3 (Winter 1951):82–96.

Inman, Samuel G. "Imperialistic America." *Atlantic Monthly*, 134 (July 1924):107.

James, Clifford L. "International Control of Raw Sugar." *American Economic Review*, 21 (September 1931):481–97.

Jenks, Leland. "Can Cuba Recover?" *Nation*, 137 (September 6, 1933):275.

————. "La influencia de los intereses americanos." *Revista Bimestre Cubana*, 35 (March–April 1935):237–50.

Jessup, Phillip. "Negotiating Reciprocity." *American Journal of International Law*, 27 (October 1933):738.

Kaufman, Burton. "United States Trade and Latin America: The Wilson Years." *Journal of American History*, 58 (1972):342–63.

Kling, Merle. "Towards a Theory of Power and Political Instability in Latin America." *Western Political Quarterly*, 9, no. 1 (1956):21–35.

León, Rubén de. "La verdad de lo occurido desde el cuatro de septiembre." *Bohemia*, 26 (February 4, 1934):28–30, 39–40.

"Letter from the Central Committee of the Communist Party of the United States of America to the Central Committee of the Communist Party of Cuba." *Communist*, 10, no. 1 (January 1931):66–73.

Lliteras, Juan Andres. "Relations Between the United States and Cuba." *International Conciliation*, 296 (January 1934):4–19.

Loveira, Carlos. "Labor in the Cuban Sugar Industry." *International Labor Review*, September 1929, pp. 424–29.

Mañach, Jorge. "Revolution in Cuba." *Foreign Affairs*, 12 (October 1933):46–56.

Masó y Vasquez, Calixto. "Una isla singular." *Aportes* (Paris), 11 (January 1969):10.

————. "El movimiento obrero cubano." *Panoramas* (Mexico), 9 (May–June 1964):69–93.

Merrifield, R. B. "The Magazine Press and Cuba, 1906–1933." *Mid America*, 34 (October 1952):233–53.

Minor, M. Carlisle. "Cuba and Congress." *Barron's*, 10, no. 3 (January 20, 1930):5.

National City Bank. *Monthly Bank Letter*. September 1928, pp. 143–47; October 1933, p. 158.

Nichols, Jeannette. "Roosevelt's Monetary Diplomacy." *American Historical Review*, 56 (January 1951):295.

O. "Cuba and the United States." *Foreign Affairs*, 6, no. 2 (January 1928):231.

O'Connor, James. "The Foundations of Cuban Socialism." *Studies on the Left*, Fall 1964, pp. 97–117.

————. "International Corporations and Underdevelopment." *Science and Society*, Spring 1970, pp. 42–60.

————. "The Organized Working Class in Cuba." *Studies on the Left*, 6, no. 2 (March–April 1966):3–30.

Omvedt, Gail. "Towards a Theory of Colonialism." *The Insurgent Sociologist*, Spring 1973, pp. 1–24.

Ordoqui, Joaquín. "The Rise of the Revolutionary Movement in Cuba." *Communist*, 13, no. 12 (December 1934):1254–62.

Ortiz, Fernando. "El deber norteamericano en Cuba." *Revista Bimestre Cubana*, 33 (January–February 1934):75.

————. "Las responsabilidades de los E.E.U.U. en los males de Cuba." *Revista Bimestre Cubana*, 33, no. 2 (March–April 1934):250.

Porter, Russell F. "Cuba Under President Machado." *Current History*, 38 (April 1933):29–34.

"The Present Situation, Perspectives, and Tasks in Cuba." Resolution of the Second Congress of the Communist Party of Cuba. *Communist*, 13, no. 9 (September 1934):875–87, and no. 11 (November 1934):1157–69.

"Revolutionary Events in Cuba and the Tasks of the Communist Party." *Communist International*, 10, no. 18 (September 15, 1933):620–28.

Rocca, Joseph C. "Agricultural Policies in Cuba." *Pan American Union Bulletin*, 67 (February 1933):109–20.

Rodríguez, O. "Our Present Tasks in Cuba." *Communist*, 10, no. 6 (June 1931):516–24.

———. "The Present Struggle in Cuba." *Communist*, 10, no. 10 (November 1931):928–34.

Roller, Arnold. "Black Ivory and White Gold in Cuba." *Revista Bimestre Cubana*, 25 (1930):281.

Roosevelt, Franklin D. "Our Foreign Policy: A Democratic View." *Foreign Affairs*, 6, no. 4 (July 1928):573–86.

"Roosevelt Sent Private Investigators to Cuba." *Business Week*, February 15, 1933, p. 22.

Rosen, Elliot. "Intranationalism versus Internationalism: The Interregnum Struggle for the Sanctity of the New Deal." *Political Science Quarterly*, 81, no. 2 (June 1966):274–93.

———. "Roosevelt and the Brains Trust." *Political Science Quarterly*, December 1972, pp. 531–57.

Rugoff, Stephanie. "The Imperialist Role of the American Sugar Company." *NACLA Newsletter*, 4, no. 4 (July–August 1970):19–22.

Schurz, William L. "Cuba's Economic Isolation." *Current History*, 36 (August 1932):545–49.

Simons, William. "Background of Recent Events in Cuba." *Communist*, 12, no. 9 (September 1933):902–21.

Sinani, G. "New Revolutionary Phase in Cuba." *Communist*, 12, no. 12 (December 1933):1221–30.

Smith, Robert F. "Cuba: Laboratory for Dollar Diplomacy, 1898–1917." *Historian*, 28, no. 4 (August 1966):586.

———. "Twentieth Century Cuban Historiography." *Hispanic American Historical Review*, 44, no. 1 (February 1964):44.

"Social Legislation of Cuba." *Monthly Labor Review*, September 1929, pp. 508–10.

Stimson, Henry L. "The United States and the Other American Republics." *Foreign Affairs*, 9, no. 3 (April 1931), supp.

Suchlicki, Jaime. "Stirrings of Cuban Nationalism: The Student Generation of 1930." *Journal of Inter-American Studies*, 10, no. 3 (July 1968):350–68.

Thomson, Charles A. "The Cuban Revolution: Fall of Machado." *Foreign Policy Reports*, 11, no. 21 (December 18, 1935):250–60.

———. "The Cuban Revolution: Reform and Reaction." *Foreign Policy Reports*, 11, no. 22 (January 1, 1936):262–76.

Torriente, Cosme de la. "The Platt Amendment." *Foreign Affairs*, 8, no. 3 (April 1930):364–78.

"Unemployment in Cuban Towns." *Monthly Labor Review*, December 1927, p. 157.

Valdés, Nelson P. "La diplomacia del azúcar: EEUU y Cuba." *Aportes* (Paris), 18 (October 1970):99.

Villarejo, Don. "American Investments in Cuba." *New University Thought*, 1, no. 1 (Spring 1960):79.

Villena, Rubén Martínez. "The Rise of the Revolutionary Movement in Cuba." *Communist*, 12, no. 6 (June 1933):559–69.

"Wage Scale for the Cuban Sugar Industry, 1940." *Monthly Labor Review*, April 1940, pp. 974–75.

Wallace, Benjamin B. "Tariff Bargaining." *Foreign Affairs*, 11, no. 4 (July 1933):621.

Welles, Sumner. "Is America Imperialistic?" *Atlantic Monthly*, 134 (September 1924):412.

Wicker, Elmus. "Roosevelt's 1933 Monetary Experiment." *Journal of American History*, 57, no. 4 (March 1971):864–79.

Williams, William A. "Cuba: Issues and Alternatives." *Annals*, 351 (January 1964):73–80.

———. "Latin America: Laboratory of American Foreign Policy in the 1920's." *Inter-American Economic Affairs*, 11, no. 2 (Autumn 1957):3–30.

Wood, Dennis B. "The Long Revolution: Cuba." *Science and Society*, Spring 1970, pp. 1–41.

Woodward, Ralph. "Urban Labor and Communism: Cuba." *Caribbean Studies*, 3, no. 3 (October 1963):17–25.

Wright, Thomas P. "United States Electoral Interventions in Cuba." *Inter-American Economic Affairs*, 13, no. 3 (Winter 1959):50.

Zamora, J. Clemente. "La unión aduanera entre Cuba y los EEUU." *Universidad de la Habana*, December 1929, p. 182.

Newspapers

Alma Mater (Havana), 1933–1934
Diario de la Marina (Havana), 1933–1934
Hoy (Havana), 1964–1965
New York Herald Tribune, 1933–1934
New York Times, 1920, 1933–1934, 1941
El País (Havana), 1933–1934.

Dissertations and Theses

Aguilar, Luis. "Cuba 1933: The Frustrated Revolution." Ph.D. dissertation, American University, 1967.

Berger, Henry W. "Union Diplomacy: American Labor's Foreign Policy in Latin America, 1932–1955." Ph.D. dissertation, University of Wisconsin, 1966.

Blasier, Stewart. "The Cuban and Chilean Communist Parties: Instruments of Soviet Policy (1935–1948)." Ph.D. dissertation, Columbia University, 1954.

Farber, Samuel. "Revolution and Social Structure in Cuba, 1933–1959." Ph.D. dissertation, University of California, Berkeley, 1969.

Fracaro, Alice M. "The Role of the Third International (Comintern and Cominform) in Latin America—1935–1951." Masters thesis, University of California, Berkeley, 1952.

Gellman, Irwin. "Good Neighbor Diplomacy and the Rise of Batista." Ph.D. dissertation, Indiana University, 1970.

Graff, Frank. "The Strategy of Involvement: A Diplomatic Biography of Sumner Welles, 1933–1943." Ph.D. dissertation, University of Michigan, 1971.

Jablon, Howard. "Cordell Hull, the State Department and the Foreign Policy of the First Roosevelt Administration, 1933–1936." Ph.D. dissertation, Rutgers University, 1967.

Jackman, Francis V. "America's Cuban Policy during the Period of the Machado Regime." Ph.D. dissertation, Catholic University, 1964.

Krauss, Paul H. "Communist Policy in Cuba, 1933–1946." Masters thesis, Columbia University, 1950.

Krogh, Peter F. "The United States, Cuba and Sumner Welles: 1933." Ph.D. dissertation, Fletcher School of Law and Diplomacy, 1966.

Lazo, Mario, Jr. "The Place of the Cuban Sugar Industry in the Trade Relations Between Cuba and the United States." M.B.A. thesis, Wharton School, University of Pennsylvania, 1952.

McHale, James M. "The New Deal and the Origins of Public Lending for Foreign Economic Development, 1933–1945." Ph.D. dissertation, University of Wisconsin, 1970.

Millington, Thomas. "The Latin American Diplomacy of Sumner Welles." Ph.D. dissertation, Johns Hopkins University, School of Advanced International Studies, 1966.

O'Connor, James. "The Political Economy of Pre-Revolutionary Cuba." Ph.D. dissertation, Columbia University, 1964.

Page, Charles. "The Development of Organized Labor in Cuba." Ph.D. dissertation, University of California, Berkeley, 1952.

Steward, Dick H. "In Search of Markets: The New Deal, Latin America and Reciprocal Trade." Ph.D. dissertation, University of Missouri, 1969.

Wills, Robert L. "A Study of the Growth of Competition in the United States Between Domestic and Off-Shore Cane Sugar Refiners, 1927–1946." M.B.A. thesis, Wharton School, University of Pennsylvania, 1946.

Wolf, Harold. "United States Sugar Policy and Its Impact on Cuba: A Reappraisal." Ph.D. dissertation, University of Michigan, 1958.

Index